Sociology of Communism

Sociology of Communism

BY JULES MONNEROT

TRANSLATED BY
JANE DEGRAS AND RICHARD REES

GREENWOOD PRESS, PUBLISHERS
WESTPORT, CONNECTICUT

Library of Congress Cataloging in Publication Data

Monnerot, Jules.
Sociology of communism.

Translation of Sociologie du communisme.
Reprint of the 1953 ed. published by G. Allen & Unwin, London.
Includes bibliographical references and index.
1. Communism. I. Title.
HX56.M6413 1976 301.5'92 76-46469
ISBN 0-8371-9309-5

The French original
Sociologie du Communisme
was first published by Gallimard in 1949

*

With the consent of the author, this English translation omits the philosophical 'digression' which appeared parenthetically as Part II of the French original

First published in English in 1953 by George Allen & Unwin Ltd., London

Reprinted with the permission of George Allen & Unwin Ltd.

Reprinted in 1976 by Greenwood Press, Inc.

Library of Congress Catalog Card Number 76-46469

ISBN 0-8371-9309-5

Printed in the United States of America

Contents

PART ONE

THE TWENTIETH-CENTURY 'ISLAM'

1. *The Twentieth-century 'Islam'* 9
2. *Failing Oligarchy and Impotent Plebs* 24
3. *A Technological Messianism* 39
4. *Structure of the Army* 46
5. *Growth of Absolutism and Concentration of Power* 60
6. *Bolshevisation* 85
7. *The Third Army* 100
8. *The 'Men of the Threshold'* 112

PART TWO

SECULAR RELIGIONS AND THE *IMPERIUM MUNDI*

9. *The Prestige of Totality* 123
10. *The Psychology of Secular Religions* 133
11. *The Political Phenomenon of Tyranny* 164
12. *Twentieth-century Absolutism* 182
13. *The Totalitarian Dynamic* 237
14. *Projections of the Sacred* 264
15. *What is a Revolution?* 293
Postscript to Chapter 15 334

INDEX 337

Part One

THE TWENTIETH-CENTURY 'ISLAM'

CHAPTER 1

The Twentieth-century 'Islam'

IN 1917 Russian Bolshevism appeared to be a stage in the Westernisation of Russia. What appeared to be triumphing in Russia was not the specifically Russian 'populist' socialism of the *narodniki*, but Marxism, which had its origin in the West, designed for a different social order, and imported into Russia at the end of the 19th century. The most prominent Marxists were Germans; and Plekhanov, Lenin, and Trotsky were clearly anxious to absorb the wisdom of the German theorists, whose mastery was not disputed. It was not until Lenin published his famous polemical pamphlet *The Proletarian Revolution and the Renegade Kautsky* that the pre-eminence of the Westerners in the theoretical field was denied. But the reversal was decisive; it was no longer Europe which dictated doctrine and strategy to Russia. Henceforth it was from Russia that commands and directives were issued and from Russia that operations were conducted. Russian Marxism of the 19th century was at first an importation, a 'loan' from Europe; but European communism of the 20th century, from Lenin's death to the 'cold war', appears more and more as an aggressive and unremitting interference by the dominant Russian oligarchy in the internal affairs of Europe, and indeed of the rest of the world. The eastward cultural expansion of Europe has been followed by a reaction, a counter-expansion, and the Marxism 'returned' by Russia to Europe is strikingly different from the Marxism 'lent' by Europe to Russia. Marxists have sharp eyes for 'capitalist contradictions', but does not the outstanding riddle of our time (Is communist strategy the revolutionary strategy of Marxism, or is it rather that the Marxist revolution is a strategic speciality of the Russian Super-State?) display a *Marxist contradiction*, Marxism being understood here as a broad sociological fact, a total social phenomenon, of which Marxist theory is but one aspect?

In the 19th century, Marx's study of Clausewitz gave him the idea of using strategy in the service of revolution. Strategy was to be one among several methods at the disposal of the revolutionary planners. In the 20th century the relationship seems to be reversed, revolutionary action becoming part of the strategic arsenal of the oligarchy that rules over the most formidable empire in the world. Encouragement of seditious elements within enemy States has always been one method of warfare. To embarrass the enemy by exploiting discontent and the discontented (fallen statesmen, ambitious younger sons, members of factions excluded from power, exiled partisans) was a familiar method both in the mediterranean world in the thousand years before Christ and in the Italian cities from the 13th to the 16th centuries in dynastic and feudal Europe. The same methods, transformed by the rapidity with which 'thought' can be disseminated (leaflets dropped by aircraft, communication by wireless and radar with those operating behind the enemy lines), can in the 20th century be used on a vast scale; this makes social life today something quite different from social life in the 19th century. The destructive force generated by human sufferings and resentments can then be *used*, manipulated by specialists, in the same way and to the same purpose as material explosives. In this sense it can be said that the affective forces which determined socialist thought and action in the 19th century have lost their absolute status. They are now no more than one specialised form of tactics competing with others within a wider total strategy. The 'Marxist' general staff exploits or provokes discord among the enemy; it is the most up-to-date form of an old tactic. Mobilising their forces in enemy territory at the same time as their own, the great powers of today can subject their opponents to simultaneous pressure from without and from within.

The distinction between domestic policy and foreign policy is thus of the same order as that between infantry and artillery. Modern heavy industry provides the material elements for psychological warfare. As an explosive weapon the word, written or spoken, is comparable to the bomb, and psychological weapons are pre-eminent in long-range effectiveness. A few rule-of-thumb psychological prescriptions and the technical knowledge to apply them make it possible to co-ordinate the blows aimed at the enemy so that they converge on his weak spots. The vast extent of modern industrial organisation makes morale one of the attainable weak spots. Since an entire nation is today in effect mobilised, the active combatants can be indirectly attacked by striking at non-combatants; the front is vulnerable to attacks upon the rear, and indeed the distinction between the two is already much less clear than it used to be, and in some cases no longer exists.

Applying Marxism to the Marxists and judging them by their own standards, it may be observed that revolutionaries are victims of an 'alienation' of the same type as that which Marx called 'religious alienation'. The affective motive forces by which values and meanings are distributed in the world by the Marxists are treated and manipulated like things[1] in a mechanistic and technical (one might say engineering) spirit, and enter as such into the calculations of the general staffs, who can speculate in them as the tycoons of the capitalist market speculate in commodities. Such a standpoint, it is true, can only be taken from the outside. The communist postulates a pre-established harmony between the calculations of the Politburo and the requirements of his faith. But the equivocation exists, and his enemies take care to remind him of it every day; and it might develop into a fatal disease at the very roots of the Faith when the great Campaign meets its first serious reverses. For since it takes the field in the dual role of both Emperor and Pope, and attacks in both capacities, any defeat it suffers is equally a defeat for both. Russian defeats react upon the religious faith of the Stalinists, and an increasing number of adepts may lose it altogether, given favourable circumstances, if the doctrine is subjected to the solvent of criticism. The class war becomes ambiguous when it is transposed to the plane of struggle between empires; inside the very country which, as communists believe, *represents*[2] the disinherited there is more social stratification and a more rigid hierarchy than anywhere else. The very war and victory which, again as communists believe, should emancipate the disinherited of the whole world, only contribute in the 'land of socialism' to widen the gulf between the small governing class and the mass of the governed; they only consolidate the 'superiority' of the higher strata.

In the Europe of the 19th century, in process of industrialisation, the Communist Manifesto distinguishes and sets in opposition to one another the *Proletariat* and the *Bourgeoisie*. The advantages of this simplification, which fosters the growth of a myth and also the development of a tactic, have been plain for all to see: it does violence to sociology but it pays dividends. But although both the dualism and the duel are religious myths, the existence of the proletariat was an historical fact, a real problem of a specific society: and until the 20th century it remained an internal concern of the society which had produced it. Nineteenth-century socialism was the reaction of the Western conscience as much to the problems of industrialisation as to the drama of proletarianisation, and it inherited elements of humanism and Christianity which it transformed but did not deny. They were the world from which it was born and of which it was one aspect; but Marxism, as a comprehensive political strategy, as the art of seizing and holding power, both was and is the art of maintaining and widening the actual schism which

[1] The brusqueness with which totalitarianism switches its policies implies a complete disregard of the difference between material reality and human reality. Men are merely lumps of material or blocks of capital.

[2] The mechanics and dynamics of this kind of representation derive from religious sociology. It is obvious that the Russia of today 'represents' the proletariat in quite a different way from that in which a French or Belgian deputy represents his electors.

gives a pretext for the theoretical opposition between the proletariat and the rest of society. Its purpose is to make the schism absolute and absolutely destructive. It is possible to discriminate in thought between what should be destroyed and what preserved, but destruction takes place in reality and not in thought; its effects are experienced by thought but not controlled by it.

After the Russian revolution, *at the very moment when the revolutionary Campaign was becoming formidably equipped for action*, its control passed out of the hands of the men who had conceived it. These men had inherited the tradition of the western European workers' movements and the socialist doctrines which, having come to birth in Germany, England, and France, *embodied elements of civilisation much older than themselves*. In theory, the control passed from them to an international body of picked revolutionaries—the Communist International. But it would be both un-Marxist and unhistorical to hold that this select body could resist the magnetic attraction and the influence of the Russian Super-State which grew up rapidly after the revolution. The victims of the successive 'purges' were drawn as freely from members of the International who were unlucky enough to be in Russia as from the Russians themselves. The Communist International was thus progressively *identified* with the ruling oligarchy of the new Empire in proportion as this new Empire and dominant minority became established in fact. The executive committee of the Communist International was composed of men who, being Russian, must by hypothesis be identified with the State interests of the new State, and of men who, although not Russian, made no distinction or else distinguished badly between the interests and aims of the disinherited of the countries they represented and those of the new State and the men in whom it was incarnated. Marxism might reject such a dualistic distinction, but reality does not. What in fact happened was that Russia gradually *obtained a control over the interpretation of world history*, which was at first effective only in some sectors and for practical purposes inoperative in others. But we have now reached a point where the men at the apex of the social pyramid of Stalinist Russia (more and more of whom are too young to have taken part in the revolution, whose conscious motivation was socialist and Marxist) are in control, from their command posts, of all the forces which are attacking all other social structures, including those which, like the political parties of the same name, are reputedly socialist. It has fallen to this *privileged class* to direct the revolution of the disinherited outside Russia and to oppose the integration of the proletariat within Western States. The integration of the proletariat is no longer an internal affair of these States; it has become the peculiar concern of an international Campaign whose real leaders are outside Western society and shaped by a different history. And this Campaign is an answer to the particular problems posed by that history. A new type of social differentiation has appeared, whose hierarchical aspect has become clearly recognisable in the course of thirty years to the lay (I mean the non-communist) observer, and with it has appeared a new type of régime, harsh towards the 'free' proletariat and inhuman towards its slave labour.[1] The proletariat can only be called free by comparison with the labour force of the concentration camps. The *revival of slavery* is one of the characteristic features of 20th-century totalitarianism: the defeated in political and factional warfare, side by side with delinquents of every kind, many of whom would not in countries farther west be liable to any penalty at all, are all alike reduced to slavery, and not by a foreign power but by their own State.

At the end of the 19th century slavery existed only on the outskirts of Western civilisation. The European colonists found it established in the countries they exploited, especially in Africa. Although they formally abolished slave-ownership, their methods of developing the land were not at first such as to improve the conditions of the former slaves. On the whole, however, a new class of proletarians or tenant smallholders increasingly took the place of the old slave class. The Marxists of the 19th century accused the liberals of being liberal only at home, but in fact there was a movement, though a very slow one, towards the extension of political liberalism to the colonies. In the 20th century, in Russia and Germany, slavery reappears in new forms. It is *State slavery*. The slaves are not members of remote tribes on the periphery of the 'civilised' world—they are members of the losing side in the political struggles within Russia and Hitlerite Germany. It is their own countrymen who reduce them to slavery, and with no better pretext than to penalise a difference of *Weltanschauung* or consecrate a factional victory.

The fully-developed totalitarian world is an industrial world; pre-eminently, a world where resources are exploited and utilised. In it, repression is a part of the methods of production. Hence one of its characteristic phenomena: a *legal system* which concerns itself with problems of manpower, and production plans based on estimates of the supply of penal labour. Twentieth-century State slavery enables the exploitation of men, as Marxists used to call it, to be carried much

[1] See Dallin and Nicolaevsky, *Forced Labour in Soviet Russia* (New Haven, 1947). See also David J. Dallin, *The Real Soviet Russia* (New Haven, 1944). The first decree calling for the greater use of forced labour appeared 26 March 1928. In July of the same year the Commissariat of Justice ordered forced labour for all physically fit prisoners. This measure was a prelude to the first five-year plan. The execution of the plan, combined with the collectivisation of agriculture, brought about, between 1929 and 1935, the first of those great forced migrations which are a major characteristic of the totalitarian world.

further than was possible under the capitalist 'iron law' of wages. Its costs of production are necessarily much lower, because the men who compose the penal labour force do not get a sufficient share of the social product to enable them to live and reproduce themselves.

Next above the slaves of the labour camps comes the proletariat, which one can only call free by contrast with the category below it. Whereas the traditions of democracy and trade unionism have enabled the Western proletariat to participate more and more in the determination of its own status, to secure a limitation of working hours, and generally to intervene in discussions of which it has ceased to be the mere passive subject, the Russian proletariat does not sell its labour at all, but *owes* it to society. The organisations called trade unions in Russia have nothing but the name in common with trade unions in the 'democratic' world, for there is no place in the régime for such an idea as opposition between employers and employed—it belongs to a different world. The worker is a mere function of his work. He has no freedom of movement, but is entirely at the government's disposal all his life long. He cannot go anywhere without a passport, and is liable to legal penalties for unpunctuality. He works harder than in Western countries, and for less wages. His children are now practically debarred from higher education.

In short, it is men who reduce a section of their own compatriots to slavery who have finally assumed, in the régime we are describing, the task of freeing from oppression the disinherited elsewhere who are not their compatriots.

* * * *

Thus the society which created both the proletariat and socialism is, as it were, denied the right to deal with its own problems. The drama of proletarianisation belongs to the society of 19th-century Europe. Thought converts this drama into a *problem*, but still a problem of 19th-century Europe, a problem arising out of its own history. The problem is circumscribed, like a figure inside a circle, within the society which determined its form. It began with the disruption of Western society by its own action, a change in its manner of self-determination. The problems of the integration of the proletariat into Western society and of the rhythm of social differentiation and the circulation of the élites are problems of Western society in the 19th century, and the opinions of the Tsar concerning them were not consulted, any more than the Grand Mogul would have been consulted in the 17th century concerning the problems of Jansenism. In the 20th century the more and more widespread and intense industrialisation all over the world tends to establish a sort of common denominator for all men by standardising their living conditions and ways of life (though this 'Marxist' factor is combined with other factors). Peter the Great sent Russia to school in Europe, and one of the consequences, at the end of the 19th century, was the assimilation of Marx's ideas by Lenin. But this end-product of Russia's relative Westernisation gave rise to a movement in the contrary direction: Russia became industrialised, like Europe, but her way of doing it estranged her from Europe. Risk, personal initiative, enterprise, private property, and the profit motive were the mainsprings of European industrialisation, not the motive of service to a more or less *sacred* State or of war against the rest of the world.

The increasing standardisation of mankind's material conditions is accompanied by a religious theory of the division of mankind into two camps. This duality is a duel, and according to communists there can be no future for humanity unless their side wins—though it is difficult for the unbeliever to conceive what meaning this statement can have for them. In any case, the separation of humanity into two camps is not the work of capitalists but of Marxists.

Whereas the 19th-century European socialist wanted to create a just society in Europe, the 20th-century European communist works for the absorption of Europe by a totally alien system which includes non-European factors and was designed to meet uniquely Russian problems. It is as though the Christian church had worked within the Roman Empire for the success of the Parthian monarchy, or as if every Christian in the Mediterranean world had been an agent of the Persian bureaucracy. Persia bordered on the Roman world as Russia borders on Europe, and Rome never succeeded either in absorbing Persia or in eliminating her.

There is, moreover, a resemblance between the use made of Marxism by the present masters of the totalitarian world and the conversion of nomadic barbarians, such as the Goths of Alaric and the Turkish mercenaries of Mahmud of Ghazna, Togrul Beg, and Alp Arslan, to the universal religion of the civilisations they threatened, namely Christianity in the first case and Islam in the second. Like Stalin's Marxism, their conversion gave them the pretext for disrupting civilisation *from within*; as converts they were able to attack in the name of the true Faith the very societies which had brought the Faith to them. In the same way the Marxist chiefs of totalitarian Russia attack Western society from within, attempting to destroy the social structure of European countries for the sake of the socialism to which these countries themselves gave birth. There is no need to question the sincerity of the Bolshevik leaders' conscious motives. We may observe, however, that in the remote depths of Russia and central Asia the conception of Marxism and communism is probably comparable to the conception of Christianity entertained by the Germanic tribes (Frisians, Saxons, Chamaves, Thuringians), who were subjected to 'mass conversion' after Charlemagne's victories.

The first object in the West is to prevent the integration into society of the proletariat. The mere existence of the 'communist' Campaign, *as it is today*,[1] implies that Western society is unfit for the task of integrating its own proletariat. *But the continued existence of Western society depends upon the accomplishment of this allegedly impossible task*. It is a precarious and alarming situation, indeed, for any nation if its 'lower' classes and all the disintegrating and unattached elements that adhere to them can be mobilised at the command and for the profit of a neighbouring empire.

The communist design can be seen to comprise in fact a two-fold campaign: to destroy one society and to construct another. In many countries the society marked for destruction is on a higher material and cultural level than Russia. The society 'for construction' begins in the Super-State known as Soviet Russia, and spreads outward from it. *This dual significance of the Campaign is revealed in its very structure and anatomy, in the fact that the privileged ruling oligarchy of the Russian Super-State is theoretically the leader of the disinherited outside the frontiers of Russia*. This is the age of general staffs, and the general staff in question is composed of the 'leaders' of the world revolution, who scrutinise the schisms and divisions of the Western world and do all they can to perpetuate, extend, and exploit them. But other members of this same general staff are concerned with constructive work inside Russia, which proceeds concurrently with the destruction abroad. There is social construction: the stabilising and reinforcing of the social stratification which set in after the revolution. And there is material construction: the industrialisation of Russia—building, machinery, factories and factory products, agriculture. This type of society is founded upon service, labour, hierarchy, and a *secular religion*,[2] unlike the 19th-century liberal capitalist society of the West, which was founded upon profit, property, risk, and personal initiative and independence. The twofold destination and function of the communist Campaign is served by two distinct groups of organs, whose separate roles were discernible from the beginning in the distinction between the Russian State and the Comintern, or Communist International. The campaign aspires to synchronise the destruction of the 'capitalist' and the construction of the 'socialist' world. Without counting the cost (in terms of

[1] Whenever this question arises it leads to confusion. Some people mean by the word communism what communism *ought* to be and others what it is; or else people use the word now in one sense and now in the other.

[2] The German sociologist Spranger was the first to use this now familiar term.

lives), it works for a unified and homogeneous world; exalting Russia and casting down everything that is not Russia, creating within Russia a hierarchical social system to be extended uniformly over the whole world, undermining by every available means the existing systems and hierarchies and also any which are developing or potentially developing in independence of her own system. This campaign recognises no worse enemies than those who resist its authority and yet call themselves socialist; and the war against the heirs of the 19th-century working-class movement, in so far as their loyalty to their traditions inspires them with a repugnance for Stalinism, is conducted as implacably as the rest of the Campaign. It is clear indeed that the struggle today is not only a vertical one between classes but at least equally a horizontal one between two different worlds and mentalities. The communist Campaign appears, if one discounts such 'justification' for it as the Marxist ideology can afford, to be an attempt to destroy outside Russia all the things which it is constructing, in a different form, within Russia: industry, social stability, the State, the political system, hierarchy, social movements, etc. In the whole period from 1918 to today wages have been low in Russia, and the standard of life inferior not only to that of the United States but also to that of western Europe. If this state of affairs continues long enough the campaign would become economically unjustifiable; for, economically, it now rests entirely upon the thesis that a totalitarian régime, by imposing a planned economy in a part of the world that is rich enough to maintain an autarkic independence from the rest of the world, can in theory eliminate the periodic slumps which are characteristic of capitalism. The task is made easier by the fact that the consumer has no political liberty, and can therefore make no effective complaints or protests. The government is not in the least concerned to satisfy men's actual demands, but only to impose upon them from above what seems good from the point of view of those above. The shortcomings of Soviet planning may be the fault of the planners and their methods, but they certainly exist; and since there is no right of assembly or meeting and no free vote the people have no way of expressing any opinion that conflicts with the orders from above—a state of affairs totally foreign even to the *aspirations* of 19th-century socialists, Marx and Engels included. *Many of the major sociological characteristics of the régime are censored or travestied by the official propaganda.*

Meanwhile, outside Russia, the Campaign canalises and fosters every class and mass and individual resentment, and tries to bring it to the decisive pitch of active virulence; its whole activity abroad consists in *organising* discontent and the discontented of every kind. By means of the unions it controls through communist fractions, the Campaign can influence the methods of fixing wage rates and their fluctuations, and can thus compromise *from within* the productive capacity of capitalist countries which—in normal times—are able to assure to their working class a higher standard of life than the 'socialist' standard of Russia. At the same time, taking advantage of 'capitalist contradictions in the age of monopolies and imperialism', it 'works' upon the colonial 'masses' and thus lowers the standard of life of the metropolitan masses.[1] The purpose is to inflame and envenom all the contradictions of the capitalist world and *at the same time* either to destroy or else absorb into the Campaign every working-class and socialist movement and also every independent movement of revolt.

By the accelerated industrialisation of Russia, Marxists have built up an economy by which the economic can determine the political; thus demonstrating at once the efficacity of their doctrine and the need to interpret it boldly. By capitalist standards of accountancy, many Russian industries have been working and still work at a loss. But the data of the problem are changed by the fact that these enterprises are totally dependent upon the State. Economic politics have been substituted for political economy.[2]

But the ultimate aim is the most absolute tyranny ever conceived by man; a tyranny that recognises no spatial limits (except for the time being those of the planet itself), no temporal limits (communist believers generally refuse to contemplate any post-communist ages), and no limits to its power over the individual: its will to power claims total possession over every man it wins, and allows no greater freedom in mental than in economic life. It is this claim that brings it into conflict with faiths, religions, and values, which are older than itself or developing independently; and then the battle is joined. We are the battle.

* * * *

Communism takes the field both as a *secular religion* and as a *universal State*[3]; it is therefore more comparable to Islam than to the Universal Religion which began by opposing the universal State in the Hellenistic and Roman worlds, and which can be said to have drawn men's hearts away from the State to itself. Its voracity is extraordinary. As universal State it would abolish all the differentiations which keep the world divided into distinct and individual units (the most recent unit of this kind is the nation); and as secular religion it canalises discontent,

[1] It cannot be denied that the relatively high standard of life of the British working man at the beginning of the 20th century owed something to imperialism.

[2] As Michel Collinet has said (*La Tragédie du Marxisme*, Paris, 1948).

[3] In intention but not in fact. The universal State is a sort of collective fantasy; the totalitarian State's image of itself projected into the future.

organises and reinforces every impulse that sets men against their native society, and works pertinaciously to aid, abet, and accelerate the self-division and secession of part of their own vital force which plunge societies into dissolution and ruin.

Although the phenomenon is unprecedented since Europe emerged from the mediterranean world and from the migratory tribes that poured into it from the East and created itself out of these elements, there was once an analogous phenomenon in the eastern part of the continent. Soviet Russia (to use the name it gives itself, although it is a misdescription of the régime) is not the first empire in which the temporal and public power goes hand in hand with a shadowy power which works outside the imperial frontiers to undermine the social structure of neighbouring States. The Islamic East affords several examples of a like duality and duplicity. The Egyptian Fatimids, and later the Persian Safavids, were the animators and propagators, from the heart of their own States, of an active and organising legend, an historical myth, calculated to make fanatics and obtain their total devotion, designed to create in neighbouring States an underworld of ruthless gangsters. The eponymous ancestor of the Safavids was a saint from whom they magically derived the religious authority in whose name they operated. They were Shi'is of Arabian origin, and the militant order they founded was dedicated to propaganda and 'nucleation' throughout the whole of Persia and Asia Minor. It recruited 'militants' and 'adherents' and 'sympathisers'. These were the Sufis. As rulers, their sympathies were recognised by other sovereigns in the same way that Stalin, head of the State, is recognised by other heads of States, and rightly, as the leader of world communism.[1] This merging of religion and politics was a major characteristic of the Islamic world in its victorious period. It allowed the head of a State to operate beyond his own frontiers in the capacity of *commander of the faithful* (Amir-al-muminin); and in this way a *Caliph* was able to count upon docile instruments, or captive souls, wherever there were men who recognised his authority. The territorial frontiers which seemed to remove some of his subjects from his jurisdiction were nothing more than material obstacles; armed force might compel him to feign respect for the frontier, but propaganda and subterranean warfare could continue no less actively beyond it.

Religions of this kind acknowledge no frontiers. Soviet Russia is merely the geographical centre from which communist influence radiates; it is an 'Islam' on the march, and it regards its frontiers at any given moment as purely provisional and temporary. Communism, like

[1] Speaking before the second congress of Soviets, 26 January 1924, Stalin said: 'Lenin was the leader not only of the Russian proletariat and not only of the workers of Europe . . . but also of the whole working-class world.'

victorious Islam, makes no distinction between politics and religion, but this time the claim to be both universal State and universal truth applies not only within a civilisation or world which co-exists with other different civilisations, other worlds, but to the entire terrestrial globe. To an educated European or American, unless he is himself a communist, it appears that communists are religious fanatics in the service of an expansionist empire which is striving for world dominion. But communists see it differently: for them communism is *what ought to be*, and the whole of history, the whole past of humanity, takes its meaning from this future event.

Communism is on its way. A religion is seen as such only by those outside it. For its adherents it is simply the highest form of truth. For the true believer Russia no longer exists as such; but he does not believe he is a believer; he believes he possesses the truth. In fact, he is *possessed* by something which he believes to be the truth; and for this truth he feels an active attachment of a kind which truth (at least scientific truth) does not usually inspire or demand. Communism is a faith, and it has in Russia a sort of fatherland; but such a fatherland cannot be *a country like any other*. Russia is to communism what the Abbasid empire was to Islam. This is only an analogy, but a necessary one. Communism is not the party of 'foreign patriotism'[1]; it is a religious sect of world conquerors for whom Russia is simply the strongpoint from which the attack is launched.

* * * *

In the 19th century politics and religion and economics were each a distinct and separate province. They were 'specialisms', separate in fact as well as in theory; and neither as subjects of study nor as activities was there much interchange or communication between them. This kind of intellectual autonomy is a characteristic feature of the liberal world; and minds formed in this tradition, even the ablest of them, will be at first perplexed by a phenomenon so complex and yet so unified as communism, which can, in a way, be described as a total social phenomenon. It is true that soldiers, historians, diplomats, and politicians, for whom imperial rivalries are a familiar subject, will have no difficulty in perceiving that this is yet another example of it: Persia and Assyria, Carthage and Rome, Habsburg and Bourbon, and now Kremlin and White House (or Kremlin and Wall Street, as communists put it). For such observers it seems a simple struggle for power; they will read the drama as a problem, and will easily grasp both its economic and its strategic aspects. But they will fail to take sufficient account of the

[1] As M. Léon Blum called it (*A l'Echelle humaine*; Paris, Gallimard, 1945).

drama which 'over-determines' the problem: the drama of the birth, development, maintenance, and transformation of a religion. Hence their conclusions will be incomplete, and any policy deduced from them may be mistaken both in foresight and in action. The economist and the strategist will need to possess 'historical tact', and to combine the penetration of the 'director of conscience',[1] the historian of religions, and the psycho-analyst. This may be too much for any one man, but it is certainly possible for a group of men. It is by no means beyond human capacity.

The paralysis of production in the 'bourgeois' countries, to whose destruction the communist Campaign is vowed, is an economic effect obtained by psychological means. The internal contradictions of capitalism are a reality, but the communists are able to aggravate them by promoting a religious schism. What is happening in the West today can be compared to what the situation would have been in the Roman world of the third century if there had been intentional and preconcerted synchronisation between the Christian refusal of obedience and the successive thrusts of barbarian invasion; in other words, if a single general staff, devoted to the ruin of the ancient world, had had command of both the Christian church and the barbarians. The historical innovation of contemporary communism is the virtual unification of the forces of an external and an internal enemy,[2] a combination of subversion with invasion—so that as it expands the system can absorb[3] simultaneously both societies and individuals, and can make not only territorial and economic but also political and spiritual conquests. The innovation also consists in raising an issue and persuading a certain number of people, by various methods of intimidation and psychological pressure, to accept it as predestined (but the word destiny is never used; the issue is described as 'necessary', 'ineluctable', etc.).

If we can see in history nothing but conflicts of power between collectivities we shall miss the meaning of the contemporary crisis. Not that there are fewer of such conflicts than before, on the contrary; but the water-tight compartments which in the liberal period preserved the autonomy of the different spheres of human activity have begun to leak. A religion is propagating itself in terms of political economy. If politics tries to remain nothing but itself while economics and religion are mixed together it is in danger of becoming completely unreal. The communist Campaign could not exist if it were not religious; it could not exist if it were not pervaded by religion through and through. The leaders and

[1] I use this term in the strict sense: I refer to the tact and psychological 'technique' of, for example, the Jesuit confessors of kings and favourites.

[2] The Stalinist, not the proletarian, is the internal enemy.

[3] That is to say, it can aim to absorb; it is so constituted as to make the attempt.

strategists of the contemporary world will ignore this fact at their risk and peril. The Campaign is what it is solely because it has proved capable of mobilising and energising a deep and powerful fund of affective impulses. The fate of the Campaign, and consequently the issue of the struggle of empires, will depend less upon strategic routes and pipe-lines for uranium and oil than upon the invisible pipe-lines by which this modern 'Islam' canalises the resentments and discontents of the world it is vowed to destroy; even the unprecedentedly powerful modern weapons of war can be immobilised by the slow and secret canalisation of resentments and discontents and the draining away of the warlike spirit.

* * * *

In this situation we shall get no help from the isolated study of political economy, history of ideas, history of religions, or plain history considered as the battlefield of men and conflicting wills. All these dimensions must be explored simultaneously, using for each of them its appropriate method. When the spirit is assailed on all fronts at once it must achieve a kind of ubiquity for its counter-attack.

Western historians and sociologists have hitherto applied their familiar categories to the phenomenon of communism. But these categories were evolved from Western history. It was only with difficulty that they could be made to embrace such 19th-century phenomena as nationalism and socialism, and amid the new realities which are closing in on us they are totally inadequate to evaluate the newness and originality of communism. An empire, or aggregate of nations and peoples grouped around one preponderant nation, which is also a kind of religious community and at the same time engaged in sectarian proselytising, underground warfare, and the care of souls—here is a phenomenon which may well baffle members of a culture based upon the two great historic ideas of the distinction between spiritual and temporal and the secularisation of politics. The Christian distinction between *spiritualia* and *temporalia* means the separation, at least in principle (for it is an ideal rather than a fact) between two powers, each of which recognises the rights of the other even though in practice they both tend to encroach. Of the second idea, the secularisation of politics, the work of Machiavelli remains the classic expression. After *The Prince* and the *Discourse on Livy*, the art of politics in the West became as free as the art of cookery, and freer than that of medicine, from any religious or magical context. Not that the leader of men really ceased to have something in common with the person in primitive societies possessed of mana, but he came under the jurisdiction of the critical intelligence. Today, as in the past, there is an irrational element in the admiration men feel for success; but there is a greater sense of the need for intellectual justification. Since Machiavelli the art of politics has consisted in a body of precepts derived from logic and experience, and it tends to be pursued in a scientific spirit. Political sphere and religious sphere, struggle of classes and struggle of empires—the meaning of these terms must be kept fluid. That the western European working-class movement should be identified with the expansion of the Russian Super-State, or even that the one should participate in the other, is a notion that upsets all the preconceptions of minds formed in European and American universities. Such minds will therefore confine themselves to a consideration of Marxism as a theory of history, whether convincing or not; or else they will adhere to the conservative and sceptical point of view that human nature never changes and that we are involved in a struggle of empires whose fundamental character is the same as that of previous struggles. Others again will accept the 'mystical' identification and participation, but will translate them into rational operations and secular concepts, and provide them with an unreal and false, though often ingenious, setting in an imaginary world—a sort of shadow of the real world; and they will reinterpret all the real facts into the dream language of this dream world. The only error of the rational and sceptical interpretations is that they are too limited. Their truth is incomplete because it lacks the true perspective. The imaginary interpretations, on the other hand, reveal the truth, but not in the way they are meant to: the truth can be deduced from them in the same way as from the hallucinations of a psychological 'case'.

CHAPTER 2

Failing Oligarchy and Impotent Plebs

THIS Campaign which splits the world into two camps did not spring to life full-grown and fully armed. It cannot have had, in the minds of its first initiators, the full meaning or, rather, all the meanings that we find in it. The meaning of any great historical enterprise arises from the fact that it *is* historical; in other words, that it happened or is happening. The intentions of its authors contribute to its meaning, but are only a part of it. An event is not at all the same thing as an intention, and may differ from it even more than a work of art from the intention of its creator. It is impossible to foresee all the consequences of an action or all the results of a change in the world, or all the meanings, unsuspected by its author, that an action will acquire in other men's eyes. So, in a sense, man is both innocent and guilty, both conscious and unconscious, of his own acts. He may do what he chooses, but he cannot choose all that he will have done. For there is no such thing, in our experience, as knowledge of the future.

The perspectives of Lenin and his companions were different from ours; they lived in a different age. We are trying to describe the Campaign, in broadest outline, as it is today before our eyes; and even if our description is factually accurate the meaning we ascribe to the facts will not always be accepted by everyone. As soon as a man reports a fact it ceases to be a pure fact, because it may appear to others to be compromised merely by the reporter's choice of words. An historical fact is related in one way to the man who reveals it and in another to the man who inspects it. If sociology makes an attempt to understand the facts historically, these types of relationship, or, if it be preferred, a sort of reflection of them, will also appear in it. Thus communists today will tell us that we are looking at the facts from outside; that a movement which they *experience* integrally, because they also enact it, is only seen by us from outside, and therefore appears to us to consist of a complex of effects which can be broken up into their several parts and elements. Our view being external and superficial, they will say our interpretations must be even more so. And, indeed, there can be no doubt that during the Counter-Reformation the policy of the Papacy, and of the Catholic church in general and the Jesuits in particular, was seen in one way by a 16th-century humanist and in quite another way by those who carried out or inspired the policy. History dictates the boundaries and course of the Campaign as the contours of the earth dictate those of a river. But the events of history did not create the Campaign any more than the river's bed creates the river. Something is given: namely the waters flowing down from the hills and meeting together, and that fact is independent of the geology of the valley. But the characteristics of the river will depend not only upon the volume of water it carries but equally upon the channel afforded to it by the countries it traverses on its way to the sea; and therefore upon the climate of those countries. And just as the flow of the river changes with the changing configurations and gradients of the land and with the variations of rainfall, so communism has modified itself in order to adapt to different geographical and historical environments. (The analogy is imperfect because men are less passive towards circumstance than a river towards the gradient of its course.) Above all, one should not think of the Campaign as a factory working with mathematical accuracy and mechanical precision on a material product according to a prearranged plan. It is tempting to do so because our age has so far produced no other political machine so perfectly adapted to its immediate tasks[1]; but we shall only be able to explain or understand the phenomenon if—instead of regarding its character as finally formed and established once for all—we trace it back to its origin. To do otherwise would be to 'fix' it in a timeless and therefore unreal world which can only be conceived as the antithesis of the historical world. The birth and growth of the Campaign must be grasped both as the development of an idea *and* as the thrust of a living thing, such as a tree, which from a seed is always adapting itself to its environment or finding a way round obstacles in its purpose of expansion and growth. When we speak of the development of an 'idea' we do not imply that this 'idea' is not also a real form that can generate new realities; and when we speak of a living thing we do not mean that it is a natural phenomenon outside human control. The human world is a real world; its phenomena take substantial form as things; and these things make and unmake themselves, are mobile and fluid. But the world is more than a world of things, for the things are related to meanings.

* * * *

There are two immediate political facts inherent in every real revolutionary situation: on the one hand the *failure of a political oligarchy* (the situation is revolutionary precisely because the ruling

[1] I do not say, to its ulterior purposes, because, seen from the outside, they partake rather of the nature of justifications; and these will be considered later.

oligarchy has lost control of it), and on the other hand the *impotence of the plebs*. What is the chief reason for this impotence? It is that the mass of the people, the plebs, is by its very nature unorganised. The Gracchi were not helped or saved at the moment of crisis by the Roman plebs, although they had wished to bestow upon it the *ager publicus* which the senatorial oligarchy had cornered. The *patres* of the Senate were able to organise the defence of their interests against an unorganised opposing force, and could not be defeated until an organised force was brought against them. *This force was recruited from the plebs, but was not itself the plebs*. It was the army. The Gracchi perished because they failed to tackle the problem along the lines which brought Marius virtually to its solution (though the definitive solution was only arrived at later, by Cæsar). When Marius, in 107 B.C., enrolled the proletarians in the army so as to meet the external danger, he did more than merely change the character of the army. He revealed the means by which plebs and free-men could be *used* to overthrow the oligarchy and make it subordinate to a new power, and this was an essential preliminary to the unification of the Mediterranean world. For the problem was beyond the capacity of the old oligarchy, which clung to its prerogatives and privileges but *no longer possessed, as a body, the political imagination which the historical situation required*. Organised in the army, the weight of the lower classes had its effect upon the transformation of power, the changes in the State, and the weakening of the oligarchy. There is a certain analogy between the Cæsars' policy of rallying the plebs to the army and Lenin's policy of rallying the masses to the Party. The revolutionary situation was implicit in the incapacity of the Tsarist oligarchy, which proved itself impotent to solve the problems set by history before the Russian government. The immense majority of Russians felt the need for a change of régime. Russia was an essentially agrarian country, yet its methods of agriculture were irrational, its equipment obsolete, and the living conditions of the peasants miserable. It was a country in rapid process of industrialisation (in 1853 there were 10,000 firms employing fewer than half a million men; at the end of the century 38,000 firms employed 1,750,000 men), and its workers' conditions were much inferior to contemporary conditions in Europe and America. It was a country whose universities were creating a swollen intelligentsia ('How disastrous,' said Marx, 'if it is true that there are 40,000 revolutionary students in Russia whose only career consists in the dilemma: Siberia or emigration to western Europe'), and the Tsarist government was incapable of integrating them into a society which was urgently in need of their services. There was a plethora of agricultural experts without land and of unemployed lawyers, doctors, and teachers. 'A hungry and ignorant *muzhik* could not afford the services of teacher, doctor, or lawyer, however much he needed them.'[1] All these discontents were brought to a head by the two wars (1905 and 1914), which came too close together. But from the beginning of the 20th century the 'revolutionary situation' was inherent in the inadequacy of the oligarchy before its historic tasks. There is a revolutionary state of affairs (in the most general and universally accepted sense of the word) whenever men in any definite social category begin to reject the social definition of that category; in other words, when they revolt against conditions of life which are experienced as intolerable. But unless the society in which these revolutionary phenomena appear is itself profoundly sick there will be nothing more than short-lived riots and disturbances. Whenever men rebel against the conditions of their life they become exalted with ideas of liberation; there is a resurgence and elaboration of myths, and the intoxication of collective activity inspires men with a readiness to fight and die. But a revolution is successful only when it acquires a stronger organisation than that of the ruling oligarchy; and from this point of view the successful revolutions of the 20th century have been made by *general staffs*. But these general staffs have known how to ensure at least the benevolent neutrality of the majority of the population.

In the Roman world it was in the structure of the army that a solution was found for the problem set by the Senate's failure. And in the 20th century we find that the communist Campaign, and also its fascist and national-socialist imitators, *have modelled themselves upon the structure of the army*. They have borrowed some of its characteristic and typical features: discipline, subordination, hierarchy, concerted exercises and methods, unity of command. But it was not sufficient to pour the proletariat into the existing mould of the army, as in the Roman world, and this was not what was done. The problem was to replace the army (and the police, who can be taken as a specialised branch of it) by *another army*. And this new army was to wage a new type of war. It was to operate in time of peace and to wage, in time of war, its own separate war, not against the enemy but against its own government; it was not intended for open campaigns or for attacking fortified positions, but for undermining a social order. Such an organisation, which ignores the definitions by which an army is traditionally described, namely the distinctions between war and peace, between military and civilian, cannot properly be described as an army. The traditional army exists to defend a collectivity both offensively and defensively; it is for use only in time of war (martial law, which treats certain kinds of internal trouble as equivalent to foreign war, is an exceptional case)[2]; and lastly, and above

[1] Martov: quoted by G. Alexinsky, *La Russie Révolutionnaire* (Paris, 1947).
[2] The special cases of despotism and tyranny are considered later.

all, it restricts itself to the use of recognised weapons (or at least this has been the case in all wars except the last one). Dynastic Europe acknowledged the rules of war, and they were observed between European countries up to the first world war; that is, until the introduction of submarines and poison gas and the device of sheltering behind the bodies of enemy civilians. From these symptoms it should already have been possible to predict, during the war of 1914, the birth of totalitarian methods. From then onwards the expression 'scientific barbarism' stood for something that Europeans could recognise by experience. The traditional army did, of course, employ spies in its intelligence service; but military decisions had to be taken openly, by men dressed in conventional uniforms which distinguished them from civilians and from enemy soldiers.

The organisation known as *the Party* (we shall refer again to the ambiguity of this word, which stands for a new political fact while still retaining its old meaning) *is an army which admits no conventions whatsoever in common between itself and its opponents.* Since it represents a partition of the human race into two camps, the word 'party' is etymologically quite appropriate. Such a party, or its general staff, has no use for declarations of war, nor even for any discrimination between the state of war and the state of peace. The mere existence of the Party reveals or implies a state of war which can only end with the final destruction of all pre-existing social structures—*and this is the sole purpose of the Party's existence.*

The war waged by an army of this type, specially adapted to 20th-century conditions, is very much more 'total' than the totalitarian warfare of Ludendorff's studies, because it is not confined to periods of military operations. It cannot conceivably stop short of the conquest of the entire planet. It is a Protean war, of unlimited duration. It is not an affair of rivalries between empires, and although the essential war may project itself, as psycho-analysts put it, in the forms of imperialist war, these forms do not reveal its meaning. The purpose is to rid the world of all rivals and rule alone. The 20th-century communist army does not absorb the proletariat as the Roman army did, but it does, like the Roman army, have leaders who are working to build a *new Imperium.* And within the new type of army called the Party the conventional army—the army of the state or of the super-state when once it has been subdued and organised—will be merely a specialised military subsection for dealing with any wars of the traditional kind that may at times be superimposed upon the permanent Campaign.

This new historical reality, whose meaning exceeds the connotation of such words as Army, Campaign, and Party, was developed in theory before it became a fact; and theory helped to make it a fact. Indeed, we can see today that a certain theory was the chief premonitory symptom of the event itself.

* * * *

In 1900 the man who was later to be known as Lenin was thirty years old. His father, who was an inspector of primary schools, bore the title of 'actual State Councillor', which places him as a member of the 'governing class' in the Russia where the system of ranks (*chin*) introduced by Peter the Great was still in force. Lenin's elder brother was finishing his science studies in St. Petersburg when, in 1887, he was condemned and executed for having taken part in a conspiracy to assassinate Alexander III and for having drawn up the manifesto to the people which the conspirators had intended to issue after the assassination. In the same year Lenin was excluded from the University of St. Petersburg, where he was studying law and political economy. Like most of the ablest young revolutionaries at that time, he preferred Marxism to the other revolutionary gospels. 'It is the most horrible torture to have your head filled with ideas that will never be applied'; the remark is attributed to Tkachev,[1] the theoretician of Russian 'jacobinism' (the original of Dostoevsky's Shigalev). Ardently studying and preaching Marxism, Lenin was immune from such torture and from such a fate, thanks to that prescient self-knowledge which is the hall-mark of the man whose potentialities are developing in subtle harmony with the movement of history. It almost appears as though such men were the answer to some unconscious historical demand, and that their personal qualities cannot come to fruition in the small successes of local politics but require, at least at decisive moments, the stage of the whole world, which will later come into the full glare of history's limelight. Pursuing his theoretical studies, Lenin translated the classic work of the Webbs during his first travels abroad (Germany and Switzerland), and during an imprisonment in Petersburg, followed by exile in Siberia. He also found time to work out his *Development of Capitalism in Russia*, an attempt to apply the theories of *Das Kapital* to the Russian economic situation, and to write for the 'legal' Marxist periodicals. Activities which suggest that the Tsarist version of prison and deportation was a liberal one.[2]

Geneva, Zürich, Munich, Brussels, London: this journalistic period when Lenin collaborated on *Iskra* and *Zarya* is of capital importance. In exile in Germany he studied with admiration the organisation of a strong, disciplined, hierarchical, and centralised social-democratic party.

[1] He died insane at the Sainte-Anne Asylum in Paris.

[2] This humorous complaint is attributed to Lenin, on his release in St. Petersburg: 'They are letting me out too soon. I haven't collected all my documents yet.' Things are different in the concentration camps today.

It was at this point that Lenin came to grips with the historical problem that was linked with his destiny; just as Marx, after the *Communist Manifesto*—concentrating on the elucidation of economic facts and on the laws which, according to him, must govern the development of capitalism—had hoped thereby to make the revolutionary movement invincible and to get even science on to its side. Cæsarism, as we have seen, was the solution of the problem as it appeared in Roman times, in the different terms of a different age and world. The failure of the oligarchy and the impotence of the plebs, however, were its essential features; and in Russia, too, the failure of the Tsarist oligarchy and the impotence of the plebs were unmistakable. Terrorism might shake the supports of the régime; but something more was needed.

Tkachev, the jacobinist and Blanquist, laid all his emphasis upon the 'impotence of the plebs'. Like the populists, he believed that the Russian peasants were the bearers of 'the seeds of socialism'. There was no need, therefore, to import Western socialist theories into Russia. Tkachev was not a Marxist, but neither was he a populist. The people could not themselves bring socialism to birth. His paper, *The Tocsin* (*Nabat*), recognised the impotence of the plebs, but looked to French jacobinism and to Blanqui for the remedy. 'Neither now nor in the future', he wrote, 'can the people accomplish the social revolution by their own efforts. . . . It is only the revolutionary minority that can perform this task.'

In the last decade of the 19th century the Russian intelligentsia literally threw themselves into Marxism. It was a legal Marxism, tolerated by the police, who found that the discussion of economic facts and theories in a jargon incomprehensible to the masses effectively sidetracked a section of the intelligentsia, who could thus be distinguished from the revolutionary agitators. Marxist literature was distasteful to the populists because of its lack of feeling. But their own lack of ideas prevented them from forming any general plan at all. There was, however, a new tendency: to trust in the spontaneity of the masses; and this led to 'economism'. Those who believed in the 'spontaneity of the masses', and who were known as 'economists', held that the intelligentsia could learn more from the workers than it could teach them. Only the 'labouring masses' were *creative*.

The process of industrialisation, and the drama of proletarianisation, gathered speed in the last decade of the 19th century, producing strikes and even riots. But these were isolated events which led nowhere. Without leadership, the aggressiveness of the proletariat achieved no real successes. Meanwhile, the aggressiveness of the intellectuals expressed itself in the literary polemics of clandestine publications in which 'position' confronted 'position' and 'thesis' opposed 'thesis'.

There was no correlation between the two types of aggressiveness; their separate ingredients remained unfused and uncreative. The groups which proliferated and split and coalesced among the intelligentsia were unable to 'awaken' or 'activate' any significant number of workers. Plekhanov's 'emancipation of labour' group at Geneva issued a few pamphlets, but they never got beyond theory and the polemics of intellectuals. Within Russia 'fighting squads' were formed, which owned theoretical and tactical principles, though not always the same ones, but were never merged into a single all-embracing organisation.[1] The so-called Russian Social-Democratic Labour Party was only just coming to birth, and the struggle against the Tsarist régime was still what it had been all through the 19th century: local alliances and isolated actions. The different types of political romanticism characteristic of backward 19th-century Russia are still recognisable in the tradition which links the *narodovoltsy* of the 'seventies and 'eighties with the *Social Revolutionaries* of the first decade of the 20th century, exhibiting the same historical oscillation between the two poles of individual terrorism and the spontaneity of the masses. Then Lenin elaborated the principles which were to make him Lenin. One may fairly call creative the period in which *Iskra* was founded. (It was set up in the presses of the German social-democrats at Stuttgart and Munich.) It was then that Lenin wrote and published *What is to be Done?*—in which he discusses the impotence of the plebs in 20th-century terms, and points to the theoretical remedy by defining the type of organisation which was, in fact, to dominate the first half of the 20th century. His language is not so original as his thought; he pours the new wine of his idea into the old bottle labelled *Party*. The word *party*, becoming now finally and totally ambiguous, enabled him to circulate the new wine without needlessly alarming the enemy or the distant friend—in other words, the liberal, whether pale pink or almost red. Yet there can be no mistaking Lenin's meaning.

* * * *

At the same time Georges Sorel was beginning to elaborate, from his studies of French and Italian strikes, the doctrine which he presented in its final form in his *Reflections on Violence*; and it was also between 1900 and 1907 that Vilfredo Pareto put forward[2] his theory of the *circulation of the élites*.[3] There was resistance to all these theories on the part of

[1] The word then acquired the political resonance which it has for the 20th century.

[2] In the introduction to *Les systèmes socialistes* (Paris, 1920–3).

[3] Élite: a small number derived by selection from a larger number. It is probable that Pareto's conception of the élite arose from his original meditations upon Vacher de Lapouge's theory of social selection. Pareto transformed Lapouge's 'zoological materialism' into 'positivist sociology'.

those whom they startled or embarrassed; but history has been kinder to them than the universities. They were all developed during the same period, and were not completely unrelated to one another. It is also worth noting that their three authors were breathing the same European intellectual atmosphere at the same time. Lenin and Pareto could have met one another on the shores of the lake of Geneva. Sorel and Pareto had a high opinion of one another's work. Pareto published many articles in the Italian reviews; and Sorel was read in Italy. Pareto's sources are in liberalism, in the economic theories of Walras, and also in Roman history (like those of two other great Italians, Machiavelli and Vico). Sorel derives from Christianity, and from Vico, Marx, and Bernstein. All three were keenly alive to the weaknesses of the Marxism of their day. Pareto was concerned to refute them; Sorel and Lenin, each in his own way, to make a 'fresh start'. All three were critical of parliamentary democracy and of the use made of it by European socialists. Lenin showed as little enthusiasm for introducing a parliamentary régime in Russia as Sorel and Pareto showed for preserving it in its existing forms in France and Italy. All three of them condemn, in their own language, the farrago of ideological jesuitry, windy oratory, and political trickery that corrupted the parliaments of the Continent—they were no more lenient to Jaurès than to the turncoats and opportunists; and all of them placed efficiency above all else. Lenin wanted an efficient Party, Sorel an efficient Syndicalism, and Pareto an efficient governing class which should be more than a mere possessing class. They all advocate the intelligent use of force, and condemn the debilitating and costly tactics of the 'spellbinder'. They look forward to a new élite. In the days of the republican bloc, when both Lloyd George and Crispi rose to fame, the best political writers of Europe showed a distrust of all parliamentarianism, even socialist. The élite hoped for by Lenin, Sorel, and Pareto are not merely new but virile; they will establish the true 'quiritary values'[1] of the 20th century and will have no inhibitions about the use of violence. Sorel was receptive to all ideas. Pareto was devoted to the 'objectivity' of science in its coldest and most ruthless form. Alone of the three, Lenin was obsessed with organisation, in addition to being a man of action. It was at this time that he reached the full conception of the passionate fixed idea which was to integrate his strong personality, and christened it 'organisation'. And by his actions he gave an historical demonstration of the validity of some of Sorel's ideas, and, even more, of Pareto's.

Pareto will allow himself no personal hopes. He claims to be a scientist and nothing more; but he reveals himself in his 'objective' language as personally as Sorel's 'subjective' language reveals Sorel. As for Lenin,

[1] 'Valeurs quiritaires' (Sorel).

he writes without any graces at all; he is not addressing the cultivated public of Europe.

Each of them is in favour of a 'hard' régime. They all express the need and the nostalgia and the presentiment of a world-view and a world organisation of an opposite kind to those which prevailed while capitalism was establishing itself in Europe. They are hostile to the ideologies and the morality which veiled behind a parliamentary curtain[1] the domination, exploitation, and fleecing of the world by a shopkeeping plutocracy. What they unconsciously stand for is a sort of revival of the war-like as opposed to the mercantile ethos, and as a result they exalt violence at the expense of cunning.

Lenin was born into the official class in a country where an official was a sort of officer. He had been influenced by Tkachev and also by Nechaev. The latter held that revolutionaries of 'the third or second rank' should be absolutely subordinate to the key people or indispensable 'elements', who would even have power of life and death over the rest. Nechaev's solution of the problem of revolutionary organisation was therefore the most authoritarian and the most violent possible. But how was complete subordination to be secured? The famous address[2] (drafted by Marx) of the Central Council of the Communist League to its members, in which the idea of *permanent revolution* appears for the first time,[3] had already postulated 'an autonomous organisation, both secret and public at the same time'[4] which should 'ally' itself with the 'bourgeois democrats' and use the alliance *in order to destroy them*. Such an organisation was necessary in order to watch and control the 'allies', whose function it was to be the host upon which the revolutionary organism would feed. On his first visit to western Europe Lenin had had a close view of the German Social-Democratic Party, for which in *What is to be Done?* he makes no attempt to hide his admiration. Now, there could be observed in this party a sort of sociological constant, which Robert Michels has called the *iron law of oligarchy*.[5] The German Social-Democratic Party tended to become a closed hierarchical society. Michels does not allow for the fact that German social democracy, with headquarters in Berlin, which was also in its own way a centralising influence in Germany, succumbed unconsciously to the pervasive Prussian influence of the prestige of the German army which was believed not only by the German bourgeois but by the whole world to be a model of organisation.

[1] Pareto, a liberal economist, at first only reproaches parliament for interfering with the free functioning of capitalism.

[2] March 1850.

[3] According to Ryazanov, Lenin knew the passage by heart.

[4] Lenin quotes these words textually in *What is to be Done?*

[5] See Robert Michels's classic work, *Political Parties: a Sociological Study of the Oligarchical Tendencies of Modern Democracy* (Engl. transl., 1949).

We see, then, that the sociologists who best understood their age devoted their attention and ability to the problem of the impotence of the plebs; being sociologists of the present, it was natural that they should be ignored by the society they studied, for it was still robust enough to defend itself 'like a living organism subjected to vivisection.'[1] Judging by results rather than intentions, Lenin also can be considered a sociologist. The situations he analysed were real ones; and the analysis suffers less from the fact that his methods were often summary than it gains from the fact of being *an analysis of a real situation.*

* * * *

If, in contemplating world history, we isolate the histories of the various civilisations which have succeeded one another but overlapped, we may conclude that Marx, and his followers, were over-impressed by the growth and culmination of capitalism and its accompanying social developments. This was an emotional compensation, the reaction to an affective trauma.[2] Technical and scientific progress and the radical transformation of the human environment, from the first steam engine to the present day, have had the effect of *confirming* a habit of messianic aspiration. Men have believed that the world was entering upon an epoch not only unprecedented but also incomparable with any previous age; and they have neglected to look for similarity beneath the differences. In such men, the messianic spirit has prevailed over the Greek spirit. The problem of the impotence of the plebs had already presented itself at the crisis of another civilisation.[3] And a similar solution to Lenin's was found for it, *mutatis mutandis*, namely militarisation. Although it is risky to make analogies between one age and another, this parallel does hold good, and Lenin was, without knowing it, the first theoretician and the first exponent of Cæsarism in our time. As a Marxist, he would have censored this impious thought if it could have occurred to him; but in our world, as in the Roman world, the most active 'elements', the special instruments of historic change, have been militarised; and in our world, as in that one, the tendency is towards an all-devouring *imperium*—an *imperium* which recognises, theoretically, no limits either in time or in space.[4]

[1] Robert Michels, op. cit.

[2] The author of this book draws freely upon a very extensive vocabulary of technical and scientific terms. We have followed his practice as closely as possible, but complete consistency in translation is impracticable. Thus, to give two examples, the French nouns 'affect' and 'représentation' have usually been translated in these pages as 'affect' and 'representation'; but in some places it has seemed preferable to translate the first as 'feeling' or 'emotion' and the second as 'image' or 'idea'. [*Translators' note.*]

[3] But historical analogies of this kind must be used only with the greatest discretion.

[4] But our world shows nothing analogous to the Roman *tolerance* which was extended to every country that participated in the benefits of the Universal State.

Marxists exaggerate the importance of the industrial revolution and the transformation of material life. It is pure eschatology to see in these things the beginning of the end, the opening stage of the transition from the reign of necessity to the reign of freedom, or from pre-history to history, or (according to certain anti-Marxists who are merely inverted Marxists) from history to post-history. Marxism can usefully be regarded as a neurosis resulting from an affective trauma: the drama of proletarianisation is the cause of the trauma, and from then on the experience is rationalised and an appropriate *Weltanschauung* and 'praxis' are evolved. The inverse and symmetrical attitude is a fatalism, whose hidden source is probably in astrology, which can act as an antidote to Marxism but which is also the rationalisation of an affective experience. In this case the trauma is *disillusionment with mankind* because it seems never to change. The two attitudes present a contrast similar to that between messianic eschatology (both Aryan and Semitic, Jewish and Persian) on the one hand, and the astrological fatalism of Babylon on the other. The dualism in man of the irredeemable animal and the indomitable deifying impulse draws the scientific spirit both one way and the other; our latter-day Babylonians are drawn towards a transfiguration of the past, and our Marxists towards a transfiguration of the future.

* * * *

It was in the course of a polemic against the partisans of the spontaneity of the masses that Lenin defined clearly his position as regards the major question of the time: What must be the structure of the Russian Social-Democratic Party if it is in fact to perform the function which justifies its existence? It was not possible simply to copy the structure of the Western socialist parties which lived under parliamentary, democratic, and liberal régimes. The field of operations was too different. Lenin, like Tkachev, and unlike the economists, thinks that a leaven is needed before the proletarian lump will rise. He agrees with Kautsky: 'Socialist consciousness is an element imported into the proletarian class struggle from outside',[1] and not an element which arises spontaneously within it. The proletariat—Kautsky continues—did not *create* either economic science or modern technology. Both these things, and socialism as well, are the creations of bourgeois intellectuals. Lenin adds that the *intellectuals are a 'revolutionary bacillus'*[2]: the intelligentsia has a real educational mission, and intellectuals are necessary for both agitation and propaganda. But history had already decided the matter. At the time when Lenin was writing, the intelligentsia was already performing this role. The very conditions of the

[1] '*Von aussen hineingetragenes.*' [2] Lenin, *What is to be Done?*

struggle implied first priority for the problem of organisation. Secret groups were a necessity. But how was the dichotomy to be overcome between what was later to be called *mass action* (which was already occurring sporadically in the form of strikes) and *conspiracy* (which was the only course open to those whom autocracy branded as illegal)? For Lenin there was one, and only one, solution: to copy the structure of the army or, more exactly, to borrow from it some of its most characteristic and typical features, those which made an army of a body of men. Only a structure on military lines can bring a very large number of men into an operation as participants, while at the same time guaranteeing unity of plan and outlook and secrecy of action. An army of a new kind is therefore the solution of the problem: or, more precisely, a new thing which, without being an army, possesses those characteristics of one which will enable it to perform its appointed task. The characteristics in question are in fact the essential military characteristics: a small 'nucleus' is in command of an obedient majority. This command and this obedience can only be ensured by a strong organisation; and this organisation must be centralised, on the army model. There must be a 'dozen tried and talented leaders (and talented men are not born by hundreds), professionally trained, schooled by long experience and working in perfect harmony.'[1] Secret work must be concentrated in the hands of the smallest possible number. Who will be the staff officers? Who will compose that small directing nucleus which shall ensure the continuity of the movement through changing events? The answer is: 'Men who devote their entire lives, and not simply their free evenings, to the revolution',[2] men whose profession is revolutionary action. It must be a true *professional army*, but an army, as they would say today, of 'cadres', for each one of the staff officers, senior as well as junior, is liable to find himself, willy-nilly, in the role of a soldier of the line. Lenin, who is the complete Marxist, always preserves the 'class perspective'; but as an empirical and practical sociologist his answer to the old problem of the Cæsars is, in fact, a cæsarian one. But it is, of course, expressed in Marxist terms, for the men of our day, unlike the Romans, must always have a theory.

The type of army Lenin requires is adapted for the typical 20th-century non-military warfare: 'We must have "our own men" . . . everywhere, among all social strata, and in all positions from which we can learn the inner springs of our State mechanism. Such men are required for propaganda and agitation, but in a still larger measure for organisation'.[3] An organisation of this kind can only maintain itself if it knows how to select its members. The selection must be rigorous. What cate-

[1] *What is to be Done?* p. 114 (London; Martin Lawrence, n.d.). [2] *Iskra*, No. 1.
[3] *What is to be Done?*, p. 83.

gories of men provide suitable recruits for this professional army? 'A working man who is at all talented and "promising" must not be left to work eleven hours a day in a factory.' We see here the first principle of selection of the new political élites. 'We must arrange that he be maintained by the party.'[1] The proletariat therefore provides raw material for the new élite, *but not the proletariat alone. The intelligentsia will retain its priority.* Lenin remembers, in a revealing phrase, 'the men who dream of doing practical work even while still at school'.[2] But the next step is to convert these heterogeneous recruits into a homogeneous unity (precisely the same problem that an army has to deal with). Among these men 'whose profession is that of revolutionists . . . all distinctions as between workers and intellectuals . . . must be dropped'.[3] Which means that by the time the Party has formed them they will be neither workers nor intellectuals but a new social, and even a new human, type. Bound by military obedience to a general staff which decides every change of tactics, trained by a long apprenticeship to all the weapons of revolutionary action, these men are under the obligation to combine legal with illegal forms of struggle; they must be members, if necessary, of an ultra-reactionary parliament and of other reactionary institutions. The party is both a machine and a machination. The picked men pick others in their turn; and wherever they penetrate, from trade unions to the most harmless-looking associations, there will be the 'small compact nucleus' which we have since come to know under the name of 'communist fraction'. This 'compact nucleus' behaves towards the rest of the association *as an organism in relation to its medium*, and thus possesses over its host the superiority of the organic over the inorganic. It uses the host for its own ends, sometimes intentionally leading an institution to disaster by perverting its direction and meaning. Lenin revives, as if by instinct, the rules of the militant sects and orders; the organisation that is at the same time both secret and public, both legal and illegal. It cannot be altogether secret, because it proposes to gain 'the unlimited confidence of the masses'. Thus it retains what was effective in Blanquism while rejecting its frankly aristocratic basis. Blanqui's active minority is combined with Nechaev's secret society. It is sensitive to the least change of mood in the masses, it lives their life, as the 'populists' and 'economists' wanted to do, but it has the centralised and hierarchical organisation of Kautsky's party. From French jacobinism Lenin took its network of popular groups, while rejecting its individualism. *His organisation combined the resources of a secret society, a democratic political party, and an army.* But whereas in an army the soldier is not always on duty, the 'organisation' claims every breath of its 'responsible' members' lives. They are mobilised not

[1] *What is to be Done?*, p. 104. [2] ibid., p. 101. [3] ibid., p. 105.

for the duration of a war but for life. Christianity allowed men a private life; and this was not taken away from them, in the West, either by feudalism or by the 'despotic' monarchies of Bourbon and Habsburg, or by the 'bourgeois' régime. But now it is abolished: for the true Bolshevik there is no inner retreat to which he can withdraw to *detach himself* even for a moment. His door must always be open, as in ancient Cuzco. Bolshevism grew up in a civilisation and a part of the world where there had never been a complete distinction between political and religious, or temporal and spiritual; it demands more than Christ, for he acknowledged Cæsar, or than Cæsar, for he was a tolerant ruler. With Bolshevism it is all or nothing, and whoever is not for it is against it. It allows nothing to exist outside itself, and anything it cannot absorb or make use of is condemned to be destroyed or to disappear. In other words, there are no duties above those that one owes to the Party, and the Party owes none except to itself. Though there are, in theory, duties towards the working class, the Party itself is in practice the sole judge of them. Those who, from outside, brought socialist consciousness to the working class are still extorting a heavy payment for the gift.

Professional revolutionaries in Russia before the October Revolution were men deprived of work and legal existence. To have been once in prison made it difficult or impossible ever to find a place in Tsarist society. The *okhrana* allowed them no destiny except to be revolutionaries. What was there to do in exile abroad, or even in Siberia (for the concentration camp techniques of the 20th century were not yet invented), except to read and meditate and exchange ideas with other men confined to the same circle? The Tsarist régime tended by its very methods of self-defence to create the revolutionary 'medium' around itself. By driving them out of society it left these men no other aim than to destroy society. There had been revolutionaries in the 19th century who had no particular profession, but they had a romantic and literary streak; they were something between the hero and the tragedian. Mazzini is the perfect example. As a rule, they were not totally possessed by one fixed idea, nor concentrated, like those of the first half of the 20th century, upon the technical problems of its realisation. They were men of literature rather than of theory, and least of all were they technicians. In *What is to be Done?* Lenin *justifies* his career as a professional revolutionary, and this apologia is also a technical handbook of the conquest of power and, perhaps, of the world as well. As organiser and theorist, Lenin refers continually to Marx, with whom no doubt he identified himself. But they did not resemble one another.

CHAPTER 3

A Technological Messianism

IN Marx the professional revolutionary of the 20th century is prefigured: in the total and violent concentration of his whole personality for the service of a fixed and passional constellation of ideas. Marx's intellectual life was in despotic control of his ordinary life; and a rigid intellectual system ruled equally despotically over his intellectual life. In him the intellectual dominated the man—and the prophet dominated the intellectual. The prophet's message, in profound accord with the spirit of the age, is a *technological messianism*. It is from the Hegelian teleology that this messianism draws its first sustenance. History has a direction. But in place of the nations, each marking a stage in the progressive Realisation of the Spirit, Marx puts the two social classes. He simplifies the Hegelian scheme down to an archetypal eschatological dualism of the type of which manicheeism is historically the most illustrious example. The relay race of the nations is replaced by the duel of bourgeoisie and proletariat. But at the same time that Marx simplified the Hegelian complexity, from unconscious eschatological motives, he revealed his messianism in that technological form which is the hall-mark of his originality and historical fecundity. He marches resolutely into the tunnel of political economy. Although he also continues to exhort and organise, his words come from the remote depths of the British Museum, where *Das Kapital* is gradually being evolved. In the hey-day of English liberalism and the prosperous capitalist *Weltanschauung*, Marx obtained all the facilities for becoming the enemy of capitalism, because he knew how to seize them. (And also because, unlike totalitarianism, which is pessimistic and suspicious and tries to destroy *ab ovo* any dangerous idea or man, liberalism is easy-going and confident.) Marx exhibited the characteristic 'titanism' of reformers in the romantic age—the preface to his doctoral thesis betrays a youthful admiration for the Æschylean Prometheus—but he was a technological titan. Marx, before Lenin, studied attentively the theorists of the art of war, Clausewitz, Jomini, the Maréchal de Saxe; and he even consulted Cluseret for street fighting and the construction of barricades. At the same time he absorbed all the political economy of his day, from Adam Smith to Rodbertus, and also the works of those thinkers whom he distinguished from himself by the epithet 'utopian' (though we prefer to call them, by contrast with Marx, the *unarmed prophets*), from Robert Owen, St. Simon, and Fourier to Proudhon.[1] It is striking that he should have been able to combine with the characteristics of a prophet those of the founder of a sect—the bitterest intolerance and refusal to understand other points of view. (One has only to remember the churlish intransigence and ill feeling he showed, and caused others to show, towards Proudhon, Lassalle, and Bakunin; in other words, towards anyone who could conceivably threaten his doctrinal dictatorship or his intellectual primacy.) One may add to this certain traits characteristic of the theologian (particularly the *odium theologicum*): ingenuity in appealing to the 'letter', or sleight of hand in substituting for it the 'spirit', in the conciliar texts and papal bulls of the new religion, and in addresses and discourses before workers' associations, and the resolutions and decisions of congresses. Further, he was perhaps the greatest pamphleteer and polemist since Tertullian, and one is tempted to compare him with Aquinas for his thoroughness in defining orthodoxy, with Loyola for his will to impose it, and with St. Paul for his fury of proselytising. There has been no one since Marx with a psychic energy whose versatility and power has enabled him to grasp a comparable number of diverse subjects or display such contrasted virtues. His intellectual omnivorousness and his titanic sense of disaster are profoundly related to the ascendant phase of capitalism and to the apogee of English liberal society. Major phenomena are often difficult to isolate.

The men who bring something to their fellows, the bearers of 'charisma',[2] seem to feel a moral compulsion or necessity to 'choose a hero'. The hero Lenin chose was Marx. After Marx's death the fields of thought and spheres of action he had brought together fell apart again. There were politicians, 'leaders', and organisers in the Second International; but to explorers and adventurous spirits the atmosphere was unbreathable. Either they passed by, or if they entered it they soon left again, like Georges Sorel—though he, in any case, came to Marxism too late to be in any sense a representative of it. There were, however, a few theorists who carried further some of the Marxian analyses or adapted them to the new situation.[3] Lenin himself was scarcely a theorist, but his *Development of Capitalism in Russia* shows both that Marx was his hero

[1] In this list Pecqueur and Sismondi, to whom Marx owes a lot, occupy a special and interesting midway position (cf. their own works; cf. also Andler: *Commentaires du Manifesto Communiste*, and Elie Halévy: *L'ère des tyrannies* (Paris; Gallimard, 1938), and *Histoire du socialisme européen* (Paris; Gallimard, 1948)).

[2] To borrow an expression of Max Weber's.

[3] cf. Rosa Luxemburg's *Accumulation of Capital* (Engl. trans.; London, 1951), and Rudolf Hilferding's *Das Finanzkapital*. Also, generally, the products of the intellectual activities of the Austro-Marxists.

and that what he wished to acquire from the West was, first and mainly, whatever was applicable to the conditions of his own Russian environment.

A man such as Marx could not easily find a place in 19th-century German society. Industry, commerce, and the intellectual professions were the only ones open to Jews. But money had no prestige or seduction for Marx. And as for politics, a Disraeli was possible in England but not in the Prussia that was soon to be Bismarck's domain. Lassalle was merely a tool, in Bismarck's eyes. But the world of ideas was less unfriendly. Another Jew, Stahl, was the theorist of feudal reaction. He systematised and attempted to rationalise the claim of the landowners to retain their hegemony and control the growth of capitalism. There is a sort of parallel between the situation of the proletariat in 1840–8 as seen by Marx and the situation of the Jews in Germany, and it may be an unconscious connection in his mind between the two that enables him to pass so easily from one to the other[1] and to make the solution of the Jewish question dependent (like all other questions, it is true) upon the solution of the proletarian question. If he refuses to acknowledge the myth of the chosen people he replaces it by another: the chosen class.[2]

Between *The Jewish Question* and the *Communist Manifesto*, from 1843 to 1847, the conception of the chosen class emerges and is confirmed. Capitalism, says Marx, has inherited the nature of Judaism. (Here, no doubt, is the origin of Sombart's theory, which Max Weber refuted, concerning the Jewish influence on the formation of capitalism.) Marx brings the Jewish question back to the proletarian question. He quotes Bauer: 'The Jew, who exists only on tolerance in Vienna, nevertheless determines by his financial power the fate of the whole Empire. [Bauer is thinking no doubt of the Rothschild influence in Europe after the Congress of Vienna.] The Jew, to whom the most insignificant German state can refuse all political rights, is the arbitrator of the fate of Europe. . . . The difference between the real political power of the Jew and his political rights is the difference between politics and the power of money.'[3] Marx concludes that the Jewish question cannot be solved in

[1] cf. *The Jewish Question.*

[2] It should be noted that it makes no sense to limit to certain semitic tribes the eschatological myths and the messianism which are, in fact, to be found in ancient religious history among (Persian) aryans before they appear among the Jews, and which seem then to be diffused over a wide geographical-cultural area from Asia Minor to the Indian ocean. Some of them, indeed, do not appear in the Old Testament until *after the exile* (cf. especially Charles Autran: *La Préhistoire aryenne du christianisme*) and during the period of Persian hegemony. The archetype to which the myth of the chosen people belongs was revived later, and displayed a vigorous creative activity, in Protestantism and in Jansenism. In Protestant countries the idea of the *elect individual* was used as a justification for capitalism in its beginnings (cf. Max Weber). It was also used to justify the particularisms of the 19th century. From oppressed people to chosen people is an easy stage.

[3] *The Jewish Question.*

isolation; as he experiences it, the Jewish problem is identified with the proletarian problem, the chosen people are replaced by a chosen class. The situation of which other Jews complain, as Jews, is experienced by Marx as a 'human' situation. The 'human essence' has been alienated by a capitalism that has inherited the essence of Judaism (we see here the reciprocal interaction of the affective, passional fixed idea and the systematising and organising work of the intellect); it will be restored by the action of that social class whose present abasement reveals it as the chosen class, just as it was by their abasement that the Jews were recognised by their greatest prophets to be the chosen people. This class is by its nature universal, 'because its suffering is universal, and it claims no particular right because it has suffered no particular wrong, but universal wrong. . . . It can only emancipate itself by emancipating itself from all other classes and, thereby, emancipating them all.'[1] One might say that Marx is here investing the proletariat with the characteristics of the Jew at the end of the feudal age: his proletarian has no country, and his very existence is a sort of negation of national particularity. (This Manchester-inspired vision has not been confirmed by history.) According to the theory, the proletarian who sells his labour in the market is no more rooted to any one place and has no more feeling for any one country than the medieval Jew. (But Marx underestimates the real particularity and partiality of proletarians in real history.[2]) Marx sees the proletarian as an element that is *in* society but not *of* it; veiling his eschatology in Hegelian language, he declares that the proletariat is '*the decomposition of society manifested in the form of a particular social class*'. His own role in relation to the proletariat is exactly the role of a prophet towards his people, except that the blood kinship is replaced by purely spiritual ties. The community between them is based upon a concept, and Marx's life was devoted to giving this concept historical substance.

Marx exposed very clearly the fact that German intellect of the first half of the 19th century, being unable to master and mould the reality of German history, was legislating universally, as though there were some implicit reciprocal relationship between the feudal fragmentation of the country and the vast and 'global'[3] character of an intellectual speculation that sought to hold theology, cosmology, and history in one unlimited embrace. The concept of the proletariat enables Marx to reconcile this aspiration to think universally with the need to provide his philosophy with an incarnation in which it could realise itself and become history. From his observation of the English proletariat, which

[1] *Zur Kritik der Hegelschen Rechtsphilosophie.*

[2] cf. Michel Collinet, *La Tragédie du Marxisme.*

[3] Kierkegaard says 'world-historical' (*Postscript to Philosophic Fragments*).

was the first of modern times, he paints with unequalled power the portrait of a sort of absolute proletariat, a proletariat-in-itself, proletarian by 'essence': and in this sense Marxism is a Western synthesis, whose elements are fused together in the furnace of his messianism.

The immediate heirs of this encyclopædic titan were no better than those of Alexander the Great. Marx himself never had the chance to give his full measure as a practical revolutionary and leader, and his only active intervention was in the Rhineland. The industrialisation of Germany was not at that time sufficiently advanced for the proletariat to be able to make much progress in the messianic task assigned to it by Marx (or so Marxists say). During the crisis of 1848 Marx hesitated politically between the 'bourgeois revolution' (i.e. support of the industrial and liberal bourgeoisie against feudal absolutism and the Prussian monarchy) and the '*permanent revolution*', which he found himself more or less obliged to expound in theory at a time when he was doubtful of its application to the facts.[1] The problem was to assist the bourgeois ally while at the same time exploiting and compromising him, to support the most radical of the bourgeois policies and push them to extremes, thus compelling the democrats to prepare the work of the communists: the maximum of nationalisation (in fact, though the word was not used) and of expropriation without compensation. In this way the democrats were to be compromised in the eyes of the moderate parties. But the 'communists', in addition to trying to turn all 'democratic' measures into so many 'attacks upon private property', must *duplicate* the legal power of the bourgeois government by 'clubs' and 'workers' committees'; and these committees must continually outbid the offers of the bourgeois power, thus driving it towards a more extreme policy, and must also try to establish themselves as a new power while undermining the democrats' efforts to establish their own (this is where the *workers' militias* make their appearance). It was typical of Marx's destiny that he himself never had the chance to put into practice this programme, which served so well as general plan and directive for 'Marxist' revolutions and revolutionary attempts in the 20th century. But it fell into abeyance, except as a theme for academic manifestoes, until the arrival of Lenin and Trotsky.

Between the death of Marx and the rise of Lenin there were a lot of politicians and a few theorists, but nothing more. Marx may be regarded as a professional revolutionary, but *bound* within the realm of theory. History imposed upon him his specialisation as a technological prophet. It was working men who had climbed into the bourgeoisie, and lawyers, and bohemians, and professors, who claimed his mantle after his death, and imposed themselves upon the workers, until the appearance of

[1] cf. *Address to the Central Council of the Communist League* (March 1850).

Lenin. At the end of the 19th century the future could be read in these two facts: *the organised discipline of German social-democracy, and the social unrest and conspiratorial politics in Russia.* The 'bourgeoisification' of the Western socialist parties—and particularly the German party, which was by force of circumstances the chief inheritor of Marxism—took place simultaneously in two ways: first, the party and the trade unions developed within the world 'to be destroyed' and prospered there; they were administered by salaried officials, they became affiliated in a thousand ways with the 'class enemy' and built up their movement upon the foundations of a soil which, according to Marxism, was not their own; secondly, the leading spirits were moulded into 'leaders' after the pattern of the bourgeois parliaments whose manners they adopted, and all the more easily because many of them, particularly in France, were lawyers, doctors, and university graduates of one kind or another, whose roots were in the petty bourgeoisie. Thanks to Russia's peculiar historical circumstances, which did not include a bourgeois period, Lenin was not faced with this problem of 'the bourgeois degeneration of socialists', but with other peculiarly Russian 'deviations' such as populism and the attachment to certain autochthonous institutions (*mir* and *artel*) from which a direct development of socialism was expected.[1] All that Lenin consciously did was to insist on a return to pure Marxism. Although Marx seldom left London, he tried to achieve by the written word what St. Paul achieved in his missionary travels. He kept looking for favourable opportunities for bringing his doctrine to bear, and he took them wherever they presented themselves; for he felt no organic attachment to any one country. No doubt Lenin also believed himself unattached. But he had not the time, nor perhaps the inclination, for the kind of world-interpretation that occupied Marx. Except, indeed, in respect of one subject, and that one of capital importance, namely organisation. For organisation acts upon the historical present, and must therefore take into account all the characteristics of the contemporary historical situation. Marx kept abreast of the whole movement of ideas in his time, but Lenin seems only to pursue knowledge in so far as it can be applied. Unlike Marx, he uses sociology only as an engineer uses mathematics.

For Marx, the primordial fact is production, and all other facts, without exception, must be referred to it before they can be understood. In the beginning was man's production of his means of existence, and production still remains the key to history. Marx proved, in his own work, that this conception makes it possible, starting from a given point in time, to interpret history in both directions, past and future. It

[1] In the preface to the Russian translation of the *Communist Manifesto*, Marx outlines a method of reconciling the two points of view. But in the end they proved mutually exclusive.

provides a basis for a science of human motives, from which the art of politics can be deduced. Upon this hypothesis the grand strategy of history and the laws of conquest and the rules for conquerors will all depend, above all, upon the historical variations in the methods of production.

New light is gradually brought to bear upon the facts of history, from the class war to the phenomena of culture, religion, and art, by referring them to this central datum. It provides a method for classifying realities and for defining and investigating problems; it is also a principle of research and an ordering principle which supplies a theory for distinguishing the primary from the secondary or, in practice, the urgent from the less urgent. It is possible, however, to accept both the principle and the method up to a point as being appropriate for certain problems and certain circumstances, or indeed it is possible to accept them unreservedly, without being either a Marxist or a socialist and without accepting the chosen class and the mission of the proletariat—in a word, without accepting the eschatology which inspired Marx in his youth or the Hegelian presentation by which it acquires the status of a system.

CHAPTER 4

Structure of the Army

UP to the time of the Russian revolution the ideas expressed by Lenin in *What is to be Done?* remained, from the point of view of the positivist historian, nothing more than ideas. The split between mensheviks and bolsheviks did not at the time appear to have the importance which, in the light of later events, we know it to have had; and it would be a mistake to think that 1917 found the instrument of revolution perfected and ready for use. It was still necessary for a small group of men 'to transform [in the words of Trotsky, the most articulate of the group] a certain world view into flesh and blood, subordinating to it their whole consciousness and the whole world of their private feelings'. Even in 1917 these men had not yet reached complete agreement among themselves. Lenin and Trotsky knew by experience what a gulf separated them from European socialists with their different historical and social background.[1] To the Germans and Austrians Trotsky seemed a crazy fanatic, and to Trotsky the Germans and Austrians, with the exception of Liebknecht and Rosa Luxemburg, appeared lukewarm sceptics and, often, unconscious conservatives. He called them 'professors and [potentially] perpetuators of bourgeois society'. And Lenin, from his exile, strained himself to reach the ears of the bolshevik professional revolutionaries in Russia during the 'period of reaction' (from 1906 to the first world war), whose only exploits known to the outer world were acts of terrorist 'expropriation'. (At European socialist congresses Lenin was at pains to avoid disowning them.) To use Trotsky's language (which later imposed itself as the language of bolshevik theory),[2] it was a period of ebb; there was nothing to do but wait for events to mature and prepare for the next round. The Campaign was not yet in being, it was still in the womb; and the time was not ripe for the engineers of history and technicians of revolution, until the German Staff, at war with the Tsar, loosed Lenin upon Russia by allowing him to cross Germany in the famous sealed coach. 'It is a measure of war no less legitimate than poison gas,' General

[1] cf. Trotsky's opinion of these socialists in his autobiography. The chapter entitled 'German Socialism' is typical.

[2] cf. Stalin: *Problems of Leninism, History of the Communist Party of the Soviet Union.*

Hoffmann is reported to have said. From this point circumstances took control. Lenin played off the soviets of workers and soldiers against a democratic bourgeois government in alliance with the 'imperialists' of the Entente and trying to continue an unpopular and mishandled war. The peasants in the army became restive as soon as there was a chance of seizing the land, for which it was essential to be on the spot. Lenin's 'Organisation', which was his answer to the question *What is to be Done?*, was not yet in control of events. But the peasants in military uniform, temporarily uprooted, confused by the war, disheartened by the mistakes of the Tsarist military administration and the conflicting orders of the high command, made an ideal medium for the transmission of catchwords expressly designed to release and justify and exploit their own natural impulses: Back to the village, seize the land, stop the war! And now the revolutionaries can see the revolution's victory on the horizon. But the social-revolutionaries, heirs of populism, and the mensheviks, attracted by Western parliamentary democracy, and the bolsheviks are not all hoping for the same revolution nor even for the same victory. Events will clarify themselves, and accounts will be paid, in action; and everything happens as though the ultimate victors were playing the others off against one another for the establishment of something entirely new at the expense of the ideologies of all alike. It is action that interests Lenin, and for him all theories that can help to advance it are good, not excluding those of Bakunin and the Communards, from which he undoubtedly borrowed.[1] But for the period as a whole the best theory was still the one which Marx had put forward, perhaps regretfully, in his *Address to the Central Council of the Communist League*, March 1850. The *duplication of power* is successfully practised, and the revolutionaries, by continually outbidding the democratic government, carry it farther and farther out of its depth. The provisional governments from February to October 1917 were entangled in a bankrupt inheritance (the problem of liquidating Tsarism and coming to some decision about the war that the country would accept). What the political situation required was the exploitation, the calculated disorientation and the control of men's impulses and appetites from moment to moment, so as to convert their energy into the driving force for historical change. Catchwords were selected to gratify and justify these impulses; they represented a compromise between the objectives in view and the collective emotions which provided the motive power to reach them. The tactics outlined in the *Address* of 1850—'permanent revolution', 'duplication of power', 'people's militias'—have the austere perfection of a blueprint. Applied to a given real situation they presuppose additional virtues which can only be awakened

[1] cf. *The State and Revolution.*

or revealed in action: the gift of handling men, for example, and not merely the demagogic art[1] of adding fuel to excitement, but the ability to take advantage of the *right moment* and to keep *in touch* with the masses. It is necessary to know just how far one can go *this time*, and not go too far or be carried away; and this implies a special sensitiveness in estimating what risks can be taken and at what moment, and how long that moment will last. It is also necessary to know how to let go and withdraw in good time, and to recognise the periods of 'ebb' and 'flow' which may bring disaster if they are not foreseen and controlled. For all this, although it is certainly better to have read and understood Marx, it is not sufficient to possess a merely theoretical understanding. The virtue of *praxis* is that in the world of physical fact we verify the science that we apply by our industry in applying it. In the world of human relations and of power, which is *sui generis*, *praxis* fills in the gaps left by theory; for theory is always general and not particular, and it is only by being continually reinterpreted that it can be applied to the changing and particular situations of historical becoming. In this world we are no longer in the precise and static realm of knowledge, and new qualities are needed. The special qualities appropriate to the military leader in a new type of war, and to the specialist of power, are not conferred by knowledge and theory alone, however 'correct'; they depend upon character, and character, as Stendhal said, 'is the one virtue that is not acquired in solitude', because it cannot be manifested except in our relations with others. In this sphere, where Marx left them everything to do, the 'great bolsheviks' had to discover for themselves that art of inventing catchwords satisfactory both to the political intelligence of professional revolutionaries and to the affectivity of the masses. The catchwords which then began to circulate among the masses played a part similar to that of advertisement in capitalist industry. Like advertisement, they depended upon suggestion, and the method of suggestion was similar. The word slogan is used today to describe both methods. But in 1917 this was not foreseen.

* * * *

Kerensky had the hardest task. It was not so easy to govern at that time as to make exaggerated promises, incite workers and soldiers to agitation, and sustain and inflame their excitement. But Lenin's instrument was not perfected until after his rise to power and during the civil war. Let us compare the Russia of the bolsheviks with the France of the Convention—neglecting the considerable differences in order to fix certain similarities: the Convention had to deal with a foreign war and

[1] Demagogic in the etymological sense. The art that we find in the earliest democracies known to us, those of the Greek *polis*.

with a civil war, and with the discontent of former officials and constitutionalists and monarchists—in a word, with the moderates. In France as in Russia what happened was that a centralised and despotic 'organism', a faction *par excellence*, emerged from the factional strife and gradually overcame all its rivals. The questions at issue were matters of life and death both for those who raised them and for their opponents. The nerve system of revolutionary France was the network of popular 'clubs' through which a despotic, though an improvised and at first a needy central power, could impose itself and command assistance, enthusiastic or compulsory, in all parts of the country. The nerve system of revolutionary Russia was the bolshevik party. But there is a major difference to be noted. The French jacobins did admittedly tend to rely upon foreign 'sympathisers' and to create 'sansculottes' wherever it seemed possible. French intervention was synonymous with the abolition of feudal rights, but it also awakened nationalisms which were very soon directed against France in a formidable coalition, which compelled the levying of burdensome taxes for defence. The Russians in 1917, on the other hand, had not invaded any foreign territory; and in the eyes of the European 'bourgeois democracies' the Tsarist régime had seemed a barbarous anachronism. Throughout the 19th century Russia had been the 'gendarme of reaction', and all through the century European liberals had been wholeheartedly for Poland against the Tsar. So it was that in his first proclamations Trotsky did not seem to be the spokesman of an empire at war with other empires, but the announcer of a people's deliverance (or so it appeared to many European liberals, if not all). The socialist parties possessing a tradition (or even several traditions) constituted a political climate which influenced not only the working and middle classes but the whole public opinion of western Europe. Although they had not been able to prevent it, socialists had not wanted the European war. The event was so contrary to their expectations, to their creed and their way of life, or, at least, their organisation, that it seemed to those of them who remained socialists that, in this clash of nations, a whole period of socialism must be coming to an end. Moreover, many people were overwhelmed by the sufferings of war, and for the more or less disillusioned adherents of optimistic rationalism such sufferings make an 'absurdity' of the world. They want the sufferings to have been 'for some purpose'. Hence the success in Europe of the Wilsonian 'ideology', and not only with the defeated to whom it promised more lenient terms of peace. Hence also the more or less ephemeral myths of the 'war to end war' and of 'the Revolution'. Many socialists looked for a reorganisation of the world on entirely new principles; and although professional diplomats looked askance at Trotsky's radio appeal, over the heads of the governments, to the 'oppressed masses' of the belligerent countries, his words awoke in those masses a profound response. As a Marxist he addressed himself to the proletariat, and as a bolshevik he flouted diplomatic usage. Revolutionary France never really won the soul of the nations, because they detected too soon the imperialism behind the mask. But for bolsheviks the Europe of the Wilsonian era was a field ploughed ready for the propagandist's seed. The bolsheviks had no claims against Germany or against the Allies, and they held a trump card in the fact that Russia was herself a defeated nation. So they were able to *fix* the general aspiration for a new socialism, cleansed of treachery and redeemed from failure.[1] The masses were in the required state of receptivity, and the technicians of popular agitation were already in existence, so that the Campaign was launched outside Russia almost as soon as within. It only needed organising. And for the first time socialism was to have the resources of an immense country at its back. While the Second International was trying to recover from the shock of the war, its battered prestige could do little against the young communist parties which were arising everywhere. But these new parties had at first very little in common with the sort of organisation desired by Lenin.

Soon after the death of Jaurès (which Trotsky regarded as the end of a socialist epoch) Lenin was writing: 'The Second International did useful work in organising the proletarian masses during the long "peaceful period" in the third part of the 19th century. The task of the Third International [which was not yet in existence] will be to prepare the proletariat for revolutionary struggle against capitalist governments and for civil war against the bourgeoisie in all countries, for the conquest of political power and the victory of socialism.' The period from the October Revolution and the birth of the Third International to the speed-up of industrialisation and the five-year plans in Soviet[2] Russia may be regarded as a new period. The series of shocks which followed the first world war were only the tail end of the cyclone; and Lenin, Trotsky, and their co-religionists, who could now be found in all parts of the world—for the Faith precedes the Campaign as the myth precedes the rite or the religious movement the Church—were soon hoping that Germany and Hungary would provide the stage for the next outbreak of 'the Revolution' (technicians though they were, the dramatic eschatological sense was still deeply alive in them). For Marx, to assist revolutionary agitation wherever it occurred, meant to study the facts and to issue addresses, tracts, and pamphlets; but these were 19th-

[1] cf. Georges Sorel: *Plaidoyer pour Lénine*, appendix to the 1930 (French) edition of *Réflexions sur la violence*.

[2] The word is still used, though without any precise meaning. It merely serves to distinguish post-revolutionary from Tsarist Russia. Communist Russia would be more accurate, for the party is more important than the soviet (or soviets).

century methods, designed to influence men who had already been educated up to them and not to act directly upon the masses in a state of profound upheaval. But the bolshevik leaders had the power to subsidise, support, and foment revolutionary agitation wherever it occurred or could be promoted; or at the very least they could influence it, both materially by the power of money and spiritually by the prestige of religion, using all the means and methods they could gradually discern and choose. They learned to specialise in playing upon those emotions which are most powerful and profitable as a spur to action.

German social democracy, which was more Marxist than any other, had been the *alma mater* of those Russian revolutionaries who now found themselves at the head of what, as Marxists, they always conceived to be the World Revolution. But those very theorists whom the Russians still admired, although they had long deplored their lack of 'revolutionary energy', now seemed to them to have gone over to the enemy. Most of them had accepted the 'imperialist war' without protest, and now they were criticising the Russian revolution and denying, on grounds of theory, its claim to be called socialist. According to Kautsky, neither the economic basis nor the historical conditioning were correct, and therefore it could not be socialism and must be something else; from the Marxist point of view, he said, it was simply an opportunist adventure. It was at this point that Lenin, without being fully aware of the historic importance of his deed, wrote *The Proletarian Revolution and the Renegade Kautsky*, and finally destroyed the ascendancy of the German theorists. Liebknecht and Rosa Luxemburg, the two who were nearest to Lenin and, even more, to Trotsky, were killed; and the German socialists Noske and Ledebour put Germany on the defensive against bolshevism, temporarily filling the role of the Junkers and permitting the rebirth of the German army from its ashes.[1] From the first there was a disequilibrium in the young International between the Russian element and the rest, with the result that the very name International, so out of fashion today, very quickly came to have a false ring. The historical consequences of this disequilibrium for the 20th century would be hard to over-estimate. The mere fact that the Russian intelligentsia came into existence had seemed to be a sign of the increasing westernisation of Russia. After European romanticism, and after Hegel, it was Marx who chiefly inspired the eagerly groping and malleable minds of Russian students and the workers whom they could reach. And although Marx was certainly the liquidator of the whole Western socialist tradition, it remains true that—in respect of its *pathos*—he was also its heir. But after the bolsheviks came to power Russia ceased to be a pupil and began to give lessons instead. The Russian

[1] cf. Benoit-Méchin, *Histoire de l'armée allemande*, vol. i.

leaders rejected their masters in the '2½ International', accusing them of treachery towards socialism, of which the Russians themselves, in their own eyes and those of their followers in all the continents of the world, were now and henceforth the outstanding representatives. Up to the time of Peter the Great the history of Russia had been quite distinct from European history. Its problems were those of a frontierless country opening upon immense level plains inhabited by still primitive peoples, which were gradually Russianised by the slow advance of the Cossacks along the great rivers. Up to the 15th century it was the corridor to the West for all the Turanian invasions. But from the time of Peter the Great it began to fight for access to the open sea and to the concert of Europe, for the Baltic and Constantinople. As protector of the Slavs it aspired to supplant the dying Ottoman empire in Europe; and, turning to the West as its teacher, it borrowed shipbuilders and military instructors and methods and equipment. Although the 19th-century autocracy banned Western publications and made war on liberalism, the aristocracy spoke French and the intelligentsia of the 1890s increasingly thought in terms of Marxism. But in the 20th century, after the triumph of Lenin, the direction was reversed. Henceforward, according to its new rulers, Russia was to be the teacher of the nations, the standard-bearer of predestined world-socialism, and the executor of Marx's mission. Bolshevism could endorse without changing a word this claim of Dostoevsky's, in which the accent of a spiritual imperialism rings through his orthodox messianism: 'For what is the power of the spirit of Russian nationality if not its aspiration after the final goal of universality and omni-humanity?'[1] The mission of the Russian people and the mission of the proletariat appeared in the years that followed as twin aspects of a single movement of expansion, and the new type of Marxists who proclaimed them made only a superficial distinction between the two. But Dostoevsky, in his speech on Pushkin, had called on the Russian people to assimilate everything human everywhere so as to become the salt of the earth, whereas the new Russia became less and less receptive to everything outside herself, and tended more and more, like Japan, to import only what could increase her material power.

In Lenin's life-time Russia was only slowly recovering from the civil war (the *cordon sanitaire* was still in force), and the bolshevik fraction of Russian social democracy, having become the communist party, comprised all the effective chiefs of Russia and, in addition, and without its ever being put in writing,[2] exercised authority over all other communist parties—or, to put it more exactly, was already a candidate, and much

[1] *The Diary of a Writer* (Engl. trans.; London, 1949), vol. ii, p. 978.

[2] The statutes, addresses, and resolutions of the first four congresses even expressly state the contrary.

more than a candidate, for the supreme authority. At first the bolsheviks owed their privileged position solely to their prestige, for had they not already begun to put into practice the things which European socialism had only been able to plan on paper? The socialists whose authority and knowledge had dominated the whole socialist movement before the bolsheviks were either dead, like Bebel, or else, like Kautsky, Hilferding, and the Austro-Marxists, were compromised in the eyes of the younger revolutionaries. For a time some of them held together in what the bolsheviks contemptuously called the '2½ International'. In France Sorel's writings quite failed[1] to drag the unions out of the 'trade-unionist rut' or the socialist parties out of the 'parliamentary rut' and the 'revolutionary decadence', which was turning 'Jaurès-ism' into a mere variety, though a particularly eloquent one, of radical-socialism. Guesde and Vandervelde were swallowed up in the 'sacred union'. All the outstanding theorists and orators of the socialist movement had either disappeared or suffered a severe loss of prestige and credit; and European socialism found itself thrown, as it were, by this eddy of history, under the domination of Russia. Now, the members of the bolshevik group who had some connection with the other European leaders, through their training and their 'theoretical level', as they themselves called it, were far from numerous all told: Lenin, Trotsky, Zinoviev, Kamenev, Joffe, Bukharin, Rakovsky, Radek, etc. The men who were to follow them in the supreme positions had not much in common with the Europeans. This situation was to be resolved historically by a radical change in the whole movement which, before the Russian revolution, had been European socialism and was in future to be called (in part) communism. The method of recruiting members and the type of member were to change. Had socialism been 'betrayed' by the lawyers and professors, the 'petty bourgeois' of the Second International? Then communists must in future be recruited, in principle, primarily from among proletarians. Had European social-democracy been seduced by the liberal, bourgeois, and parliamentary democracy of Europe, whose manners, individualism, indiscipline, and hedonism it adopted? Then discipline must be supreme, a military discipline modelled on that of the Russian party which had been forged in the fire of revolution and civil war, and was the realisation, as we shall see, of the doctrine set forth in 1901 in *What is to be Done?*

But when European socialism was reborn as communism[2] it broke with its own traditions; the elements it borrowed from Russia were to

[1] For an obvious reason: only intellectuals could read them.

[2] We leave aside the reorganisation of the democratic socialist parties, which does not here concern us. It was of importance only during the period between the last wave of revolution (Germany, 1923) and the effective industrialisation of Russia.

prevail increasingly over its original elements. It was now Europe who became the borrower. The Russian revolution did not really set a directorate of men of every race and nation at the head of the workers of the world whom it was calling to battle. What it did in fact was not what it had done in theory. It founded the Communist International. But in the first place it was the Russian section of the International that possessed the *sinews of war*, and war was the business in hand; and in the second place the very structure of the parties and the unwritten but gradually established rules of promotion assured the Kremlin of a supply of *new men* who, though certainly more and more enfranchised from their 'own' bourgeoisies, were also more and more helpless against the specifically Russian organisation, which in effect co-opted them and identified them with its own interests. In the end it became impossible for them to look after the interests—in the geographical sense—of which they were the ostensible guardians; or to envisage them at all except from the point of view evolved by the high Russian bureacracy which developed in the 'twenties and gradually substituted its élite of officials for the old élite of professional revolutionaries, who were too few in number and had been decimated by the revolution itself and by the civil war. The new men, the leaders and delegates of the communist parties of other countries, were indeed not subservient to 'their own' bourgeoisies as the former socialist lawyers and professors had been; but being born of the 'Party' and being nothing apart from it, they merely experienced a *new kind* of dependence. Instead of being bound to the ruling élites of their own countries they were bound to that of Russia—and the new dependence distorted the nature of the European working-class and socialist movement quite as much as the old.

The Catholic Church has maintained itself in spite of the fact that the Popes have too often been Italian. But it was a definite advantage for Catholicism in the days of the Spanish or French or Habsburg hegemony that the Pope should not be a Frenchman or a Spaniard or an Austrian. It meant that the interests of Catholicism were saved from being absorbed in those of the Habsburg or Bourbon monarchies to the grave detriment of the Catholic clients of the other great powers.The situation of communism in our day is not unlike what the situation of Catholicism would have been from the 16th to the 19th century if the Pope had been always a Frenchman or always a Spaniard.

During the 1920s the inevitable development of a new 'governing stratum'[1] took place in Russia. Inevitably, because when the State took

[1] In Pareto's terms, a new 'élite'; in Gaetano Mosca's, a 'political class'. But the word 'political' in this context must bear its most general, or Artistotelian, sense. It refers to the political class of a régime in which the 'autonomy of the spheres'—economic, political, ideological—is tending to be merged into one comprehensive power.

over the whole of the governing functions of society, it was bound to produce a sufficient number of functionaries to perform the functions. The new State powers—essentially the control of production, the collection and requisitioning of the country's wealth, and its allocation and distribution—were in the hands of a group of men bound together by interest, way of life, and consciousness of a common task. And this under a régime which abolished private property, supervised and controlled the exchange of goods, and was to carry through in a very short space of time the industrialisation of a country whose population had hitherto been for the most part unfamiliar with such tasks and such a way of life. When Trotsky after his fall anathematised the creation of the soviet bureaucracy, he spoke less as a 'scientific socialist' and politician than as a man in whom sentiment had somewhat obscured a clear sociological view of the situation. The victories of the bolshevik vanguard had created the very conditions that necessitated such a bureaucracy. How can totalitarian State control and the compulsory industrialisation of an immense country be imposed by any 'human material' except officials, by men who become officials by virtue of the functions entrusted to them? How could it be possible to create the strict yet multiform control which such an organisation presupposes without at the same time creating a bureaucracy?

The attraction exerted by Europe upon Russia had always been consciously felt, though there had always been certain resistances to it both on the part of the autocracy and of the slavophil and populist and economist revolutionaries, but henceforward it was to be reversed. Whereas Russian intellectuals, as well as the Tsars, had previously felt the need to resist a foreign influence, it was now the West that would have to repel, consciously or unconsciously, an influence from the East; or, alternatively, to surrender to it. This reversal of roles was not at first intentionally brought about; it was not the development of a conscious plan. On the contrary, Lenin had been the ardent pupil of Kautsky and German social-democracy, and at first both he and Trotsky believed that the Russian revolution would not be secure until confirmed by a revolution in Germany which would unite industrial Germany to agricultural Russia and then spread over the whole of Europe. But when the bolsheviks initiated the Third International the *balance* of the socialist movement was upset. No Marxist can deny that the weight of material resources ensures and will increasingly ensure a privileged position for the bolsheviks. And this privilege reaches the point of establishing between the directing brain of the International and that of the Russian Super-State an identity such that the International becomes a system in which the various non-Russian communist parties are merely satellite organisms; *the ideal of interdependence becomes the reality of subordination.* The military structure of the Russian communist party, developed under the fire of revolution and civil war, was extended to the parties outside Russia, though not immediately and not unchallenged. And the effective general staff of the Russian communist party was to become in fact the supreme staff of the whole international army of communists, while it was at the same time building up a Super-State—the first and the most complete of 20th-century tyrannies—and establishing itself at the summit of the Russian bureaucratic pyramid. 'The Communist International undertakes to support by all the means at its disposal every socialist republic wherever it may be established.'[1] But in fact only one republic was established; the Russian one, heir of the tsarist power *for which the metropolis and its colonial possessions constituted a single empire under a single sovereignty.* Tsarist centralisation was reinforced by the bolsheviks even more strongly than was the monarchic centralisation of the *ancien régime* by the jacobins and by Bonaparte. The fact that the heterogeneous and non-Russian parts of the Empire are granted 'cultural and linguistic' autonomy cannot disguise the rigour of centralisation through the Party, which is totally dependent upon its headquarters. Quite the contrary, in fact, for the apparent decentralisation of the 'Soviets' has no real historical meaning except against the background of communist centralisation. Every soviet organisation is paralleled by a corresponding communist organisation. The soviets, like the trade unions, merely provide the material for the activity of the Party, which lives off them and recruits its members from them. It also selects from them the suitable executants for policies handed down from the 'summit'. The technique of the *fraction* consists of a preliminary meeting of all the Party members to take note of the directives to be applied (which to an ever greater extent are handed down to them from above) and to discuss them, but only briefly. The point was soon reached where there could be no serious discussion except of the best manner of applying the directives. New recruits to the Party had nothing to do but listen and obey. By the time of Stalin's ascendancy the proceedings of every soviet and trade union meeting were immutably fixed and predetermined.

The foreign communist parties are enfolded within the International, but there is no interchange between the Russian party and the others. The Russian party is not in any way westernised and borrows nothing from the other parties. Its evolution is an integral part of the evolution of the Russian Super-State itself, whose characteristic organ it is, while the other communist parties are progressively *bolshevised* by a process which offers a typical example of what ethnographers call 'borrowing'.

[1] *Statutes of the Communist International.*

Being modelled upon a single prototype, all these parties come to resemble one another to an ever-increasing extent. And the material weight of Russia makes this development inevitable. The Communist International shall 'integrally and unreservedly uphold the conquests of the great proletarian revolution in Russia'. The supreme tribunal of the International is nothing less than the world congress (but after 1935 the world congress never met). The Executive Committee, which has supreme control and takes all decisions subject to ratification by the world congress, comprises five representatives 'of the communist party of the country in which the world congress has fixed the seat of the Executive Committee'. The twelve most important communist parties have only one representative each; and the others have one delegate whose function is merely consultative. These statutes, taken together with the prestige of bolshevik success and the resources accruing from the despotic control of the Russian empire, made it finally certain that the majority in the executive were always favourable to the Russians. 'The Executive Committee of the International has the right to demand the exclusion from affiliated parties of any groups or individuals who fail in proletarian discipline.'[1] The Executive Committee, in which the Russians have the preponderating voice, is the judge of such transgressions. It is true that the affiliated parties have the right of appeal to the world congress. But this procedure of appeal will be found to remain in the realm of theory.

The general staff of the bolshevik party very soon ceased to tolerate the existence of other parties in Russia, except 'in prison', as Bukharin said; and it had the upper hand in both the International and the Executive Committee, which were specially concerned with the maintenance outside Russia of a 'secret organisation' or 'clandestine organism', because it was 'absolutely necessary to combine illegal with legal action'.[2] For the strictly centralised communist parties 'an iron discipline bordering upon military discipline'[3] was prescribed. The 'illegal organisations' were to carry out 'illegal action in the army, navy, and police'. In this way the rulers of the Russian Super-State would be able to undermine from within the armies, police forces, navies, and merchant navies of all other States; and they would achieve this through the intermediary of nationals of those States. All this, for the sake of the 'proletarian revolution'.

All the chief Russian leaders of the International soon disappeared: Lenin died; Trotsky, Zinoviev, and Bukharin were successively

[1] *Statutes of the Communist International.*

[2] *Thèses, Manifestes, et Résolutions adoptés par les i, ii, iii, et iv Congrès de l'Internationale Communiste* (Paris, 1934), p. 46.

[3] ibid., p. 40.

eliminated. Control finally passed into the hands of men of a different historical and social type, who were to make a brutal use of these methods of permanent interference in the history and existence of all other societies. Trotsky was later to make bitter criticisms of this machine, of whose installation and perfection he had been one of the agents. But the psychological and social type of which he was the most eminent representative was progressively replaced by new types; and this development, which could have been foreseen and was in line with historical precedent, involves all Trotsky's polemics and arguments in a vicious circle of inconsistency which he never succeeded in breaking. He had faith in the proletariat's mission and in its 'historic fertility', and believed that it guaranteed the survival at the summit of the pyramid and at the heart of the whole system of a certain type of man—the man in whom Marxism was incarnated, the man who had not merely 'assimilated passively certain parts' of the doctrine but had experienced 'total psychological transubstantiation and the re-education of his personality in the spirit of Marxism'.[1] But, as it turned out, a new kind of life produced a new kind of man.

'As soon as the authorities of the party have decided upon an action, all the comrades must obey the decisions of the party and carry out the prescribed actions. Criticism of such actions may only begin after they have been completed, and then only within the party and its organs.'[2] This is in accordance with the theory of *What is to be Done?*—and also with all military regulations all over the world.

'Every communist member of parliament signs a formal undertaking to resign his seat immediately at the bidding of the central committee.... Every communist member of parliament must remember that he is not a "legislator" seeking a common language with other legislators, but an agitator posted among the enemy with the object of applying the party's decisions. The communist member of parliament is responsible, not to the anonymous mass of electors, but to the communist party, both legal and illegal.'[3] These pronouncements reveal the unbridgeable gulf between communists and any bourgeois liberal parliamentary democracy; by 'organic dispositions' of this kind the 'apparatus' of the communist parties of all countries, with their hierarchy of members, are placed in strict subordination to the real general staff of the International. Although they are responsible in (Marxist) theory to the proletariats of the countries they represent, the will and aspirations of these proletariats require interpretation; and the interpretation is supplied in directives handed down from the Communist International. The Executive Committee of the Communist International, controlled by the bolsheviks, is the judge of the

[1] Trotsky, *Ma Vie*, vol. ii, p. 54. [2] *Thèses, Manifestes*, etc., p. 102. [3] ibid., p. 69.

overall situation, and therefore of the directives appropriate for each section of it. None of the other parties is in a position to achieve a view of the whole and make decisions upon it. On their visits to Moscow—it is no secret that they are sometimes imperatively summoned there—the representatives of other countries very soon come to appear as mere regional executives. They may have supposed that their problems as representatives of the proletariat in this or that part of the world rated a certain priority, but at decisive moments it often happened that they had to yield to more urgent priorities—of which, no doubt, their hosts always succeeded in convincing them, but in the long run there was no question of their refusing to be convinced. The resolutions and theses of the first four congresses of the Communist International urgently enjoin upon the communist parties to promote 'new men' (so many militant socialists had been compromised during the war!), and it is recommended that these new men should be recruited from the proletariat rather than from the petty bourgeoisie. They will therefore owe *everything* to the party and will be *nothing* apart from it, and they will thus be in the hands and at the discretion of the bolshevik general staff in a way that their predecessors[1] could never be. Through them the central command will address communists, workers, and people of all countries. *It is the realisation upon a world scale of the theory of a centralised, hierarchical, and simultaneously legal and illegal organisation of professional revolutionaries.*

From this point, the natural consequences of the system evolved as was to be expected; and the fall of the revolutionary tide after 1923 contributed still further to the dependence upon Russia of the non-Russian communist leaders.

[1] Who were then to be found in the 'nationalist right wing' of the remaining socialist parties, or in the '2½ International'.

CHAPTER 5

Growth of Absolutism and Concentration of Power

IN the 1905 revolution, during the October strikes, the mensheviks originated the idea of soviets to represent 'the workers in struggle', or as 'representative organs of revolutionary self-government'.[1] And it was against the opposition of the bolsheviks, who disapproved of the *girondin* flavour of the slogan (Lenin was abroad at the time), that the Petrograd soviet, of which Trotsky was a leader, came to birth. But in the course of the 'twenties there was a change in the very conception of a suitable representation of the embattled workers. By the end of that decade the soviets were strictly and in every respect subordinate to the party. Like the trade unions, they were simply the 'transmission belts' by means of which the Party of the State could set in motion or restrain society as a whole. No initiative of a soviet or of a trade union could have any real political significance except through the initiative of the corresponding party organisation. The true originality and importance of Lenin do not reside in the insurrectional victory of the soviets over Kerensky, nor in the ideas he expressed in *The State and Revolution*, which provided theoretical justification for the use of the soviets. They consisted in his application against Kerensky of the tactic of 'dual power'. The soviets were made to act, in relation to the provisional government, as forces of shock and disruption to the precise extent that the apparently spontaneous mass excitement of a crowd in process of formation could forward the plans and decisions (constantly modified in the face of changing circumstances) of a single calculating will with one purpose in view: the seizure of power. It was the will of a general staff. The original form of the *Politburo*, which became at once a sort of central committee of the central committee, was that of a 'secret insurrectional directorate'.[2] Thus the optimum conditions were achieved. In the given historical situation, its military structure and discipline made the bolshevik 'fraction' the only strictly organised

[1] Dan's articles in *Iskra*, June and July 1905.

[2] cf. Souvarine, *Stalin* (Engl. trans.; London, 1939). The Politburo was created on the initiative of Dzerzhinsky, the first head of the Cheka.

power; yet at the same time it was flexible enough, and Lenin and Trotsky were perspicacious enough to modify its tactics very rapidly whenever resistance became so strong as to make a temporary halt desirable. Then, in order to secure a free hand, demands for 'maximum' democracy would be advanced, maximum democracy meaning the maximum disorganisation of the State system which was the object of attack. Democracy of that sort means, in effect, a battlefield; and precisely because bolshevism was not democratic it could manœuvre effectively in such 'democracy'. Defined in this way, democracy means pitting the concentrated will of a strong organisation against the haphazard improvisations of unstable spontaneity.

After the revolutionary seizure of power, Russia's historical development was not in reality that of a soviet society, for such a society would have been a sort of decentralised producers' republic. What did in fact develop was a *Party State*: that is to say, a dictatorship not of the proletariat but of the party—and to identify the proletariat with the party, as someone has said, is like identifying the horse with the rider. There are in Lenin's work two tendencies, of opposite historical and sociological significance, and in the event it was the tendency so forcefully expressed in *What is to be Done?* and not the tendency of *The State and Revolution* that was to prevail. The full extent of its triumph was seen only when the extreme centralisation of the party was complemented by the decentralisation, 'de-co-ordination', and 'disconnection'[1] of everything outside the party. The way the system was applied in practice was such as to make impossible the formation of any group or association or any manifestation of social life independent of the State. The division of communist Russia into soviet republics and the compulsory grouping of the workers into 'soviets' at their place of work prevented the possibility of any spontaneous social manifestations, any movement from below, and therefore any resistance or any autonomous social life, whether industrial or national (for the Russian empire is an aggregation of nations). The *partisan State* is seen, therefore, to be a technically skilful solution of the governmental problems of an empire in which the metropolis is contiguous with the colonial possessions, the cultural and linguistic decentralisation merely emphasising the centralisation of politics and religion (i.e. communist orthodoxy). And this system of soviet republics has the further advantage of being an effective weapon of imperialism, for any foreign country may in time be converted into a soviet republic and take its place with the others as a strictly subordinate republic in the pyramidal structure of the partisan State. It is for the party to pick out the potential national leaders in the 'soviet republics' and either assimilate or

[1] The only advantage of these neologisms is their precision.

destroy them. The important chiefs of the soviet system and the Party in the various soviet republics are primarily representatives of the Party: they stand to their own nationals as representatives of the Party rather than to the Party as representatives of their nationals. But an unceasing struggle has to be waged, especially in the Ukraine, against the apparently ineradicable tendency towards 'bourgeois nationalism'.

Let us examine the purely political aspect of the new pyramidal social power established in Russia after the October Revolution. From 1919, in violation of the constitution promulgated the previous year, the Central Committee of the bolshevik party assumed in practice the powers which constitutionally belonged to the Council of People's Commissars and the Executive Committee of the Soviets. Already at that time[1] the government of the Central Committee was more centralised than the Venetian Council of Ten or even the French Committee of Public Safety. 'One man, Lenin, held all the strings of politics and another, Sverdlov, all those of administration.' This system, justified by the necessities of civil war, was continued after the war, as we shall see. 'The local committees of the party usurped the authority of the executive committees of the soviets.' Party and State were ruled by six men who were responsible to nobody: Lenin, Zinoviev, Trotsky, Kamenev, Bukharin, Stalin (Sverdlov had died prematurely). All political parties except the bolsheviks were suppressed. The freedom of the press and the right of association recognised by the constitution of 1918 are the freedom of the government to make use of the press, and the right of the people to assemble together when, and only when, the government requires it. The Central Committee consisted of nineteen members, but was subdivided for efficiency into two even smaller units: the *Politburo*, and the *Orgburo*, created in 1919 for administration. The soviets are, in fact, appointed, from the highest to the lowest, by the corresponding party committees. *Long before the rise of Stalin* the real political method was the accumulation of power at the summit, so that the dual soviet-communist system was, in fact, a functional dualism and not a real division of power; and the accumulation of power at the summit made it fundamentally impossible that a dual power should ever arise. The *Politburo* was in fact supreme not only over the Council of Commissars and the Executive Committee of the Soviets, but also over the Council of Labour and Defence, the Supreme Economic Council, the Military Revolutionary Committee, and the Cheka.[2]

[1] cf. Souvarine, op. cit.

[2] The Council of People's Commissars was in fact an 'executive commission of high officials' (Souvarine, op. cit.). The same author pertinently compares the Executive Committee of the Soviets to a 'rump parliament'. Among other examples of organisations which had no political independence are the Planning Commission and the Workers' and Peasants' Inspection.

In 1919 another new organ was created, the secretariat of the Central Committee of the party. It was in theory an executive organ, but it acquired in fact a dictatorship over public appointments. Souvarine describes it as a 'commissariat for official promotions'. Stalin succeeded to this post in April 1922, and it became his function to co-ordinate the work of the Orgburo, the Central Control Commission, and the Cheka—in other words, the supreme authorities of the Party and the police. His colleagues in the Politburo, each absorbed in his own task, usually had no time to study the ready-made decisions which he laid before them. For the same reason, when the effects of these decisions appeared, they could not always understand how they had been arrived at, nor could they accurately judge how far they were in line with accepted doctrine, or with the directives they had agreed upon in common, or with justice. In theory, the Central Committee controlled everything, but it was in the nature of things that it could not, in fact, control the secretariat. How can one supervise the thing whose function is supervision? Moreover, the capital importance of this function did not immediately appear. The general secretary controlled neither the International nor diplomacy, nor industry, nor agriculture. In other words, neither policy nor production was in his hands. And the man who held the post was a tried and active bolshevik who had only rarely and for very brief periods been outside Russia, knew no foreign languages,[1] and had to his credit no theoretical work on revolutionary tactics comparable to those of Lenin or Trotsky. And as for administration, it was Sverdlov, now dead, who had seemed, in the heroic period, to be the great administrator.

Nevertheless, Stalin's position enabled him in effect to present the Politburo with accomplished fact in respect of a whole series of measures, each of which might be only a detail but which, taken all together, reveal a definite *tendency* (in the sense of both meaning and direction). When Lenin perceived the need to control Stalin's activities, and perhaps terminate them, it was too late.

When Stalin entered upon his secretarial functions there was already a pyramid with one man at its summit; and the political character of the leadership derived from the Party's military structure which was the historic expression of the doctrine of *What is to be Done?* The personality and the peculiar virtues of Lenin, however, helped to obscure the true nature of this leadership. Lenin's initiative and his tactical theories had been successful at times of crisis; he was known as the founder and unchallenged leader of the bolshevik 'fraction' which had triumphantly passed the test of history: a relentless fighter and formidable polemist, he had yet made no irreconcilable enemies among

[1] Like Hitler.

his comrades of the Central Committee. All this had combined to make Lenin's power a recognised and accepted fact for the revolutionaries of Russia and of the whole world.[1] But this power did not derive from any specific function. It was attached to the *personal* authority of an inspirer and supreme arbitrator, who was esteemed not so much in virtue of his powers and functions as in terms of 'human value'. Lenin, in fact, was invested with a sort of supreme authority above and beyond the constitution. No major decisions were taken unless he agreed, and everything of importance that was done from 1918 until his health failed was done either on his initiative or with his approval. So it can be said that both the immense Russian collectivity and the world-wide 'diaspora' of communism had already acknowledged one supreme head before the death of Lenin; and, indeed, the number of complicated and interpenetrating interests that had grown up while he was still alive made some such supreme authority historically necessary. Lenin was the commander-in-chief, allotting to others their tasks, defining and co-ordinating their functions, and when necessary taking the final decisions himself.

The twelfth congress of the communist party of the Soviet Union, in 1923, increased the membership of the Central Committee to forty. The Control Commission had fifty members and, in deference to a wish expressed by Lenin on his sick-bed, there were to be joint plenary sessions of the two bodies. If Lenin's idea was, as the opposition have maintained, to subordinate Stalin and his secretariat to the Central Committee, then it failed in its purpose. Plenary sessions of the two committees could not be held frequently, and the effective power lay with their two *bureaux*, each of seven members with four deputy-members; and at that time both these bureaux were controlled by the 'Troika', namely the alliance of the old bolsheviks, Stalin, Zinoviev, and Kamenev, against Trotsky. They had in common the fact that they had been bolsheviks when Trotsky was a menshevik, and that they would not accept that he should inherit Lenin's undisputed position, although his actions, his personality, and his gifts had made him during Lenin's lifetime the second outstanding figure of the régime. We learn from this that an undisputed first place, independent of the constitution, was in fact a feature of the still insecure régime, and that there was no normal constitutional procedure to ensure, as in the Western democracies, that vacancies are automatically filled by an election, and to prevent the death of the head of a State from causing a political crisis. By this sign we know we are in presence of a new type of power. When, at about the same time, Mussolini was entrusted with the

[1] World leadership of communism and the revolution was an inherent function of the new Russian power.

supreme power in Italy by King Victor Emmanuel, everyone realised that he was not going to be just another normal prime minister.

To the 'old bolsheviks' Stalin seemed to be one of themselves. He did not put them in the shade, as Trotsky did. But he differed from them in two characteristics whose importance was to be fully demonstrated by events.

In the first place, while he was in charge of the secretariat, or 'commission for official promotions', of the party at the time when the State was becoming the first of the 20th-century partisan-states (the partisan-state being the preliminary stage of the totalitarian state), Stalin was also a member of the Politburo; and in this way he had a more complete view than anyone else of the situation as a whole.

Secondly, although he was not a legendary figure like Trotsky, he was the man who could make or mar promotions, and was therefore known to all who had been, or wished to be, promoted. There is no question that the old bolsheviks failed to detect the true importance of the secretariat. For the fact is that at the very moment of Lenin's disappearance from the scene Stalin was establishing himself as the supreme agent for the recruiting, advancement, and replacement of officials, and this at a time when the whole of Russia was becoming officialised. The State that emerged from the civil war had assumed to itself all the important social functions, political, economic, administrative, and ideological, and it was bound to find for itself a personnel adequate to operate and make effective this *total* domination and control over society.

The Secretariat and the secretary would preside over this *political stabilisation* and *social differentiation.* To *re-compose* a collectivity in this way is, so to speak, to repeat—*mutatis mutandis,* on a vast scale and with much greater complexity—the hierarchical, vertical structure outlined in *What is to be Done?* The army which is the Party became the animator of the State, which was assuming every important social function. Stalin found himself placed—and he knew how to stay there—at the very point of concentration of power, in a key social position of the new ruling élite that was emerging and stabilising itself. There was soon to be developed an effective solidarity between a rising élite, an institution (the secretariat), and a man; and this élite, faced with an uncertain future, would come to regard the institution and the man as a point of security in a troubled world whose horizon was still veiled by clouds of the recent storm. Once elections, from top to bottom, became a mere formality, and junior secretaries were appointed by senior secretaries, the general secretary became, in the eyes of all who depended on him, the very personification of the Politburo and the Central Committee of the Party—in other words, of the one and only political power in the whole immense empire, in which no other power was allowed to exist. In their eyes it was through Stalin that this power made its decisions, decisions which could raise a man to great responsibilities with a great future or cast him into outer darkness. The great majority of new members and candidates for the Party, and for all official positions, was composed either of converts, people who had come over from the old governing class, and intellectuals (who, being pliable by definition, were most often only too anxious to forget their past and the days of their ascendancy), or else of political illiterates. These last, when they opted for the 'victorious revolution', were in fact opting for a normal social life in society as they found it; they were 'in favour' of a chance to earn a living and put an end to their acutely physical anxieties. All that was necessary was that these men, who had been rescued from want and offered the hope of a career, should remain at the discretion of the secretariat. And the structure of the empire made it inevitable that this would happen. The secretary had only to give his mind to it—as history proves he did—and he could rally round himself a crowd of clients who were for the most part unable to grasp the true political situation (which would have required unusual insight) and in any case not at all anxious to do so (as one can well imagine). The historic test was the struggle with Trotsky and the opposition. It appeared to prove the 'class solidarity' between the secretaries, or new élite, and the general secretariat. By definitely establishing the ascendancy of the secretary (though there was still an attempt to save appearances), it placed in the forefront of the historical scene the solidarity between a rising élite and one man. Thenceforward, in the period of the *Nep*, when private enterprise was permitted in agriculture and internal trade, the political tide was favourable to a secretariat whose whole concern was with the public service. The selection of congress delegates was in reality a monopoly of the secretaries; the regional or local secretary was regarded as the spokesman of the centre and could rally round himself the floating mass which comprised, owing to the state in which Russia then was, only a very few men of any real education or political experience. It was therefore in the power of the Secretariat to make and unmake the men in charge of production, to give or withhold the means of livelihood, and to conscript and direct the whole population of Russia as though it were an army.

Russian society appeared, then, to have entered upon a process of recomposition, of which the driving force was the nucleus of professional revolutionaries grouped around Lenin. But after it came to power the functions of this group were both extended and transformed. There occurred a phenomenon which had already appeared before in Russian history. Under the Tsars the public service conferred nobility, and the system of ranks introduced by Peter the Great had created a hierarchy of the upper classes. Thus we can see that Lenin's solution of the world problem of the impotence of the plebs 'over-determines' a specifically Russian phenomenon, a phenomenon which the conditions of Russia produced twice (though certainly in different forms) in two centuries. There was only one method by which the bolshevik general staff could encompass and penetrate and animate the whole life of the country—organising the production of goods and ideas alike and controlling equally the distribution of produce, personnel, and thought—and this method was the creation of a centralised and hierarchical staff of officials; which meant, inevitably, a bureaucracy (for without bureaucracy there can be no control). This system may be described, for the convenience of our analysis, as a *second recourse to the military type of structure*. It is the Party that energises the bureaucracy; one must be a partisan, whether a party member or not, before one can become an official. By a major internal crisis the régime gets rid of the opposition, which consists of men who are still theoretically in agreement with the Party, though in significantly varying degrees, but who are, nevertheless, '*objectively*' *opposed to the existing social trend*. Theoretical points cannot at this stage be taken so literally as in the preceding period, and hence the mixture of hypocrisy with ferocity in the struggle between the two factions. It was war to the knife between parties who fought in the name of the same ideals (a war which saw the first, and sinisterly ominous, intervention of the State police against Party members), and it took the form of disagreements about tactics and disputes about methods while all concerned accepted the same ultimate objective of 'world revolution'. The aim of Trotsky's opponents was, in fact, to uphold and pursue an existing social trend, but since this trend was in contradiction with accepted theories there was a strong temptation not to notice it. It was the glaring weakness of Trotsky's position that it could only be maintained if the five or ten thousand leading Party members and their subordinates were 'great Marxists' like himself, instead of being, sociologically and statistically speaking, normal men. It was impossible for Trotsky to appeal to the working class against the Party apparatus and the 'secretarial hierarchy', *because the organisation of the working class was precisely that apparatus and nothing else*. The distribution of his pamphlets[1] and articles was already in the hands of the Secretariat, which took care to sabotage them by losing them or drowning them in a flood of refutations and side-issues, which of course enjoyed all the advantages of the distributive facilities of a régime that monopolised the press and the

[1] Notably the famous *New Course*.

book trade. Events had moved swiftly, and real-life history was playing one of its familiar tricks on its ideological phantom. As a result, Trotsky became involved in a confusion which lasted to the end of his life, for when he speaks of the Party and the U.S.S.R. he is sometimes speaking of them, ideologically, as they ought to be, and at other times he is speaking of them as in fact, in real-life history, they are. In appealing to the Party against the Party apparatus, and also, in some degree, to the Party apparatus against the Party secretariat and Stalin, he is already in fact appealing from the real to the ideal. He is appealing from the Party as it is, and as he himself, in point of fact, had largely contributed to make it, to the Party as it ought to be.

The sociological phenomenon of *concentration of power* has occurred at various times in various civilisations. It appeared in Europe in the first half of the 20th century, first in the reign[1] of Lenin, then of Stalin, and finally in Hitlerism; and Fascism appeared in Italy at the same time as the rise of Stalin. We have already seen how there was a tendency for power to be concentrated in Lenin; and in this particular case the personality of the man played a part in creating the function. Although the constitution of 1918 contained no hint of such a person, the death of Lenin meant the disappearance of a man in whom supreme power was concentrated. The sociological significance of this fact was obscured—wishfully in the case of communists, who were in a position to know the truth, and of the whole European and American Left—by the particular personality and record of the man. The 1918 constitution was based on the doctrines, principles, and standards consciously accepted by the leaders of the new régime; but the concentration of power pursued its course in spite of ideology and doctrine. There was, however, a specific difference between Lenin's rise to power and the accession of Stalin to the supreme position left vacant by Lenin's death. Lenin was the leader of a successful revolution and also a personality in a class by himself, whereas Stalin emerged victorious from a 'struggle of Diadochi' that lasted thirteen years. (Although his success seemed assured once Trotsky had been eliminated, he was not safe beyond all question until the end of that period.) His position only became inexpugnable after the Moscow Trials and the violent and dishonouring[2] deaths of the last of those companions of the prophet in whom there inhered a fragment of the 'revolutionary legality', which was the only legality the régime could claim. If we examine the matter, as is customary in the West, from the point of view of public law, we

[1] This is an intentional exaggeration. The phenomenon was not so clearly marked at the beginning.

[2] At least in intention.

find that Stalin transformed the soviet constitution of 1918 in the way that Cæsar, Augustus, and their successors transformed the republican constitution of Rome. The mere proliferation of magistratures and functions can change a republic into an empire and turn a constitution into a sort of academic text. What *was* the Roman imperium? An accumulation in the hands of one man of republican magistracies whose content had either been transformed by the mere pressure of history or been modified in unforeseeable ways and in a sense undreamt of by their founders, or else been totally voided of its original meaning. The first Cæsars successively combined in their own person:

(1) The tribunitian power, the essentially plebeian magistrature in virtue of which the tribunes were leaders of the plebs.[1] (It has been described by a German historian as the 'institutionalisation of tyranny'.)

(2) The pro-consular *imperium*,[2] which soon became the *imperium majus infinitum*. This was the origin of the use of the word 'empire'. It was an extension of the power of a commanding general to protect or conquer the province legally assigned to him. It is the source of military power, and is the power that enabled an imperial candidate to make good his claim. The imperial power was made an effective reality through the efforts of great military leaders.

(3) The office of *princeps senatus*, which bore the same relation to the oligarchy as the office of people's tribune to the plebs. The *princeps senatus* was the oligarchy's traditional leader. (But, in fact, unless he had a powerful personality the function remained purely titular.)

(4) The sovereign pontificate. The emperor was a member, *ex officio*, of all the religious colleges, and therefore had the chief position in the State religion.

To this nucleus there were added other exclusively imperial powers which owed nothing to the republican magistracies and were indeed a negation of them: the right of peace and war, of 'presentation to magistratures', of conferring Roman citizenship, founding colonies, coining money. And finally the emperor became *princeps civium*, thus acquiring for himself the *potestas populi romani*.

Just as the Roman imperium appears to a constitutional lawyer to be an accumulation of republican magistracies, so the unique position of Stalin in Russia seems to derive from an accumulation of functions. In 1922, when he began to build up the power of the secretariat, Stalin had been a member of the Central Committee since 1912, and a member

[1] The senatorial oligarchy succeeded in profoundly modifying this function, and was sometimes able to turn it to its own advantage; but not before suffering some rude blows from it.

[2] 'The alliance between democracy and military power, which gave rise to the Empire, was permanently incarnated in the emperor himself' (Léon Homo, *Les Institutions romaines*: Paris, 1933).

of the Politburo and of the Council of People's Commissars since 1917. He had belonged to both the Committee of Five and the Committee of Seven which planned the insurrection, and during the civil war he had belonged to the military revolutionary committee. And in 1925 he became a member of the Executive Committee of the Communist International. If the same names appear again and again in the committees, it is Stalin's which appears in all of them; and the secretariat was to add the final weight which would make him preponderant after Lenin's death both in function and personality. But in the eyes of the old bolsheviks, and, still more, of the other 'companions of the prophet', it was Trotsky who personified the threat of dictatorship. They had no fear of Stalin, or, more precisely, so long as Trotsky was on the scene they did not think that Stalin could take Lenin's place. Thus it was possible for Stalin, by allying himself with Zinoviev and Kamenev and by setting Bukharin against Trotsky, to secure a majority against Trotsky in all the important committees while at the same time the apparatus of the secretariat—press, wireless, and the verbal propaganda of the secretaries—was at his disposal. The organisation supported him. Very soon, when Kamenev and Zinoviev turned against him, it had become too late. They had so weakened Trotsky and the opposition that neither could give effective support. It was in vain that Kamenev sounded the alarm at the 14th Party Congress (December 1925): 'We object to the creation of a headship theory; to the setting up of a "head". We object to the Secretariat, uniting policy and organisation in itself, being placed above the political organism. We stand for an internal organisation of the supreme power so as to assure full power to the Political Bureau, which contains all the political brains of our Party, and subordinate the Secretariat to it as the technical executant of its decisions (*uproar*). . . . We cannot consider normal, and think harmful to the Party, the prolongation of a situation in which the Secretariat unites policy and organisation and, in fact, predetermines policy (*uproar*). . . .'[1]

But Kamenev could no longer count on help from Trotsky and the opposition, whom he and Zinoviev had helped Stalin to defeat; and his attitude made him suspect to all who were identified with the Secretariat. He was threatening the *status quo*, which meant that he was indirectly threatening the secretaries' standard of life.[2] Should Kamenev succeed, there would be a reorganisation of the apparatus which would

[1] Souvarine, *Stalin*, p. 404.

[2] Henceforward every criticism of the Secretariat was liable to be taken in this sense, and the Secretariat became more and more identified with the very organisation of the Party. Kamenev's complaints recall only too vividly Trotsky's letter of 8 October 1923 to the Central Committee, in which he denounced the structure of the system with the perspicacity of one who was beginning to suffer bitterly from it.

endanger the whole of Stalin's clientèle and all their dependants as well. On Lenin's death it was Trotsky who had appeared to Zinoviev and Kamenev to be the man who must be eliminated at any price. It would be a blow to all of them if Trotsky inherited the mantle of Lenin's moral and political authority. Trotsky had opposed the bolsheviks in the heroic days of illegal activity and exile and expropriations, when they themselves had been the very backbone of bolshevism. Trotsky's caustic arrogance had spared no one. As chief of the Red Army and Commissar for Transport he had shown a dictatorial streak. He was a success, but at the cost of many people's self-esteem. He had emerged victorious from a serious conflict with Stalin, and he had been opposed in less well-known quarrels to every member of the Politburo at one time or another. Naturally, therefore, his position was challenged; and even his virtues—no doubt one should say, especially his virtues—were such as to raise the suspicion that he would claim Lenin's power, and also the suspicion that he was capable of wielding it, though without any of Lenin's tact. So that when it became clear that Stalin might take possession of the supreme power, and was in fact already doing so, it was too late for effective resistance. That is why Kamenev and Zinoviev submitted, and Bukharin also, though hoping no doubt that the chance would arise later of reversing the situation. Unlike Trotsky, they would remain inside the Party. Retaining their prestige as the original men of the revolution, the Party could always turn to them as an alternative to Stalin. But once Trotsky was broken neither Zinoviev nor Kamenev, nor yet Bukharin, had the power to reverse the trend of evolution. They were discredited in the eyes of both the opposition and the secretaries; and their collapse and recantation were a warning to all who had allowed themselves to become identified with so unsuccessful an opposition. What Kamenev and Zinoviev seem to have desired after Trotsky's elimination was a sort of institutional reform implying a directory of several heads without the primacy of any one. That at least is what Kamenev clearly indicates in the speech quoted above. But just as Trotsky's frontal attacks on the bureaucracy and the 'apparatus' bore witness rather to his ideological zeal than to his sociological sense, so Kamenev and Zinoviev, and Bukharin also from another angle, must, if they seriously contemplated a directory, have quite misunderstood the nature of the power that Stalin was about to assume.

Probably Stalin himself was not aware of the true significance of his own rise; such meanings only become clear in the light of later events, and it is possible to be the man of a situation without being fully aware of the situation. Indeed, history provides many more examples of this than of the contrary. Stalin became identified with a certain social function at the very moment when that function was emerging and acquiring importance. There had already been an accumulation of power at the summit before the secretariat was created; and the secretarial function gave to its holder, who then began to reveal fully his particular qualities, a weight that did not become decisive until after the fall of Trotsky. After that event it was Trotsky himself, Commander-in-chief of the Red Army and formerly, during the civil war, the incarnation of the authoritarian menace, who was to become the incarnation of the ideology and the doctrine and the revolution that had been betrayed. But the fact is that when he clashed head-on with the secretariat he broke himself against a social force in full acceleration. In this conflict there is revealed one of the fundamentals of political success: the gift, which is only proved by results, of moving with the stream of events instead of against it. Events will seem to 'play into the hands' of the man who possesses this gift. The moral is underlined the more emphatically by the fact that Trotsky was a brilliant figure. (Stalin's qualities were of a different kind.) The position of Stalin was always solidly based on real power, and neither ideology nor doctrine could confuse his knowledge—perhaps a purely empirical and almost instinctive knowledge—of where that power lay. Stalin did not speculate about the historical fertility of the proletariat. He stuck to his function and to reality—in other words, to a process of political composition and social differentiation. In this his behaviour resembled that of Augustus. What appears remarkable about his rise is that he seemed to be placed *at the very point where power was coming to a head.*[1] His method consisted in belonging to all the most powerful bodies, becoming the first to hold a position which corresponded to the rise of a new social force, and successively reducing all those of his colleagues whose accumulation of similar powers made them possible rivals. Hitler was later to apply the same accumulative technique when he insinuated himself into the already existing republican political forms.

* * * *

The transition in Russia from the period of revolutionary excitement to the period of stabilisation in which the new régime could begin to settle down was a two-fold social process: a recomposition and a series of social differentiations. The various parts of a new social whole were fitted together and began to become specialised. The fluid improvisations of the revolutionary period were gradually replaced by more solid conceptions such as *job* and *function*, and the growth of the Secretariat illustrates particularly clearly the history of this special development. The swift rate of stabilisation can be measured by the

[1] It is difficult to distinguish the 'subjective' from the 'objective' factors of such a situation. The two manifestly converge.

internal transformation of the revolutionary party. All other political parties having been abolished, the political life of the country inevitably took the single-party form. It may be said, indeed—oversimplifying for the moment and leaving details and complications until later—that since the Party had left no living social forms outside itself *the Russian counter-revolution was not directed against the Party but was an internal revolution within it.*

The comparative lack of social differentiation in the old Russia provides a partial explanation for this fact. Unlike the monarchies of old Europe, Tsarism was a landowners' government, or tyranny, based chiefly upon an oligarchy in which nobility and function went together (function conferred nobility, so the Tsar could and did create nobles); whereas in Europe the king himself was only one of the nobles, and they did not hold their titles from him (hence the long-standing prejudice, inherited by the bourgeoisie, against the recently ennobled). Over against this dominant oligarchy, which was outweighed by the Tsar, the Father of all the Russias, stood the mass of the peasants, whose legal status was still servile until 1861. Even in the industrial sphere initiative usually came from the tsars who, since Peter the Great, themselves created factories and State workshops and inspired 'private initiatives', which deserved the adjective very much less than their Western analogues. In the non-Russian parts of the Empire 'primitive societies' still existed, and in central Asia, for example, the Moslem social structure had changed little from what it was during the Islamic Middle Ages. Russia had nothing resembling the age-old and vigorous social differentiation of western Europe; its history had brought to maturity no bourgeoisie comparable to that of Europe, with its creative achievements in economics, law, and culture—and even politics. The first truly political manifestations in Russia were the revolutionary political groups of the early 20th century, the social-democratic party and the social revolutionaries; but not the constitutional democratic party, which was based only on the liberal nobility (that is, a small minority of the oligarchy), and on a small and heterogeneous and sparsely scattered bourgeoisie which had no historical experience behind it. The bolshevik dictatorship made short work of eradicating these parties, whose roots were shallow; and Russia's 'modern' social structure took shape entirely under bolshevik auspices. Although it is convenient for the purpose of descriptive analysis to distinguish between composition and social differentiation on the one hand and the rapid process of industrialisation on the other, they are in fact merely two aspects of a single historic phenomenon which is still in process of emergence. Historical developments in the West may bring into conflict two or more social forces each of which has its own political 'formation' to represent it, and, therefore, civil war or revolutionary disturbances are not impossible; but in Russia these clashes occur within the one and only Party and lead to internecine struggles and purges. The entire political field of the whole Russian world is comprised within the Party. Consequently all Russian phenomena, compared with those of the West, appear *synthetical.* But the true character of the internal conflicts of a despotic régime is not revealed to the light of publicity. The version of them given out by historians and journalists usually bears much the same relation to political truth that hagiography and sacred history bear to historical truth as conceived by a scrupulous contemporary Western historian.

The appearance of new élites is a sign that a valid society is in process of formation. The bureaucracy derives its power from the fact that the State (which means the State apparatus) has monopolised the economic functions of society. The social analyst will therefore observe an interpenetration of economic and political functions; but the sociologist will note rather the assimilation of all the forms of power into one comprehensive power, accompanied by an increasing specialisation of social tissues. And the power to which the new specialised organs are subordinated is an *absolute power*. The unprecedented importance attaching in such a régime to the State police is an objective demonstration of this fact.

The State is all-embracing, and therefore the State police must supervise everything, including culture and art and, above all, the arts of representation and expression of opinion. These latter, the cinema, the theatre, and literature for example, work upon opinions and feelings in their raw and equivocal and undetermined state, and *form* them by providing patterns to which they can be moulded. Since mankind always 'looks for a hero', the ruling oligarchy of a State which has absolute control over every social activity must itself select the models towards which the affective energy, in other words the working energy, of the people is to be directed. This energy being the capital of which the State is the monopolistic exploiter, the State will try to canalise and direct it towards its own purposes, and the control of the arts is a means to this end. Even allowing for some psychological miscalculations, a control of this kind will produce results. The bureaucrats select the types of hero to be *starred,*[1] and they are held up as models for the formation of whatever new type of man the government believes itself to require.

A social recomposition is always accompanied by the appearance of

[1] Communist writers outside Russia did the same thing, but often without very much tact. The result was a 'literature of edification' in which the 'right attitude' towards Party and (Russian) State not seldom had to make up for a lack of talent and invention.

a new élite, emerging from the masses which are set in motion by the revolution but only becoming clearly identifiable after the revolutionary excitement has died down. Inevitably, this élite is hostile to the old régime to whose death it owes its own existence. The new Russian élite of the 1920s was composed of converted members of the intelligentsia, deserters from the former oligarchy, and new men. These new men may previously have been workmen or proletarians, but they soon ceased to be. Passing through the army into the bureaucracy, they became first military men and then bureaucrats. And the workmen's sons who received their training at universities and institutes and technical schools became something different from workmen. So it was from among the poorer peasants, numerically the largest section of the population, that the huge proletariat necessary for the industrialisation of Russia was recruited. In its results, therefore, the October Revolution was seen to be, as the new social composition emerged, the functional equivalent of a 'bourgeois revolution'. In the France of 1789 there was already a bourgeoisie prepared to take power, but in Russia it was only from the moment of revolutionary upsurge that there began to be a selection of officials. It was an example of circulation of élites on a vast and accelerated scale. As in the United States in the heroic age of capitalism, great numbers of proletarians had their chance to 'get on' and cease to be proletarians.

A time would come when technicians would be appointed on grounds of competence, but to begin with—after the new batch of members admitted at the time of Lenin's death—the Party selected its members more strictly than ever by co-option. In other words, the Party 'apparatus' selected Party candidates and recruited its own members from the Party (an election very soon became nothing more than a nomination coupled with a formula of assent). *The Party structure is vertical and business proceeds exclusively along vertical lines.* Officials of the same rank in different departments are isolated from one another by water-tight compartments. Here the resemblance to an army is striking ; at a given level men of the same rank and way of life have no means of combining against their official superiors. As Stalin himself put it, the trade unions and soviets are simply 'transmission belts' by which Party members can control the rest of the population in the same way that they themselves, within the Party, are guided by a system of controls passing down by stages from the highest levels to the lowest.[1] On every level the most important function socially is the

[1] Souvarine (*Stalin,* p. 318): 'Committees of all sorts abound . . . become more numerous, jostle one another, and build up a many-storied machine. The executive institutions of the Soviets, on an analogous but even more complicated model, are under the orders of the corresponding Party institution. Generally *the directing element is identical in the two.*

secretariat, and all the secretariats from top to bottom are in two-way communication. At the top of the pyramid or, better, the *Ziqqurat*, is Stalin, the secretary of the Party. The oligarchy at the higher levels recruits its members by co-option. All initiative comes from the top. Such is the final stage of an evolution which had already begun before Lenin's death.

One has only to describe the system to see clearly how it stifles opposition. The secretaries, each of whom owes to the one above him his privileges, functions, social status, and livelihood, are appointed by one another according to the tacit formula by which ostensible nominations from the 'rank and file' are, in fact, directed from above. Trotsky was outvoted and driven out of political life by delegates appointed in this way. Behind the formality of election they had, in fact, been appointed by secretaries who depended upon the secretary of the Party, the very man whom Trotsky was attacking and whom, if he had been successful, he declared he would eliminate from political life along with the institution he represented. Now these secretaries, many of them 'new men', who had raised themselves out of insecurity and were just beginning to enjoy the stability to which they aspired, felt responsibility for one another from the highest to the lowest. Any 'new course' threatened to plunge them back into the uncertain and the unknown, into insecurity, unemployment, and perhaps worse. It may be that Trotsky was not precisely aware of this social situation. The position was certainly confusing, for the Party *qua* organisation *was* this social situation, and Trotsky was obliged to appeal against it to the Party as a tradition and an ideal. He did not call upon the proletariat to attack the Party, but he appealed to the Party against those who were, in fact, its head. In so far as he recognised the authority of the Party, he could not treat it as an enemy, and this was an impasse from which he never escaped. He must have known later on that his attacks were useful to the enemies of the Party (and of the U.S.S.R.), so, while he assembled an array of reasons for attacking them, he kept on proclaiming that they must be defended.

* * * *

The Cheka was created in 1917. In origin it could be defined as a political police, and its original functions were merely repressive and

[Our italics. This statement is the key to the whole system.—J. M.] In factories, State institutions, dwelling-houses, schools, trade unions, consumers' co-operative societies, the army, the militia, the police—communists are grouped into cells and sections which delegate their authority. [Delegated from the summit and relayed down by stages.—J. M.] The Comsomol, with its 400,000 members, has its own cells everywhere. Where communists are not numerous enough, "sympathisers" act as auxiliaries. This extraordinary network extends irresistibly.'

supervisory. It was a specialised organ of the Party. The doctrines and plans of a general staff in charge of a total transformation of society can only be imparted to, or understood by, a very small minority, and the Cheka was the organ for detecting and denouncing any movement of opposition and for unmasking and suppressing malcontents. The great and rapid growth of the institution bears witness to the extent of public incomprehension of the government's policy. And here we come upon a characteristic phenomenon of tyranny: the uneasiness of the government at not being a product of peaceful evolution and at not being able to retain its position without violence; and also its distrust of its subjects, a distrust expressed in inquisitorial police methods which lead in their turn to a general suspicion of all against all. Universal surveillance proves universal mistrust; acts of disaffection are expected and must be forestalled. Hence the development of an institution to organise the prevention of such acts and to collect and systematise the delations arising from a general state of suspicion. In this state of affairs, delation acquires a sort of independent existence 'for its own sake', for everyone learns by observation or experience that it is an easy method of getting rid of people who are in one's way or of revenging oneself on those who are or seem to be one's enemies. The Cheka, having now become the GPU, was intended to operate among the general population, but as the apparatus of Party and State embraced an ever larger part of this population, the GPU increased correspondingly in size and complexity until it became not merely a Party organ for use against the rest of society but also an organ for use inside the Party and the army. It became a sort of state within the State and party within the Party. This development dated from 1923; and in the following years, up to the elimination of Trotsky, inquisitorial police methods were used against the opposition within the Party.

A second phase in the development of this institution, and one whose importance can hardly be exaggerated, came to light in the decree of 26 March 1928 (just after Trotsky's deportation to Alma Ata). This decree prescribed a greater use of forced labour, and was followed, in July, by a further decree prescribing the extension of forced labour to all physically fit prisoners. These decrees had been preceded by an anonymous article in *Pravda* stating that the methods of the *Nep* were failing to supply adequate provisions to the urban population and the army. From November 1929 it became obligatory for judges to include forced labour in all sentences of internment; [1] and in July 1934 the GPU, having become the NKVD, was invested with the right to order expulsion, exile and imprisonment in 'corrective labour camps', without preliminary trial, for a period not exceeding

[1] D. J. Dallin, op. cit.

five years. This police force thus acquired new functions which differentiate it from all other police in the world at that time.[1] One can no longer regard the GPU as simply a police force. It becomes a new and original institution of the 20th century.

The penal labour force played such a large and active part in the empire's economy that the institution in charge of it had to be given other powers besides the normal coercive powers of the police. Indeed, the distinction between the police and the administrative personnel of prisons and correctional establishments did not exist in the same way as in non-totalitarian countries. In so far as it was decided at the summit that the plans for accelerated industrialisation required a certain proportion of the population to be deprived of the status of 'free worker' (a privilege the collectivity could not afford to bestow too lavishly), there had to be a new and historically unprecedented system for organising forced labour. There could not even be any absolute distinction between the economic enterprises for which forced labour provided the 'human raw material' and those functions, purely coercive in the one case and purely supervisory in the other, which in the Western democracies are allotted respectively to the police and the personnel of prison administration. There did, in fact, occur a certain confusion and intermixture of the two social functions, and since they are not pure ideas but social realities, they gave birth in the Soviet empire to a new and original organism of which the police, even in the highly developed and specialised form it had assumed, was only a part and not the whole. This was the institution known successively as GPU, NKVD, MVD. (The frequent changes of initials represent functional reorganisations but are also a sort of euphemistic magic to ward off curses.)

By this phenomenon not merely the economic but also the human aspect and geography of whole regions was to be transformed. In the Russian system there is usually not one camp but a *system of camps* covering an entire region and modifying its whole character. The camp is merely the penal aspect of the phenomenon. In its economic aspect it is a system or network of co-ordinated enterprises.[2]

[1] Except the Gestapo, which existed only in embryo in 1934, and which seems to have owed a great deal to the example of the GPU.

[2] Dallin (op. cit., pp. 158–61) gives a list, though not a complete one, of these penal areas. For conditions of life in the camps and the numbers inhabiting them between 1928 and 1948, see the works of D. J. Dallin and of Dallin and Nicolaevsky already referred to. To gauge the accuracy of their figures one can only rely on probability, compromises between various estimates, and guesswork. When official statistics exist at all, they make no distinction between the large concentration areas and the others. But the fact that the government keeps the true figures secret argues in favour of the estimates in the books referred to. The camp population has fluctuated, and estimates of its numbers vary in the proportion of three to one. But no one (except the blindly faithful and 'fellow travellers' influenced by them)

The phenomenon as a whole can be seen as one aspect of the rapid industrialisation and the five-year plans. It was in order to expedite the plans that the 'correctional camps' of the earlier period were transformed into economic enterprises.[1] (It should be noted that in Hitler's Germany the 'substructure' was quite different although the concentration camp system was very similar. It too served the purpose of providing cheap labour in addition to being a repressive measure. Equally there was similarity in the camp populations: a mixture of political prisoners and common law offenders.)

The institution continued to develop by the acquisition of new functions. In the 'concentrational' areas the political authority of the heads of these important enterprises naturally came to overshadow that of the local authorities. The construction of airfields, barracks, factories, roads, railways, and canals implies heavy budgets and a specialised personnel. The provisioning of such a population raises complex administrative and transport problems. Moreover, this vast organisation of police supervision must also supervise itself, so there is a special armed force of picked men, in both the political and military sense, whose functions are very much wider than those of our own 'republican security companies'. It has its aeroplanes and armoured cars, and in the last war it even had the monopoly of a certain 'secret' weapon.[2]

The point to note is the combination in a single organism of all these functions, which in other contemporary societies are kept separate, and also the method of self-aggrandisement or, one might say, 'self-proliferation' by which one function creates another by making it necessary. The institution has also the right to retain its prisoners after their terms have expired, so that in effect it is able on its own sole initiative to impose sentences of administrative deportation of practically unlimited duration.

Moreover, special political and propaganda tasks are entrusted to it. In time of war, for example, the additional economic burden has the effect of further expanding the institution by widening the scope and extent of its work. Prisoners of war and 'wartime prisoners' (deserters, suspects, military offenders) are incorporated into the system. In the

denies that the figures run into millions. In Hitler's Germany concentration camps and penal labour only became a part of the country's economic life as a result of the transition from peace to war. The war corresponded in Germany to the first five-year plans in Russia as a factor in transforming the function of the police into an economic function. And in Russia, too, the war helped to develop the system further. The fact that 'free' labour can be quickly transferred and distributed completes the system.

[1] 'The method of work established in the camps derives from two factors: the need to stimulate the worker's activity by making his rations proportionate to the work accomplished, and the need to keep the work as cheap as possible.' Dallin, op cit. See also Margarethe Buber, *Under Two Dictators*.

[2] Dallin, op. cit.

last war prisoners were added to the penal labour force; and the institution was given the task, on account no doubt of its acquired skill in dealing with the 'prisoner mentality', of organising the 'Free German committee'[1]; in other words, it was required to work upon the German military sensibility in such a way as to produce the results anticipated by the Politburo's policy.

It would be true to say that what links this institution to the Party summit is the central axis of the régime. 'Opposition at the summit' would threaten the entire system. It may be noted that after Dzerzhinsky and up to 1939 more than one head of the institution has suffered the death penalty.

* * * *

The power relationships in this society are clear. A small number of men possess, as opposed to the majority, the power of distributing consumer goods and of fixing, according to standards of their own, the place of each man in the social scale and the status of each category in the social hierarchy. This small group of men wields, in fact, over the majority a power which has so far known no limitations either by custom, as in all older despotisms, or by 'natural' associations or 'intermediate bodies', as in Western constitutional monarchies. The majority enjoy no benefit of custom, franchise, privileges, or freedoms. Trade unions are nothing but channels of communication between the Party and the masses, and they only serve to hold the worker more strictly to his job. Regional diversity is tolerated only so long as it does not interfere with centralised activity.

The system is a whole whose parts are interdependent and mutually determined. The superior living conditions of those who live well presuppose the inferior conditions of those who live badly: the wage-earning proletarians whose conditions are no better than those of the workers who built up[2] the great capitalist accumulations of 19th-century Europe—conditions which aroused the public indignation reported by so many socialist and Christian writers. The standard of life of the ruling élite presupposes not only the conditions of the workers, tied to their factories, and of the collective farmers, tied to the

[1] Note the (grim) humour of totalitarian nomenclature. There is a gulf between the 'free French' of General de Gaulle and the 'free Germans' of von Seydlitz. They do not seem to refer to the same kind of freedom.

[2] Apart from the question of political tyranny, the present Russian system ought, according to Marxism, to come to an end when the phase of intensive industrialisation is completed. The conditions of labour, both compulsory and 'free', ought to improve in the same way that the standard of life of the western European working class improved during the second half of the 19th century.

kolkhozes, but also of the convicts whose status is comparable to slavery (especially to the State slavery of the Pharaohs' workshops). It is not true that there must be slave-owners before there can be slavery or that there must be private property before there can be 'exploitation of man by man'. To think so is to give precedence to legal conventions and *a priori* notions over established fact and lived experience; it is to suppose, contrary to sociological findings, that the absence of slave-owner, boyar, or private capitalist implies the absence of exploitation. The slaves of Pharaoh's workshops were in no way personally dependent upon the Pharaoh, but the harsh relationship of master to slave existed nevertheless. It was personified in the eyes of the slaves by the foremen and overseers and directors of the work. Even though the territory belongs to a divine monarch or to a god, mediated by temple and priesthood (to keep to the Egyptian illustration), men are still physically related to one another in the same way, as masters who command and slaves who obey. It may be agreed by all that the supreme master is some remote and scarcely conceivable entity, but the slavery of the slave and his servile condition are still realities.

In Russia both wage labour and forced labour are, in fact, under quasi-military control. The remote entity called the State is incarnated in a government and administration which control the production and distribution of goods, and also the lives of the people, who can thus be transferred from free labour to forced labour or vice versa, and can be immobilised or displaced as higher authority decides. Marxists refuse to describe the minority which thus disposes of the majority as a governing class, but this is a doctrinal rather than a sociological problem, and it cannot affect either our description or our judgment of the facts.

It is important to bear in mind that the argument that 'everything belongs to the State, which merely represents the collectivity, and therefore everything belongs to everybody', is a purely abstract one and is completely unrelated to what actually happens. What happens is entirely different from what happens in a co-operative where each member is joint proprietor of the whole enterprise, or in a hypothetical joint-stock company in which all the shares are equal and each shareholder possesses the same rights (i.e. opportunities, for a right is nothing if not an opportunity) as all the others. The reality in Russia is the social differentiation of a stratified society. It is true that everyone, or almost everyone, is in equal danger from the totalitarian police, but this danger also is hierarchically stratified. There is a governing élite, and then there are the middling and petty officials, and then the wage earners, and lastly the slaves. Though there may be a circulation between the wage earners and the medium officials, the governing élite is tending to become a caste, or hereditary élite. There can be a hereditary élite without hereditary landownership.[1] In Russia the difference between highest and lowest wage is in the proportion of 50 : 1 (in France it is 8 : 1). The higher standard of life of the Russian élites does not rest upon private property in land, capital, or slaves. It is a function of membership of the oligarchy which plans, decides, and distributes. M. Carcopino[2] has shown that Cato, the author of *De Agri Cultura*, got more wealth from his *possessio* of a portion of the *ager publicus* on which he raised herds than from his private inherited patrimony. But in law the *ager publicus*[3] was the republic's property, and Cato's *possessio* was a class privilege. The oligarchy had, in fact, arrogated to itself the lion's share of the *ager publicus*. Oligarchical privilege was worth more than private property. In contemporary Russia private property does not exist, but oligarchical privilege does. It is useless to reply that this privilege is a reward for performing the most socially valuable functions, because, in the first place, such a claim would be hardly in the spirit of the programme which the bolsheviks set out to realise in 1917 and, secondly, what reason is there to suppose that the *patres* in the time of Cato the Elder were not performing the most necessary and valuable functions of the collectivity of their day? Quite obviously, they were doing so. The special privileges of the governing élites in Russia are equivalent to a *possessio* conditional upon function.[4]

Between the Russian system and a system based upon private property (which, in any case, is being increasingly curtailed in the West 'in the public interest' and ever more drastically taxed) there are many intermediate stages. A great trade-union organisation may, as was typically the case in the Germany of the Kaisers and of the Weimar Republic, be the owner of real estate, banks, printing presses, and other businesses[5] which are no one's private property. But one cannot deny

[1] cf. Peter Meyer, *The Soviet Union, a New Class Society* (*Politics*, New York, April 1944), quoted by Arthur Koestler in *The Yogi and the Commissar*: 'The decree of 2 April 1940 fixed the fees for secondary schools (medical, technical, agricultural, normal) at 150 and 200 roubles a year. This eliminated 600,000 poor students. Cadet schools have been created to which officers' sons have special entry; and there are special schools reserved for the sons of officials. Other children on leaving school are mobilised for four years (compulsory labour, preceded by an apprenticeship varying from 6 months to 2 years). To obtain a scholarship a pupil must be marked 2/3 excellent and 1/3 good. The selective character of these measures tends to keep the leadership in the hands of the same families.'

[2] *Histoire romaine*, vol. ii: *Des Gracques à Sylla* (Paris, 1935).

[3] The historical importance of the problem of the *ager publicus* is well known; the Gracchi attempted to preserve or even to re-create the rural middle class by dividing the *ager publicus* into small holdings. Such proposals threatened the *possessiones* of their own class, the oligarchy, and were persistently opposed and defeated by it.

[4] We make no demagogic objection to this fact. We merely request to be allowed to see it for what it is and not pass it off as something else.

[5] Today the major American trade unions are great collective capitalists and 'big business men.'

that the high salaried officials of the union enjoy a larger share of the common property than the ordinary paying members. The ancient Egyptian temples and the Catholic Church in western Europe, both feudal and monarchical, were great landed proprietors, but their property belonged to no one except, in Egypt, to the god, and in Europe, according to ecclesiastical doctrine, to the community of the faithful. It was the clergy, however, who administered the property and enjoyed what was left over when due charges had been met; and it is only by a legal fiction that the community of the faithful can be said to have been the owner of the clergy's property.

Social stratification and differentiation can survive the disappearance of private property in the means of production and exchange. There is no clear-cut distinction in the U.S.S.R. between a 'managerial' group of technical experts in organisation, administration, and production, and a 'political class' in Gaetano Mosca's sense, or political élite. There is inevitably a certain division of functions, but one should not try to see more in it than is really there, for the fact is that power of every kind converges at the summit of the pyramid in the Politburo: economic planning and organisation and planned production are strictly coordinated with the general policy, both internal and external, of the Super-State. If analysis still reveals a distinction between economic power and political power, the fact remains that the two are interconnected. No Russian political leader can ignore the problems of planning, and no economic chief can ignore those of general policy. The Marxist ideology itself forbids it. At the lower levels there can be a certain degree of specialisation, though not so much as in the West. But in the neighbourhood of the summit the ruling élite, which has created and is still creating itself, tends towards a certain homogeneity. This is the opposite of what happened in the liberal Europe of the 19th century where, in the highest economic circles, it seemed to be theoretically possible to treat politics as a mere series of obstructions to be circumvented. But this was appearance rather than fact; and it has been a favourite theme of Marxist criticism to detect, behind a variety of ideological camouflages, the repercussion of the economic upon the political. (These criticisms have been among the most fruitful products of Marxist thought, except when their purpose has been purely agitational.)[1] The tendency towards homogeneity at the summit appears in the fact that all forms of power seem to lead to one another. Men can pass from what we should call the legal sphere to the diplomatic.[2] And,

[1] As has been too often the case in France, but less so in Germany and Austria.

[2] cf. the case of M. Vyshinsky, the most recent in date. It may be the same in the American 'super-state'. During the war Mr. Byrnes (cf. *Speaking Frankly*) was transferred from the Supreme Court to the State Department.

moreover, the highest industrial technicians are kept under particularly strict police observation. The distinction between the experts in the administration of things and the experts in governing men is less clear in practice than in theory. The leaders of 'Kombinats' have to manipulate men, and some of the heads of the police are concerned with certain economic problems. There is no place any more for the pure technician of mass action, like the pre-revolutionary agitators whose sole purpose was to bring down a régime and who could afford to be pretty ignorant about everything else. Mass propaganda today is closely linked to general policy and production. It would be ingenuous to imagine that there is a class of men called technicians subordinated to a class called politicians (or vice versa).

Meanwhile, for the proletarian or the man in the concentration camp the State may appear to be an ineluctable reality, like the changes of the seasons and the succession of night and day. All he can do is to try to accept his destiny as a providence.

CHAPTER 6

Bolshevisation

THE bolshevik party 'began the revolution with "human baggage" amounting to between 5,000 and 10,000 men'.[1] The civil war decimated the élite of professional revolutionaries. Yet although the bolshevik party had only 23,000 adherents in 1917, it had as many as 200,000 after the capture of power. 'Russia was run by 150,000 proprietors, so why should not 240,000 bolsheviks be able to do it?' asked Lenin. In 1919 the Russian communist party had 313,000 members; it had 611,000 in March 1920, and 800,000 in 1925.[2] The million mark was passed in 1926; and in March 1928 there were 1,304,000.[3] A great purge in 1929 liquidated Trotskyism and the opposition, and cleared the way for a 'new course' of a very different kind from the one Trotsky had hoped for. A few years later it was possible to give a name to this trend: totalitarianism. But the party grew even as it purged itself. It had 1,852,000 members in 1930, and although the purge of 1935–8 expelled hundreds of thousands there were 3,700,000 by the end of 1939. During the war the membership drive was intensified: 4,600,000 members by 1943 and 5,700,000 by 1945. The young communists, an auxiliary organisation of the party, had 4,000,000 inscribed members in 1938 and 17,500,000 by the end of 1943.

These figures seem to make the days of the 'clandestine circle' and the 'military organisation' of professional revolutionaries look very remote. But not at all. All that has happened is that the meanings of words have changed. The party, the Russian State, and the International are still controlled by a handful of men. The supreme staff (the real one) is no larger than it was under Lenin. In 1904 Trotsky made his famous 'anti-bolshevik' sally: 'According to Lenin's plan, the working class is replaced by the party; the party is replaced by the party organisation; the party organisation is replaced by the Central Committee; and finally the Central Committee is replaced by the dictator.'[4] This gives a better account than the figures we have just cited of what really happened

[1] According to the menshevik Dallin.
[2] Although the purge of 1921 had removed 175,000.
[3] The figures for the 'young communist' organisation increased proportionately.
[4] *Nashi Politicheskie Zadachi*, p. 54.

after 1917. Indeed, it gives an explanation of the figures themselves. It is within the party itself that we must now look to find the true statistical relation between the organisation of professional revolutionaries and the working class and then the 'labouring masses'. To the new member who has no special recommendations the party membership card gives a chance of obtaining work and lodging, but nothing more. There is a plebs within the party. The structure has not really changed. Witness Stalin himself: '*Three or four thousand men of the high command*—the generals of our party. Then 30 to 40 thousand intermediate commanders; these constitute the officer corps of our party. And a further 100 to 150 thousand of the leading elements of our party—these are, so to speak, the subaltern officers of our party.' Quoting these words, Dallin justly comments: 'Of the 30 to 40 thousand party directors . . . fully one half are scattered throughout distant provinces. . . . They have no part in the formation of party opinion. Only about 10,000 to 15,000 . . . constitute the *real party*.'[1] It is clear that in spite of appearances the numbers have hardly changed since the beginning. The general staff constantly endeavours to counteract the effects of the executions, deportations, and purges inherent in the régime by recruiting new élites as revealed in productive work and, later, in war, and by supervising and encouraging them. It was decided in 1934 that no party candidate should be accepted unless he had 'taken courses in political education and was grounded in the fundamental principles of Marxism-Leninism' (Kaganovich); but Stalin had this clause abrogated, and it no longer appears in the statutes of the party as modified in 1939.

The 'spontaneous disappearance' of the International (or Comintern) in 1943 made no difference at all. Russian history can be distinguished from Western history by the fact that in Russia every initiative comes from above; and what distinguishes Tsarism from the post-revolutionary régime in Russia is that the former was only able to carry out imperfectly its desire to circumscribe and penetrate and control and inspire every social activity, whereas the latter achieves this objective more completely.

The government had to fight against the vestigial remnants of the old régime and to keep on guard against the malevolence of the capitalist world; it also aimed to industrialise at record-breaking speed an immense country, with vast natural resources, most of whose population had remained hitherto quite untouched by modern industrial civilisation; and these activities all tended towards the same goal as the theory expounded by Lenin in *What is to be Done?*—namely a gigantic, centralised, hierarchical, pyramidal apparatus whose purpose would be

[1] Dallin, op. cit., p. 226 (our italics).

to establish over 'one-sixth of the earth's surface' (to begin with) a state that might be described as a sort of modern Sparta, industrial, warlike, and bureaucratic.

And just as the evolution of Western capitalism produced new middle classes[1] in place of those it disrupted or destroyed, so the conditions of post-revolutionary Russian capitalism, in the form of State capitalism, have produced new middle classes who resemble their analogues in the private industries of the West in being classes of officials and employees. But as distinguished from those of private Western capitalism, the Russian bureaucracy is uniform and hierarchical. In contrast with the new uniform and hierarchical *chin*, the conditions and ways of life to be found among the new middle classes of Western capitalism seem to be heterogeneous and varied (though only by comparison with Russia). Differences in standards of life are more obvious to the naked eye in Russia, and the expression 'industrial army' is literally true. There is no distinction, as in the West, between workers in private industry and State employees; there are only State officials, and these officials are integrated into a system which cannot well be compared to anything except an army. The bolshevik élite, the hard nucleus of the Marxist intelligentsia, was obliged to undertake the militarisation of 'cadres' drawn from the plebs in order to effect a frontal attack upon, and real *occupation* of, the State power; but the achievement of power merely necessitated a further militarisation on a larger scale, though masked this time by the new and less heroic conditions. Nevertheless, the tone of the propaganda for the five-year plans remained militaristic, and it compared to a series of battles those plans of 'socialist construction' which the unbeliever calls the industrialisation of Russia.

The 'apparatus of production' is not identical with the party. A great many non-party technicians have occupied high posts in it since the resumption and acceleration of industrialisation in the late 'twenties. But such technicians, whose promotion is solely due to their professional competence, are naturally careful never to oppose the party; and many of them join it because party membership is of such enormous assistance to their careers. Hence, necessarily, a change in the character of the party, which began to appear immediately after the victory; one no longer joined the party in order to conquer the world, but to conquer for oneself a place in the world. This is a familiar historical pattern. When a revolutionary party is successful it begins to recruit into its swelling ranks the very type of men it has just been fighting against: the men who always support whole-heartedly whatever is well able to support itself, namely any powerful constituted authority—of whatever tendency. Meanwhile, one particular part of the State apparatus, the

[1]As is now well known, Marx did not foresee this phenomenon.

police, increased and multiplied in complexity until it acquired that preponderance in society as a whole which characterises the police of totalitarian régimes.

That 'the party' came to mean something quite different from what it had meant between 1910 and 1920 is proved by the fact that party membership, especially from 1926 onwards, although it still conferred facilities of work and lodging and was a sort of certificate of loyalty, was of no avail whatever as a protection against the inquisitions and persecutions of the political police. On the contrary, in the great purge of 1935–8 party members were in greater danger than the rest of the people. Both party and State apparatus were purged, and the personnel of the two was generally the same.

Between the capture of power in November 1917 and the exile of Trotsky, a 'ruling stratum' came to the fore: officials both high and middling began to adopt a new way of life, no matter whether they were old revolutionaries or deserters from other parties, or men without any political past. The State which promoted and employed them had from the very first the structure of despotism and tyranny. They owed their places neither to elections based on universal suffrage, as in the United States, nor to competitive examinations, as in our own democracy. At that time there were more places to be filled than there were men with sufficient education to fill them. The *sine qua non* was political loyalty. But loyalty to whom? For those who had not fought in the revolutionary ranks the question was obscure, and for those who had it was complex. By the force of events the party itself was in full evolution. It could not remain the same after the conquest of power as it had been before. It must transform itself to adapt to the new functions imposed on it by history. And so the 'revolutionary' institutions begin to take on a new meaning, begin to become just plain institutions and to play their part as given historical functions in a given historical organism, ignoring if necessary their original revolutionary purport and ideological justification. It is true that the functions develop rapidly, and so does the rhythm of the organism's growth. But the fact remains that the situation as a whole has begun to stabilise itself by contrast with the revolutionary excitement of the previous period, which is now held to be prejudicial to the interests and affairs of the State. A society resumes its vital functions and reconstitutes itself by means of the reciprocal adaptation of the social functions to one another and to the social organs. The most urgent problem is not to ascertain how much 'democracy' the party can tolerate without disintegrating, but to reconstitute society and solve its vital problems. In this case, reconstitution meant a stratification with the newly differentiated social strata arranged in hierarchical order. In his autobiography Trotsky speaks with a disillusioned contempt of the 'careerism' which revealed itself without compunction once Lenin was dead. Society at the summit of the pyramid was becoming extraordinarily mixed, thought the former chief of the Red Army: time-servers and new men were already on equal terms with the original leaders of the revolution. But it was no longer for a revolution that leaders were required.

* * * *

Marxists use the term 'revolutionary ebb' to describe the return to relative social stability of the belligerents of the first world war. Failure in Hungary and then in Germany convinced the Comintern that it could now only wait in patience and prepare for the next revolutionary wave.[1] Lenin had hoped that the wave he had ridden would continue and submerge Germany, which would have meant that Marxism had re-entered its main channel, so to speak (for Germany was the most highly industrialised country of Europe).

But on the contrary, it was signs of 'counter-revolution' that increasingly appeared in the West during the 'twenties: the rise of Stalin and Mussolini, and the curbing of the European communist parties, which included the wholesale jettisoning of their original traditions as being insufficiently revolutionary from the point of view of Russian conditions. Indeed, the process that has been called the 'bolshevisation' of the communist parties consisted in bringing them to heel. Under Stalin's reign the evolution of the bolshevik party has been a determining factor in the evolution of all other communist parties. The time has come for Russia to repay her debt to the West. If Marxism did violence to Russian ways, it is under the banner of Marxism that Russia will now return violence for violence. To 'vertical determinism' there is added a 'horizontal determinism', and the resultant is the phenomenon which we know here and now as 'communism'.

* * * *

History offers many examples of the arrest of the evolution of a particular human group or social structure as the result of external intervention. The autonomous institutions of a conquered people are overlaid by those imposed by the conquerors. But the former are repressed rather than destroyed. They do not disappear without leaving traces, but what remains of them is profoundly adulterated. Ethnography shows us the sensible, material aspect of this general law of cultural phenomena: a conquered people is introduced by its conquerors to the bow or the outrigger; but while the conquerors confer some items of culture they destroy others. Historians since Herodotus have

[1] Which proved to be the capitalist crisis at the beginning of the 1930s.

merely related these facts, but ethnography displays them in picturesque form for all to see. The process is not confined to technical inventions. Art, language, religion—philosophy even—can be transmitted or destroyed.[1] Ideas do not reproduce themselves like living creatures; a new idea is born of the adulteration of old ideas. In the same way, civilisations are transformed by adulteration; and this is true in detail as well as in general. Because the various components and factors of a civilisation are interdependent, an alteration of any one factor involves the alteration of another, and in the end 'society' is changed (though whether the change is an advance or a decline, an integration or a disintegration, may be a matter of opinion).

The west European working-class movement was profoundly changed by the adoption of rules, practices, and customs properly belonging to the new absolutism which came to birth in Russia during the 'twenties.

Henceforth, non-Russian 'revolutionary communists' were no longer guided solely by the circumstances of the concrete historical struggle they were waging in their own parts of the world. The non-Russian communist parties were finally 'bolshevised' by the end of the 'twenties, which means that their very history was in a sense 'liquidated', and with it all their particular characteristics and everything in them, however new and alive, that distinguished them in any fundamental way from Russian bolshevism. In the eyes of those who carried out the policy of bolshevisation, the history of these parties was nothing but 'pre-history'. In France it was not only 'parliamentary degeneracy' that the 'bolshevisers' swept away.[2] They also swept away 'revolutionary syndicalism' with its hope of a genuine working-class education to be provided by the unions,[3] uninfluenced by parliaments, headquarters, and parties, and its hope of a 'producers' republic' whose functions would be divided between professional and local organisations, leaving no function for the State except that of co-ordination, and in which there would be socialisation without State domination and co-ordination without hierarchy. Admittedly, the matter-of-fact world of history had always given short shrift to the aspirations of Proudhon and his followers, but who knows what fruitful seed they might have sown? In the event, they were pitilessly stamped down by the bolshevisers of the French communist party. The new order of the day was the conquest of the State—a way of dispossessing the wealthy and disrupting the ruling classes which was to be pursued by methods as radical as those

[1] Or adulterated, which, in the realm of ideas, produces syncretism, and in the realm of words a '*lingua franca*'.

[2] The excuse for the neologisms in this book is that history has been presenting us with new facts to be named.

[3] Concerning this aspiration cf. especially Fernand Pelloutier, *Histoire des bourses du travail.*

of a foreign army of invasion. The appropriation of the revolution by the general staff of the Kremlin led to a standardisation of revolutionaries. There was mass production of the prevailing 'Stalinist' type, and all over the world revolutionaries were converted into career soldiers of a new kind: officials who are always in principle on a war footing, but officials nevertheless. The French communist party, like the Russian, relays down to the base of the pyramid, i.e. the mass of the workers, the initiatives received from the summit; but the French summit is itself only an intermediate authority. The International becomes identified with the Russian State at the real summit, and it is only there that decisions are taken on a world scale. The general staff draws up the general plan, allots to each his role, and plans the 'world revolution' in the same way as it plans the economy of Russia. If anyone opposes the plan he is requested pretty sharply to reflect on the fable of the members and the stomach. The part cannot rebel against the whole, and no sacrifice by a member is too great if it contributes to the welfare of the stomach. 'You must trust the International,' said the Russian emissary to the Cantonese communist who complained that the International had practically betrayed his comrades to Chiang Kai-shek. 'Whoever does not trust the International is not a revolutionary.'[1] A world strategy is worked out in Moscow for every period and it is there that the roles are distributed. Those who get the ungrateful ones soon find that they are not free to refuse them.

The struggle of the 'rising bureaucracy' against the 'opposition'—that is to say, against the untimely spectre of the earlier period—did not take place only in Russia. The bolshevisation of the foreign communist parties meant (among other things) the elimination of all oppositionists, who were treated as schismatics. The prohibition of 'fractions' in the Russian communist party, which practically abolished open opposition, was automatically extended to the foreign parties. It enabled these parties to exclude from their ranks all who wished to judge situations for themselves, according to their own revolutionary tradition, historical formation, knowledge, and critical ability. So bolshevisation of this kind practically amounted to 'de-Westernisation'. The type of communist who so far from being a mere executive was inclined to interest himself in the affairs of the Russian communist party and to interpret literally the word 'International', was doomed to rapid extinction. The 'fight against the opposition' was succeeded by the fight for the five-year plan and for the rapid industrialisation of Russia, which implied for Russia a greater centralisation, a more disciplined and more tentacular State apparatus, and a stricter obedience on the part of every executive.

[1] Malraux, *Man's Fate*.

Revolutionary communists in other countries were not directly exposed to the same necessities, but indirectly they were. The Russian party finding itself exposed to new necessities, these necessities must be reflected in the foreign parties. The preoccupations, the state of mind, and even the behaviour current in the parent party were reproduced (so far as possible) in all the other parties, which came more and more to resemble under-age children subjected to a strict and vigilant guardian. 'Bolshevisation' was supposed to be part of a world revolutionary strategy, but it was in fact the product of a purely and specifically Russian structural change; so the structure of the other communist parties appears no longer to be determined solely by the needs of their own particular campaigns, but to take instead the form of what ethnographers call a 'loan'. By the end of the 'twenties the system of promotion in these parties had become characteristic. The men of the earlier period, whose revolutionary past of campaigning for socialism had often added lustre to the party, were succeeded by a new race which seemed to have been bred within the party itself. These new men were selected on the spot, but were then sent to take courses in political warfare at Moscow or Leningrad. From cell secretary to national secretary a regular political *career* became possible, a sort of *cursus honorum*, and the real power behind the top men in this career was the prestige accruing from their honours in the Stalinist schools. 'Opposition' receives the same treatment as in Russia. If dissident members try to make their protests public they are accused of 'splitting tactics', and are isolated by being cut off from any possibility of explaining themselves or putting their case. As a result of bolshevisation the parties had been left with none but official channels of communication from above to below, and therefore any direct appeal to the rank and file became, as in an army, the supreme offence against discipline. Word is passed round, or rather received from above, and the dissidents or alleged dissidents are depreciated in uniform terms by the entire party press and spoken propaganda. To be in conflict with the party authorities is considered to be playing into the hands of the party's enemies, i.e. of capitalism and 'reaction'. These methods are mechanically and slavishly applied outside Russia by men who seem to represent the new upper strata of Russian society rather than the masses of their own countries. It will be claimed that they are 'bringing socialist consciousness to the masses from outside'; but is it really socialist consciousness that they bring? For those who wish to remain in the party there is no way but submission. The guilty must sign full and formal recantations which are so framed that if those who have signed them should ever again wish to criticise or differ from the line imposed from above they will only be able to do so with greatly diminished authority. (This was what happened to Kamenev, Zinoviev, etc., in the U.S.S.R.) Thus an opponent of party policy, if he wishes to be restored—and how precariously!—to grace, must first contribute to discrediting himself. If such a man possessed any authority outside the party, he loses it by his recantation. Having himself, by recanting, undermined his past authority, he can in future possess only the authority conceded to him from above, and this may be revoked as easily as it was conferred. These proceedings are the expression of a phase of social composition and stabilisation peculiar to Russia, and in other countries where the social structure is still intact and where the communist parties are in theory struggling to change it they represent a 'loan' in exactly the same sense as would the wearing of a three-piece suit by the inhabitants of the Trobriand Islands. We see here a sort of *secondary* social phenomenon, a 'superstructure' not based upon its own 'substructure' but *imitating another superstructure based upon a different substructure*. The internal contradiction, and the drama, of the International consisted in the fact that the structure of communism all over the world was *identical* with that of the Russian communist party, except for the difference that the former *was not*, while the latter *was*, based upon a real economic and sociological substructure, and a real historical past, namely the Russian 'twenties, when a new ruling élite emerged from revolutionary upheaval and chaos.[1]

The assumption of control by this new élite was reflected in the modification of the Russian communist party, for in Russia there was organic continuity between the social substructure and the political superstructure. The latter could still be an expression of the former. But the customs of the Russian party, when extended by decree from above to the other parts of the International, modified their superstructures without affecting the substructures of which they were supposed to be the product. As a result of bolshevisation, the foreign communist

[1] This contradiction was quickly detected. In 1924 three members of the German communist party (of whom two, known as 'Boris' and 'Samosch', were of Russian origin) published some 'theses' in which they examined the relation between Soviet foreign policy and the policy of the International in a period of revolutionary ebb. Their conclusion was that a divergence was possible between the interests of Soviet foreign policy and those of the non-Russian communist parties, and that therefore the Communist International should be kept separate from the Soviet State. The headquarters of the International should no longer be in Moscow, and all political and organisational links should be severed. The non-Russian communist parties should renounce Moscow's financial support and should pursue their own policies without regard to the changing requirements of Moscow diplomacy. The Russian communist party should be a member of the International on equal terms with the others.

Although 'Boris' and 'Samosch' were young men without much influence, these propositions aroused a storm of protests in the Politburo (and in particular a very violent 'open letter' from Zinoviev). See Ruth Fischer, *Stalin and German Communism*, p. 395 (Harvard, 1948).

parties tended to become organically alien to their own milieu; and in spite of their genuine efforts they are never quite successful in disguising this fact nor in allaying its awkwardness. Where communism becomes strong it is at the expense of the working-class movement, which loses its autonomy to an external leadership. The conception of revolution as an eruption from the depths of the masses is replaced by a new and hybrid conception. What is now required is revolution to order, eruption by instalments, spontaneous effervescence controlled by written instructions. Insurrection tends to be given the status of a conditioned instead of a spontaneous reflex. In this sense it can be said that the popularisers of Marxism are a living refutation of their own theory, for they introduce an uncovenanted stage into the process by which capitalist society should create the conditions of its own destruction. The power of decision and command is transferred, as it were, to a brain outside the body to be moved. It is acquired by a despotic general staff which presides over the destinies of an empire or developing totalitarian Super-State in which capitalism (in the form of State capitalism) has only just come to birth and in which the proletarian condition is disseminated by ukase. And it is a bolshevik general staff composed of Marxists (that is to say, of men whose self-imposed mission it is to abolish the proletarian condition) which issues the edicts. The leaders, both central and local, of the non-Russian communist parties are in the last resort co-opted or upheld by the Russian secretariat on the same grounds, the same conditions, and, *mutatis mutandis*, by the same procedure as Russian officials. It was a freak of history that combined the traditions of Tsarism, Byzantinism, and Western socialism. The ubiquitous photographs of Thorez in France are inspired by the ubiquitous photographs of Stalin; and when the Renault workers presented a motor-car to Duclos in 1936, they were following the workers of the Putilov factory, who presented one to Stalin. 'Loans' of this kind correspond exactly to the definition of *pseudomorphosis*. The cult of the leader was an imported cult in France, where there was still a lively libertarian tradition. A new composition of society was historically necessary in Russia, and this explains the need for a hierarchical and docile bureaucracy in which nothing is expected of the lower ranks except obedience; but outside Russia there was no necessity for vertical 'Stalinisation', and the natural tendency might be better described as 'horizontal'. Hence an internal contradiction in international communism. The qualities required of the Russian bureaucracy are necessary to the operation of a general plan which embraces and predetermines the entire life of the Russian collectivity, but in the 'borrowing' countries *no such conditions exist*. It may be objected that all that was involved was a tightening-up of discipline which was necessary in view of the battles to come. But battles fought by whom? And, really, in whose interest? Here is the central ambiguity. By his organisation of professional revolutionaries and his creation of the Party, Lenin had found a modern solution for the problem of the organic impotence of the plebs; and after the capture of power in Russia the nucleus of professional revolutionaries was the headquarters of a double enterprise: the composition of a new Russian society and the campaign for world revolution. This nucleus had to be the co-ordinating centre for two campaigns which—according to the theory which was improvised to fit the facts, in spite of the doctrinal difficulties it involved—were held to presuppose and complement and mutually determine each other, but between which it is, nevertheless, possible to make a distinction.

And this is the reason for the 'alienation' and 'mystification' of foreign communists of the lower ranks who are in no way related as clients to the new soviet ruling élite. They see that the campaign which is in theory *their own* is being directed from above by men who can only look down on them from above. But does this matter? Is it not world revolution that is at stake? True; but here there enters in the factor of *becoming*, the time factor. It was not Lenin's conscious intention to create a new *chin* in Russia, which would take up with even fiercer energy the task of Peter the Great and carry it through, in an age of greater efficiency, by even more radical methods. Lenin's intentions were quite different. He wanted, first in Russia and then in the rest of the world, to change the impotence of the plebs into its opposite. But this long-drawn-out game of world revolution has to be played by men who change and replace one another as time passes and who are changed by history as much as they change it. Moreover, who, in the last resort, is really in charge of the game? Is not the revolutionary campaign on the way to becoming something that might not be easily recognisable by those who first conceived it in the surroundings of a society totally unlike the society of contemporary Russia? And do not the very methods employed amount to new facts which, judged in the light of the original conception, might be said to be a distortion of that conception itself? And if a 'Marxist' completely rejects, or is fundamentally incapable of, this kind of examination of conscience, then how far can the word 'Marxist' be said to have retained the same meaning in the 20th century that it had in the 19th? Or is this corruption of ends by means an inherent characteristic of all historical enterprises of very long duration? It is only by leaving the time factor out of account that we can avoid noticing that the leaders of the communist parties outside Russia are coming increasingly under the jurisdiction of an élite of officials in place of the former élite of revolutionaries. The leader is still a 'bolshevik'; but the men who serve him in Russia are more and more the products of the new social requirements. They are officials in the authoritarian system of a State bureaucracy; and this system which they apply and serve and live off has created the very atmosphere they breathe. Being unable to imagine any other system, they do their utmost to extend the one they know. In Russia five men give orders to eighteen. These eighteen command five hundred; the five hundred command twenty thousand; the twenty thousand command one million two hundred thousand, and so on. . . . Foreign communists are set in motion on the same principle, and the position of their leaders is comparable to that of Russian officials. Initiatives from the Russian summit are transmitted outside Russia to men who are chosen for conformity to a certain pattern, that of the 'Stalinist leader'. From the highest to the lowest the select cadres are ever more closely modelled upon this prototype. It is the emergence of a new social type. At all the control points and responsible posts, there are men who have good reason for never opposing the initiatives from above. They are *party products*, and the confidence reposed in them by the lower ranks is based mainly on the fact that they are considered to 'represent' the Party. In due course, having faithfully followed the party line and all its turnings, how much sense of consistency and continuity will such men retain? How much sense of self-consistency, even, apart from fidelity to the Party? It would seem that if this one thread should break, such men must literally fall to pieces. Once they break with the Party their very coherence as persons seems threatened, and it calls for an unusual type of courage to withstand such a disaster. Their personality was only manifested in and through the activity of the Party as a whole, and their capacity for independent judgment or criticism of the Party is almost atrophied. Only the very strong can find their way back from such an impasse.[1]

The ritual and ritualism of unanimous congresses and demonstrations at which a whole crowd repeats the same words with the same gestures; mechanical applause for leaders (who can do no wrong, for they are the Party); ready-made opinions and the synchronisation of changes of opinion leading to action or inaction; all these specifically totalitarian features are imported by communists from Russia into their own countries.

Socialism made little headway before 1918, and communism has made rapid strides since 1930. The reasons for the failure of the one explain the success of the other. Where socialism preached abstractions, communism creates symbols; where socialism called for reflection, communism controls reflexes. Communism makes the expression 'working-class movement' sound like an anachronism, for today there

[1] This is not by any means to say that all those who leave the Party are men of great courage. There are other and quite opposite motives for doing so.

is a world-wide army of revolutionary officials, disciplined leaders, under the control of an 'apparatus' whose master switches are in Russia; and the chiefs of this army, from top to bottom, are selected by co-option. As in most armies, it is not the men who select the officers. The rise of the communist parties and the decline of the working-class movement are the same thing, for before there can be said to be a working-class movement there must be a minimum of self-determination and autonomy. And by the end of the 1920s the International was going the same way; it had become a pawn in the game of Russia's internal politics, in the struggles taking place within the supreme command.[1]

* * * *

Although they will have to deal with differing situations, it is always men of the same psychological type[2] who are co-opted and *appointed* for other countries by the high Russian bureaucracy. Men who, as Trotsky says, are often 'fundamentally imitative and organically opportunist'; men who, although they are found in different social régimes, possess the qualities necessary for social success in an absolutist and bureaucratic State of the Russian type. Who have led the International since Lenin's death? asks Trotsky, and there again he notes the appearance of a new type of 'leader'—'the adaptable type in search of protective colour'. Just as the men of the Politburo are concerned simultaneously with the most diverse aspects of Russian life and with the widely varying mechanisms of the Super-State and Party, so 'the same man [Raskolnikov] was in charge at the same time of proletarian literature and Asiatic revolutions'.[3] The Comintern leaders who are not Russian and therefore do not divide their time between the International and Russian internal affairs are members of the 'Executive of the International' who have been banished from their own countries after unsuccessful revolutions, such as Bela Kun (who has since 'disappeared'), Kolarov, Dimitrov, and Kuusinen. They live in Russia, and Trotsky calls them *pensioners*. They are selected, chosen

[1] In addition to Trotsky and Souvarine, see Borkenau, *The Communist International* (London, 1939), and Ruth Fischer, *Stalin and German Communism* (Harvard, 1948). Souvarine goes so far as to say that the hopeless putsch at Canton was carried out on orders from the International so that the news of its failure could coincide with the 15th Congress of the Russian communist party, thus providing Stalin with a triumph over the opposition and with a temporary justification—to last for the time of the Congress—for his Chinese policy. The price: a hundred thousand victims. Our own information does not allow us to agree with Souvarine; but that such a view could be advanced and could be held by many of the opposition is significant. Even if it was imagination, what was imagined was by no means impossible.

[2] The truth of this statement, in so far as it is true, can only be statistical.

[3] Trotsky, *L'Internationale après Lénine*.

from among their competitors, and finally co-opted according to the same standards [1] as high Russian officials; and they belong in the same way as these officials to what Souvarine calls the 'hierarchy of secretaries'. They are exposed to the same risks, and are liquidated, if need be, in the same purges.

As for the local leaders who live in their own countries because they are the 'chiefs' of parties which are still legal, their case is not so very different. We have already tried to show why they are unlikely to be able to draw inspiration or energy from their own native traditions and culture. The signatories of the theses of the first four congresses of the International have nearly all since dropped out of the communist ranks. The bolshevisation of the European parties was a *Gleichschaltung*.[2] After it, practical subservience to the Russian bureaucracy was an essential condition for the job of leadership of a non-Russian communist party. The fact that there can be no criticism or judgment of directives and orders received from above produces a type of men whose chief aptitude is for the justification and execution of orders in whose drafting they have, at the most, only a consultative voice. The professional revolutionary of the 1920s either vanished of his own accord or else was 'liquidated'; he had become an anachronism, a mythical figure. His place was taken, in France, by a type which combined the cautious official, the astute parliamentarian, the genial orator, and the professional agitator. These 'stars' are selected on very different principles from the professional revolutionaries of the heroic period (of whom a few 'converted' specimens still survive). During the period which Trotsky calls the 'period of domestication of international revolutionaries', when Bukharin's quarrel with Stalin came to a head at the Sixth Congress of the International, Bukharin 'read out a letter of Lenin's to Zinoviev and himself in which Lenin warned them that if they began replacing independent and intelligent men in the International by docile imbeciles they would infallibly kill it'.[3] There is certainly one accurate observation in this outburst. It is represented by the word 'docile'.

It is possible to divide into two periods this process of bringing the communist parties to heel and absorbing the leading members of the International into the soviet bureaucracy by turning them into a sort of special class of officials. The first period is that of the 'fight against Trotskyism', and by the beginning of the 1930s the enemy was defeated, although not annihilated. Of the second, and totalitarian, period the most striking episode was the collapse of the German communist party —a collapse which had very much the air of a suicide. With Hitler in

[1] This is true at least in part.

[2] The Nazis may have invented the word but certainly not the thing.

[3] Trotsky, *L'Internationale après Lénine*.

power, a certain number of militants who continued to work illegally were caught by the Gestapo, and others, banished from Germany and living in Russia,[1] disappeared with as little ceremony as many of their Russian colleagues at the same period. The purge that began in 1935, after the assassination of Kirov, the leader of the Leningrad soviet, was of unprecedented scope and severity, and the foreign members attached to the high soviet bureaucracy were in no less danger than the Russians themselves. The future of both alike depended upon the outcome of those coterie struggles which are the totalitarian equivalent of court intrigues. Moreover, the leaders of the foreign parties depended upon the favour of one or other of the big men at the summit of the Russian communist party, the International, and the Russian State, and if any of them failed to disentangle themselves quickly enough from their fallen protector they too risked falling into disgrace. This explains why the sudden disappearances and the 'trials', at the end of which Stalin remained the sole survivor of the great bolsheviks of the heroic age, were accompanied by a reshuffle, in the administrative and diplomatic sense, among the high personnel of the International.

Both in Russia and abroad, therefore, it is all one single bureaucracy; with this sole difference: that the ability of officials inside Russia can more easily be estimated by their superiors. Docility is not enough, because efficiency can also be taken into account. But it is not so easy to appraise the value of a foreign communist leader as of the director of a *Kombinat*. Indeed, almost the only complaint that can nowadays be brought against the former is failure to carry out orders or to keep his superiors adequately informed. If he can prove that he has always done his best to carry out his instructions it is not easy to blame him for their non-success. Such a leader is protected by the 'interior régime' of communist parties from any criticism from below, and towards those above him in the *de facto* hierarchy he has no rights except the right to plead his good intentions.

Such is the background of the Campaign as we know it with all its familiar characteristics. The pre-1914 socialist movements, the Russian revolution, and the foundation of the Communist International are related to it as ancestors, and we shall not be able to understand the Campaign if we ignore its ancestry. But we shall misunderstand it if we see it only in terms of these bygone historical phenomena which enabled it to come into existence, but which it transcends. Indeed, it can best be understood *by contrast* with its antecedents, for any attempt to explain it in the light of them would oblige us to neglect the time factor—in other words, to neglect history itself.

[1] cf. the lists (incomplete) given by Barmine, *One who Survived* (New York, 1945), and by Krivitsky, *I was Stalin's Agent* (London, 1939).

CHAPTER 7

The Third Army

THE twofold apparatus, part legal and part illegal, from being doctrine and theory became, after the early congresses, institution and fact by virtue of the statutes of the Communist International and the conditions for admission to it of the various communist parties of the world. There must be two types of organ or apparatus, the communists say,[1] to correspond to the two forms of their struggle; and 'bourgeois' legality cannot be valid for those whose purpose it is to destroy it. Not merely the occasional recourse to illegality but the permanent existence of illegal alongside legal activity is a constitutional feature of communism, and this division of labour calls for specialisation, dual functions, and dual organs. The right hand must, or at least must be able to, ignore what the left hand does. And if the right hand, the openly declared communists, and the left hand, or illegal apparatus, are to co-operate towards the same end, there must be a central nervous system to order and co-ordinate the work and grade its priorities. The whole is under the control of the supreme authority which, as we have seen, is not in reality the directorate composed of proletarian leaders and revolutionaries of the whole world, which, ideally, it seemed to be. The constitutional delegation of power on the principle of universal suffrage was not possible, nor, even if any such legal formalism had not been utopian in the circumstances, would there have been any point in introducing it; for the purpose was not to consult the opinion of the masses as they then were, but to awaken and win them, to spur them on to agitation and activity. The reality of the Russian revolution, which placed vast resources at the disposal of the Campaign, prevailed over any theoretical considerations prescribing equality among the revolutionaries of the world. By the same token, Nechaev's doctrine triumphed: that there must be a hierarchy based upon the relative value to the revolution of the individual revolutionaries; those who were most necessary must be at the top. And who could these be but the Russians, who had given the world revolution its 'operational base'? Nechaev also foresaw that in

[1] We may note here the preference of communists, in their choice of terms, for assimilating the animate to the inanimate. The word apparatus, which refers to machinery, supplants organ, which refers to living beings.

such a hierarchy the least necessary revolutionaries must be at the disposal of the most necessary, as capital which they can invest or spend. And that is certainly what happened; nor can it be said that those who have this capital at their disposal have ever shown any great reluctance in expending it.

'To carry out its task, the revolutionary class must be able to master *all* forms or aspects of social activity, without the slightest exception . . . must be ready for the most rapid and unexpected substitution of one form for another.'[1] If for Lenin's phrase 'revolutionary class', which can be endlessly debated and the use of which presupposes adherence to his own *credo*, we substitute 'Comintern', we get the formula which was in fact applied; and which could be applied only if action were not restricted to legal channels, so that the right hand could if necessary be unaware, or only half aware, of what the left hand was doing. The doctrine (and in this context doctrine is strategy) shows consistent development from *What is to be Done?* to *Left-wing Communism*. 'Everyone will agree', continues Lenin, 'that the behaviour of an army which does not prepare to master all types of weapons, all means and methods of warfare which the enemy may possess, is unwise and even criminal.' Going further than Clausewitz, from whom he drew his inspiration, Lenin here does more than merely express, he actually embodies, what is a characteristic phenomenon of the 20th century—the complete fusion of politics and strategy. 'If we do not possess all the means of struggle, we may suffer a heavy, perhaps even a decisive, defeat.' To object that Lenin is speaking of *class* is a verbal quibble (frequently indulged in by those who discuss class in terms of Marxism); for did not Lenin write as early as 1901: 'We must have "our own men" . . . everywhere, among *all* social strata, and *in all positions from which we can learn the inner springs of our State mechanism*.'[2] If they are to do their job, these men must cease to be proletarians, if they ever were, and become specialists. But in doing so they will not merely come to *resemble* the secret service agents of a great power; whether they are aware of it or not, that is what they will actually be.

Two special organisation conferences were held in Moscow in March 1925 and February 1926.[3] Among those who met the Moscow factory representatives were Paul Merker and Ulbricht for Germany, Viola Briaĉco for Italy, and Maurice Thorez for France. One result of these conferences was the 'atomisation' of the communist parties; that is to say, the destruction of 'horizontal' connections and the reinforcement of 'vertical' connections. The basic unit, the cell, was no longer to

[1] Lenin, *Left-wing Communism*, p. 75 (London, 1920).
[2] *What is to be Done?*, p. 83 (our italics). [3] cf. Ruth Fischer, op. cit., p. 500.

communicate with other cells, which meant the virtual elimination of regular 'broad' discussions and meetings; communication was to be vertical, from top to bottom; a secretary was to represent the superior body within the inferior body (and not the other way round), and at information meetings, to which the delegates were carefully nominated, the party line was not *decided* but was merely brought to the knowledge of those who had to apply it.

Ruth Fischer estimates that at this time (1925) almost one-twelfth of the membership of the German party was in direct Russian pay. 'From then on conferences of responsible party officials were meetings of employees in support of their employer.' They were, she says, 'the most active elements in every sphere, in action, organisation, and propaganda'. Particularly significant: these 'Russian cadres within German labour' were co-ordinated and had 'direct affiliation with the centre in Moscow'. This 'network of Stalinist agents became so dense' that on the one hand it destroyed the 'autochthonous' traditions of the German movement, and on the other it 'strangled all anti-Stalinist forces, eliminating every potential anti-Stalinist'. It was at the time of the 'struggle against the opposition' in Russia that this sytem was organised and set in motion.

In 1926 the 'Lenin School', which was not the only institution of its kind, was established in Moscow. No one was admitted to the school who had not faithfully followed the party line for years and passed severe tests. The course lasted two years. The graduates became the élite of the secret service, and were given 'the most responsible tasks in the most important regions'. In this way, Ruth Fischer continues, 'side by side with the open party functionaries . . . there grew up a parallel invisible hierarchy, a secret élite whose every aspect was antithetical to the workers' representatives elected in the pre-Stalinist era. This body of G.P.U. officers had a life of its own, a solidarity apart from the parties it manipulated. Rank and title, and corresponding salary and privileges, depended upon the value of the services to the Russian state'.[1] This description underrates the incentives of these 'superior cadres' and is to that extent incomplete, but nevertheless it cannot be regarded as inaccurate. Ruth Fischer relates how this new institution proved its value in the struggle against the opposition (or rather, the oppositions). Known as the N-Apparatus, it organised raids on the opposition,[2] surrounding their meetings with detachments of armed men, searching the participants for 'oppositional' literature or incriminating letters. The agents of the apparatus were also used to search private homes and

[1] cf. Ruth Fischer, op. cit., p. 514.

[2] These methods have more than one feature in common with those used at roughly the same time by Mussolini.

bring comrades to headquarters, where they were interrogated, not by members of the legal party but by members of the secret service. This same service also organised slander campaigns, whose victims were represented as the personification of evil; inside and outside the party organisations they were defamed by the written and spoken word—both 'made in Moscow'.

There were different kinds of punishment, Ruth Fischer tells us; dissidents were sometimes removed for a year from responsible positions or participation at meetings; or they were forbidden to speak or write on political subjects, either in the party press or elsewhere. Some were banished to Moscow or to the interior of Russia; others were sent on remote missions to the Far East or Latin America.[1] During their exile they were forbidden to read anything coming from Germany.[2] Not merely individuals of the 'opposition' but entire cells were expelled from the Party as 'counter-revolutionary', and 'Party members were not permitted to have any relations' with them whatsoever, on penalty of '*expulsion for contact*'.[3] Karl Korsch was expelled for contact with Ruth Fischer; and both Zinoviev and Trotsky had to make declarations that they had not had contact with her. (In the case of Zinoviev this was not strictly true, according to Ruth Fischer herself.)

* * * *

All this may be regarded as simply a special, and rigorous, application of the theory of the 'professional revolutionary'. But the placing of these 'specialists' in the organised 'vanguard' of the proletariat is satisfactory to the theorist and reassuring to the faithful only because each of them is so much in need of being satisfied and reassured.

Doctrine became institutionalised; the theory of the professional revolutionary took practical shape in the foundation of genuine *military colleges* (the one in Leningrad being the most famous). Their object was to select from the mass of foreign communists an élite to serve the Campaign. But whereas in Russia the 'elements' recruited were those most suitable for *building* a society, the criterion for the new professional revolutionaries outside Russia was their fitness for *destroying* other societies. Their task was to aggravate the 'inevitable contradictions of capitalism in the epoch of imperialism' by 'nucleation' and sabotage (the Comintern's pet panaceas), by organising strikes, by the

[1] The Russian 'opposition' were being dealt with in the same way at the same time.

[2] This statement of Ruth Fischer's seems exaggerated. We know of no written evidence to corroborate it.

[3] Our italics. This 'prohibition of contact' is a typical tabu. Contact with the infidel, the gangrenous member, is held to corrupt the healthy member.

removal of troublesome persons,[1] in short by methods requiring other kinds of expertise than philosophy, economics, or literary style. By throwing sand judiciously into the machine, communists tacitly admit that the 'ineluctable effects' of capitalist crises, as foreseen by Marx and Engels, need to be helped along; and the work of these technicians who commit sabotage to order fits in perfectly with the communist propaganda and agitation carried on by selected officials and individuals or by ordinary party members, and with the assistance provided by certain bourgeois whose intellectual sympathy is the product of their masochistic complexes. Therefore when these specialists in consciousness and conscience are unaware, or pretend to be unaware, of what is going on, they should be severely judged according to the principles which they claim as their own, according to the logic on which they pride themselves. For those who perform decisive acts and those who merely talk interminably are collaborators in the same campaign.

Up to 1923 the leading bolsheviks hoped for a revolution in Germany, which would be the victory of the revolution in an industrially advanced country where the forces of production had reached a high level and the proletariat had been politically trained by decades of trade-union struggle and socialist education. With the revolution successful in Germany, the bolshevisation of Europe was sooner or later inevitable. So a military organisation was more than ever necessary; but it is characteristic that when the revolution seemed likely to happen at any moment this organisation was far from perfect and still left a lot of scope for that 'spontaneity of the masses' which so appealed to Rosa Luxemburg. It was the period of revolutionary ebb that saw the real establishment of the new type of 'apparatus', adapted for acts of war such as strikes, sabotage, penetration into non-working-class associations, or terrorist raids. The mere existence of such an apparatus gives rise to a state of masked civil war wherever its action is clearly felt; and it operates so as to effect a real convergence and synchronisation between material and social construction in the Soviet Union and the systematic destruction of the material, economic, social, and political systems of other countries.[2] And this *Freikorps* is directly

[1] According to Krivitsky (*I was Stalin's Agent*) and Jan Valtin (*Out of the Night*, Heinemann, 1941), whose evidence, manifestly fictionalised, can only be used in so far as it agrees with other less doubtful evidence. The main defect of fictionalised material of this kind is that it is difficult, if not impossible, to disentangle fiction and fact. That is why I have not used Victor Kravchenko's *I Chose Freedom* (New York, 1946), in spite of the interest of his story.

[2] A former Comintern agent, Jan Valtin (*Out of the Night*, p. 178), describes the organisation in these terms (since his statements have not, to our knowledge, been denied and have been corroborated by other witnesses, for example Ruth Fischer, we may cite them here, with due reserve): 'The Communist Party of Germany had at that time a quarter of a million members. It published twenty-seven daily papers, with a total circulation of about

dependent on the Executive Committee of the International. The presidium of the committee had five members in 1920, of whom three—Zinoviev, Bukharin, and Radek—were Russian, one German, and one Hungarian. The substitute members were Lenin, Trotsky, Chicherin, Pavlovich, and Berzin. In fact, since the foundation of the Third International its real leadership, the people who gave the orders and provided the money, were invariably Russians.

Those leaders who were not Russian by birth were in effect incorporated into the soviet bureaucracy and differed from it less and less, or rather had ever less opportunity and desire to make the difference felt. Militants from other countries, selected from among those who had shown in practice that they knew how to handle matters and had little taste for revelations or indiscreet questions, or that they possessed unusual gifts as agitators or propagandists, received special training in Russia in these new military colleges. When they had finished their

five million. A dozen weekly and monthly publications and hundreds of factory sheets augmented the regular party press. Nearly four thousand communist cells functioned in Germany, with over six hundred of them in the city of Berlin alone. Surrounding the Party was a belt of eighty auxiliary organisations which received their orders from Moscow by way of the Karl Liebknecht House. Working silently and efficiently in the shadows of the ponderous communist edifice was the underground G.P.U. network of the German Party. Its divisions included the "*S-Apparat*" for espionage, the "*M-Apparat*" for communist penetration into the army and navy, the "*P-Apparat*" for disintegration of police morale, the "*BB-Apparat*" for industrial espionage in favour of the Soviet Union, the *Parteischutzgruppen*—the armed bodyguards of party leaders, the "*N-Apparat*" for passports, party censorship, courier service and communications, and the various *Zersetzungs-Apparate* for counter-espionage work and disintegration work in the Social-Democratic Party, the Catholic Centre, the Monarchists, and among the military formations of the Hitler movement. Every department of the Party and every auxiliary organisation was directed by a special emissary from Moscow, invested with extraordinary dictatorial powers.

'The expressive word "agent" is never used in Comintern circles; the official title of the foreign Commissars of the Kremlin is the awkward "International Political Instructor". Each of these international agents was a specialist in a given field. There were specialists in propaganda technique, in strike strategy, in industrial organisation, women's specialists, espionage specialists, advertising experts, Red Army experts, business managers, police specialists, and specialists for each of the basic industries—steel, shipping, railways, mining, textile, public utilities, agriculture, and the chemical industry—and expert accountants sent to clear up financial tangles. Rarely were they known by their true names. All these instructors were well dressed and well paid, and seldom did any of them appear in a meeting without the protective escort of a personal courier or an alert-eyed girl who served both as secretary and mistress. It was this elusive corps of Comintern agents that formed the real leadership of the Communist Party.

'But Berlin was more than the centre of German Communism; since 1929 it had become the field headquarters for the whole of the Communist International. Moscow was too remote from western Europe and the Americas to carry on a close and constant supervision of the activities of its Foreign Legion. Besides, the laws of conspirative work demanded that the broad stream of international agitators in and out of Russia should be reduced to only the most necessary trickle. It was decided to let all threads end in Berlin, and to retain only a single line of communication between Berlin and Moscow. A Western Secretariat of the Comintern was therefore established in Berlin, whose jurisdiction reached from Iceland to Capetown. Appointed to act as its political chief was Georgi Dimitrov, who was responsible only to Molotov, the real ruler of the Comintern.'

training they were the equivalent of staff-college officers in the underground war. These men are of a palpably different type from the intellectuals whose adherence to communism is based upon theories about the 'course of history'; they are a corps of élites inured to an insidious underground war which will end only with the total elimination of the enemy; and, as the military élite of the underworld, they are dispensed not only from bourgeois morality but even from the normal obligations and behaviour expected from ordinary rank and file communists. Each member of this élite is answerable only to his superiors, and the very rules of their war forbid the comradeship which is a feature of open warfare. So this new application of the theory of the professional revolutionary assumes the form of a State institution for the training of a special kind of expert. It includes preliminary tests, theoretical study, and practical work; and finally this international order of modern warriors is let loose throughout the entire world. One of the more important jobs of these underground communists is to keep an eye on the 'legal' communists, thus acting as a kind of internal gendarmerie; and the 'legal' apparatus makes their work easier by more or less voluntarily closing its eyes to what they do. They represent the final stage of the 'militarisation on all planes' which was conceived by the small original group of revolutionaries as the 20th-century solution for the problem of the impotence of the plebs. But Lenin's solution of this problem, like Cæsar's,[1] does not alter but rather confirms the theoretical conception of the impotence of the plebs. The 'political soldiers' share the life of the proletariat when necessary, but only when necessary; more often they appear as business-men, confidential agents, condottieri, mercenaries; and if their job requires them to be workers, they are like secret service agents acting the part rather than real workers. By their very specialisation they fall short of Lenin's ideal of the professional revolutionary. For times have changed, and they have gone too far along their own road; they are no longer truly members of the Party 'living outside the Party'.[2] No one who has studied the history of the Campaign from its beginning can believe that it was really put an end to by

[1] It should be noted that the solution of education (as opposed to agitation, which is its contrary), regarded as utopian by the revolutionaries, has never been tried on a wide enough scale or with sufficient depth and continuity to make a judgment of its efficacy possible.

[2] cf. Valtin, op. cit. This book is one of those 'semi-documentaries' which are nowadays steadily encroaching on the novel, no doubt because they meet the same needs more satisfactorily. He describes these seeming business-men and their clever and beautiful secretaries who spy on the spies and wield great influence, auditing accounts, granting or withholding supplies, and acting as messengers of promotion, disgrace, and sometimes death. Their lives are wholly subordinated to the supreme mission: no personal ties, but only such material pleasures as are essential to offset the strain of their work. According to Valtin, the Comintern has its agencies in all countries open to this kind of penetration, and so far as possible in others as well.

the 'spontaneous' official dissolution of the Comintern in 1943. If there were some innocents who believed this, their belief cannot have lasted long ; or else their 'innocence' was of a most peculiar kind. The fact is that the Campaign is still on. But its character has changed since the far-off 'twenties ; its secret apparatus has been purged along with the Russian communist party, and to the same end. Its members from being bolsheviks have become Stalinists.[1] At first, the only resemblance between these soldiers of a new myth and the secret service agents of the great modern States was in the kind of activity undertaken; but today all differences are tending to disappear.

* * * *

Men make their own history, but not the history they anticipate. In studying and interpreting history, it is neither intentions nor plans, nor rationalisations after the event, which provide the starting-point. These are part of the evidence which has to be interpreted and do not themselves supply the key to the cipher. On the contrary, they make the evidence more difficult to read, and the apparent simplicity they lend to events must first be set aside. The communist Campaign which is active around us did not spring fully armed from the head of any one man—neither from Marx nor from the founders of the Third International. Looking back, it can be seen to have a structure which was created gradually, and a glance at its history enables us to list in order those who contributed to it, and to identify which parts they added and which features of the design they did most to elaborate. When Comte dreamed of the 'alliance between the intellectuals and the proletariat', he conceived it without reference to historical exigencies as a sort of diplomatic negotiation or conference; Marx conceived it practically, but what he helped to bring to birth was totally different from his conception. He founded a religion of the chosen class (a class which is a collective messiah, for the proletariat is to make philosophy real), whose mission is revealed to it by messianic individuals, men who become messiahs by contact and 'participation'. Academic social-democrats pass over this strictly religious aspect of the doctrine with the same embarrassed haste as 20th-century Hegelians in dealing with the 'Philosophy of Nature'. They dismiss certain Marxist propositions as the product of Marx's youth, 'when he was not yet Marx'; and at the end of the 19th century, when positivism and science were in the ascendant,

[1] cf. Krivitsky, op. cit., particularly his account of the Spanish war. His evidence can be used only with caution. There is inevitably more chance of error in sociological interpretations of what is secret than of what is not. However high the probabilities, little can be proved.

the religious idea became unrecognisable under the scientific and positivist cloak in which social democracy enveloped it. After the *Communist Manifesto*, Marx himself increasingly used (except in the 'Addresses') the language of economics and politics; and Lenin, as a maker of history, and concerned only with the transformation of the world, required for its understanding no more than a narrow beam of light to illuminate his field of action. If he had also the ambition to think and to legislate for the proletariat as a whole, he grasped—since he was at close grips with the social realities of Russia—the historical opportunities afforded him by Russian realities; and it was chiefly the theoretical ideas of Lenin, Trotsky, and Zinoviev which dominated the International. But Lenin's theories of organisation anticipated an historical development which it would be too bold to claim was foreseen by Marx. Lenin himself spoke only of 'class organisation', but in the more and more frequent use by the bolsheviks of the term 'organisation of the masses' there sounds a note that is foreign to Marx. It was Marx's opinion that the soldiers of the proletarian army were trained by factory discipline; and he was right in the sense that factory life inculcates certain habits of discipline and obedience. But with the transition from plebs to army, the recruitment of the world communist forces owes less to factory discipline, which can be only as it were a predisposing influence upon the proletariat, than to the new type of military organisation commanded and manned by professional revolutionaries. Organisation proceeded upon several planes successively. First there was the Russian bolshevik party, whose leaders issued the 'correct' instructions with decisive effect; and next, as a general staff, they laid the foundations of the world revolutionary organisation, within which they behaved towards the newly fledged communist parties as a creator towards his creatures.[1]

The structure of the International was such that by the early 'thirties the various national communist parties had become branches of the Moscow head office. A re-reading of the statutes of the International and the theses and documents of its first four congresses (ignoring intentions and rationalisations and examining the simple historical facts) will show that from this time onwards the fact was undeniable. The subordination of the national parties to Moscow was facilitated by the unquestionable superiority of the early bolshevik leaders, who stood head and shoulders above the other revolutionaries of their time. (They owed their 'mettle' to the extremely rigorous political climate of Tsarism.) Once subdued, Russia was placed at the service of historical conceptions of vast scope, which were essentially the work of one man assisted by a

[1] cf., for example, the 'Zinoviev telegram' to the Congress at Tours, and the various interventions of Trotsky, Zinoviev, Manuilsky, etc., in the following years.

staff of five or six; but at the same time these conceptions were intended for the service of Russia.

The military structure prescribed by Lenin was worked out successively for three different organisations: the Russian State, the communist parties, and the secret apparatus which has its outposts all over the world. On this third plane, even more than on the two others, the communists resemble a professional army; and we may note the deviation, or coefficient of deflection, imposed by history upon those Marxist ideas which make class the measure of every political phenomenon. This specialisation of organs, of apparatuses, of an active élite who are removed from proletarian life and from the working-class environment, is implicit in the very nature of social realities as revealed by history; ostensibly a triumph of the plebs, it really confirms the impotence of the plebs. It is a differentiation from the plebs of a new élite, who proceed to exact obedience from it. Great historic changes are effected, *but they fall far below the level of messianic hopes*; and, indeed, events follow quite a different course. Where communism is strong though not yet triumphant, the plebs may make inroads upon the power of their industrial employers; and they achieve this through strict obedience to 'political employers' who themselves obey higher political employers, in another place. In countries which are not within the soviet protectorate the communist has still the choice of changing his party; but he is held within a strong web of habit and tradition, of mutual supervision and comradeship, which makes it very difficult for the average man to take such a step, unless the communist party has suffered a severe reverse. Communism is a machine which grips people and holds them in a state of impotence, so that they can neither get free nor even seriously wish to. In its own revealing language, the Party treats them as 'elements'. In 1917 the Western socialist movements which called themselves revolutionary were dispossessed of their historical initiative, and they have never regained it. German socialism, the *alma mater* of European socialists, was destroyed by Hitler in the 'thirties, and Stalin was the beneficiary. But the outcome of the German communist party's suicidal policy was the complete disappearance, after 1933, of any historical possibility of a revolution in the West on communist lines.[1] Henceforth,

[1] That is to say, of the very thing for which Lenin hoped; cf. Ruth Fischer, op. cit. In 1919 when Radek was in prison in Berlin he met a great many Germans who were not by any means all communists. With them he discussed plans of a 'national-bolshevik' character, in which social revolution supported by Russia was closely linked with the struggle against the Versailles Treaty and for the national recovery of Germany. Lenin forbade any further consideration of these plans (cf. *Left-Wing Communism*). The contacts between the Russian and German general staffs are well known. Up to 1933, arms were manufactured for the Reichswehr, and tried out by German experts, in Russia. After Hitler, nothing is known of these relations. The world was aware only of the violent clash between the two brands of propaganda. On the origins of the 1939 pact, in addition to the German archives

the revolution could only be conceived as the world-wide triumph of the Campaign conducted from Russia. On the other hand, if a change in human relations can really take place in Europe, it must now be of a completely different kind. During the 'thirties both Stalin and Hitler liquidated the opposition in their own countries, and the culmination of this period in which the oppositions were destroyed was the short-lived pact between the two leaders. The destruction of menshevism, the bolshevik attacks upon European socialism, and the annihilation by Hitler of both socialism and communism in Germany, all these seem to be a part of the same 'process of liquidation' of Western socialism. The result could only be a still closer dependence of the other Western communist parties, and particularly the French, upon Russia. But in view of the 'theoretical and scientific' superiority of the Germans, the victory of German communism—if it had allied itself with social-democracy against Hitler in the 'thirties—might have restored the initiative to European socialism.

During the 19th century world history seemed to be at the mercy of economic forces: but the 20th century has been remarkable for a determined effort to control history by ideology, and the bolsheviks have undertaken, in the name of historical materialism, to impose the will of a few individuals upon the entire human world. Lenin inaugurated the *era of staff campaigns*.

The military staffs of the 19th century performed a specialised function. They could influence general policy, but nowhere did they completely control it. In the great capitalist countries economic interests influenced politics and represented the whole of the material side of human life. The soldier was subordinate to the shopkeeper; and learning, instead of being a caste prerogative, was like an auxiliary service, available throughout society, a reservoir into which every party could dip. But in the 20th century there appeared a new type of 'intellectual warriors', claiming to bend history to their own 'view of the world', claiming to know its direction and to possess the qualifications for leading men along the road. It was they who planned and effected the transformation of the plebs, turning the working class into a new kind of army; and it was they who, later, carried out the planned transformation of the Russian economy. These were two attempts to impose upon history a thought-out and predetermined order: and by their policy of sweeping away the values, traditions, and institutions which were accepted until they, and those whom they claim as their forerunners,

published by the American State Department (*Nazi-Soviet Relations*, 1948), see A. Rossi, *Deux ans d'alliance germano-soviétique* (Paris, 1949). Rossi is anti-communist, but he relies entirely on facts and documents. One is tempted to reconsider the underground struggle of the German communists against the Nazis in the light of the pact with which the period ended; and this is what Rossi appears to do.

appeared, they revealed themselves as a *new type of conqueror*,[1] *the destroyers of a culture*. Our knowledge may be superior to theirs, but knowledge is of no avail against religion; and, among the oppressive determinisms they have established, the one from which the others draw their chief strength is—in my opinion, and contrary to appearance and to the generally accepted view—a determinism derived from a religious sociology.

[1] Here again, we are strongly reminded of incipient Islam, with obvious differences.

CHAPTER 8

The 'Men of the Threshold'

THE centralised and hierarchical organisation of professional revolutionaries must be able to assume that its initiatives will command the active sympathy of the masses; wherever it operates, it must call forth assistance and collusion. The sympathy, support, and collusion of the working class—it is all set forth in *What is to be Done?*; but Lenin also said: 'We must have "our own men" everywhere', adding, to make it more precise, 'among all social strata, and in all positions from which we can learn the inner springs of our State mechanism'. Here the expert on organisation went further than the disciple of Marx; for when Lenin wrote this the posts he had in mind were far from being in the hands of the workers, so help had to be looked for outside the working class. Marxism still comes first; it is still, above all, a question of transforming the proletariat into an army. But the man of war is foreseeing a new kind of war. In order to arouse the masses, Marxism is transformed from a philosophy into a religion, from a doctrine of the élite into an ideology for the masses; and, thanks to a series of distortions and simplifications, it is made more easily assimilable and more acceptable to those whom it is intended to exalt. But precisely to the extent that this is achieved, it departs from the definition of Marxism which an historian of philosophy, if no one else, would arrive at through the rational interpretation of Marx's texts.

But if the drive of the new 'Islam' is not to be slowed down, it must find traitors within the citadel who will open the gates; and this is why, from the very first, the bolsheviks attached so much importance to the 'intellectuals'. They were intellectuals themselves, and had overthrown a régime on the strength of having found—or so they thought—a 'correct theory'.[1] The bolsheviks apparently never doubted that they would have the help of the bourgeoisie in its own destruction, or that the bourgeois 'bad conscience' would powerfully assist the 'socialist consciousness' which the intelligentsia was to bring to the workers 'from outside'. They still thought that everything was being done 'for the workers', but as practical men they already understood that every-

[1] In such matters, as we have seen, the bolsheviks are strict pragmatists: the 'correct' theory is the successful one, and the 'true' propaganda is the propaganda that 'pays'.

thing cannot be done *by* the workers. The truth is that the Campaign could not have developed as it did by relying exclusively on disruptive shock tactics based upon proletarian aggressiveness; and descriptive historians of communism have not paid sufficient tribute to the role of the 'sympathisers'. But it has, of course, been often observed that the bad conscience of the bourgeoisie played into the hands of socialism and Marxism, and that there was less good conscience on one side of the barricades than on the other. The bourgeoisie relied upon the 'rights of man' or upon Christian ideas; they never thought of themselves as an hereditary aristocracy, but justified their position, in their own eyes, by work and merit. Thus the accepted morality of the bourgeoisie was itself a factor in the psychological mechanism of bourgeois conversions to communism—because it identified the cause of the workers with the cause of justice. With the appearance of communism in history the question arises '*Can faith without works be sincere?*', and from then on the 'sympathisers' (who got their name at this point) require for salvation something more than a tender heart. They must act, or help others to act. They are conscripted into the army, although 'not for active service'. They must help to seduce by propaganda, and to promote, within bourgeois society, the interests of the besieging army outside; and should the need arise, even more active forms of complicity will be required of them.

It is a design of war and conquest, as 'political observers' have had no difficulty in showing; but how is it that such a design can find accomplices everywhere? If we look below the political surface we can see that while this Campaign is like the 'secret service' of a great empire, it is also something more. The motives of secret service agents are of three kinds—patriotic, official, or mercenary; but the Campaign brings other motives into play, and on a world scale; and therefore the uninterrupted state of war which its mere existence inflicts upon the world cannot be reduced to an ordinary rivalry of empires. It is a half-truth, and therefore an error, to explain the Campaign in terms of Marxism and of ideas, and it is an equal error to confine it to a case of imperial rivalry; but both points of view are necessary to its understanding, and neither can be ignored with impunity. The latter has the positivist limitations, fixation upon the past and upon results, and the former suffers from the characteristic intellectual lack of realism; it fails to see that the influence upon men's behaviour of even the best and truest, the most brilliant and profound and noble of ideas, will probably not be in direct proportion to all these virtues; it may even be, statistically, quite restricted. Nor can it be said that men pursue their own interest, for they do not clearly know their interest. The most that one can say, and it is not the same thing, is that so-called 'interested' motives are very powerful. But the claims of the working class would have had less weight in history if they had not been approved by the bourgeois conscience; and the men of the 'secret apparatus' and the 'activist' groups would have been a mere handful of outlaws at the mercy of any repressive power, if it were not for the existence of *something more* than the motive of self-interest. But for this *something more*, the fact that they had no scruples and shrank from nothing would have caused them to be regarded as 'nothing more' than public enemies. The soldier in an army, whatever he may do, is not regarded as a common bandit if he is obeying his superiors; and those who embrace ideas, to which, in all simplicity, they attribute the power of nerving the activist's arm, will be forced—although incapable themselves of performing the deeds for which the ideas call—to admire those who act them out to the end; and the more they value the ideas, the greater will be their admiration. And this is the explanation of the congenital weakness of all 'leftists' and 'radicals' when confronted with communists. For once a man has admitted any sort of causal link between Marxist ideas and communist actions, and once he has surrendered, even against his will and knowledge, to the ideas, he finds himself disarmed and strangely impotent in face of the actions. The 'men of the right', on the other hand, are positivists; they fall into the opposite error and see the facts as nothing more than facts. They cannot fight communism effectively because they do not understand it. It was because Marx understood and deeply admired capitalism (an admiration which dominated his life), and also those whom he too summarily described as the bourgeoisie, that he was able to fight effectively against them. Without the faithful and the 'sympathisers' communism as a political problem would be simply a matter for the police. But the existence of sympathisers—possibly even in the police itself—makes the problem essentially other than a police responsibility.

Where there are 'believers' and 'sympathisers' we may deduce the presence of a religion. The sympathisers, or *proselytes of justice* (to use the language of the Jews disseminated at the time of Jesus throughout the Mediterranean world), may be called the *men of the threshold*. They stand before the door of the temple. Attracted by the 'true God', they have yet not entirely broken with heathenism. There is still something that holds them back; and those 'within the threshold' take good care that most of them remain outside, for that is where they can be most useful.

If this religion is to be fought, it must be criticised; but criticism is not enough. The religion fulfils an emotional need, and can only be replaced by another religion.

The real wars of our time are fought on every level at once; and it is a mistake to consider only the military dimension, on the pretext that the casualties are greatest there. The military importance of the psychological dimension has steadily increased, to a degree still unsuspected by most observers. Anyone who reads James Burnham's *Struggle for the World*, for example, may well wonder how there can still be any communist sympathisers; but that is a problem about which everything remains to be said.

The temporary superiority of the communists over their opponents is strikingly seen in this simple fact. The Americans are manufacturing certain bombs which we have all heard about, and so far there has been no Russian reply on the same scale; but the Russians have, all the same, a devastatingly effective answer. Using psychological methods, and playing upon religious, moral, and 'metaphysical' motives, they direct their attack against the scientists whose work enables the bombs to be produced. They try to make it a moral imperative, for those whose research and discoveries underlie the manufacture of the new weapons, to deliver the formulas not to Russia or the Russian army, but to the servants, messengers, and supporters of a new and 'more just' conception of the world. This line of action completes that of the Russian secret service in foreign countries; and in this sense it can be said that the 'psychological arm' might be able to defeat the most deadly weapons of destruction that the world has known.

The bolshevik general staff reaped what Marx had sown, and the harvest is a religion which owes much to all its antecedents in the West, and notably to Christianity; but the Russians added to it their immense capacity not only for obedience but also for faith. This religion, whose roots were in the West, is misinterpreted and outraged by them in their own country; but they have revived it and made themselves its champions all over the world. Outside Russia they continue to present human problems in Marxian language—which is identical, in its *pathos*, with that of the 19th-century European socialists, and especially those whom Marx called the utopians (whose influence, in fact, helped to make him what he was). To accept the terms in which communists present the problems of our time—for example, that the struggle is simply between capitalism, or bourgeoisie, on the one hand, and communism, or proletariat, on the other—is to accept terms which are necessarily false, if only because their significance derives from a world which has greatly altered since Marx's day, and it amounts to an unconscious endorsement of the communist Campaign. If we grant them everything at the outset and accept all their premises, is it surprising that we should have some difficulty in avoiding their conclusions?[1] Western Europe has not yet been able to repeat the effort it made in the 19th century. But the communists, still living in that century, and to this extent out of date,

[1] Their two grossest assumptions are the dichotomy and duel between bourgeoisie and proletariat, and the identification of the communist party with the proletariat.

endeavour by every method of pedagogy, drill, and obsessional technique to imprison us within the false dilemmas of the mental universe—no longer a true one—in which the Marxist claims were formulated; that is to say, within a world which is not the real world in which Russian society and the Russian State and its will to expansion are, in fact, operating. Within this false world, if once we accept it, whether consciously or not, we shall either become the tools they want or else be hopeless and sterile rebels and misfits. The intensive cultivation of obsessional and repetitive propaganda for the purpose of conditioning reflexes, as developed by Stalin after the industrialisation of Russia and in imitation of Hitler and Mussolini, is effective and dangerous, because the true communist is possessed by a faith strong enough to withstand his own lies and to protect him, so far, from the dissolvent action of the ridicule they can provoke. These devices are held to be necessary for rousing the masses; and it is indeed true that it is not by difficult ideas, which must be protected by a constant intellectual effort from the encroachments of error, that the masses can be mobilised, kept on the alert, and stimulated or restrained as tactics require. 'Lies for barbarians' are a necessary weapon of those who seek to 'put philosophy into effect' and 'accomplish the purposes of history'. Behind the diffusion, which is to say the vulgarisation, of an ideology lies the propagation of a religion, and among those who are touched by the simplified propaganda there will always be an élite who will 'transmit' the religious current. To become a member or supporter of a political party is often an interested act; but when men today succumb to the intoxication of propaganda it reveals rather that they are particularly vulnerable to that type of suggestion. Nevertheless, men who are possessed by a faith must have certain qualities which do not belong to all men; and the lies of the propaganda experts are only able to be effective because there are also men of faith who *believe* in 'truths' which they persuade themselves to accept as 'scientific'. Communism, too, has its 'knights of faith'. The difference outside Russia between the 'man of faith' and the 'propaganda animal' is reflected on the intellectual plane in the distinction between an 'esoteric' communism, which is Marxist and is reserved for those who are qualified to discuss the theory and also later developments in the history of science and ideas and in history itself, and an 'exoteric' communism, which is a popular version adapted to the masses' affective needs at any given time.

* * * *

We must have the strength of mind to think about our situation in terms relevant to it and to ourselves ; it is for us to discover these terms and to justify them as Marx justified the terms he used. The chief danger is not what is wrongly called Macchiavellism (it should be 'gangsterism'); for this, indeed, in spite of appearances, is not really dangerous. But what is dangerous is the fact that men of every kind can be found to condone and connive at the behaviour of the gangsters. The strength of communism does not lie in its desperadoes, nor in the secret cadres which know how to foment and exacerbate a strike, or wreck a machine, or carry out a raid; it lies in the 'innocents', and especially the 'sympathisers', who form a safety-curtain behind which the active specialists of the world conspiracy can co-ordinate their work.

The communist Campaign resorts to the traditional devices of secret societies—cells and 'fractions' among them—and Marx, who rejected secret society methods, is of no help in understanding them. The originality of communism consists in its being, so to speak, a social fact existing in several dimensions and on several planes at once; it is both a mass organisation *and* a secret society, a perpetually active electoral army *and* a *Freikorps* in the social struggle, a parliamentary party *and* an underworld *Bund*. It is a religion against religion, and an education for obscurantism. In being one thing it does not cease to be the other ; and it always has an ace up its sleeve because it is always playing two games at once. Indeed, the very conception of fair play is completely foreign to its nature, and when it pretends to conform to this enemy custom it is merely confirmed in its contempt for the enemy and in its conviction that an opponent who abides by the rules is doomed to defeat. To stick to the rules of the game, whether parliamentary or military, seems to our contemporary totalitarians of every brand to be a custom as obsolete as the chains by which the French knights at the battle of Agincourt are said to have bound themselves together. The idea of not using *every* weapon at one's disposal against a weaker enemy is outside their comprehension. To refrain from crushing the weak would be 'liberal' and 'bourgeois'; and the communists are the heralds of a new and harsher dispensation. Communist leaders cry aloud for democracy, before they come to power, in order to have a free hand; but it is only a field for manœuvring, and the bolshevik army can make all the better use of it for not being itself democratic. For it, democracy is a way of preventing its enemies from combining, and here the tactic of the 'fraction' is invaluable. The opposing forces, being democratic, are neither organised nor hierarchical, and can therefore present only a dispersed and confused resistance to concerted manœuvres.

Reviving the psychological imperialism of the militant sects, the communist politicians who are its latest exponents are well aware that every man is most easily caught by playing on his weakness, his characteristic wants or passions or vices; the *weak point* of the individual, which it turns to its advantage, becomes the *strong point* of the group that wins him. Then there is also the bond of *complicity*, one of the strongest of all, which men can hardly break when once they have acted, or connived at, or profited from, an action. The second world war, which enabled the communists to get rid of the 'anti-communists' in Europe who had supported Hitler, also enabled them to purchase the obedience of all those to whose past they consented to shut their eyes (and such a decision was only taken for good reasons). Thus there begin to appear, especially after the German defeat, *satellite men*, *obedient to communism in action but not in thought*. What is required of them is not intellectual agreement but practical co-operation; and in view of their official positions it is undesirable to advertise their subservience, for that might lead to their dismissal and so destroy their usefulness. It is not even desirable that their co-operation should be accompanied by a *secret* conversion to communism, however sincere. Better that they should remain the bourgeois they are, for that is how they are most useful; and self-interest is the best guarantee of docility. In this way, too, they are most likely to deceive those whom they can only betray in so far as they resemble them. These satellite men are incorrectly described as 'crypto-communists'.[1]

There are also other kinds of satellite men. For example, those useful innocents who are perhaps too useful to be completely innocent. Their critical faculty being in other respects quite well developed, their naïveté and credulity seem to be too specialised, too localised and consistent, to be generally accepted as sincere. They appear to see only what they wish to see, and the relation between what they consent to see and what they refuse to know reveals what they are; for this kind of game can hardly be played unless there is all-round collusion, and would collapse without it.

The types of 'nucleation' employed at the present time are easy to recognise. Its purely political forms are the more innocuous. Ever since the late 'twenties 'socialists' and 'radicals' have been appearing at communist meetings to denounce the socialist and radical leaders; and during the 'thirties this practice was so thoroughly organised as to acquire almost the status of a formality. The tactic of the 'popular front' brought in some Catholics to join the socialists and liberals; and since the last war these Catholic fellow-travellers are in a fair way to eclipse all the other performers, both by their numbers and by the vehemence of their emotion. The rallying of well-wishers has now become a major operation. The 'popular front' tactic, which was elaborated in Moscow after the defeat of the German communist party and under pressure of the war scare, was replaced—once Russia was in

[1] These men have no claim to the respect which, in our opinion, is the due of communists.

the war—by 'national fronts' in the German-occupied countries. The minimum of 'common ideology' in the popular fronts disappeared completely in the national fronts. These were based upon the absence of any common idea at all except opposition to the Germans. All these 'fronts' multiplied the contacts between communists and non-communists, and thus spread a wider net for the capture of useful 'sympathisers'.[1]

The behaviour of some of these non-communist dupes strengthened the already robust contempt of their peculiar allies. Great results were obtained by abandoning the tactic of 'class against class' for that of infiltration by organised confusion, adapted according to circumstances; and it is to this new tactic that the Campaign owes its present bizarre and picturesque appearance. The spectacle of a collection of their dupes, temperamentally disposed to seek the limelight, but unversed in analysing a historical situation in terms of forces and their relations, or in assessing the true nature of the forces in play, was no doubt what suggested to the communists that it is convenient, since it is possible, to choose one's enemies rather than let events impose them; for when peace had (more or less) returned they did their best according to their means, which were by now considerable, to 'place' their least dangerous enemies in good positions. Both the 'Resistance' and the 'purges' gave them opportunities for this. The fact is that what they really object to is anything that has the kind of power that can resist them. What they cannot tolerate is the existence of any *hard* nucleus except their own; and therefore if anyone shows the slightest sign of challenging this monopoly they raise the cry of 'Fascism!' The only associations they tolerate are the kinds in which they can find friends for themselves; and all others, whether present or future, are anathema. They want a uniformly soft and relaxed environment within which only one single hard structure, their own, is to develop; and they still practise the old blackmailing technique which Hitler once used with paralysing effect: 'If you try to stop us, you are a warmonger.' Besiegers have never advocated vigilance among the besieged; they prefer them asleep.

[1] Krivitsky, a former G.P.U. general, writes: 'With the thousands of recruits enlisted under the banner of democracy, the communist party Ogpu espionage ring in the United States grew much larger and penetrated previously untouched territory. By carefully concealing their identity communists found their way into hundreds of key positions. It became possible for Moscow to influence the conduct of officials who would not knowingly approach a Comintern or Ogpu agent with a ten-foot pole. More challenging perhaps than this success in espionage and pressure politics is the Comintern's penetration into labour unions, publishing houses, magazines, and newspapers—a manœuvre accomplished by simply erasing the Comintern's label and stamping anti-Hitlerism in its place (*I was Stalin's Agent*, p. 90; London, 1939).

Part Two

SECULAR RELIGIONS AND THE *IMPERIUM MUNDI*

CHAPTER 9

The Prestige of Totality

WITH Hegel, philosophy was expanded so far as to leave nothing outside itself. Art, religion, history—it explained everything; and Hegel tended to make a future Hegel impossible. But the speculative character of the system turned against it; for although the system explained everything, it could do nothing. The completion of the system makes the system itself futile; and the totalitarian unification in the world of ideas only makes the fragmentation in the world of facts more irritating. This intellectual totalitarianism calls for *orthodoxy*, but does nothing to create it; so recourse must be had to history if philosophy is to be made effective. Writing at the same time as Kierkegaard, Marx was to expound the necessity for a *leap* outside the system and beyond speculation, and was to attempt the leap himself. With both these thinkers it is a question of a leap into existence; in the one case the existence of the individual, in the other that of the Species. If the word *dereliction* is not to be found in Kierkegaard, the thing itself is there; and the concept is not really clear except in relation to sin and grace. But Marx's perspective is that of Feuerbach; with him it is not a question of the salvation of the individual, but of the Species. The role played in the Christian universe of Kierkegaard by persons corresponds to the part played by groups in the atheist universe of the 'Left Hegelians'. According to Marx, the intercessor and mediator is a collectivity: the Proletariat. The system has burst apart and philosophy overflows into history; but on the historical plane of the real man, Marx and Marxism continue to pursue the same ambitions as the system. There is, however, the difference that what in Hegel was philosophy becomes, after Marx, religion. *A philosophy lived collectively cannot remain philosophy but is transformed into religion.* It is here that Marxism, which takes up again on its own account the Hegelian search for the unity and homogeneity of the world, can make an ally of the need for intellectual unity, coherence, and tranquillity, which has moved men at different periods of history to look for a key and to believe that they have found one. The aim is to enclose everything within a circle, leaving nothing outside; to enclose literally everything, beginning with life itself. It is then no longer a question of a purely speculative system, but of an orthodoxy which shall be at one and the same time a vision of the world and a practical imperative, both science and conquest. Orthodoxy is a system which satisfies the need of activity as well as the feelings and the intelligence, and saves man from the atomisation of his faculties which corresponds with that autonomy of the separate spheres (political, economic, and cultural) which characterised the liberal epoch. In this sense the negation of the liberal atomisation of man proceeded steadily (making its way underground for more than half a century) from Hegel to communism. When the system is able to attract and nourish affectivity and to include *praxis*, it becomes apparent that philosophy in action is religion. The communist Campaign is a religious campaign.

* * * *

Those who sought to bring the clear, cold eye of the classifier to bear upon the so-called 'primitive' phenomena of 'religious life' were, for the most part, after the end of the 18th century readily sensitive to the 'belief in omnipresent impersonal forces'.[1] To this category of forces belong the famous *mana* of the Melanesians and the 'equivalent' forces identified in other 'primitive'[2] societies, the *orenda* of the Iroquois, and the *wakanda* of the Sioux; but it also includes quite different representations, such as the *rta* or 'order of the world' of the Vedic aryans; the *asha* of Zoroastrianism; the μόιϱα of the Homeric poems, which bears witness to beliefs far more ancient than the poems themselves; or that omnipotent Δίκη which, according to Heraclitus, keeps the sun 'within the boundaries of its empire'.

If we remember that the physical concept of energy, as elaborated in the 19th century, includes implicitly the obscurer concept of dynamism, we shall better understand the resonance of words or expressions[3] like History, Forces of Production, the Goal of Evolution, the End of History, the Realisation of Philosophy, the Dialectic (with a capital letter). Such impersonal entities as these—Auguste Comte called them 'metaphysical'—place the real history of men and their worlds within a domain completely intelligible ('in law', though not in fact) and completely penetrable to the mind of the Marxist (and to his alone), and they afford him the kind of certainty and security which can only be derived from dogma. These 'forces', often as slow and tortuous as Providence,

[1] 'God is not only a late arrival in religion; it is not indispensable that he should come' (Van der Leeuw, *Phénoménologie de la religion* (French trans.; Paris, 1948)). Durkheim reached the same conclusion by other ways. Cf. *Année sociologique*, 1897–8; *De la définition des phénomènes religieux*.

[2] I use this adjective with the utmost caution (cf. *La Poésie moderne et le sacré*, pp. 191–6) and only for the sake of immediate intelligibility.

[3] It is essential to distinguish between the two, but resonance may be common to both.

to which they are undoubtedly related, are ineluctable, and will sooner or later make short work of the frivolous wills that oppose them. Not that such wills cannot have any effect; but in the long run they can only produce at the most (and it is much) a delaying action.[1]

It is not, however, unthinkable[2] that the bad wills may triumph; but in that case, say the Marxists, though not all of them, it will be 'chaos' and the triumph of 'barbarism'. And the words 'chaos' and 'barbarism' give eloquent expression to the angry impatience that the real future would provoke if it dared to thwart the dogma and condemn the believer to frustration. Our believer refuses to see beyond the classless society. It is his horizon, and everything seems to suggest that he is afraid of imagining what lies beyond it. This in itself is enough to indicate that his outlook is an eschatological one. While Hegel's thought proceeds from the spirit to the spirit and forms a cycle or closed circle, Marxist thought stops irrationally at a *result*—which is unadmittedly, and also, for those who claim to be scientific, inadmissibly, presented as a sort of absolute. That at least is how it is presented in fact, though not in theory; for Marxists admit that there will be 'post-revolutionary problems'. Only it is obvious that these problems do not interest them. Those who do show signs of an interest in this kind of problem are under suspicion of not being 'true Marxists'; and rightly so. For it is futile to foresee or to imagine, and it is vain to speculate about what will happen after the coming of the kingdom. There will be a change comparable to the change one likes to imagine (but it is only an optical illusion) between history and pre-history. It cannot therefore be foreseen and, as Georges Sorel would have said, the manner of it eludes description.

Marxism of this kind starts from a theory of progress. The mythical proletariat, which is a kind of universal legatee, preserves all the attainments of the civilisation which precedes, prepares, and engenders it. But the transition from class interest to general interest after the revolution is a process upon which we have none but 'dialectical' light.

For these believers the idea that the impersonal, omnipresent, and ineluctable forces might come to nothing is the very essence of the absurd. It reduces the world to absurdity, because it makes it unthinkable. In saying this they seem to be unaware that they misunderstand the working of the human mind, which can think everything. There is nothing that is not thinkable or that cannot be explained—after the event. This is implied, indeed, by the anthropological concept of man,

[1] Note that we are merely examining the outlook of 'intellectual' believers.

[2] This word is not part of our vocabulary. We do not believe that anything is unthinkable.

in which he is both an *interpretative animal* and a *political animal.* A brief and superficial and rapid examination of the latent content of this theology without transcendence and without God is, in fact, sufficient to reveal that it takes its bearings from a dynamism inherent in the world or in History or in Man (as the case may be; but they all refer to the same reality). History, therefore, is believed to lead somewhere; and we too believe that, but we believe that history leads somewhere, and then leads somewhere else, and we are always ready to take liberties with our preconceived ideas, so that we may make use of our ideas instead of being enslaved by them. A first glance at this latent content of Marxism informs us that there are in fact classes (or one class), institutions, events, and also individual men who are as it were charged with *mana* or, in other words, with a prestige which cannot be adequately accounted for in terms of experimental and logical thought. Impersonal forces (productive forces, productive relations) raise up the believer and should cast down the unbeliever. In relation to these dynamic equivalents of divinity, the functions of the church (this is merely a comparison) are assumed today by social groups, such as the Party, the socialist State, and the whole organisation which claims the combined role of universal Church and universal State. And the total believer, following Marx who was the seer, forerunner, and prophet, surrenders himself to these forces and adheres, or wishes to adhere, to them with all his strength—to the point of *identifying* himself with them, living in them, and suffering physically and raging murderously when they are betrayed. Here again we see an impersonal and more or less omnipresent dynamic immanent within man, and man within it.

* * * *

Lenin felt the attraction of this unity and totality, this coherence in which all human potentialities would converge and be realised. He too understood that *everything hangs together*. The 'hero' image which he chose and which formed his ideal was Marx, the technological prophet, the intellectual conqueror, the welder of human unity.

But this is not, in fact, what Lenin was to be. He was rather a kind of engineer of history and technician of the revolution, subdued to a limited task. On the plane of knowledge it may be said that, although he inspired a few notable theoreticians, the encyclopædic prophet has had no successor. The movement of ideas in the 20th century has not been dominated by any of his followers as he dominated the movement of ideas in the middle of the nineteenth. Marx had set himself to recover the unity for which his studies of Hegel had awoken the aspiration, and to recover it in the form of a doctrine which should be a weapon of history, explaining what had to be explained in order to fight and to conquer. In the 20th century the fight itself was to devour the doctrine, and the philosophy was to become a religion. Marx was totally identified with this doctrine, in which he may be said, using his own terms, to have *alienated* himself, as every creator alienates himself in his work. (If we modify the derogatory sense in which Marx uses the term, which counts for so much in his critical work, the sense of the criticism will be changed, and this part of his work will be brought in close relation with what is now known as *psycho-analysis*.) As a Hegelian, Marx held that force brings societies to birth; and as a critic of Hegel he wanted philosophy to play an active part ; he wanted it to erupt into history. The logical conclusion was that the army of those who would make philosophy actual must be organised and then led into battle for the *Imperium mundi*.

* * * *

At the beginning of the 20th century Marx's doctrine was what enabled the professional revolutionaries to mobilise the workers for a holy war. But its impact upon the intellectuals counted for more than its impact upon the workers, because in fact the latter impact is transmitted through the former. Politics, economics, religion, and the 'world of culture' were able to appear in the liberal epoch as so many separate realities or 'spheres', linked together it is true and reacting upon each other, but capable of being kept apart and treated, up to a certain point, as distinct from one another; and at the same time, as has happened at certain periods in other civilisations, philosophy became a 'speciality'. But with the decline of the liberal era there began a change which became more and more definite; the long-delayed success of Schopenhauer, and more especially of Kierkegaard and Nietzsche, bore witness to the return of philosophy from the lecture-room to life. Between Hegel and Marx, as between Hegel and Kierkegaard, philosophy leaves the university and comes back into everyday life. But Marx, Kierkegaard's contemporary, scores on two targets which seemed by definition to be mutually exclusive: he combined the prestige and attraction of the 'lived philosophy' with the prestige and attraction of the System; in other words, he added the prestige of the single totality to the separate prestiges of totality and of Unity. In the critical social phase which began before our time and which we[1] ourselves represent, the attractive power of Marxism is that of an *orthodoxy* manifested simultaneously on the intellectual plane as a *system*, on the religious plane as *Einfühlung* (or affective communion), and on

[1] In this context 'we' means our opponents as well as ourselves.

the plane of *praxis* as an adventure of the whole man which gives human existence a goal, a meaning, a direction, and a flavour. Such a doctrine, like all religions, tells the individual not merely to exist and develop within his own limits, which was an ideal of mercantile society and of the liberal epoch, but to *surpass himself*. The individual is stimulated to overcome his limitations and never to regard them as final limits. The movement is from the relative to the absolute, *and the way to the absolute is not by 'merging' but by action*. Faith is manifested only in works. Since the Reformation the efficacy of works has increased to the point where individual salvation is finally forgotten, and the individual in the movement of history is no more than a drop of water in a torrent.

When one man or several, whether or not they form a real or virtual group, project their aspirations upon an external reality of which they were unconscious hitherto, they recognise in this reality—which, like themselves, is a living thing in process of development—the progressive realisation of their aspirations, which henceforward will be partly shaped by the external reality. Henceforth they have a better picture of it and can find words to express it. All that is necessary is that the external reality or historical movement should be an appropriate one (there cannot be haphazard projection of anything on to anything), and this means that certain of its features must be able, so to speak, to 'attach' the aspirations in question. What occurs is a *phenomenon of convergence*, a sort of line along which external reality and aspirations meet; and the aspiration, being by definition in search of a form, will assume the form which the reality seems to offer. This illustration enables us to understand the conversion to Marxism, or, in effect, to communism, of a certain number of 'intellectuals'. It also explains how Georges Sorel, at the beginning of the century, saw the trade unions as something which they were not.

Until the end of his life Sorel sought, as though instinctively, for the group of men 'free of all ambition, ready to give their lives on every battlefield, prodigal of their strength',[1] determined to break with the rest of society, and to act within it as a foreign body feeding on what it destroys until it can take the place of what it has destroyed. He sought for it in socialism, in revolutionary syndicalism, and even among the young men of the 'Proudhon circle', whom in the end he failed to prevent from joining the Action Française. Here Sorel's example has a prophetic quality; he foreshadows the attraction followed by repulsion which Marxism and communism (a combined religion, church, philosophy, and army) have inspired in certain 'men of ideas'.

A few resemblances, which may be quite superficial, are enough to

[1] Fernand Pelloutier, *Histoire des bourses du travail.*

enable an external reality, like a signal, to fix the aspiration and provoke a reflex—though it does not follow that the reflex will be appropriate for the subsequent action. The projection in this case is the function which permits the man of action to substitute one 'world' for another while he acts, and thus, by virtue of a misapprehension prolific in results of every kind, to perform a real act in the real world. The phenomenon is well known to historians of religion. Projections may be conscious or unconscious, and there is an indefinite number of degrees between the two; they may attach themselves to people, to doctrines, to objects (as in fetishism), or to human groups. In this way fantastic rumours are born, and myths which may be ephemeral or more lasting; and this is how 'god-ideologies' and 'devil-ideologies' arise and flourish. While the projection is in force or at the height of its power, the person projecting censors, unconsciously, certain parts of his experience; and he often uses his eyes for not-seeing and his ears for not-hearing. Meanwhile he will *over-value* other aspects; and some will be directly interpreted, though in this case interpretation does not take place at the level of reflective consciousness, as in delusions of reference, but at the level of perception, as in hallucination. Thus the man who projects is composing his fields of perception and reflection in such a way as to exclude all those phenomena which would prove, if fully registered, that the projection was an illusion.

Finally, legends are created, and facts imagined which do not, or do not yet, exist. Thus it can be said that those who are under the influence of projection do not live in the same world as other people; there is a sense in which their state can be compared to a *state of suggestion*. They are a privileged example of the extent to which in the animal called man, when certain of his faculties are not yet developed, being *is* sensation: between being and sense of being there is no difference of plane, or depth, and as he sees the contour in the object so he sees in what is the meaning of what is.

What usually happens is that the phenomenon becomes organised: certain features disappear, while others are definitely *transformed through adaptation to the real group*; but others become finally detached from reality and ascend into a region immune from the pinpricks of experience, where they can perform all the better their rationalising function.

* * * *

The projection which tends to merge the 'internal' with the 'external', the idea with the fact, and the ideal group with the real group, corresponds to a psychological function of societies and individuals, a function that was long performed by religious cults. But in the religions of historical peoples of high culture, projections were to some extent recognised as such; they did not introduce into the world of facts those elements of anxiety, equivocation, uncertainty, and instability which are characteristic of contemporary societies in thrall to secular religions. On the contrary, they promoted mental stability by insulating the human function of creating gods and demons and thus placing a distance between man and both the projection and its contrary,[1] his identification with god or demon. Now that these religions no longer perform their regulating function, messianism has become endemic; and the philosophies of enlightenment have done nothing to suspend or moderate this function of creating gods and demons; they have merely displaced it. Such projections may be conscious or unconscious, they may be attached to doctrines or to objects, to human groups or to individuals; and this whole world of spirits and demons, guardian angels and evil geniuses, is immanent in the real world, in our own day and in our own cities. It will not be long before the American President becomes the devil. Every incompatibility between ourselves and another—and this is even truer of collectivities than of individuals—may determine the projection into that other of the 'diabolic dominant.'

The external reality on which the aspirations are projected possesses in its own right a power which over-rides ideas, however just, and imagination, however ingenious. It exists, and instead of banishing man from the world and from action it leads him back to them ; and so the intellectual is able to glimpse, in a kind of phantasm, the reconciliation of dream and action. He then conceives that to introduce the motive forces of affectivity and imagination into reality is a process partaking of reality itself; and the danger of schizophrenia is averted. He seems to have found the point of application; and the self-opposing and (if it remains subjective) self-destroying dynamism is set free. It is thus that man creates, out of materials drawn from his own substance, the being of an imaginary group which constitutes the ideal means for his own purposes. But the group, in its turn, evolves autonomously—and this evolution confronts the individual with a dilemma; the development is usually an annoying one and if he admits it fully to his consciousness he will become cynical, but if, on the other hand, he represses his trouble it will find an outlet in a religious distemper which, in its extreme form, may *destroy all communication* between himself and 'the others', those who inhabit a 'different world'; for dialogue is difficult without a minimum of consistency in the use of words; that is to say, without a minimum of common ground between the speakers. The individual delegates, as it were, his power to the Party; and this proceeding recalls what Marx, combining Hegel with Feuerbach, described as 'alienation'. The individual worships his feeble power in the great

[1] In technical language: *intrajection* and *introjection.*

power in which it reappears without its feebleness. There is often a tendency for the powers thus accumulated to become incarnate in one man who, by degrees, is deified. But this does not *necessarily* happen, for there are conflicting forces within the constellation of power.

If intellectuals are easily attracted by Marxism and then by communism,[1] it is because they are projecting an aspiration for orthodoxy upon an actual living phenomenon which combines within itself a doctrine, a church, and an army. This phenomenon possesses the attraction of totality and of unity; it is a new form which can present itself to our imagination, if we allow it, as an integrating force capable of embracing everything without exception, so that the historical nostalgia for orthodoxy and the human yearning for atonement can be merged together in it and find fulfilment. Here, as in the laws of Manu or the republic of Plato, there are the same laws for the human and for the cosmic realms (according to Hegel, for example, his dialectic is a method for the general resolution of the problems of being, and therefore nothing is left outside its scope). In the process of quietly absorbing everything that is not itself the living orthodoxy becomes transformed. It works in the same way as human affectivity works in the shaping of the passions; fitting perceptions and intuitions into the dogma, as passion places within the form of the beloved all the reasons for living. Paulina 'had too many virtues not to be a Christian' and in the same way every new piece of knowledge appears, to minds that are still hopeful, too cogent not to be Marxist. This is what nearly happened to psycho-analysis and, in general, to all the famous 'bourgeois' theories or fashionable ideas. But at this point the System harshly asserts itself: members corrupted by eclecticism, or by an equally undesirable syncretism, are in extreme cases amputated from the healthy body by the doctors of the Law.

Existence, on the plane of lived experience, and science, on the plane of controlled experiment, are both of them by definition *open*, and, compared to them, the System has today the appearance of a closed sepulchre. But such comparisons belong to the sphere of cold factual observation. The new orthodoxy projected on to Marxism by certain intellectuals is arrayed in seductive colours: it offers knowledge, but a kind of knowledge that by its very nature satisfies and mobilises affectivity; it offers method, but a method capable of integrating all the bold and triumphant acquisitions of science, a method focused on the future and at grips with stark living reality. And so they hope to combine the infallibility of science with the fervour of religion.

* * * *

[1] We are dealing here only with some of the factors of this elective sensibility.

In this place we have been considering ideas only from the point of view of their emotional charge; their power of nourishing the sentiment or, more accurately, the subjectivity (so to speak) of an age and a civilisation. The truth of our observations does not reflect upon the letter of Marx's writings—which, in any case, represent the interaction of ideas developed at different periods of his life and may therefore appear contradictory. We are not writing the history of a philosophy but of the historical development of a living complex. Without Marx there would have been no Marxism, but the written philosophy—as we have already seen—cannot by itself adequately explain the developing complex that goes by the name of communism (whose connections with Marxism are sometimes erroneously conceived). What we are concerned with is a sociology of Marxism. One may legitimately attempt to determine the latent content of a doctrine or, more precisely, a religion whose passional dynamic is conspicuously perceptible. Such an undertaking entails risks and it must lack precision, but it can be fruitful—as will soon appear. For the moment, however, we are operating only at the most superficial level, and leaving to another place our exploration of the deeper strata.

It is not false to say that 'interest guides the world'; nor is it false to say that 'ideas guide the world'. The quest, both historical and logical, for the truth at the heart of these two formulas leads to the following proposition, which represents, as it were, a middle term: men are only moved, by ideas on the one hand or by interest on the other, through the medium of affectivity (there is a *point of fusion* at which by definition ideas and feelings no longer exist or are not distinct, or cannot at any rate be discerned). This third proposition is thus the middle term which demonstrates both the truth and the inadequacy of the two previous propositions; it includes them both implicitly, and also something else, something new. It is more true. One may put it like this: *ideas guide the world of today, provided always that they have been previously assimilated.* Hegelianism, once it had been assimilated by the affectivity of an epoch and a civilisation, and deflected, moreover, by the potent Marxist index of refraction, could only mould the sensibility and imagination of individuals and masses by taking the form of mythology, catechism, and pious images and legends; and the explosive power of Marxism derives from the same fermentation. Outside the textbooks it only survives at the cost of many an adaptation. What began as the doctrine of one man became the doctrine of a sect, and finally partook of the semi-hypnotic prestige of an advancing multitude whose magnetism draws in the spectators who watch it pass.

CHAPTER 10

Psychology of Secular Religions

IF certain observations about the Soviet Union are presented before an attentive audience, and if the speaker next proceeds to show that a certain number of propositions accepted by communists, which they derive or think they derive from Marx, are obsolete or doubtful, then a characteristic difference between two categories of men will come to light. The first will take the observations as observations and the proofs as proofs, behaving in the same way as they would if different observations and a different doctrine were in question. They divide them into the certain, the probable, and the doubtful; but a fact is still treated as a fact and a proof as a proof. The second category refuse to listen; they shout. Or, if they consent to listen, what happens is even more remarkable: like an elastic body which yields to pressure but resumes its original shape when the pressure is removed, they return to their original position as soon as the intellectual pressure of proof is withdrawn. For this phenomenon, which it is easy to provoke in France nowadays, there is an analogy. The same feature is included in the clinical definition of delusions. The delusion seems to yield momentarily before intellectual or visible evidence; but when the patient has what psychiatrists call *une idée fixe*, the effect of that kind of thought is different from the effect of the other thoughts which he shares with so-called normal people. Whereas the normal subject yields to evidence and considers the matter closed, the paranoiac (for example) will reoccupy, so to speak, the positions from which reasoning had expelled him. It is not that he has forgotten the evidence. He may remember it completely, and is often able to repeat the demonstration it led up to; but although he is aware of all its intellectual aspects the proof as a whole has no weight with him. It has lost all cogency, and cannot influence him. This is what psychiatrists mean when they say that the delusions are refractory to logical arguments and to arguments drawn from reality (to use Freud's words). Such arguments lack the power to mobilise energy. But the idea that has been refuted a hundred times by logical arguments and arguments drawn from reality can mobilise sufficient energy to reinstate itself in that privileged position which is incomprehensible to anyone not specially trained in the matter.

But what is characteristic of the paranoiac (to use the same example) is that the paranoia is his *own* paranoia. There are as many paranoias as there are paranoiac people. Delusions may be grouped in clinical categories; but such classification can only refer to what they have in common—the style, rhythm, and mechanics, and even the dynamics, of the delusion—and not to the particular character of each delusion: its history, its biographical meaning, its irreducible singularity, and everything that makes it characteristic of one particular and unique human being and not of any other. Delusion is to some extent contagious, and the patient can very often convince his neighbours, but paranoiacs cannot all agree among themselves upon a single paranoiac view of the world. In our civilisation there is some possibility (though this possibility should not be exaggerated) for so-called normal people above a certain level of scientific culture at least to reach agreement about duly established facts, even though they may differ as to their interpretation. For us, laws like those of Joule or Faraday or Ohm, or Mendeleyev's table, are not continually undermined by fancies which oppose them and which nothing can dispel; and the same is true of established historical facts, for example those concerning Hammurabi, Aurung Zeb, or Clemenceau. But it is not universally true as regards a certain number of equally well-established facts concerning Russian history between 1918 and the moment of writing these words. One example is the existence in the U.S.S.R. since the five-year plans of a system of forced labour in many respects similar to that which existed in Germany under Hitler. And the privilege extended to facts like this seems to be shared by certain ideas which might be called 'theoretical'. If one maintains before an audience of communists and 'sympathisers' that to affirm the proletariat's 'mission' is an *act of faith* (which is obvious, for a mission can only be proved after the event), and that 'logical arguments' and 'arguments drawn from reality' cannot confer upon this theory the same cogency as upon a geometrical theorem or a fact established according to the canons of historical method, then one runs the risk of incurring indignation, insults, and worse. Everything seems to suggest that those who become enraged and shout insults, etc., *know* that they cannot safely engage in debate in terms of logic and experience; but in their case the word 'know' is hardly applicable.

We must be careful not to exaggerate the unusualness of such behaviour. As everyone knows, we are all subject to passion; and between the delusional belief and the passional belief the difference is only one of degree. Consciousness itself is sustained by passion, and would not exist without it. We know, too, that the expression 'collective passion' is something more than a *flatus vocis*: the despotic control of one individual 'psyche' by passion may be the model for an indefinite number of copies. But in collective passion all the 'fixations' and 'obsessions' have a certain common intellectual content, and in this they differ both from the delusions classified by psychiatrists and from the individual's passions, however obsessive, because these latter have the effect of separating their subject from the rest of society. In this way the individual passions act as social solvents; but collective passion, on the contrary, in addition to unifying the individual psyche of each of its subjects, has also the effect of bringing men together. And when a number of men are knit together by a common passion, this difference in quantity becomes a difference of quality. Collective passions are not completely asocial, but are, on the contrary, socialised, and therefore *their nature changes*. The victims of collective passion form a social group, an ensemble, and not a collection of 'cases', like the general types of delusions classified by psychiatrists. The existence of all the other addicts of collective passion confers upon each individual addict a force and an authority which allow him a 'good social conscience'—the very thing which the victims of asocial individual passions lack. The latter see in each of their contemporaries a sort of judge.[1] The addict of collective passion, on the other hand, meets the judge with absolute defiance. The collective passion is sustained by frequent communion, inflamed by periodic rites, such as meetings, processions, and demonstrations, and fed each morning by newspaper and radio. Certain fundamental traits of passion become modified in collective passion through the action of publicity and 'good social conscience'. Indeed, the effect of reciprocal suggestion is to make collective passion something specifically different from individual passion; it is enhanced and transformed in each of its subjects by the mere fact of its existence in all of them. Now, it is a fact that the critical spirit is a specific character of the intellectual organisation of *individuals*, and there is no such thing as a collective critical spirit. So it follows that the barriers erected by a critical mind against the power of suggestion are *individual* defences, and it is a *collective* passion that breaks them down. Individual passion is restrained and resisted by a social force which compels it to flow in a sort of channel which it only overflows when in a state of flood, or crisis. But collective passion, on the other hand, can count upon social force to strengthen and swell its current; so the restraint which maintained passion in equilibrium, while it was individual passion, is removed, and from being simple passion it becomes something more like delusion in the psychiatric sense. Personality is the psychological organisation of the individual, and the elements of this organisation are derived from the

[1] Or they may divide their contemporaries into two categories, judges and accomplices, as perverts, drug-addicts, and gamblers do. But in any case they lack a 'good social conscience'.

human milieu. In other words, it is by means of culture, or, more precisely, of a particular culture, that it comes to be what it is. But personality, defined in this way, can be overwhelmed by the force of reciprocal suggestion which raises passion, with the help of social reinforcements, to a power which the individual's resources cannot withstand. So the personality, especially at times of crisis, is like a wall that can be scaled.

In collective passion, as in individual delusions and passions, the subject is aware of his impressions, volitions, and desires, but not of their cause. And in the same way, where our individual passions are concerned, we are not interested in the explanation of our erotic 'fixations' (the explanatory images offered us by psycho-analysis, for example), nor in the interpretation of our 'choices', which reveals how a 'complex' was formed; what interests us is the 'object'—that 'other' which seems to become a part, and the most vulnerable part, of our own ego. It is the same with the intellectual who adheres to a secular religion; being unaware of what moves him, he is all the more obsessively aware of what it moves him to. Here we see the importance of ideology, because its offers a *different version* of the relation between the motive and what it motivates. The materials which compose an ideology, and which it organises, can face the full light of day, so to speak. They are not only avowable but honourable, and they constantly seek to affirm their relationship with the recognised social values. Thus in our own society they appeal by preference to justice, goodness, truth, and reason. The Marxism to which communism relates itself, however, is not merely a demand for the establishment of a just, or a less unjust, society, but is also 'scientific'. It combines science with morality, thus identifying itself with the great idols as well as the great ideals. So all the arguments one can bring against communism are of no avail and cannot affect the motivation of the 'communism' of the true believer. They can only touch its intellectual content—in other words, the conscious content which is over-valued at the expense of all the rest and especially of what has been repressed. The ideology can be regarded as the systematic organisation of this conscious content and of the exaggerated value attached to it. So logical arguments and arguments drawn from experience are as impotent here as they are when directed against the delusion of the individual; they can no more affect the real motivation than direct fire can hit soldiers in a trench. Men in a trench can only be reached by oblique fire, and in this sense psycho-analysis can be compared to a weapon that shoots obliquely. The motivating dynamism is sheltered from ordinary argument; it can go on working under a shower of arguments, just as soldiers can go on firing when the enemy is shooting over their heads. 'Motivations', said Freud, 'continue to transmit their characteristic power to the motivated while themselves remaining immune to attack.' It is not necessary to share all Freud's ideas about the unconscious to agree with him that in such cases the real motivations are out of range and that the communist will remain a communist, just as the victim of obsession will remain obsessed even though he is faced with arguments which 'ought' to dissipate his obsession—but cannot do so precisely because it is an obsession and nothing else. The communication of ideas is only possible within a limited field, and our desire for universal communicability is baulked equally by mental derangements and by secular religions. Such anomalies imperil the foundations of any human fraternity based upon intelligence.

Up to now we have been considering the case of the intellectual. The working-class communist is in quite a different position. If he is offered a way of escape from conditions with which he is dissatisfied (and rightly so, in our opinion), and if he is told that he has nothing to do but obey and follow, what grounds has he for resisting the temptation—if the civilisation in which he has too small a share has not suggested any such grounds to him?

When an individual creates for himself a passional or delusional system, this might be described as an 'individual ideology', because what the word ideology stands for is nothing but a collective passional or delusional system. All the constituent elements of an ideology may, in theory, be intellectual, but the law which organises them into a system and the dialectic by which the ideology 'wins' the individual and proliferates in society are of a different order. Ideology is, as it were, deflected by passion, and all its rational elements experience a sort of inner compulsion which does violence to their rational nature, deflecting and warping them and making, as it were, curves of all their straight lines. The ideology or system professed by the communist[1] believer may therefore have a completely rational intellectual content,[2] but it has also a 'sense', an orientation, or perhaps one should say an 'intention',[3] which is alien to the intellectual content and more especially to the 'scientific' or 'rational' part of it. To understand this orientation we need to know the subject's individual history, and it then appears that the motivations of his communism are incongruous with the definition of communism as presented to us in the form of a system of rationalisations. The relevant realities are not of a doctrinal or intellectual order. But the subject systematically deceives himself about the motivation and origin of his passion and represents himself, when he talks

[1] Communism is only one example of ideology. It is used here because it happens to be a present historical danger.

[2] This is not, in fact, the case. Such elements as revolution, the mission of the proletariat, and the classless society are not rational elements.

[3] Freud's word; cf. *Introduction à la psychanalyse* (French ed., p. 275).

ideology, as a man of intellectual and rational impulses and motives. In his case, communism is *symptomatic*; it has a meaning apart from its intellectual meaning, and what it really represents is something quite different from what it claims to be. Communism, in this sense and in relation to such a man, is a 'syndrome'. The familiar mechanics of passion can be very clearly observed. Everything to which a positive value attaches is drawn into the orbit of the beloved object and incorporated in it (this is the process of 'crystallisation'). Thus the reason for adhering to Marxism is because it is 'true' or 'scientific', and the reason for supporting the Soviet Union is because it is 'socialist', because it is a 'just society'. Communism, and communists, can provide all the answers. If there were any doubt that communism is a religion, this fact would suffice to remove it. Science only answers particular questions, and in doing so it raises others. Philosophy claims to account for everything, but only on the plane of theory. Human action, like science (the one implies the other), raises a new problem for every one it solves. Only religion solves everything on all planes. There are obstacles of course, but secular religion enjoins a confident belief that all obstacles will be removed (for history is leading towards a sort of absolute emancipation); and it provides two ways of dismissing problems. First, by action: when one acts one has no time for 'profound' thought; one thinks in terms of the situation. Secondly, the doctrine enjoins the belief that when it has been fulfilled many problems which appear today quite unrelated will be found to have been solved *ambulando*, or else they will no longer arise; the 'new situation' will resolve them by making them pointless, or, failing that, they will appear in quite a new light and will then be easily solved.

Exclusiveness and monomania are characteristic of the believer. His activity is concentrated and unified while it converges with a great number of similar activities working in the same direction. Accumulated energies tend to discharge themselves all in one direction. Here the 'absorption of the mind in a few ideas' which conduces to practical success is accompanied by 'manifestations of generalised and contagious mythomania' and waking dreams of massacres. Facts are systematically distorted, and given always the same bias, to the profit of imaginings which experience is powerless to refute. There is a partial confusion of wish and reality, and the dividing line becomes obscure between things as they are and things as one would like them to be, or between the concrete results produced by work and the ideas produced by wishful thinking. Imperceptibly, the optative transforms itself into the indicative. This is how it becomes possible to take for granted that the U.S.S.R. is a society in which the exploitation of man by man has been abolished, and that it is a 'proletarian State' . . . and so on.

The negative and destructive aspect of this passional state appears in two ways: as a selective blindness, of 'pathological' type, towards those features of the beloved object whose recognition would make impossible the intellectual rationalisation of passion; and as an equally pathological selective clairvoyance as regards the shortcomings of everything which opposes the object's triumph. 'Blind' passion has eyes for some things and clairvoyance sees others; but in his clairvoyant hatred the victim of passion notices things that would escape him if he were only clairvoyant without being impassioned as well. And from this point of view ideology may be defined as a mixture of pathological blindness and pathological sharpsightedness. The critical faculty is suspended in certain directions but intensified in others. A similar use of the critical faculties is seen in the criticism of psycho-analysis and of the psycho-analyst indulged in by the patient during the course of psycho-analytic treatment. Excessive criticism in one direction accompanied by absence of criticism in the other reveals the presence of an element of collective hysteria. Freud describes this 'localised' criticism as 'an expedient in the service of affectivity',[1] an expedient guided and inspired by 'resistance'.

An ideology which is the vehicle of a secular religion appears as 'the effect of a compromise resulting from the interference between two opposing tendencies'; namely collective passion on the one hand and the tendency to scientific objectivity on the other. An ideology will therefore represent 'both what was repressed and also whatever was the cause of its repression'.[2] So the success of an ideology is, in a certain state of society, a significant symptom; and so also, in regard to the individual concerned, is the individual's choice of one from a number of 'competing' ideologies. 'The symptom . . . replaces an external act by an internal action', or an act by an adaptation. This external constraint, compelling the interiorisation of what would otherwise externalise itself, reacts 'upon all the systems of organs and all the functions'. And Freud was impressed by the analogy with what happens 'in cases of intoxication and abstinence'.

Psycho-analysis admits in practice a rough distinction between the natural being (which Freud calls the *id*) and the *ego*, which represents a sort of permanent compromise between the natural being and the outer world. The ego does its best to mediate between the world and the claims of the natural being. If it fails in its task the natural being will be broken by the world, and this means that the ego will lose all the strength that sustains its own activity; because the natural being is the source of that

[1] Freud, *Introduction à la psychanalyse*.

[2] Freud, op. cit., p. 387. Thus the symptom originates as a compromise. It is an equivocal phenomenon, being the greatly deformed product of the unconscious satisfaction of a libidinous desire—cunningly selected and combining two diametrically opposed meanings.

strength. Freud gives the name of 'super-ego' to the ego in its official capacity, in which it conforms to the prevailing morality and social imperatives. It is the model ego which we try to make ourselves appear, but which we also try to be. To maintain this super-ego in existence, the energy of the natural being must be diverted and must submit to direction and control in accordance with the norms and images, or *patterns*, suggested to us by the civilisation in which we live. In this way communication is established between the natural being (the secluded area which Freud calls the *id*), and the socialised moral area which he calls the super-ego. The aspirations of the natural being are translated into ethical and social terms by ideology; and in this sense ideology is a kind of trickery, for whereas it is supposed to flow with perfect smoothness into the ethical mould, its whole purpose is, in fact, missed if it fails to satisfy the natural being. Indeed, there is no ideology unless the *id* is more or less satisfied; instead, there is science or morality. The purpose of 'rationalisation' is to present the *id*'s aspirations in terms of the super-ego; and when the *id*, or natural being, has in fact made no concessions at all, then the scientific and rational aspect is reduced to pure fantasy, and the ideology will prove on examination to be meaningless.

The ideologies preached by secular religions exhibit typically this compromise between the 'pleasure principle' and the 'reality principle', between fiction and truth, and between myth and science. In a society where science is supreme, no 'system of illusions' can be acceptable unless it wears a scientific livery; and that is why, at the present time, religious myths are being increasingly replaced by ideologies with a similar function but a different content. These ideologies do not appeal so directly to the emotions; but their similarity of function is revealed in the fact that they can no more be refuted than the myths could be. It is useless to criticise them on the scientific level, because their strength lies elsewhere. The true nature of ideology is also revealed in the contradiction between theory and practice which is so familiar today in the form of incompatibility between ends and means. The ideology is used to justify acts which are incompatible with the aspirations it officially represents.

An ideology like the communist ideology draws together a number of diverse and complex trends, many of which have themselves been evolved by compromise, and provides them with myths, or *ersatz* myths. Judged purely as myths, these are poor ones; for the ideology itself must necessarily weaken them because of all the concessions it is forced to make to rationality in order to exist at all. But the æsthetic disappointment of amateurs of mythology is beside the point, for myths rely upon the affective energy supplied by men, and their force is measured by the amount of energy they draw upon and mobilise. Those words ending in 'ism', which designate at the same time a body of beliefs and a group of men, represent a reality that is charged with power. Renan's saying, 'the principle of mythology consists in giving life to words', applies literally to these 'isms'. Thus 'communism' may possess a vitality, a prestige, and an authority which do not depend upon the actions of 'communists'. One has heard 'sympathisers' in all sincerity reproaching communists for being unfaithful to communism, and one might conclude that these 'intellectuals' attribute priority and superiority, or in any case primacy, to 'essence' over 'existence'. Thus communism is no longer the sum or epitome of the morals and behaviour and beliefs and customs of communists, but a sort of self-subsistent entity which can be known by contemplation and in the light of which the behaviour of communists can be judged; so that the intellectual whose good intentions place him, in his own eyes, upon a pedestal, can remonstrate: 'Communists, what have you made of communism?'

These words, and the modern chimeras and dragons they reveal, may seem to live a life of their own; but in fact they are parasites. They grow fat and prosper at the expense of human affectivity, feeding like vampires upon men's misery and resentment and distress. Today, no less than in the past, men give their flesh and blood for the nourishment of deadly phantoms; and under the ægis of these monsters there is no political outrage that may not be, and is not, perpetrated. Nor is the worship of idols confined to the faithful, for unbelievers have their idols, too.

The life we bestow upon a word is our own life, for we have no other. These chimeras are anthropophagous; they are man-eating metaphysical entities. How can one pretend that there is less magic in the world today? These words seem to work miracles: the child leaves its parents, the lover abandons her beloved, and brother is denounced by brother. Is there any more powerful drug today than certain words administered in regular doses? They are administered according to the most efficacious magic ritual of our time, by men who well know their effects. In massive doses, following well-tried prescriptions and a carefully perfected technique, these words can inspire heroism or the most craven inertia. They can turn whole crowds of men into lions or into sheep. They are our modern vampires.

* * * *

The partial analogy we have revealed between the believer and the victim of delusional beliefs is undeniable. But the most striking difference between the two is a difference between the individual and the collective. Whereas neurosis and psychosis *separate* the individual from the various groups with which he is connected, the secular religion whose main outlines we are trying to describe may be said to work in the opposite direction. Beyond a certain point the victim of obsession becomes a total loss to society, whereas the believer is *restored* to society—as is shown by the fact that after the crisis which accompanies every genuine conversion the believer ceases to feel useless and begins to feel he is useful.[1] So it appears as if the individual neurosis or psychosis, which is still in the formative stage, were going to be defeated by its own weapons; as if the collective obsessional neurosis (let us describe it so, in the hope of throwing some psychological light upon it) represented, at the individual's level, a method of treatment, an individual therapy for individual obsessional neurosis, and was, indeed, in the given case and circumstances, the best preventive treatment for the particular individual obsessional neurosis in process of formation. The socialisation of obsessions and delusions effected by secular religion is a remedy for the isolation and the social withdrawal, both subjective and objective, which are a factor in individual neurosis. Thus the neurosis is dispelled. One of its most noxious components, being severed from the others, is 'reabsorbed'; and the others—fixed ideas, delusions of reference, paranoiac projections—being lived and exteriorised *communally*, lose some of the characteristics which make them so harmful to the individual. Rites, processions, litanies, and communal celebrations are in this case both a symptom and a release[2]; they are a way of leading the individual back to the world of men and action and affairs, the real historical and social world. And in this real world of real men to which he has been restored the potential neurotic finds himself in contact with sane and well-adjusted individuals. In the case of communism, his contact will be with proletarians who see in communism a way of improving their conditions or escaping from them (they may be mistaken, but the calculation and the impulse behind it are not morbid ones); and in addition to proletarians he will meet people who have become communists purely from 'self-interest'—and these are shrewd and adaptable men. Mutual contagion results. The potential neurotic experiences the influence of his fellow-believers' mental health and also of social activity which, simply by being social, reintegrates him with his fellow-men; and, inversely, the men of 'sound mind' experience a collective intoxication and begin to exhibit, in a minor degree, the hysterical traits characteristic of believers (imperviousness to logical arguments and

[1] In 'official' and 'orthodox' communist literature, the fiction that deals with individual redemption through joining the Party contains many passages describing this emotional rehabilitation.

[2] A symptom is merely a temporary expedient, both inconvenient and costly from the point of view of the psychological structure; the symptom of disease is also a defensive reaction against disease.

arguments drawn from reality). The professional revolutionaries who created this religion were intellectuals who had failed to adapt to the existing régime and therefore had no responsibilities towards it. Such a situation is conducive to neurosis, for *if neurosis makes its subject asocial, it is also true that the fact of being in an asocial state is an essential precondition of neurosis and a first sign of its onset*. There is 'intraversion' of the repressed activity, which is to say that a major human function is thwarted; and this is a condition which is always present at the onset of neuroses. Neurotics are people in whom a major function is inhibited and who have lacked, at decisive moments, the strength or the assistance required for surmounting the obstacle. This throws light upon the violence of the polemics among exiles and 'illegal' revolutionaries, in which every disagreement on doctrine or tactics leads to accusations of treason.[1]

Lenin realised his potentialities in his role of statesman, but the neurosis of which he was permanently relieved by his conquest of power became 'socialised', and propagated itself among the intelligentsia of the 'capitalist countries'.

The characteristics common to all believers are strengthened at the expense of the individual characteristics of each; thus they are reinforced, as though by an effect of resonance, at the expense of the control mechanisms which resist suggestion—for these are the property of the individual. It is by means of a transference that the individual dispels the most threatening aspect of the neurosis; he converts his trouble, and also a part of his own human substance, into a power. And this power, which is equally the product of the suffering and the human substance of other believers, is immune to his criticism; for criticism is individual and cannot operate against a super-individual power, which is created out of the very energy which the individual would need for the purpose of criticising it. But as regards everything outside the secular religion, everything that does not come too close to this forbidden zone, the individual's critical faculty becomes sharper and more penetrating. A pathological clairvoyance is achieved at the price of a pathological blindness. The secular religion is created thanks to the affective communication which circulates energy among individuals, those open monads. And by a similar circulation the affective forces which resist the critical faculty in individuals with no original predisposition to neurosis are strengthened, until the critical faculty is as completely subdued in them as in those who *are* neurotically predisposed. Once this has happened we know that the neurosis has become effectively socialised. When a secular religion has reached a certain point of development and power, it can be described as an endemic neurosis; for it confers certain

[1] The 'furious' tone of these polemics sometimes recalls the tone of persecution mania.

neurotic characteristics upon all its new adherents, no matter what their individual predispositions may be (for example, an uncritical attitude towards certain subjects, suppression of certain facts and certain 'representations', and projections which make certain events, countries, men, and institutions divine and certain others diabolical).

The Party can be regarded as a real entity in the sense that it possesses a real psychological energy. This psychological energy is not the property of any of the individuals who compose the Party. It is from these individuals that the Party draws the energy that makes it a reality; but at the same time it transforms the energy, canalising and concentrating it, and directing it outwards. So the last state of this energy has no resemblance to the first. The Party has thus the appearance of a large-scale transference,[1] and this transference is continually in progress. It is a circulation; it is both a transformation and a transformer of energy. The energy of the Party is the product not only of the quantity of energy it draws in, but also of the use of this energy which transforms itself in action. If the Party were to stop it would collapse. Its nature is dynamic, and it is only by the continual process of circulation and transformation that it can continue to tap the energy it requires. Thus we see how true it is, in a sense, that the Party is a psychological reality, and also how there can be such a thing as a psychological reality, in the clearest and most definite sense, quite apart from the psychology of any individual. Such a psychological reality could not exist in the absence of individuals, but it cannot be reduced to the individual scale. So it is possible to give a true description which is not true of any given thing, or of any event, or of any particular moment. The Party thus belongs to a psychological order which cannot be confined to any particular manifestation. The relation between such manifestations and the Party is analogous to that between a man and his action. This real psychological being really lives in the real lives of its component individuals, but it cannot be reduced to them. There is *participation* between the Party and the secular religion; and the Party *is* the continually developing realisation of the religion. When vows of world conquest are made to the Party, when men sacrifice to it their enemies or their friends or themselves, it is all dedicated to the secular religion; but it is only we, as outside observers, who make this analytic distinction. The religion is immanent in the Party, and the Party in the religion; and one can see that in such a situation politics will come to partake of the sacred. The very purpose of the Party is totalitarian, and religion is the only known historical framework that can embrace the sum total of human activities.

[1] This example shows clearly the extent to which it is a mistake to regard the social fact which is the Party as if it were a thing; it also shows how much of the Party will be incomprehensible to the student who makes it a rule to treat social facts as things.

For its members, the Party takes the place both of civilisation and of society (though there are conflicts and the Party's supremacy is not unchallenged); and it is the secular religion (the Party) which provides the model, or pattern, to be conformed to. When such a substitution has taken place within it a civilisation is really threatened with scission (to use Sorel's term) or schism (to use Arnold Toynbee's).[1] An increasing part of the civilisation's human energies, which constituted its historic force, is diverted to a different purpose. Christianity effected this kind of displacement of psychological force in the classic civilisation and turned the force against the civilisation. It must be said that the communist 'Islam' is an historical form much less well equipped for bringing about a similar general disintegration and reintegration.

When the believer 'chooses his heroes', the Party takes possession of the 'ego-ideal'. It can happen that all Party members appear to the observer *identical*, and this is because they have all made the same identification. When they identify with the same model, they also identify reciprocally,[2] and the result is an *average type*, of which the observer can recognise the embodiment in every believer. But this phenomenon of reciprocal induction, of resonance, cannot appear without the appearance of leaders. It is only then that the 'circuit' is created.

The great leader is a man with an exceptional power of infecting others with his own obsessions. The fixed idea which unifies such a man's psyche corresponds to a passional state which is prevalent in those around him. What is characteristic of this new type of 'possessed' being is that his most personal passions are the most generalised passions of some social group. The general characteristic which others have in common is in him a special and particular characteristic; and the sphere of his personal passion is the sphere of other men's collective passion. If, further, he combines with this particularity an almost physical flair for the most effective attitudes and words, then we have a 'leader' who will seem to the crowd to have broken through barriers which they have not dared attack, but which, by identifying with him, they obtain the illusion of overcoming. Revolutionary situations which stir up crowds also evoke the appearance of such leaders, who seem to be 'selected', as it were, by the march of events. Their historical importance and practical effectiveness do not derive from any personal qualities that would set them apart, but from the fact that they are *personally* obsessed with the *collective* anxiety. They are both 'transmitters' and 'receivers', and what they transmit they also amplify and transform. Thus a contemporary society re-creates for its own use the

[1] cf. Toynbee, *A Study of Histc.* ": 'Schism in the soul, schism in the social body.'

[2] cf. Freud, *Psychologie collective et analyse du moi.* (Reference to this work will show in what respect we disagree with him.)

age-old figure of the person endowed with *mana*; and thus there is a sort of natural selection of suitable figures to incarnate the ego-ideal of men who feel themselves disinherited. The transition from feelings of humiliation to feelings of aggressiveness is visibly manifested in the advent and in the conduct of the leader. He makes the circulation and transformation of energy manifest, as a spectacle visible to the naked eye.

Men of this kind act as the mediators through whom the realisation of the characteristic aspirations of a given social group, or period, or milieu, is linked with the idea of the 'Party's' accession to power. And the Party demands complete and unreserved confidence.

The nascent religion remodels the believer's ego-ideal, and shields it from the influence of models proposed by the culture which the religion is tending to disintegrate. Thus a secular religion can be analytically resolved into a number of myths each of which corresponds to a certain psychological need or function, and *also*, as used to be said, to a certain 'category of souls'. Moreover, they correspond to the needs not only of different 'social species' but also of different 'social types'. The one does not contradict the other. On the contrary, there is a 'composition' and an *over-determination*, the same myth being charged with various meanings. Each meaning is *aimed* at a certain kind of men. But when a certain meaning has appealed to the ideal of a certain kind of men and confirmed it, these men will in their turn modify the original meaning until they can recognise themselves in it. So meanings not only converge but are also appropriated.

* * * *

When an entire category of events and people and ideas becomes *immune from criticism*, we are in the presence of a religious phenomenon; a distinction is being established between a sacred sphere and a profane one. In secular religion (and also in the totalitarian State, for the two are connected) this phenomenon is recognisable by the active presence of a *faith*, and of *myths* and *dogmas*.

According to Vico a myth is the 'representation' natural to primitive man. Georges Sorel goes a step farther; for him it is the *natural* representation of men whose *affective situation has made them primitive*. He points out that modern myths are connected with war: national myths with wars of nations, and social myths with class war. This is because pure emotivity enjoys a pre-eminence in war situations which it loses in times of peace. In war, modern man is menaced—like primitive man—by incomprehensible powers and unforeseen dangers. Many men today experience in war a state of strict dependence comparable to that in which technically primitive societies live. If myth is the 'thought of primitive man', the thought of modern men becomes mythical when they have been made primitive by a sufficiently vivid affective situation. Violent emotion sets up an internal vibration which will in due course impress upon the myth that grows out of it, as man from the living germ, the stamp of life itself. For this reason, if a myth is reduced to intellectual terms its essence is missed. The strength of the myth lies elsewhere, in the fact that it is a vital response to an affective situation. In the *crowd psychological situation*[1] the barriers which the personality's organisation opposes to suggestion and affective invasion are lowered, and this makes such crowd situations ideal *conductors of myths*; which explains why there are myths wherever there are masses, and why the 19th century, the age in which the masses appeared on the scene, was also—one has only to compare it with the 18th century—an age of myths. To the extent that affectivity is a preponderant feature of mass phenomena, so also are myths. The historic upheavals which mobilise and release the primarily affective elements in society give rise to myths at the same time. For example, the 'explosive' social situation which dates back to the French Revolution (when the train of powder was lit) began to break down the partitions of society and precipitated myths as well as masses in the resulting 'effervescence' (these words are used intentionally in the sense in which they apply to chemical reactions). Speaking of the faculties of the ancient poets, Vico says: 'In that human indigence, the peoples, who were almost all body and almost no reflection, must have been all vivid sensation in perceiving particulars, strong imagination in apprehending and magnifying them, sharp wit in referring them to their imaginative genera, and robust memory in retaining them. It is true that these faculties appertain to the mind, but they have their roots in the body and draw their strength from it.'[2] 'If this is so,' comments Georges Sorel, 'it is not easy to see how the domain of imagination, the use of the will in representation, and the faculty of creating imaginative genera, could disappear.'

One of the principal inadequacies in the theory,[3] which distinguishes 'civilised man' from 'primitive man' and the culture of civilised societies from that of primitive societies, consists in this: that in order to eliminate the culture of our present society it would not be necessary to kill off the majority of the population. It would be sufficient to remove a small number of men who are only a minority in relation to the whole of society considered quantitatively. One might, therefore, advance the

[1] In English in the original [*Trans.*].

[2] *Nova Scienza*. Book III, Section I, Chapter V, p. 280 (Engl. trans.; Ithaca, 1948).

[3] The outstanding representative of this theory was M. Lucien Lévy-Bruhl, but he began after a time to add continual new refinements to the distinction, until, in the end, in his notebooks published in 1948, the theory itself was questioned. I have criticised that theory in my book *La Poésie moderne et le sacré* (Paris, 1945).

proposition that it is possible for a society to be, in part, a stranger to its own culture. Western civilisation used to be described as 'dynamic' by contrast with 'static' civilisations. But the science and technology in which this dynamic quality is expressed were at first the work of a very small number of men. Subsequently, *organisation* incorporated more and more people into scientific and technological activities, and thus enabled these activities to extend their transforming powers beyond the limits foreseeable a century ago. Meanwhile, although Europe began to make great progress from the beginning of the 19th century, thanks to the efforts of a dedicated minority, the greater part of the European population remained static in relation to this active minority. Nevertheless, dynamic minority and static majority were parts of one whole, for a society in process of industrialisation can only live thanks to the labour of peasants still ignorant of industrial techniques. This remoteness of the minority from the majority obtains throughout all departments of the culture, which means that there is a primitive society (as the term is used by Lévy-Bruhl and the French school of sociologists) *within* the civilised society. Every high culture or highly developed material civilisation contains within itself a primitiveness, and it is essential to remember this if we wish to understand the history of Western civilisation since the industrial revolution, which is to say: the history of our world. The appearance of the masses upon the stage of history means that the primitive will play a more important part both in history and in the actual behaviour of collectivities, for it means the appearance of individuals with less rigid standards of self-control and less respect for 'form'. Their emotions are less formalised and less integrated within the unitary and hierarchical system of the personality, which only becomes a system thanks to the discipline and self-control acquired through education. It also means the appearance of 'crowd situations' propitious to the growth of myths, and the frequent recurrence of such situations enables the myths to be kept in being, to be 'recharged', and to grow. With the breaking down of the partitions of society and the eruption of the masses, primitiveness was no longer segregated and contained but became diffused throughout society; and in this sense the new society in process of formation was more *primitive* and *barbarous* than the old, giving these words their full significance, positive as well as negative, in relation to current standards of value. For primitiveness is society's reserve and reservoir of energy, and its relation to the 'higher levels' is like the relation of Freud's 'unconscious' to the 'super-ego'; the power and efficiency of the super-ego depend upon its communication with the unconscious, whose energy it draws upon. If communication ceases, the super-ego will perish; and with it the psyche as a whole.

When all the elements of an old order are dislocated by such an eruption of forces and scattered to the four winds, then it can be said that a civilisation—that is to say, the product of a certain unique historic civilising endeavour, and the men in whom it was embodied,[1] the men in whom its life was expressed—has been submerged like the town of Ys. After which, or so it has been up to now, a new civilisation is formed (and the formative period is a time of troubles). This new form of civilisation may be judged by future historians to be as high as, or higher than, the old. In any case, comparisons between the respective merits of two or more historic societies are quite subjective (and each period may have its own subjectivity).

Conditions of violence strip man naked. The affective state of a large number of men becomes the state which, according to Vico, pertains to the primitive. They feel themselves the playthings of forces which dominate them and dispose of them at will; and they deify these forces, inventing modern equivalents of magical incantations to invoke or banish demons and to make allies or slaves of them. In the 19th century there was a vast resurgence of 'mythical thinking'.

We interpret through their rites the myths that are remote from us in time or place. But this method fails to explain the major and even the lesser characteristics of the myths among which we ourselves live. In fact, if we examine the modern myths we shall always find the trace of a social upheaval, an historic 'traumatism'. War is the situation that favours the creation of myths. All the 19th-century myths are connected with wars; the various national myths are related to the wars of liberation waged by the peoples, especially the German people, against Napoleon, and to the armed struggles of oppressed nationalities against their oppressors; and all the myths of national consolidation refer to victorious wars waged by the nation, or by the empire if or when it was one. Thus the romantic poets and historians of the 19th century revived, as myths and with mythical grandeur, the 'great ages' of the Holy Roman Empire, Greece, Ancient Rome, Serbia, Hungary, Bulgaria, Poland; and even the least-favoured nationalities contrived somehow or other to dig up some such reference from their past history. It is the same with social myths. They arise from an event which impinged upon the European sensibility as a profound 'affective trauma': from the fact that the industrial revolution seemed to condemn great masses of human beings to conditions of life which their fellow-men judged (consciously or unconsciously) to be appalling. This is the heart of the socialist myths; and Marxism is simply the technique by which the energy they mobilise is given historical application. It organises them more effectively both from the point of view of aggressive action and also of intellectual justification. Here we can observe the effect upon a myth of

[1] e.g., the 18th-century French aristocracy.

the age in which it is born, for the 19th-century myths are obliged to make concessions to science and the scientific outlook, from which older myths were absolved; and this observation recalls once again the function of ideology, which *reduces the myth's emotional impact but enhances the more durable qualities which emotion finds tedious*. It is of the essence of myths that they spread by contagion, but they themselves are contaminated by the supremely contagious device of language *multiplied* by methods of diffusion (which are themselves the creation of modern industrial technique). The effect of ideology appears as a toning down of the myth's affective violence, and Sorel could even maintain (though not in these words) that in the socialism of the end of the 19th century the ideological element had ended by suffocating the mythical. His ambition to be the prophet of technology urged Sorel to restore the myth to pre-eminence by translating socialist ideology back into mythology; and this was the intention behind his theory of myth. Ideology emphasises the intellectual justification of the present state of affectivity, or feeling, at the expense of that imaginative justification of present and future activity which the living modern myths exist to provide. Whereas ideology *enters into combination* with other intellectual—and affective—elements, it is the tendency of myth to embrace only those affective elements which are *congenial*. Myth is recalcitrant to combinations on the intellectual plane; as a method of ordering data it is uncompromising towards rival methods (such as the established faiths), and summons the individual to make a choice. But in ideology the mythical element tends to become detached from its emotional context; in other words, from its direct dialectical link with the basic affective situation—from the actual tragedy that is being lived. The 'natural' end-result of a myth is an act, but ideology is soon entangled in a network of theoretical relations in which the mythical element becomes diluted, exhausted, and deranged. This is the triumph of the casuists, heresiarchs, and learned doctors; and the 'man of the myth' is robbed of his act.

In the extreme case, ideology can become a mere *compensation* and nothing more than an excuse for inactivity. Its tendency is soporific, whereas myth is a call to action. It is only necessary to recall the history of German and Austrian social democracy from the end of the 19th century up to the bolshevik attack. Myth tends to realise itself in action, but ideology is reflective. One might say that myth is the field in which imagination is applied to historical reality, or the spearhead by which it enters. But in ideology the myth's impact is softened by diffusion. Ideology is *thought* charged with *affectivity*, and each of these two elements corrupts the other. Only those outside a myth can dissect it intellectually, and that is why the reductive criticism which exposes myths as *errors* always fails of its anticipated effect. Direct intellectual attack upon a myth is like therapeutic treatment of a symptom. To be effective, analysis must be applied to the causes of the myth; and as a general rule it is only as the result of a profound change in their historical conditioning that myths become amenable to intellectual reduction. This is a victory of 'reason' in appearance only.

'We should not attempt', said Sorel,[1] 'to analyse such groups of images in the way that we analyse a thing into its elements.' And indeed this could only result in isolating *elements of which the myth is definitely something other than the sum, and which, in isolation, are definitely something other than elements of a myth*; for the elements, when isolated, lose their affinity with the myth, and their mythical quality evaporates. A myth can never be reduced to what can be explained in words. Intellectual analysis reduces a myth to truths, errors, probabilities, and so on, all of which are obviously not mythical, and misses its distinctive characteristic. We get an equally unreal representation of the myth if we try to explain it as a sum of historical details. 'It is the myth in its entirety which is alone important,' says Sorel. 'Its parts are only of interest in so far as they bring out the main idea.'[2] 'A myth cannot be refuted' because it is 'identical with the convictions of a group, being the expression of these convictions in the language of movement'.[3] Belief in a myth does not imply belief in any particular event. Such belief is accessory. A social myth is born out of the basic affective situation of a given social group. The situation is a grave one, and it weighs upon all the members of the group as an immediate datum and a constitutent quality of their affective experience. The myth spreads within the group. It gains as a myth in proportion as it wins to itself the psychological powers of individuals: their power of identification, their power of rising above past events and of rising to meet future ones, their ability to recognise their own past experiences when recounted by another although at the time they may have understood them only confusedly, if at all. By the extent to which it is diffused, then, the myth defines a *social species*, and also certain *psychological varieties* within other social species. The different individuals affected by the contagion of the myth are like the neurons, susceptible of isolation by analysis, which form a 'neuronic system' with a specific rate of excitability. But here the psychological intervenes to complicate the social phenomenon: individuals whose social variety should make them non-conductors of the myth become conductors for psychological reasons, like the bourgeois magnate's son who turns communist *against* his father. It is harder to trace the circuit of the myth's current than the path of a nervous excitation, for there is not only a *social threshold* but also a *psychological threshold*; and neither of them is absolute. Moreover, it very often

[1] *Reflections on Violence*, p. 22 (London, 1916). [2] ibid., p. 136. [3] ibid., p. 33.

happens that an individual not predisposed to it, either by his social species or by his own psychological history, becomes a conductor of the myth *because of another individual*, from love or from hate. As Freud says, and this is of capital importance: 'Faith repeats for this occasion the story of its own birth. It is the fruit of love.' He adds that most men do not and never have allowed their lives to be influenced in the slightest degree by the arguments of people they do not love.[1] So, in general, man is only accessible intellectually to the extent that he is capable of passion.[2]

It is not only 'magical' thought and 'primitive' civilisations that can exploit the creative power of sentiments and resentments.

Thus, for example, a man or woman may seek a distraction from some trouble or look for an outlet for their need to act and be busy and 'start something'. They speak words and make gestures designed to please. Either of them might behave in many different ways with the same intent, but it so happens that it is these particular gestures and words that please. They pay attention only to the immediate effect of their behaviour, the effect they are aiming to produce. But it would be a mistake to think they are doing no more than what they actually do. They are in reality contributing to build up a force of an overwhelming kind—a force comparable to the power of money, but 'directed'. Thus from the 'all-too-human' something 'inhuman' is fashioned.

When the current of the myth meets non-conducting elements it is either arrested or else the myth itself is so profoundly recast that it becomes almost a new myth running in a new circuit. And this happens so often and in so many ways that it makes the sociological process of myth-propagation considerably different from the physiological process with which we have been comparing it.

* * * *

The modern myths are directed towards control of the future, even though they may appeal to the past. They are prospective, and not retrospective like the nostalgia of the past, which always peters out in literature. They are tools fashioned to grip the present and impose a certain shape upon the future. Their activity, one might almost say their volcanic activity, erupts in deeds, and not in musical choruses which relieve emotion by sublimating its vitality in misty sentiment. And although myths give rise to the poetry of the 'impossible, yet conceivable', this poetry pours forth like lava from a volcano. If the myth is a

[1] But it can also happen that mere skill in argument may evoke what Stendhal would have called admiration-love.

[2] Freud's own words are, 'of investing objects with libido'.

valid one, it is a faith for those who create it and live and die by it—and a tool for those who make use of it.

* * * *

According to Lalande's *Vocabulaire technique et critique de la philosophie*, the first meaning of the Greek word 'dogma' was: 'political decision of a sovereign or an assembly'. The secondary and derivative meaning in which the word is commonly used today 'probably comes from the fact that the ancient schools of philosophy often had the character of religious sects, so that, for their adepts, the doctrines had the same compulsive authority as a political decree for the citizens of a State'. Ours is an age in which dogma is reverting from its secondary to its original meaning, and it is also an age in which myth is escaping from the gilded cage of literature and asserting itself aggressively in life. (Above all, it is a tragic age; but it would only cease to be so if there were no longer any heroes equal to the oppressing powers, and if men became resigned to destruction by mechanical forces and allowed the spring of their resistance to go slack for want of use.)

As myth loses its vitality when it becomes literature, so does dogma in those societies and historical periods when it becomes school philosophy. But when the spiritual becomes indistinguishable from the temporal, then the word dogma attains its absolute significance, as in Hitler's Germany and Stalin's Russia. Excommunication reaches its maximum force, for its victims are not only banished from the group, but from the world as well and from life. The stark etymological origin of the word dogma is revealed once more, and the word can be used today in strictest conformity with its first, compulsive meaning. Historical and dialectical materialism are working hypotheses and heuristic methods, when examined critically; but when they are removed from critical jurisdiction they become dogmas. Myth operates in the field of affective energy, and dogma in the field of intellectual organisation, justification, and rationalisation. Dogma is ideology which has become fixed and, as it were, petrified: it tends to 'objectify' ideas which owe their existence to faith, but which, once they have become dogma, acquire a sort of autonomy and social existence in their own right. The points of a dogma may sometimes appear as so many judgments awaiting execution, and it often happens that when a believer has become possessed of a new dogma he feels himself its executor. There is no discussion of dogma, but only *about* it. In our society any scientific proposition is expected to be able to stand on its own feet. But dogma calls for armed protection; it is full of fear, and only persecutions can reassure it. Science expects no such consideration but, on the contrary, is always ready to reopen and re-examine every question. The irresistible force with which scientific truth impresses the mind is exercised by dogma upon the actual conduct and behaviour of men in society. Dogma goes with intolerance and science with tolerance. The high priests and militant missionaries of a dogma are emotionally identified with it; any blow struck at the dogma is like a physical pain to them, and if they dimly feel—what it would be hardly possible for them to perceive clearly—that they have been intellectually defeated, they tend to take, if they can, *an unanswerable physical revenge*. Whether we like it or not, we are no longer living in a liberal age; the active presence of a great dogmatic power which knows no scruples is sufficient to substitute war, whether latent or open, for the liberal habit of discussion. The world-wide facility of communications today makes impossible the co-existence of two separate worlds as distinct from one another as were, at the beginning of the Christian era, the Rome of the Cæsars and the China of the Hans. In a world where natural obstacles have been abolished—for oceans, mountains, and deserts no longer count—the intellectual liberalism of those who have remained liberal is changed in its very nature by the mere presence of a vast intolerant expanding power which is active outside as well as within the empire to whose triumph it is vowed. So liberalism—from being optimistic in the weak and shallow sense of the expression 'optimistic rationalism'—becomes tragic. The liberal remains an 'optimist'; he still aims at better things, but it is now a tragic sort of optimism. It is an incessant struggle to safeguard the freedom and sovereignty of the mind, and we see them abandoned by an increasing number of men who might be considered more than well-endowed with intellectual resources. Which only shows that intellectual resources are not everything.

During the liberal and capitalist era science achieved such an assured position and acquired so much credit that a modern dogma has to pass itself off as science before it can be safely established—even if it has to employ in the process those methods of terror which give the lie to its claim. Marxists claim to be scientific, but if Marxism were science it could not be Marxism, for in that case it would meet criticism more than half-way and would thrive upon it instead of fleeing it like the plague. Science takes note of errors, but dogma only takes note of crimes; and where dogma exists research itself becomes a crime. Since there is no sure and incontrovertible way of establishing dogmatic propositions they can only become incontrovertible by the extermination or, at the least, the muzzling of critics. So the reign of dogma implies the existence of fanatics to enforce it; and a pitiless *militia* of the faith is indispensable to the totalitarian party which enforces its dogma *manu militari* in the 20th century. Some dogmas enjoin prayer and meditation (if not speculation), but not this dogma; it issues imperatives and *watch-words*, which are rules for action in the task of transforming the world. The Marxist dogma in its compulsive aspect makes it unlawful to follow Marx's own example in sifting the treasures of human knowledge and separating gold from dross (I refer to Marxism in its positive aspect and not to the negative aspect, the *system*, in which the error becomes irreparable). It is the peculiarity of dogma at its most virulent, and is indeed the contradiction which makes it what it is, that it implicitly forbids anyone to follow the example of the very men to whom it owes its existence. Human lives are sacrificed, in the name of the dogmas of secular religions, to the knowledge which is possessed by the depositaries of Truth (or rather, which possesses them): namely, the knowledge of the final end of history and of the best means of attaining it. These dogmas, therefore, are contradictory in the sense of being both immanent and transcendent. They deny fact in the name of transcendent realities (for placing them in the future does not make them any the less transcendent), and at the same time they assert that fact is the test of truth. Believers believe they know; they believe only in knowledge and do not know that they believe. Whenever events seem to suggest that messianic hope is about to be fulfilled, it will be found on closer examination that what they really reveal is that he who tries to be an angel becomes a beast. The grand inquisitor and supreme thug of the world of today is the man who believes he knows.

These dogmas are rife in the 20th century. And, contrary to the belief of heterodox communists and Marxists, who often inspire sympathetic respect, it must be admitted that Marxism, as a unitary doctrine which hinges thought strictly upon action and tends to integrate every part of man and of human knowledge within a single whole, was able to provide an effective totalitarianism with the justification it needed. Both totalitarian and liberal Marxists are legitimate offspring of Marx, as right and left Hegelians are of Hegel. But it is nothing, or very little, to criticise dogma. We are no longer so ingenuous as the 18th-century *philosophes*. If dogma were accessible to criticism as science is, it would not be dogma and would never have come into being. Dogma is the intellectual sheath of a mystical kernel; its only purpose is to justify a faith—and faith can hardly be vanquished except by another faith. Criticism of their dogma is, by itself, of no avail at all against religions. Yet certain particularly aggressive and determined criticisms imply something new; they mean that the dogma is threatened with a decline. They may be premonitory symptoms of a disaffection such as the power of ideas alone would be unable to create.

* * * *

It has been observed more than once that each of the Oriental religions transplanted to Rome nourished the affectivity, or, one might say, the subjectivity, of a particular social or psychological species: Mithra for soldiers, Isis for women, Cybele for worshippers of the Great Mother.[1] Hard upon these came Christianity, offering itself as supernatural ransom for the dereliction of each man and of all humanity; and perhaps it was because its propositions were addressed to all men, excluding none, that Christianity ended by eliminating all its competitors. *One is immediately struck by the difference from communism, which publishes daily lists of persons and social categories condemned to perdition.* In so far as communism remains Marxist it adheres to the mission of the proletariat, in other words to a doctrine of social predestination. Not only is there a class of reprobates who are pulverised by the march of history and have no place in the future, but according to popular Marxism (the form in which it became an effective living power) all the other classes are composed of servants of the chosen class. They are not self-subsistent, but must choose between disappearance or serving the proletariat. There is no real future for them as classes.

Socialism before Marx, claiming the Christian heritage and claiming to transcend national and, later, racial particularism, represented itself as bearing towards nation and race the same relation as the universal to the particular or the open to the closed. The mood of this socialism was optative. Marx changed it to the imperative, and was not so much concerned to win the best men as to create and assemble upon a world scale a huge and invincible army for a holy war. The penalty for this radical change of mood was that particularism installed itself, like a worm in the fruit, and rotted it from within. Marxism will long remain a doctrine of sociological predestination, as the 'racial' theory is a doctrine of biological predestination.

Marxism wants to promote the (*future*) salvation of humanity; that is, of all men, through the realisation of the *present* desires of some men. Instead of a next world there is an earthly future; and when an individual falls in the fight the dogma has it that he has given his life for the entire Species—since the future of the entire species is contained potentially within the 'proletariat' to the present exclusion of all other men. This future, which is salvation, will come—as through a strait gate—through the agency of interests which are necessarily selfish and narrow. So, in regard to the present, Marxism is a doctrine of sociological predestination (one must cleave to the proletariat or, at the very least, do everything to hasten its necessary advent), and in regard to the future it is a Messianism of the human species. There is no salvation outside the

[1] These are only typical examples. In fact, there were several divinities for each social category and psychological type and species of man.

proletariat, and everything is destined to happen in this world. The chosen people, the oppressed proletarians, will see the punishment of their oppressors, and then perhaps they will see an unlimited and unimaginable perspective of happiness and delights. The (world) revolution will 'liquidate' the present, instal the future, and inaugurate a new era in which private property will not exist. '*Magnus ab integro sæclorum nascitur ordo*.' But there is no question of waiting for the Promise to be fulfilled; it is necessary to work for it. And when there are setbacks there is only one conclusion to be drawn: it was not the moment, the times were still not ripe.

The deification of man, conceived as a promotion of the Species instead of an individual incarnation, calls for the accomplishment of *works*. One must participate, either in the ranks of the proletariat or at their side, in the class struggle transformed into an unceasing holy war.

In the secular religion of communism the operation takes place at the level and for the profit of the *Party*, and not of the *Class*. In this sense the rise of communism is the downfall of Marxism. One can judge the distance that communism has travelled from the communism of the pre-totalitarian age by the fact that it recommends itself today as a principle of order to those who have need of order, such as technicians, officials, scientists, and professors. At the same time it appears as progress to those who reckon they have nothing to lose and all to gain from a radical change; and these are not only proletarians but also the disinherited of every kind, and not only the disinherited but also those who, without being exactly disinherited, nevertheless feel themselves 'outsiders' (this is the particular case of the intelligentsia). Whereas the technicians and officials conceive themselves as incapable of existing without order, and fear lest it should fail them and turn into disorder, the 'intellectuals' have no such fears, but find the communist order attractive precisely because it would be a *different* order, and their own. Moreover, the social destruction of a class is not the same thing as the physical destruction of its members, and therefore even those whose class is threatened may hope for salvation as individuals; and party membership or, anyway, good relations with party members may be the means to it. So the 'treachery' of a class may be, in fact, merely an aspect of the self-interest of individuals. In any case, whatever the dogmatic issues involved, adherence to the communist 'Islam' offers an almost physical relief from the anguish of being alone, the sense of being abandoned. In such cases the meaning and intellectual tendency of the 'ideas' which the Party is advocating do not matter. What matters is the opportunity for communion and work in common. At first the convert may have wished that the ideas offered to him had been different; sometimes he is conscious of the shocking cheapness of the myths he must accept. He may even find them sordid, and admit to himself that they are intellectually degrading. But he hopes that all will be somehow transmuted in the glowing warmth that so attracts him. At least, this is what he tells himself by way of excuse.

In listing the 'categories of souls' who become underground conspirators by choice, Nietzsche begins with 'the unsuccessful'. These are the socially disinherited, whether their handicap be personal or social, who find in 'conspiracy' a way of socialising their resentment. (Such was the 'internal proletariat' of Roman society. A common servitude effaced the original differences between the conquered Barbarian and the Greek in his fallen state.) Next come those who are 'intoxicated with morality', those who, judging their own world to be wicked, are always ready to assist its most promising adversaries. And then there are the 'men who are weary of politics'. These are the men we have already described, who are not concerned about the quality of the myths and ideas they embrace but only with the need to end their loneliness; they are aware of nothing except the void from which they must somehow escape. And this brings us to the party of the 'self-disgusted', the men with a thorn in their flesh, the broken men, who have no faith in any reasonable cure but on the contrary are attracted by the absurd. To them, if a doctrine is questionable or even untenable, this only increases its chance of success. And finally, when the conspiracy has become sufficiently powerful, it is joined by the careerists, the 'normal men'.

As a church, the conspiracy attracts the religious natures; as order, it attracts average men; as a war, it attracts the warlike. Each man is caught in a trap for which his own imagination supplies the bait, and they all find in the conspiracy what they themselves have brought to it. As for the gospel, it is protean and polyvalent. A doctrine can be self-contradictory, but propaganda never is. Propaganda says at any moment whatever it suits the propagandist that it should say. Logically confronted, the various propositions it advances would cancel out. But such a confrontation would be like an algebraic addition of terms that have nothing to do with algebra.

Communism does not say, 'To each according to his need', nor does it say, 'To each according to his work or his deserts'. It says, 'To each according to his desire'. But it is true that it offers only emotional nourishment and ideal food. Of secular religion, too, it may be said that 'each has his part in it, and all have it entirely'. This miraculous distribution is facilitated by the feat of imagination which makes affectivity content to feed upon its own desire. But their internal contradictions place secular religions at the mercy of more effective conspiracies. (The fact that no such conspiracies exist today proves nothing about the future.) The social neurosis canalises forces that were otherwise wasted, and gathers up resentments which had hitherto poisoned only the resentful themselves and the objects of hatred they have conjured up; but in the process of socialisation it becomes transformed and takes on the colour of a secular religion. The anxiety of the neurotic turned believer is changed into a certainty which is too aggressive and too passionate to be really sure of itself.

Modern life, especially in the great cities, has a harmful aspect; and there comes a point where the frustrated man, however docile he may remain in appearance, becomes an irreconcilable. He cannot become a rebel because the springs of his rebelliousness are broken. This, however, is not the condition of the active section of the proletariat; it is that of the unemployed proletarians and of the various other types of unemployed—the floating plebs of the great capital cities, uprooted people, human particles set free by the collapse of social barriers, whose freedom is the freedom to drift. Masses of such people are rescued from dereliction and reinstated in society by the secular religions which cater for them.[1] They are the typical development of proletarianised man in the first half of the 20th century. It sometimes happens that the victim of frustration, when he has reached the point of being incapable either of revolt or of reconciliation, draws a line, like a man who has added up a bill. He has reached the total, and it is too big ever to be paid in the world as it is. The offence that has hurt him, the humiliation that has degraded him, have become inexpiable. When the *irremediable*, to this degree, has become general throughout a collectivity, then the time may appear ripe for a totalitarianism—a complex social phenomenon, of which the triumph of a secular religion appears to be an integral part. This is what happened in Germany in the 1930s; and in this sense religious phenomena certainly are 'conditioned', in so far as they are also social phenomena, by the economic structure; but *condition* must not be confused with *cause*.

The irreconcilable man, when he has been produced in sufficient numbers, consents to invest his resentment; he will invest it in a 'conspiracy' or in an 'Islam' which becomes a general agency for injuries to be revenged. Responsibility for the evils he has suffered is laid at the door of individual men or groups of men; and thus sadism begins to appear as a collective function. The totalitarian State will provide this function with official organs.

Just as the secular religion is immanent, and participates in the party, and vice versa, so there may be reciprocal immanence and participation between the Party and the Leader. There is a *dialectic of Incarnation*. Models are indispensable for any real morale, and the 'ego-ideal' must

[1] Communism and national socialism both functioned in this way; and Stalinism provides a Marxist camouflage for the process.

have *images* upon which to form itself. Ideas do not suffice; they must be emotionally *treated*, worked upon by affectivity, until they have been converted into images. A 'leader cult' emerges as the proper and normal result of the process. In national socialism the cult of the leader was established before the capture of power; the absence of doctrine favoured a rapid incarnation of the power that united the militants. But this makes it all the more remarkable that a leader cult should have developed in communism, for both the Marxist doctrine and the whole outlook of the prophets of the new Islam were fundamentally opposed to such a cult. It is true, however, that the cult was largely reinforced by the influence of a purely Russian emotion which had been directed previously upon the Tsar. Hitler had such a direct hold upon the Germans' unconscious that people of all other nations took him for its actual emanation; but Stalin, who emerged from the bolshevik ranks and reached the leadership by way of the secretariat, by the accumulation of functions, by ruse and manœuvre, is to some extent the object of a similar cult; and this seems to show that the cult of the leader in the 20th century is a *phenomenon of convergence*. A collective emotion or affective need *accommodates itself* to the person whom history provides for it.

In communism the ultimate stage, the incarnation of the Party in the Leader, is of less importance than it is in national socialism; the role of the institution tends to outweigh that of the incarnation. In national socialism the party seems to draw its life from the leader, but in communism this impression is reversed. The process of deification is counteracted by optimistic rationalism, the secular philosophy of 'progress', and the spirit of technology. So the great transformation seems rather to take place on the level of the Party. Instead of an incarnate God, the communists offer a sort of 'incorporated company God'.

* * * *

When morbid phenomena which are dangerous and destructive on the individual level are transferred to the collective level the disease is transferred to the collectivity, and the individual is to some extent relieved of ailments and weaknesses with which he could not cope by his own individual strength. Thus the individual and the collectivity may be likened to communicating vessels. A really firmly established order, a compartmented and stable society, condemns those whom a neurosis has cast adrift to remain imprisoned within the neurosis, whereas an unstable society whose barriers have broken favours his re-socialisation; but the re-socialisation of the neurotic involves the socialisation of the neurosis. This dialectic, and this problem, reveal a tragedy peculiar to our age: the more neurotics or potential neurotics are saved in this way from the most destructive effects of the neurosis, the more society itself becomes infected. It becomes charged, as it were, with obsessional and neurotic 'currents'. So those who try to put up an effective resistance to secular religions are in the end more or less obliged to adopt some of the most powerful and, so to speak, profitable characteristics of the neurosis: frenzied activity and fanaticism, for example. In this way they necessarily become infected by what they are fighting against. Each camp infects the other, and *since the contagious external symptoms are connected with internal states, the latter also tend to be reproduced in both camps*. Spinoza says somewhere that one should be able to act violently without being violent, to perform the acts of a fool in the spirit of a sage—to act without being corrupted by one's action, without becoming the instrument of one's instrument. And Nietzsche laments that the great Napoleon failed to rise above this remorseless dialectic. (But to judge Napoleon from this absolute standpoint is to remove him from the plane of history to that of art.)

When an individual affective trouble is transformed by its incorporation into collective behaviour, the result appears as a cure for the individual but as an illness for society. So it is too simple to say that secular religions (in the language of sociology) or group neuroses (in the language of medicine) serve to 'gather up the neuroses of individuals'. It is an over-simplification which verges upon error. I believe rather that there is a relation between individual psyches and what one might call the social psyche[1] comparable to the relation sought for by the pioneers of 'psychosomatic medicine' between 'psychic disorders' and 'somatic disorders'. As we know, the American Dunbar, combining Freud and Pavlov, starts from this postulate: If psychic tendencies fail to find a satisfactory release in action, there may result not only psychopathological disorders but also somatic changes which appear first as functional disturbances and later as lesions. Therefore, although they start from different points, the historical sociologist (ourselves), the physiologist of reflexes (Pavlov), and the dynamic psychologist (Freud), all arrive at the same idea: that there is a *mutual dependence*, a general interdependence of a *dynamic* (and no longer a mechanical) type, which indicates—to put it in well-worn terms which are clear enough in this context—that man is not *in* nature but *of* it, and that the respective contents of physiology, sociology, psychology, etc., are not themselves worlds but simply ways of seeing the world.

Here at last it becomes fully clear what is meant by our expressions

[1] It should by now be possible to use this expression without fear of misunderstanding. The reader who has followed our thought will know that no reference is intended (as is still the case even in Durkheim) to some sort of 'great being'.

'the canalisation of resentments' and 'the diversion of aggressive impulses'. To understand them one must adopt a viewpoint from which the so-called 'normal' and the 'pathological', the physiological and the psychological (or better, the physical and the moral), the social and the individual, the substructure and the superstructure, do not appear as distinct domains but as analytical abstractions and types of meaning which the seeker of knowledge can make use of to light his path. Historical changes and social movements can only avail themselves of the energy that exists—and it is equally true to say that the energy that exists can only express itself through the social movements and historical changes. Secular religion of the Islamic type—the virulent conjunction of a religion and a people each of which is 'new' and at the disposal of the other and each of which transforms the other—affords a vital outlet. According to Dunbar, affectivity repressed as the result of a too-painful tension gives rise to energy in a different circuit. Instead of issuing in exteriorisation,[1] it is liable not only to 'intravert' and produce psychoses and neuroses but also to enter the 'reduced circuit' (the subcortical centres and sympathetic system) and to influence that part of the nervous system which controls sympathetic reactions. Then the organs begin to speak in their own 'language', which takes the form of illness (the disorders are at first functional, but the functional disorder eventually modifies the organ itself). Adherence to a secular religion would thus be an individual therapeutic solution; the psychic trouble is cured and the danger of somatic trouble removed. So religion effects a *transmutation of human suffering*, and the religion that triumphs is the one that best satisfies the emotional needs of the greatest number.[2] The energy that fixes upon images continually debases and alters them, investing them with new meanings and even paradoxically taking advantage of their contradiction by events. Thus the early Christians accommodated themselves to the postponements of the Second Coming and took advantage of these successive accommodations to create new and different representations. In communism, a secular religion, and also in the crude and brutal religion that was inherent in national socialism, the function of the *beyond* is performed by the *future* (the future millennial or multimillennial Reich and the destiny of the master race correspond functionally to the classless society). Each of these secular religions must be described as 'materialist'; in the one case it is historical materialism and in the other zoological. They seek the 'beyond' in the 'here', and

[1] Dunbar's physiological demonstration of this is outside the field to which we are restricting ourselves.

[2] According to Arnold J. Toynbee, the universal or '*higher*' religions emerge from the depths of the '*internal proletariat*' of a society and are the product of the accumulated miseries of a prolonged '*time of troubles*'. Themselves the product of suffering, they tend 'absurdly' to deny suffering.

thus the intellect is brought up short before a mystery. (This also happens in the great other-wordly religions.) But they immediately make the mystery more absurd[1] by the fact that they seek the transcendent within the immanent. It is true that the emphasis on *praxis* and action serves forcibly to distract the mind from this fundamental absurdity. The tendency of the faithful to provoke an historical upheaval which shall translate their confusion into act is a measure of their need to escape from an ever-increasing inner incoherence. But this reveals another internal contradiction of secular religions, for they are exposed to the risk that events will mock and give the lie to their claims. If Feuerbach's proposition is true, that God is made in the image of man, the contrary proposition that God is conceived in contradistinction to man is not less true; for in contrast to man, the very type of the insufficient, God is the sufficient. Hence the ever-threatening disillusionment that undermines the secular religions. They have placed all their hopes in this world, and yet every time they stretch out a hand to grasp what ought to be sufficient, its insufficiency is glaringly revealed. So the secular religions decline into a materialistic cynicism and begin to appear horrible. There is no longer any justification for the human sacrifices they call for and make. Lapsing into final absurdity, they make men suffer and inflict tortures upon them in order that mankind may be rescued from suffering and torture.

[1] If the faithful of these religions are not *comic*, it is solely because they are strong.

CHAPTER 11

The Political Phenomenon of Tyranny

IN 19th-century Europe political liberalism advanced and extended its influence, and parliamentary institutions continued to develop with the development of capitalism. Progress was not continuous, but if we examine Europe and Russia from the French Revolution to the end of the 19th century, it is clear that this was the general trend of political change. Nicolas II held out; but he could only do so by sealing Russia off from Europe, and in any case there were still chinks through which ideas could pass. The counter-revolution that followed the storms of 1848 was more a stabilisation than an attempt at wholesale re-establishment of the old European order, such as followed the defeat of the first Napoleon; and even the abortive Second Empire in France, which, as we can now see, prefigured in some respects the absolutisms of the 20th century, culminated in a series of concessions to political liberalism.

All this makes the reversal of the trend in the 20th century the more remarkable. For we now note, everywhere from Russia to the Atlantic, the signs of a transformation of power and the appearance of new absolutisms; and these absolutisms have something in common over and above the features which distinguish them from 19th-century liberalism and from Europe's *ancien régime*, in which society was partitioned into 'orders' or 'estates'. By contrast, the 20th-century absolutisms are the product of a period in which social partitions collapsed, a period of confusion, fusion, and excitement. The determining influence in this situation appears to have been the industrialisation of the western part of the continent, which involved an exodus from the country into the towns and the appearance of new forms of urban life and new kinds of towns. The old social barriers were broken down; the 'estates' (formerly the 'orders') were mixed together; society became more fluid and unstable; and there gradually arose *a new type of cosmopolitanism, of manners instead of intellect*. It was not a consonance of soul or of intellect, but a growing uniformity of way of life over the whole area of diffusion of a common material civilisation. The new absolutisms followed upon a process of relatively rapid disintegration of social relationships whose development had been long and slow, a process of atomisation and 'mobilisation' (in the literal physical sense of the word) within society of its constituent human particles. Movement of every kind became more rapid, and from this all-round acceleration nothing was excepted and nothing spared. Even values changed more quickly; and with the growth of credit and speculation and limited liability companies wealth acquired an unprecedented mobility.

The midwife of the new absolutisms was the first world war. It greatly accelerated the rate of decomposition and dissolution both of social régimes and of territorial States, and in some cases it completed the process. It rang the knell of the Habsburg monarchy, the last of the dynastic accumulations of countries and peoples; and by endangering the existence of old-established historical forms it put the States which embodied them through a severe test—a test which the Tsarist and Habsburg States and the Ottoman Empire failed to pass. As a constellating force in the post-war period, historical and racial particularism was quite as powerful as economic necessity; and the peoples of the former Habsburg monarchy seem to have felt simultaneously the attraction of the two great historical ethnic groups, Germanic and Slav. The attraction exercised in the 19th century by Russia upon the Slav nationalities of eastern Europe appeared to fail with the revolutionary political change in Russia; but it was in fact a relaxation and a 'repression', and not a failure of the attractive force. When the Russian power expanded again after the German defeat in the second world war, the attraction was revived and politically organised. But this movement was carried through hastily and by force, so its results may be as deceptive as the preceding indifference. Intervention by armed force achieves rapid conversions, whose only drawback is that they are liable to be reversed by the intervention of another armed force.

After 1919 a large number of authoritarian régimes came into being in Europe. The 'young Turk' revolution had seemed to conform to the general law of liberal and parliamentary progress characteristic of the period; but it ended by establishing Turkish society on an authoritarian basis, though with certain distinctive features and without the non-Turanian populations which fell away when the Ottoman Empire finally collapsed. East and south-east Europe were split in fragments in the name of the principle of nationality; and the fragments were new nations which could only hope to exist politically (not economically) in relative independence in times of peace. For they were incapable, if attacked from either side (and the more so if attacked from both simultaneously), of maintaining their new political forms unless supported unconditionally, and at the price of total mobilisation, by the great Western democracies. The reserves and hesitations of the West after the second world war precipitated these nations into the Russian orbit.

The various authoritarian States brought to birth by the first world war had in reality very little in common except authority. To describe them all indiscriminately as 'fascist', as liberal and socialist journalists too often did, was an error of judgment which has since had to be paid for. Alone of the new States, Czechoslovakia tended towards a democracy which conformed, *mutatis mutandis*, to the Western pattern. On the other hand, in the Balkan States the reigning monarchies were not challenged, in spite of the changes in landownership (the episode of King Carol's abdication did not put an end to monarchy in Rumania), and the new authoritarian tendency was expressed, in practice, in the reinforcement of the royal power. In the Poland of Pilsudski and the Lithuania of Valdemaras, which had barely regained or acquired a precarious national independence, the remedy for weakness was sought for in a stronger and more stringent executive power. Along the whole chain of new States stretching from north to south, from the Baltic to Hungary, between defeated Germany and bolshevik Russia, the executive (which practically displaced the legislature) was kept in a perpetual state of alert both by the fear of a return of Russian domination, in the aggravated form of bolshevism, and by pressure from the West. From the very first the machinations of communism were a major and unambiguous national peril for these States. And we have no need to call upon imagination to picture this peril, for memory should suffice. At the very most, then, we should call these States dictatorships; but we ought not to describe them as fascist, and still less as totalitarian. In the same way, it is a piece of mental laziness to call Primo de Rivera's régime in Spain a fascist one. All through the 19th century the anarchic Spanish impulse towards liberalism was counteracted by periods of authoritarian reaction. Moreover, the army in Spain is not an historic necessity as it is in France (Spain has not faced an external threat for more than a century), but is, on the contrary, a serious social problem; not being required for war, and being a more stable organisation than the political parties, it has been on several occasions a determining factor in Spanish internal politics.

But in the Italy of Mussolini we can clearly discern some of the specifically new features of the 20th-century type of absolutism—though here, too, they are qualified and combined with purely Italian characteristics. The real distinctive features of 20th-century absolutism are those common to Stalin's Russia and Hitler's Germany. But one may say that Italy proved her receptivity and historic inventiveness: she provided, as it were, a brilliant and spectacular dress-rehearsal of the phenomenon; and although it remained superficial because certain essential conditions were lacking, it established the *décor* of 20th-century tyranny. The talents of the new condottieri both as actors and as producers cannot be overrated; they launched a mode, and they remain unchallenged as masters of style and spectacle. Italian fascism is a sort of political Spring Fashion show.

* * * *

We have spoken of *tyranny*. Were we merely echoing a piece of liberal rhetoric learned at school, or were we making an accurate sociological observation? We propose to justify the second alternative.

Admittedly, the humanist tradition we have imbibed encourages us to call any power, against which we have or think we have a grievance, a tyranny. And in this sense one uses the words 'tyranny' and 'despotism' indifferently as style or euphony may require. Such was the practice of Etienne de la Boétie, and of the 18th-century *philosophes* (except Montesquieu, who was a sociologist). But it is possible to give each of these words a precise meaning, and for this we are indebted to the historians who, from the 19th century to the present day, have made it possible for us to be, or try to be, sociologists.

Here we must refer to certain fundamental data of political sociology and the theory of power. The earliest political powers, whose counterpart has been recognised among certain populations described as primitive, were exercised within a group which it is convenient and simple to call 'natural'—a group in which *blood ties*[1] determine those relationships of subordination which are the first image of what is going to be a political power. Blood is prior to soil, and the relationships within nomadic 'clans'[2] were determined in this way before they became attached to any particular soil. Such, in the earliest Hellenic civilisation, is the power of the *genos*, in which politics still partakes of the sacred. From this point of departure we may observe in the Near East two types of evolution. In the first, among certain nomadic peoples, there emerges and becomes established an aggregation or federation of tribes under a war chief; and this chief is soon the head of a warlike organisation capable of shattering empires with a long history of civilisation behind them. Once victory has been achieved, the next historic step is to found a territorial empire. We will take the empire of the Medes and Persians as a typical example of the territorial and seignorial empire. The political and warlike organisation of these aryan nomads was diluted and extended, as well as transformed, by their occupation of the countries previously subdued to the ancient Hittite, Mitanni, Assyrio-Babylonian, and later the Egyptian States. The lieuten-

[1] We will not enter here upon the complex problems of 'kinship'.

[2] For the sake of simplicity, we will not enlarge here upon the notion of 'clan'. For the purpose of our demonstration, it is only necessary that the proposition should not be untrue.

ants of the warrior chief, who now became the *Great King*, occupied and governed the various regions of the new empire; ruling them as satraps, they were responsible for their external defence and internal organisation. The authority of the *Great King* was in principle absolute, and was in practice subject to no limitations except those imposed by the physical nature of things. But the extent of the empire and the rudimentary means of communication, which made the transmission of orders slow and difficult, obliged the satraps and the local authorities generally to take on their own initiative decisions which might be of capital importance for the whole empire. Moreover, profiting by any reverses to the power of the Great King, the satraps tended to convert their satrapies into autonomous political units and thus establish a *de facto* independence. Such an empire may be called a *despotism*, because the authority of the Great King or Despot is without limits, in so far as nature and the force of things permit it to be really exercised. The major characteristics of such a despotism are that it is seignorial and territorial: seignorial because the satraps hold their power in virtue of their military functions, their position as lieutenants of a warrior chief, and because the power conferred on them is a total power over the entire life of a region. Territorial, because when an empire of this kind reaches the sea it meets problems which it cannot solve. The Persian Empire never overcame the Greek world, which barred its access to the sea, and the conflict with this world led to its ultimate downfall. It was a hellenised Macedonian king, with the flower of the Greek military world as his followers, who destroyed the Achæmenid empire. So this empire remained seignorial and territorial to the end. It never reached the stage of hegemony which later enabled the Roman empire to become the unifying force of a world or an entire sphere of civilisation, or, if it be preferred, of a *universal* empire or State. It appears, then, that the territorial character of the Achæmenid empire was a *handicap* to its aspirations for hegemony.

The Greek world, starting from the same point, presents a different type of evolution. In it, too, the groups within which the earliest forms of political power were prefigured were groups in which relations of subordination were determined by ties of blood.

We find 'kings', and some of them powerful, in the very earliest known periods of Hellenic history. There were as many as twelve in the little island of Ithaca.[1] Indeed, 'kings' seem to have been as common in the early Hellenic world as 'princes' in 19th-century Georgia. In the expedition against Troy, Agamemnon was 'king of the kings'; but as a warrior king he held this position only in time of war (and the Homeric poems make it clear that even so his authority often met with consider-

[1] cf. Homer's comparative and superlative: *βασιλεύτερος* and *βασιλεύτατος*.

able resistance). Moreover, in addition to being a military chief, the king of kings seems also to have been a high priest, a sort of king of the sacrifices, to use the later Roman term. More than one passage in the Homeric poems shows the king of kings as only *primus inter pares*, with no more than a preponderating voice. It was probably an alliance of γένη (clans) with a common military organisation for war, whether for the common defence or for a profitable foray. But the component elements retained a relative autonomy within the whole; so the secondary kings pursue their private quarrels and disputes about precedence and, in the Homeric poems, threaten on more than one occasion to withdraw from the enterprise. Then the Mycenæan civilisation, which saw the exploits of Achilles and Odysseus, was submerged under the Dorian invasions, and they in turn were followed by a 'middle age' which completed the cycle, as it had begun, with powerful γένη and private wars. These private wars, like those of the stormiest feudal periods of ancient China and Japan, or of the 'Rajput chivalry', or Europe's middle ages, were devastating. Whenever the perils of remote expeditions or the danger of invasion had been overcome, the knightly power resisted and repelled the power of the military and religious kings. This was possible because of the virtual absence of economic connections between the different domains within the kingdom, or more exactly because of their almost complete autarky. In Attica it was wars of this kind that the Draconian code was framed to abolish. It is impossible to accept unreservedly Marx's proposition that the history of mankind is the history of its class struggles. The fact is that the history of the Greek *polis* is at least equally the history of struggles within what Marxists would call a single class—and this is only one example among many that could be given. If we admit a continual 'vertical' struggle, latent except at times of crisis, between lower and upper classes, we must also recognise a '*horizontal' struggle between equals*; and we must admit that the history of mankind is as much the history of its clan struggles as of its class struggles.[1] (By 'clans' I mean here single collective units in horizontal strife; struggles between cities, between kingdoms, or between nations, are, *mutatis mutandis*, successive concrete instances of the same 'form'.[2])

[1] This error of Marx's might be called his 'Manchester' error. It explains his completely wrong, because incomplete, appreciation of the revolutionary movements of 1848.

[2] This is what Gustave Glotz says: 'The most powerful γένη tried to make their own tradition and their own interest prevail. They transferred their cult to the *demes* of the City and to the City itself; and they extorted from the City as well as from the *demes* the recognition of their hereditary right to their religious ministry. The petty disputes between neighbouring γένη grew into rivalries between two or three large γένη each commanding the support of a party, who fought one another for the government of Athens. *In the civil wars which were to take place, sometimes between different regions of Attica, sometimes between social classes, sometimes between political factions, we find again, as always, beneath the surface the struggle of clans*' (our italics) (*La Cité Grecque*; Paris, 1928).

The defeated in these private wars and clan struggles, reduced to poverty or slavery, finally strained to breaking point the political framework upon which the strength of the great γένη was based; and henceforward all progress in the art of war was accompanied by an increase of the *disinherited* class of unattached men.[1] This was how the two great powers without which the 'Greek miracle' could not have happened—money and spirit—emerged, as from the waves, and grew to greatness. Commerce and industry arose to stimulate exploration, and also the bold expeditions of Greek navigators in the tracks of the Phœnician traders. Deprived of a future on terra-firma, men took to the sea; deprived of land, they created mercantile wealth. A part, but only a part, of the landed nobility joined the movement; and in the maritime cities the established and increasing urban population of craftsmen and manual workers threatened and undermined the power of the γένη, from which they were practically emancipated. So the nobility was faced with an alliance between 'proletarians' and 'bourgeoisie'. But the urban population was too mixed (except perhaps, in some degree, at Athens) to be able to establish what was later called democracy. This struggle between the maritime and monied bourgeoisie and the land-owning and warlike nobility of the γένη was to last through two centuries, which were a period of social revolution. From it emerged the two new and specifically Greek political forms: tyranny and democracy—the latter usually turning into the former.

Tyranny appeared, between the 8th and 6th centuries B.C., in the great industrial and commercial cities of Æolia, Ionia, and the Archipelago. It spread from east to west, from the Asiatic coast and the islands to the continent of Europe; and Sicyon, Corinth, Megara, and Athens all knew tyranny in their turn.[2] In the Italy of the 12th to the 16th centuries, which offers, *mutatis mutandis*, another example of city rule, we see

[1] In Attica, the *thetes*.

[2] 'From the coasts of Asia Minor bordering upon opulent Lydia to the shores of Europe, from the gulf of Salonika to the gulf of Corinth, the list of tyrants corresponds, so to speak, to the list of great ports' (G. Glotz, *La Cité Grecque*; Paris, 1928).

When tyranny first appeared in their history, the Greeks conceived iti n the image of Oriental despotism (of which the Persian empire was in their eyes the eminent example). The word Turannos (which appears in lyric poetry) comes from the Lydian, and is a synonym for Δεσπότης. Like the thing itself, the word appears at the western periphery of Asia Minor. In the Greek world the word means: 'A chief who has risen to power by taking advantage of violent party strife' (cf. A. Dies' Introduction to Plato's *Republic*, coll. Guillaume Budé). The pejorative sense of the word seems to come from the oligarchs and their lyrical spokesmen, who knew the thing by experience. The evil associations of the word were revived by democrats for whom tyranny had smoothed the way to power. In the Western world the word 'republic' has had a comparable evolution, though in the opposite direction. The *sans-culottes* of the great French Revolution appealed to it, and also to Cato and Brutus, who used the word incessantly; but these modern 'republicans' completely misunderstood the true historic role and political position of those defeated Roman oligarchs.

tyrannies, side by side with 'democracies' and to the same extent as them, expressing a movement from below directed against the great landed and warlike families which still embodied in the pre-renaissance period the main features of the feudal age. And this movement added strength to a brilliant bourgeoisie of captains of industry and bankers. The same, or at least a similar, evolution of money fortunes, major and minor arts, and an urban populace, gave rise at the same time to 'tyrannies'[1] in northern Italy and to 'democracies' in central Italy; though these latter were extremely turbulent, and alternated between periods of plutocracy (the urban patricians continually absorbed the ancient nobility into their ranks) and popular movements. The history of Florence is a characteristic example. The same economic development gives rise in one historical context to tyranny and in another to democracy; and therefore the struggle between the new monied powers dependent on the sea (or at any rate upon the development of the means of communication) and the old land-owning oligarchies gave rise, according to the phases through which it passed, to one or other of the two types of régime, tyranny or democracy, which characterised the political age of the 'City State' both in Greece and in Italy. In both of these worlds there were frequent transitions within the cities from the one political form to the other.

In general, tyranny arose from the violence of class struggles; it appeared at the moment when the opposing factions in the city (both of them frequently enjoying foreign support) were on the one hand irreconcilable and on the other sufficiently strong and aggressive to make it impossible for the city to continue to be governed according to the forms and methods found suitable hitherto. At such crises the city is not so much a city as a battlefield; and civil war is confused and exacerbated by foreign war. At first the future tyrant was usually a member of one of the factions. (According to Plato (*Republic*, Book VIII), it is always the leader of the popular faction, the 'stinging drone', who becomes tyrant; a proposition which needs to be interpreted in the light of Plato's own circumstances and aims.) But this was not always the case. Quite frequently, indeed, the process of a tyrant's accession to power would begin with the exercise of a high magisterial function or a military command (the tyrant was often a member of the oligarchy, as also very often was the leader of the popular faction, whether or not he later became tyrant). Before Cæsar, these popular chiefs and tyrants were often drawn from the ranks of adventurers—younger sons, bastards, 'classless' men produced by the oligarchy itself (Catiline was the last example of the type)—and also from among the deserters from the

[1] As we shall see later, the 'signorias' of the 15th and 16th centuries are a more complicated case. We leave aside also the history of Venice, which is altogether special.

ranks which provided the natural leaders of the opposite faction (and Cæsar was the last example of this type). The tyrant sometimes had recourse to foreign aid, and he was invariably the leader of a troop largely composed of foreign mercenaries. Usually he possessed personal merit; his value was his own, and not entirely derived from his membership of a clan. It did not depend, or not exclusively, upon the ties of blood that linked him with other men. Sometimes, even, he was an *outsider* (a former slave) to whom the collapse of the old social framework offered the chance to play an historic role. So the tyrant was the leader of a predominantly mercenary armed force, which was equally detached from both the factions and equally ready, when the time was ripe, to intervene in its own interest against either of them; and the men of this troop had linked their destiny with their leader's. With tyranny and perhaps even more with democracy (which usually preceded it), there was born—and it was its first appearance in the Greek world—a power that was primarily, and properly speaking, *political*. It was sacrilegious from the point of view of the pre-existing power, being based solely upon material force.

Therefore, in the eyes of all who were attached, even unconsciously, to the ancient forms of the sacred, it appeared as a supremely impious usurpation. Since legitimacy in the cities of antiquity was derived from religion, the appearance and rise to power of the tyrant was an insult to the ancient divinities. And this is why, all over the Greek world, the tyrants often imported foreign gods into the cities they ruled. Certain agrarian cults were imported in this way, particularly that of Dionysos. These cults were available to all comers; and the purpose was to counteract the power of the city's ancient gods, which were those of the *γένη*. In the Greek world from the 8th to the 5th centuries B.C., the sacred source and religious justification of the oligarchic power of the *Eupatrides* was the 'possession of hereditary priesthood and celebration of traditional cults'.[1] It was therefore the aim of the tyrants of antiquity to *deconsecrate* the divinities which endorsed the nobles' power.

So tyrannical government is a synonym for usurpation and illegitimacy. (When democratic government was successful, it was because the cults of the city were able, after being separated from the *γένη*, to become a focus for general unanimity.) Of the absence of legitimacy the tyrants were the expression; their existence was the historical proof of it, but it was not their doing. The appearance of tyranny reveals that the old authority is dying or dead in the hearts of most men, and that henceforth it will hardly be possible to secure their obedience except by constraint, and then perhaps only temporarily.

The humanist tradition is more interested in individual types than in

[1] cf. G. Glotz, op. cit.

social facts,[1] and has therefore been satisfied to define tyranny as the arbitrary act of a single man, which is an incomplete definition. It is necessary here to indicate rapidly the social nature of this arbitrariness. Tyranny demonstrates that the city is divided; it is a phenomenon of social war. It indicates also that the specifically political State is emerging from the natural community founded upon blood and soil; it is a political power that tends to emancipate itself from the ancient concept of the sacred, and to resemble, more than the older power of the nobles did, the institution that we today call the *State*. Tyranny demonstrates with intolerable exaggeration, which has never been tolerated for long, that the State can be a form existing for its own sake, pursuing its own aims with reference to nothing beyond itself. But the State in this form, so far as it is identified with the personality of the tyrant, remains detached from society; and this fact is symbolised by the position of the acropolis, which overlooks and threatens the city. In this citadel, surrounded by his bodyguard composed largely of foreign mercenaries, sits the tyrant. He has 'cut off all the tallest heads', banished all those from whom he had anything to fear, especially the most powerful, popular, and noble of the oligarchs, and he has assured his hold over the rest of the oligarchy and the rest of the city by keeping hostages with him in the acropolis. This man, who has imposed himself by force of his own personal quality and ability, is history's instrument, so to speak, for the destruction of the older powers. Meanwhile, he will tolerate no armed factions, and he represses the very forces which helped him to power. He disarms the citizens, thus giving his armed guard of mercenaries the monopoly of armed force and, consequently, of repression. He identifies himself with none of the factions or classes whose struggles he turned to his own profit. No doubt he is unconscious of the historic role which, to our eyes, he is playing, and, in any case, he is not con-

[1] The humanist tradition, being essentially moralistic, approves of the 'portrait' of the tyrant given by Herodotus in his description of Otanes: 'irresponsibility, extravagance, envy and violence'. Ever since antiquity, it has contrasted with the tyrant the figure of the *heroic law-giver*, endowed more than the tyrant or the great demagogue with 'charismatic power', the founder (of society) and promulgator (of laws). The type of Solon.

From certain passages in his work it would appear that Nietzsche sometimes dreamed of a *social conqueror* of this kind.

Behind this legendary figure a real historical phenomenon can be discerned. In Asia Minor the function of the *ἀισυμνήτης*, which Aristotle saw as an 'elective tyranny', was of this kind. But it differed from tyranny in two major respects: it was a temporary power, and it was not imposed by force but was *solicited* by its subjects. It was conferred for the accomplishment of a definite task (promulgation of a constitution or ending of a troublesome litigation), or else for a limited period, such as ten years. The *aisymnete* was called in as an *expert* is called in today. These *arbitrators* were usually foreigners to the cities that profited from their political wisdom. (The function also existed in Italian city life.) Arbitration of this kind seems most often to have been solicited by 'sage' conservatives who wished reform rather than revolution. The *aisymnete* was invested with a mandate, and his quality as a foreigner constituted a presumption of impartiality.

cerned. Since his band is unconnected with the old factions and ready to act against any of them, he is in a position to switch his alliances whenever convenient for the purpose of maintaining and strengthening his power. One has only to read Guichardin to see how easily some of the Italian tyrants changed sides when it suited them. Between 1250 and 1264 Martin de la Torre, a nobleman at the head of the popular faction, founded the 'Milanese State'. To begin with he used the support of the 'popolani' against his own class; but later he won over the moderate nobles and the commercial bourgeoisie, and used his power against both the extreme parties. At Lodi, Como, Bergamo, Vercelli, and Novara 'centre parties' were formed, and adopted what we should today call an inter-urban organisation, grouped around the party of the most powerful city, Milan, which was Martin de la Torre's own party. We may call this, if we like, the triumph of business and the arts (or crafts) over feudalism; but it was also the State asserting itself against private interests. If the State is identified with the strongest party, this is, in a sense, quite against its will. By choice it would exist for itself alone; and wherever the State is found in history in its purest form, it can be said to be achieving this aim.

But their very tendency to become independent of the struggling factions and opposing social forces explains why the ancient tyrannies were short-lived. The same forces, whose assistance or benevolent neutrality or passivity had enabled the tyrant to overthrow the political monopoly of the old oligarchies, withdrew their support in the ensuing period when he became their oppressor. Tyranny became an obstacle to the 'productive forces' whose development it had originally favoured; for commerce and industry were very often hampered by the tyrant's propensity (frequently self-interested) towards regimentation. Moreover, the policies of town-planning and public works by which the tyrant recommended himself to the citizens were not sufficient to incorporate the tyrant himself effectively into the life of the city. Therefore one may say that the ancient tyrants—except those few who reacted towards oligarchy (for there were some who did this, and they resorted no less than the others to banishments and expropriations)—fulfilled the historic mission (to use the language of Marxism, though without any mystical reference) of expropriating the great territorial domains which were the basis of the aristocratic power of the γένη. In this sense the appearance of tyranny, which, we must emphasise, was often preceded by an experiment in democracy (Athens is the most famous example), is a symptom of what would be called, *mutatis mutandis*, in Marxist terms, a bourgeois revolution. More precisely, tyranny is the first phase of such a revolution—a passing phase in which many of the characteristics of the previous period are only repressed but not eradicated. The beliefs that prevailed during the supremacy of the *γένη* are still powerful in the city. The tyrant only holds his position *de facto*. He has suspended the laws which obstructed him, and has been prodigal of festivities and holidays in order to ingratiate himself with the lower classes; but his power is based upon a relation of opposing forces, and since his own success has disturbed that relation, a new relation is tending to establish itself which works to the detriment of the tyranny. The rising plutocracy and the small men could tolerate the tyrant only as a champion against the powerful oligarchy; and when he begins to limit the profits of industry and commerce and to control the banks, in his own interests and in those of a power external to society itself, then the alliance of the bourgeoisie and the small men, when it can be formed, will work against the tyranny—and the remnants of the old oligarchy will do nothing to defend it. A more democratic régime is then called for in the name of the 'development of productive forces'; and the more so because the tyrant sometimes strikes at the oligarchy by substituting territorial groups for the hereditary clans, thus creating the necessary foundation for democracy. The plebs of artisans and manual workers which composes the urban groups, being detached from the *γένη*, becomes very susceptible to the seductions of money, so that the commercial bourgeoisie is able by means of electoral largesse to establish a certain number of 'democratic régimes'. The same considerations which explain the ephemeral character of the Greek tyrannies of the 5th century B.C. also explain the rise, in 15th- and 16th-century Italy, of the atypical and specifically Italian tyrannies described as 'signorias'. With these signorias Italy left the régime of the City-States behind. A signoria was composed of several cities grouped around a chief city, which the others had been compelled, by a mixture of ruse and force, to accept as their protector. Owing to the violent particularism of the different cities of which this essentially unstable State was composed, and also to the complex vicissitudes of factional strife, the sovereign and his signoria were in the position of arbitrators. They relied upon a mercenary armed force, for the experiment of civic militias, upon which Machiavelli set so much store, had come to nothing. Thus it was possible for the sovereign successively to pacify the different warring sections by the alternating use of force and diplomacy. And what, meanwhile, would be the attitude of the city patricians and the middle-class bourgeoisie? Having overthrown and absorbed the feudal nobility and achieved and taken advantage of a great opportunity for economic advance, they would leave the sovereign *to govern in his own way*.[1] This

[1] This clearly suggests that no group is essentially predisposed, except as moved by interest, towards any particular political form—the only exception, if indeed it be one, is a religious faith.

was how the Visconti were able to found their State at Milan; and the Medici took advantage in the same way of the vicissitudes of Florentine factional strife in the early 16th century. From the end of the 15th century the foreign danger was increased by the addition to the 'imperial' enemy of French and Spanish 'barbarians', and this played into the hands of the perpetrators of these partial and artificial unifications around which Italian political life was constellated. Politically, Italy remained dormant within these forms right up to the French revolution. Just as the Persian menace, which evoked and stimulated the efforts of the Greeks to ally and federate themselves, was not sufficient to overcome the particularism of the cities and produce a united Greece, so in Italy too the unification of the whole country was never achieved. Thus everything worked to the advantage of the signorias, *no matter what the political origin and social backing of the signori might be*, and no matter how often they changed their colours in the course of their struggle, in order to carve out for themselves a principality.

So tyranny, as a particular configuration and type of political phenomenon, appears as a function of the relation between antagonistic powers, or of the fact that no one power or coalition of powers can dominate the others sufficiently to re-establish normal political and social life—or, more exactly, to establish a way of life that can be called peace rather than war. In such a case, one of the two powers (for the sake of a clear example we reduce the problem to its simplest form, to a sort of 'elementary case') must develop a coercive apparatus to restrain the other; and when this coercive apparatus begins to become an end in itself and to develop on its own account and acquire a sort of existence for its own sake, it will be able to maintain itself at the expense first of one power and then of the other, or to treat both of them with contempt. But it finally collapses because it has 'cut itself off' from society, when its only chance of acquiring permanent historical existence would have been to become the interpreter of a new form of society. Sometimes tyranny had reached such a point, and the tyrannical State had become so detached from society, that the breach was complete; the tyrant was able to hold every antagonistic force at bay and to reduce everything to the same level. But the history of the Greek cities from the 8th to the 5th centuries B.C., and also that of the Italian cities, proves that tyranny cannot long maintain itself at this pitch.

Of tyranny as defined by certain traits to which we shall return, of tyranny as a political form and specific phenomenon recognisable in different periods of history, of tyranny as a type and general pattern or, in short, as an essential element in a sociological reading of history, we may say that *it makes no difference from what kind of social force it takes its origin*.

In Plato's theory (*Republic*, Book VIII) tyranny follows democracy; but in Greek history tyranny more often preceded democracy. However, the contradiction is not so great as it appears. Tyranny is generally found between two differing forms of régime, and it may mark the violent transition from the one to the other. It abolishes or suspends the earlier legitimacy, and is a proof of the existence of a subversive social movement. It may be itself a product of this movement, or it may be a reaction against it; but in either case it represents the diversion of this movement to purposes which are not, or are not directly, relevant to its deepest motives. (This is an example of what Vico calls a 'trick of providence' and Hegel a 'trick of reason': namely, the dialectic by which men are involved in doing what they do not mean to do or do not know they are doing.) Tyranny exists in fact when a group, or party, or man —and the three cases are not so different in practice as in theory—has attained certain major objectives without which no tyranny can be efficient, and especially the monopoly of armed force, which means the power of effective coercion. There is tyranny whenever a relation of forces, which was established because a group or a man seized a favourable opportunity, is able to be maintained only by constraint and violence and terror when once the favourable situation has passed away. So it follows that tyranny is a phenomenon which reveals a certain relation of forces, of which it is itself a function, irrespective of the nature of the forces concerned and of the values they represent for their friends or foes. Therefore, *tyranny may be the symptom of very different kinds of historic change, just as fever is a symptom of very different diseases.*

* * * *

The study of the relation of forces and the relation of the tyrannical authority to their interplay has enabled us, by tracing the features common to the Greek and Italian tyrannies, to discover a *general pattern* of the phenomenon of tyranny. We must now ask whether this type is found only within the City-State which, in one form or other, was the milieu of both the Greek and the Italian tyrannies, or is it general and are our observations valid for other political spheres as well? We believe that they are, and we will now attempt to justify this belief.

Their remoteness in time has enabled us to draw a simple picture of the ancient tyrannies in the fewest possible lines. The societies of Greece and Italy were simpler than our own, and thus they offer less interference to a clear view of the picture. By contrast, the 20th-century societies, in which a *new absolutism* has appeared, are like complex figures composed of an indefinite number of simple figures—of which the general pattern of tyranny as we have found it in the Greek and

Italian cities is one. If we first isolate this pattern in our mind and then reinsert it within the more complicated pattern with which it is combined in the 20th-century absolutisms, we shall be able to distinguish how far the simple pattern can explain and throw light upon the more complex 20th-century pattern and how far it fails to do so. The difference, both in degree of complexity and in scale, between the ancient tyrannies and the modern absolutisms may be compared to the difference between classical and modern military campaigns, which are also differences in complexity and scale. But students of strategy have been able, in spite of these differences, to establish a certain number of typical data for all possible military engagements and to recognise these data, *mutatis mutandis*, at a distance of thousands of years. The value of x may vary, but the concept x is always possible and always functionally useful. But the two cases are not analogous and can only be roughly compared. The Greek and Italian cities must not be thought of as perfect microcosms, or test-tubes containing a chemically pure specimen reduced to essentials and hermetically sealed against external interference. Nevertheless, it remains true that the relative economic independence of each collectivity, its much more clearly defined contours, and the smaller number of elements involved, which makes it much easier to reduce the phenomenon to essentials, do give us a sort of microscopic view of these ancient societies. We see them isolated and enlarged.

The ancients defined tyranny by opposition to law. For them, tyranny was synonymous with illegitimacy because the law rested upon *sacred* foundations. The tyrant was without the law, and therefore did not and could not rely upon any law to protect him, but only upon force. The old oligarchic power rested on belief and cult and priesthood; and the democratic power, in its pure form, and despite the abuses of every kind that are interwoven with the actual history of democracy, rests upon the two foundations of the people and the law—*Demos* and *Nomos*—neither of which is anything apart from the other. If they are not brought to accord, or if they fall apart, then Demos without Nomos will produce anarchy, followed by tyranny—and this inevitably brings foreign intervention which endangers the independence and even the historical existence of the *Polis*; or alternatively Nomos without Demos will produce oligarchy. In this case, as in ancient Rome before the laws were published, the reading and interpretation of the law will be a privilege of the few, and *the others* will be mere objects upon whom the law acts from the outside. The Greek tyrants, as a matter of fact, usually paid little attention to the laws; they simply suspended them in so far as their application or execution was inconvenient to the tyranny. The law is an inadequate protection for the subject in times of tyranny, just as the civil laws are inadequate in war-time today, for tyranny is a state of emergency. Tyranny can afford to let law exist because it simply ignores it and refuses to be influenced by it in any way. In general, tyranny tends to pay no attention to things that offer no concrete obstacle to its actions. But it cannot tolerate the unconditional, and therefore it always comes into conflict with the sacred. From this point of view, the opposition between tyranny and law is a particular case of the general conflict between tyranny and the sacred. Tyranny is sacrilege. The tyrants of antiquity put their enemies to death within the walls of sacred buildings, just as modern absolutism scoffs at the 'rights of man' and uses torture, when it serves its purpose, or violates human personality. For tyranny knows no restraints; it goes to the limit of its power, and one must never expect it to refrain from doing anything it has the strength and the opportunity to do. It knows no 'invisible obstacles'.[1] To have any scruples of any kind whatsoever is to be, by definition, at a disadvantage in fighting against a tyranny. The failure of the law of succession in tyrannies (and also in despotisms, in so far as they were arbitrary) is like a revenge taken upon them by the law they have insulted. In the Western monarchies authority was tempered in fact by usage, custom, and religion; which is a way of saying that the State took account of society and appeared as a sort of organic development from society. The Western monarchies that arose out of feudalism do not deserve the reproaches of despotism and tyranny[2] hurled at them, in the borrowed language of classical rhetoric, by the 18th-century pamphleteers. The mere fact that they could call Louis XV a despot and a tyrant without running any great risk is a proof that he was nothing of the sort. Voltaire and Rousseau could declaim against the despotism of the *ancien régime* precisely because it was not despotic but was, on the contrary, an enfeebled régime which it was pretty safe to attack. But it was much more dangerous to attack the Convention, and the government of Napoleon I does exhibit the features of tyranny—though very mild compared with the 20th-century totalitarian absolutism. The Napoleonic régime can be seen as a precursor; the strict regimentation of public education, the transfer of all administrative power to the central authorities (mayors, as well as prefects, being appointed from above), the mass levies, the mobilisation of the whole population for war, the Cæsarian interpretation of the Concordat, and the conscription of seminarists—by all these measures

[1] In general, tyranny recognises no human solidarity, no common conscience, between itself and its victims. When Gandhi went on hunger strike, there was an unwritten agreement between English society and himself. Under a tyrannic régime he would have died of hunger the first time he did it, and the world would never have heard of him.

[2] Except the Spanish and French absolutisms of Philip II and Louis XIV; and even these were much less absolute than the totalitarian régimes of the 20th century.

the successor of the Jacobins reveals himself as the precursor of the totalitarians.

Tyranny does no more than *strengthen* the element of coercion that is inherent in every kind of social organisation. It strengthens it to the point where the relation between ruler and ruled is the same as that between master and slave[1]: the ruled is at the ruler's mercy. The power of the State is manifested in the monopoly of armed force; and in tyranny the armed force treats the population as an enemy. (The development of the specific organism of the police is simply the specialisation, in the armed force, of a tissue adapted for the internal struggle against the civil population.)

In tyrannies, this armed force cannot confine itself to the rigorous punishment of actions; it deals equally severely with words—and even with words which are not known with certainty to have been spoken. It is sufficient that a 'competent authority' believes that they were spoken or that they might have been. Having postulated a hostile intent in the suspect's mind, authority then proceeds to prosecute this intent as criminal. But the hostile intent is merely a projection of the tyrannical authority's own knowledge of the precariousness and unpopularity of its power. It objectifies the threat to its power by localising it in individuals and groups, trying in this way to 'fix' it and so get rid of it. But the relief afforded by such operations is short-lived, and they must be repeated incessantly. A thought may be regarded as a potential act. And from a spoken word a thought may be deduced. But one may also deduce a thought from one's own interpretation of the spoken word, or even from a man's silence when he could have spoken. And again, it is always possible to suspect that the word actually spoken was false; in which case vigilant tyranny will feel justified in substituting a word of contrary meaning. And the contrary meaning is criminal. So everything always points to crime and calls for the appropriate punishment.

Let us confine ourselves to the case of actual spoken words. An opinion once expressed propagates itself, for opinions are contagious; and this is already one reason for prosecuting the spoken, or written, word. Further: openly to criticise a tyrannical government is virtually to conspire against it. And if it be objected that words are only words, the answer will be that the speaker has used words only because he is *unable*—in present circumstances—to do anything more. But tomorrow the circumstances may change. Either the foreign menace or the internal crisis, or both together, may come to a head; and the man who today can only talk will then be able to do something more. So, in view of this possibility, which may easily materialise, the world being what it is, would it not be better here and now to put this potential enemy out of

[1] This is not a Hegelian echo. I am using the words in their plain sense.

the way of being able to do any harm? There is a sort of 'unwritten law of suspects' inherent by definition in every tyranny. A law which is the antithesis of law, because it is impossible to codify; nevertheless, it overrides all codes. A law of suspects and a dialectic of suspicion. The social bond, which is the pre-eminent fact of society, includes a certain minimum of confidence, prior to all the reasons which may later be adduced to justify or invalidate this confidence. It is like the confidence which a sane man places in his own thought. Such a man, even if his critical faculty is highly developed, would still be *able* to doubt many more things than he actually does doubt. Whereas the 'doubter' (in the psychiatrical sense of the word) must always make everything certain by reason; he has lost that minimum of confidence in his own thought which everyone possesses who is able, like Descartes, to doubt because he has previously made up his mind to do so. The tyrannical government is a 'doubting' government, and exhibits on a vast scale symptoms comparable to those of pathological jealousy; it reads into the actions and behaviour of individuals the proofs of conspiracy or, at the very least, of hostility; and against the supposed conspiracy, and even the potential conspiracy it sees in hostility, it takes preventive action. Both in individuals and in governments pathological suspicions are a sign that those who entertain them are conscious of their own weakness. And in tyrannical régimes, just as the government suspects its subjects, so every subject suspects the others—either of conspiring themselves or else of intending to denounce him for conspiracy. There is a general suspicion of all by all. One anticipates a possible denunciation by denouncing one's future or potential denouncer, and so on . . . and the tyranny sifts all these denunciations according to its suspicions and fears of the moment. Tyrannical fear is like an epidemic: the government fears its subjects and the subjects fear one another and the government as well, and the preventive actions taken by all against the dangers suggested to them by their fears will finally culminate in a terror. Aware that it rules by force, tyranny suspects any loyalty it receives of being an unwilling loyalty, and therefore it takes further precautions against the state of mind revealed by the unwillingness of this loyalty. Such is the dialectical movement by which tyranny grows more tyrannical.

CHAPTER 12

Twentieth-century Absolutism

ON the spiritual plane, the new absolutism of the 20th century is religion; on the temporal plane it is militant imperialism. Within its empire it concentrates power and rejects the liberal forms of government whose growth and extension were characteristic features of the 19th century. It is both an '*Islam*' and a *tyranny*; '*Islam*' being taken to mean the union of a religion and people for the purpose of conquest (the chiefs of this people tending to wield power beyond its frontiers by means of the religion), and *tyranny* meaning a régime in which a victory in factional strife is consolidated and ensured, by an apparatus of power and social coercion, against the fickleness of history and changing circumstances.

The very nature and actions of a tyrannical régime reveal its fear of the forces which it has defeated and upon whose defeat it is founded. Its recognition of the power of these forces is proved by the fact that it is a régime of war against them; it goes on fighting them and carries the fight even into the psyche of the people. The very structure of the régime reveals a fundamental *self-distrust*, which can be observed—with differences of scale—in the Greek tyrannies of the 8th to the 5th centuries B.C., in the Italian tyrannies of the 13th to the 16th centuries, and in the great absolutisms of the 20th century (the Russian and Nazi régimes). Tyranny is essentially no more than an accomplished fact; an illegitimate absolutism, and the more absolute because it is illegitimate. It may make its own claim to the sacred, but it will be a *new* sacred and, in the first instance, opposed to the old[1] (as when the ancient tyrants introduced new cults, especially the Dionysiac, in place of those of the γένη). The only legitimacy a tyranny can claim lies entirely in the future, instead of the past. It is a legitimacy that only time can confirm; and this makes a radical distinction between tyranny and any legitimate government. (Even the most absolute of legitimate governments is not so absolute as a tyranny.)

We have also defined one characteristic variety of absolute government, namely despotism—a territorial and seignorial empire established by conquest, comprising a number of different peoples and dominated

[1] In due course there will be cases of syncretism.

by a *de facto* élite which possesses very wide powers and has, in fact, the complete disposal of the populations under its authority. These powers take very different forms in such different despotisms as the Persian, Ottoman, Tsarist, and Soviet empires; and it is by the quantity of power at the disposal of the *de facto* élite that they are comparable with one another, and not by the form it takes. It may be based on land-ownership or, as in contemporary Russia, upon *possessio* distributed in various forms among all the members of the élite. (The policy and control of distribution is in the hands of this élite, though there is no personal ownership of landed property.) In this sense, and with this difference of content, one of the major traits of the soviet empire may be described as *seignorial*. Another trait of despotism, as we define it, is that it is a territorial power. But its ambition is to be something much more than this; it aspires to become a Universal State, which means (among other things) being a maritime as well as a territorial empire; in fact a world empire, as the Roman empire was. In its evolution towards a Universal State, the territorial despotism becomes painfully aware of its limitations, and therefore of what it, in fact, is and of what it would have to become in order to achieve universality. The Persian despotism broke itself against the Greek world, which was essentially a world of sea-board and islands. It could not absorb this world, as it would have had to do in order to become universal. It failed at the historic test because it could not combine the maritime with the territorial character; and in our day this has so far been a stumbling-block to Russia, which remains, very much against its will, a continental and territorial power. It seeks to absorb those sea-board worlds—western Europe on one side and the littoral of China and eastern and south-eastern Asia on the other—which confine it within its territorial bounds. The Persian empire resorted to the two classic devices of military adventure and corruption. (The word 'daric' became a by-word throughout the Greek world, from the circulation of a gold coin stamped with the image of Darius Codoman. It was referred to in much the same way as the 'Cavalerie de St. Georges'[1] in France during the Revolution and the Empire.) There is no reason to attribute to Soviet Russia (or to Hitler's Germany) any objection in principle to the use of either of these methods, but their efficacy is greatly increased when combined with a third: the systematic exploitation, beyond the frontiers of the empire, of the secular religion which is the spiritual aspect of every militant 'Islam'.

In terms of these definitions the Russian empire today is, at one and the same time: a *tyranny* (an internal régime imposed by a minority upon the majority, intended to maintain and strengthen by coercion a

[1] Money supposed to be used for subversive purposes in France by the English secret service [*translators' note*].

success which the minority has won thanks to a favourable conjunction of circumstances), a *despotism* (seignorial and territorial), and an '*Islam*' (the militant alliance of a people and group of peoples on the one hand and a secular and missionary religion on the other). Those who work, beyond the frontiers, for the triumph of this active alliance of an empire with a secular religion may be regarded as a *diaspora*; by contrast with the faithful who are *concentrated* within the State where the secular religion is supreme, their most immediately obvious characteristic is that they are *dispersed*—as the word *diaspora* exactly conveys. They are attached to the centre of the Empire rather as pious Jews throughout the Mediterranean basin were attached to the temple of Jerusalem, and they have something that corresponds to a holy city such as Mecca was for Islam. The Empire is entirely dedicated to the religion's triumph and the religion to the Empire's. And the heads of both are the same, which is the characteristic 'Islamic' feature of the system.

Hitlerism also was the combination of a secular religion and a temporal power. The national-socialist party imposed itself upon the other forces in Germany—army and junkers, industrial and liberal bourgeoisie, workers and intellectuals organised in the communist and socialist parties, and liberal republican associations—but the leaders of the régime knew that the most they could hope for from all these forces which they had broken or restrained was a passive acceptance. Therefore this inquisitorial police régime remained consistently tyrannical, and war could only make it more so. The secular religion associated with this tyranny—unlike the 'socialism' that became 'communism', which possessed and retained a rigid dogmatic framework—had not acquired stability and was still in process of formation. In so far as it had a system, it was the paranoiac systematisation of the themes of political 'activism'. The mainspring of the system is clearly passion, obsession, and hysteria; and its ideological justifications are quite perfunctory. The 'mythical content' is governed by the fixed ideas of 'encirclement' and 'aggression',[1] as in certain persecution manias. Both within and outside the régime resentment is projected, focused and fixed upon devils and bogy-men; and the images thus formed of the 'Jew', the 'Anglo-Saxon capitalist', or the Frenchman can fairly be described as 'collective paranoia'. Hitlerism organises and activates themes that existed before it, and although the whole system remains unstable it possesses among its fluctuating characteristics certain others that can be 'fixed': a sort of zoological materialism and doctrine of pre-

[1] The communist and the national-socialist secular religions have several traits in common. One of the most striking is the 'obsidional' complex. The more they expand, the more they feel themselves encircled. They are incessantly organising a 'defence' which tends by its very nature to become aggression.

destination, linked to a *praxis*. This doctrine asserts the pre-eminence of a certain race and, within that race, of a 'chosen people'; and in conformity with these premises it calls for a hierarchically organised world. Hitlerism suffered eminently from the typical vice of secular religions: the lack of transcendence. Its exclusive faith in immanence condemned it to a sort of positivism, which led it to appeal to fact as the supreme test and arbiter—and the verdict went against it. An essential difference between Hitlerism and the communist secular religion is its *promotion of the irrational*. It thus deprived itself of one of the best defences and principal consolations enjoyed by its rival secular religion. Communists can admit a defeat, even a very serious one, and yet communism as such will survive. For the communist believer thinks his doctrine, as a system of dogmas, is rational; and the rational, in his opinion, is an anticipation of the real. Therefore the irrational element in the world must be progressively reduced *until the rational and the real are completely and finally equated*. This conception eliminates time and is strictly eschatological. It leads to the 'realisation' of philosophy and the 'end of human prehistory'.

German national socialism, like communism, combined a political tyranny, an 'Islam', and a doctrine of predestination. But the Hitlerian predestination was such as theoretically to repel the assistance of all those whom it classes as 'naturally inferior', and the more so because the proclaimed purpose of its activity was to inscribe its dogma for thousands of years in history and in the flesh of humanity. In Marxism it is at least possible for the individual to adhere to the chosen class; but there is no such possibility in the other secular religion. The individual's social status and his chances of improving it are defined in advance by his biological structure. No doubt the belief of some of the Nazi leaders in these still fluid and inchoate dogmas was a different thing from the 'iron' faith of Lenin and Trotsky in Marxism. But the dogmas uplifted them, and when a certain pitch of emotional fervour had been reached they were swept off their feet by fantasies they could not control. The behaviour of some of them at the Nuremburg trial rather resembled that of men just awoken from a somnambulistic trance. In the days of victory it had seemed possible that the Nazi dogmas would be confirmed by the future and would materialise into a caste system; and this prospect was like a threat and a challenge to every variety of the human species, for it defied them to prove that they were not inferior. But the Hitlerian irrationalism acknowledged the jurisdiction of the crudest fact, and had consequently admitted in advance the legitimacy of the verdict that would condemn it. It is true, however, that there was another alternative: if Hitlerism had triumphed the dogmas might have become obsolete or attenuated, for they were still unformed. And this is what the 'collaborators' tried to believe when they found themselves inwardly revolted by the dogmas.

The historical crisis for which the modern tyrannies are a provisional solution is another point of resemblance between them and the ancient tyrannies. The characteristics of tyranny appear when the victorious group possessing the monopoly of armed force is aware that the rest of society, which it now dominates, does not *accept* it. So, instead of coming to an end with the victory of the successful group, the state of war continues. Such is the historical paradox of tyranny. But as there is in fact no enemy, because there is not and cannot be any armed resistance, military war is replaced by a sort of hidden war—and the presence of this war can be detected, in the 20th-century absolutisms, in the incessant activity and the growth and development of the police, which is the State's specialised organ for making war upon its own people. In the ancient tyrannies the phenomenon is much simpler and therefore even more distinct. There is one and the same armed force for operations abroad and within the city. The tyrant's mercenary guard combines the functions of police and army. In the contemporary absolutisms, the picture is much more complicated but still recognisable.

One may usefully compare the crises in ancient and modern times to which tyranny came to put an end and offer a provisional solution. In both alike there is a social order as it were in abeyance, and seeming to survive posthumously as a static negation of dynamic reality. Along the eastern coasts of the Mediterranean the period from the 8th to the 5th centuries B.C. was one of social crisis. A floating and unattached mass of men, continually increasing, lived outside the bounds of the *γένη*, which had provided the original social structure of the cities. Society was breaking out of its social frame; the content overflowed the form. Commercial and maritime progress created new powers which had no place in the old order, and the mere fact of their power showed that the form of society was no longer adequate to its content. The same thing happened in France at the end of the 18th century; the political structure of the *ancien régime* was still formally regulated by a social hierarchy which no longer reflected the social weight and potentialities of the various classes. The 'advance guard' of the Third Estate, which has been described as the bourgeoisie (though the term is only applicable when certain historical distinctions have been made), attempted to equate the form of society with its content, which meant: to free itself from the influences that opposed its 'dynamism'. So the breaking down of the social orders and estates began; and the bourgeoisie, freed from the restraints which the historical form of the old order had imposed upon its dynamism, accelerated the rhythm of this departitioning of society. The suppression of the guilds gave a new impulse to industry just at the moment when important technical inventions were going to make a great advance possible. And this great advance, known as the 'industrial revolution' of the 19th century, the matrix of our contemporary life, intensified and accelerated the process of social departitioning. Then a part of the rural world was uprooted and became mobile. Men left the country and crowded into new towns or the suburbs of old cities, abandoning their old social status without becoming reintegrated into society. Their situation resembles that of the Attic *thetes* and the corresponding classes that existed contemporaneously throughout the Greek world. These men had no longer, in the 18th-century sense of the word, a 'condition'; and their new condition was that of proletarians. The word 'proletariat', which is borrowed from the ancient world, described originally what it still describes: a group of men whose place in society is one to which no corresponding 'condition' attaches. The ancient proletariat was composed of the vanquished, both foreign and native, prisoners of war, and former free peasants reduced to slavery for debt or to a precarious vagabond existence. Since the new maritime prosperity offered a solution for some of them, they crowded into the new or reviving sea-ports and provided the human raw material for Mediterranean commerce and piracy (the two were not at first entirely distinguishable, and many intermediate forms have since been known). This class provided the artisans of the new crafts, the mercenary soldiers of the tyrants, and the sailors and needy populace of the great ports. In antiquity, as in modern times, we find the breaking down of social partitions and a sudden expansion of the methods of production and exchange and communication. In his *Capital* Marx described 'primitive capitalist accumulation' and the formation of the 19th-century proletariat; but one effect of the tremendous process escaped him—an effect of which we today are particularly aware: the appearance of those so-called *mass* phenomena which, it so happens, have been responsible among other things for the transformation of Marxism itself into a religion. These phenomena to some extent invalidate the strict application of Marx's and Engel's historical materialism, for *mass phenomena distort class phenomena.*

The society of estates had held its human particles in a state of cohesion; but once the partitions were down the liberated particles became exposed to currents which bore them in various directions and tended to regroup them. These were affective movements; they belonged to what historical materialism calls the superstructure. In the 19th century they were essentially either 'national' or 'social' movements, and Marx had eyes only for the latter. In the light of the dogma which he affirmed and succeeded in imposing, it was the social movements which appeared 'in the last analysis' the more important. National movements, according to this theory, were a survival, and the future was with the 'denationalising' social movements.

The patterns into which men grouped themselves would change or be changed, and be replaced by new ones; and new poles of attraction would be formed. The new social situation appeared, by comparison with the old, as an unstable one; it was traversed by currents and lines of force to which human beings adhered like iron filings. The lines of force were short-lived but recurrent, and certain major tendencies remained constant. National and racial particularisms, for example, reached their full force in the 19th century. It was not essentially, or even at all, around a dynasty that the 19th-century patriots would rally; it was rather, so to speak, around their own particularity, or characteristic difference, which had become sensitively aware of itself through being subordinated to a foreign particularity. Thus it was that the Germans became conscious of their own particularity through its 'oppression' by Napoleon and the French. And the same phenomenon occurred in other countries at this time and later. In Germany it next took the form of resentment against the princes, who impeded the realisation of Germany's uniqueness as a whole, as a particular phenomenon different from any other in the world. So in Germany it was a factor making for unification. But in the dynastic and multi-national empire of the Habsburgs it worked in the opposite sense. Each of the component peoples of this empire aspired to exist on its own account and not for the sake of the 'dominant people' or, if it be preferred, the people to which the Emperor himself belonged. (Germany was unified for the sake of the 'German people'; whereas the national unity of Hungary and Bohemia was asserted against that same people.) The 'awakening' in Greece, the Balkans, and the Danube countries tended, on the same so-called national principle, to disintegrate both the Habsburg and the Ottoman empires. The most obvious of what are called national particularities is the consciousness of participation in a common historical past or, more exactly, the belief that such a common past existed; and whatever the true facts about the past may be, the members of national movements feel this sense of community in the present as an insistent spur to action. The role played by poets, writers, and historians in developing this kind of national consciousness is well known.

In the 19th century there was, in fact, an interconnection between social movements, or movements resulting from the breakdown of the estates and orders, and the national movements; an interconnection, one might say, between vertical and horizontal movements. There is a sense in which the social movements were also particularist, for those who found themselves reduced by the industrial revolution to identical conditions of life became aware of this community of condition as *against* those who had a different way of life. In several countries the common conditions experienced by men of different nationalities had the effect of uniting them together as a single proletariat. Already in the middle of the 19th century Marx was forcibly struck by two tendencies that worked against the division of the world into separate States and peoples: the pressure of capitalism from above, which tended towards concentration and monopoly, and an answering pressure of the proletariat from below, which tended to impose homogeneity upon an ever-increasing section of humanity. Since the proletariat was produced by the development and concentration of capitalism, the end of the process should be the complete internationalisation of the world. Capitalism, becoming concentrated on a world scale, would override the boundaries of States and nations, while the proletarianisation of the middle classes would transform an ever-increasing number of men into proletarians without a country.

But that is not what happened. All through the 19th century the impulse to associate was exposed to the contrary attractions of social and national influences; and the resulting movement was always an original historical evolution in which both a national and a social factor could be discerned. Instead of a uniform development, of mathematical or scientific regularity, there were a number of movements—each with its own specific and complex character. It looked as though men were seeking for some new principle of association—having lost the principles afforded by the *ancien régime*, by the society of estates and orders, and also, to some extent, by religion—and as though their indecision, under the influence of rival solicitations, was expressed in these complex and fluctuating movements. Proletarianisation involved, to a great extent, dechristianisation; and a similar process, which had commenced with the 18th-century philosophy of enlightenment, was taking place, though with intermittent periods of 'reaction', among the cultured classes.

Within the old society there were small societies, each of which had a place of its own; but when the old order broke down, the human monads which composed the smaller societies were thrown together. The social landscape, instead of being divided into clearly defined scenes, became shapeless and fluid. In a continual agitation, like brownian movement, the animated outlines flowed together before they could define any clear picture, and the new scenery constantly in process of formation seemed to be in a perpetual state of flux. In the midst of all this, social mobility became much greater than in the preceding period and the circulation of the élites more rapid. Social mobility and complexity were favoured by the preponderance of the industrialists, merchants, and financiers, and of the group to which, for want of a better word, we must refer here as the 'intellectuals' (in 19th-century France they were principally the members of the liberal professions, teachers, scientists, and writers). The livelihood of all these men depended upon the mobility and exchange of goods, upon monetary and fiduciary symbols, and upon concepts, words, and combinations of words. Such were the social categories that now rose to the surface of society or appeared, as we say, in the forefront of the historical scene. But in the depths below the surface the elements set in motion by the breakdown of the old order, the industrial revolution, and the appeal of rising capitalism to fortune-seekers,[1] were charged with a variety of currents. The Western societies became unstable to a high degree—as is clearly seen in the European political revolutions and in the nationalist agitation which mobilised the patriots of Germany, central Europe, and the Balkans, both within and outside the frontiers of their oppressed countries, from the North Sea to the Black Sea and from the Rhine to the Ægean. The Russian empire championed nationality outside its own frontiers (the Danubian principalities and the North and South Slavs) while oppressing it within them (Finland, the Baltic states, Poland).

The stable social forms of the *ancien régime* gave place in the 19th century to an amorphous mobility which seems to represent an experimental groping for new forms and new principles of association. Human monads are mobilised, in the literal sense of the word, and set in activity by diverse currents which produce diverse and temporary regroupings. The whole of Western society, activated by these divergent currents, seems to be groping tentatively towards equilibrium. The phenomenon of the *crowd* (a momentary congregation of human particles betokening a state of agitation) occurs much more often in the 19th century than in the 18th ; and when this phenomenon becomes endemic within a society it proves the society to be disequilibrated and in search of equilibrium. Crowds, or more exactly the 'movements' or 'currents' that activate, multiply, and tend to organise them (thus changing their character), have their psychological origins in anxiety, confusion, impotence, resentments, contrarieties, and a sense of forlornness, and their special characteristics and potentialities derive from that same human affectivity whose dynamics are studied on the individual level by psycho-analysis. And the source of the various movements and secular religions is the same, for there is no other. There is no supply of new energy from outside; there is simply a transformation of energy by which the compounds become 'phenomeno-

[1] The chief form taken by this call to adventure was the invitation to emigrate. It was in the 19th century that the United States of America first became rich and powerful, and also the great dominions of the European countries (South Africa, Australia, New Zealand, French North Africa); and at the same time China, India, and South America were also attracting fortune-seekers.

logically' different from the components[1]; or, to put it differently, 'quantity' becomes 'quality'. (These are merely two different ways of describing the same phenomenon.) The frequency of crowd situations is therefore a diagnostic symptom of social troubles; but a social trouble is only a trouble that has become more or less general throughout society and is not something of a different order from the psychological troubles of the individual. But the social trouble cannot be simply reduced to the individual trouble, and the individual trouble needs to be seen against the social background.

Revolutionary crises are always accompanied by an outbreak of crowds. The excited atmosphere generated by the crowd reinforces the pressure brought to bear upon the public authorities, who give way. This is how the fall of the French monarchy of the *ancien régime* was brought about. But the art of directing crowd-enthusiasm and harnessing it to a purpose is learned *at the same time* that the crowds themselves are multiplying. The Jacobin clubs or 'popular societies'[2] in the French revolution came into existence at about the same time as the revolutionary crowds.

We may note the remarkable fact that this art of crowd manipulation attracted so much interest that it pushed into the background, so to speak, the study of the characteristic traits of the crowd itself. When the chiefs of the *ancien régime* were threatened by the crowd they concerned themselves only with the actions of the leaders, as if they regarded the rest of the crowd as a passive thing. It is true that the leader is with and inside the crowd, and appears to be, to all intents and purposes, essentially an unseparable part of the phenomenon. But all the same, when they chose to notice only the action of the leaders, the conservatives were underestimating more or less consciously and hypocritically what Marxists call the 'objective factors': the affective motives, reduced to the form of *interests*, which incited men to demonstrate in this way and to pass from the individual to the crowd state. They equally underestimated the special character of crowd states (as also did the doctrine, if not the *Praxis*, of Marxism), in so far as it is a symptom of a social trouble and represents a new form of determinism added to those already in play. The scientific study of these states was also neglected by revolutionaries. The more romantic relied upon a mystical confidence in the 'spontaneity of the masses',[3] while others, in reality no less romantic but more individualist and somewhat 'aristocratic' in their

[1] The school of Durkheim insists especially upon this.

[2] They were the product, no doubt, of more secret groups recruited from among the élites towards the end of the *ancien régime*.

[3] It was the day of the *Volksgeist*, when the fashion was to deny and, as it were, exorcise the individual authorship of the great epics of civilisation, such as the Homeric and medieval heroic poems.

romanticism (like Blanqui), put their trust in certain individuals who would lead the peoples to the attack. For others again, such as Marx, the psychological factors give way before the 'objective'; they are rationalists, and they hold that such events are determined *from beginning to end* by necessity and interest. Making use of the Hegelian notion of the 'cunning of reason', Marx thought that even if the masses were not aware of what they were doing, they were, nevertheless, obeying 'historical necessity'; and this necessity was not external to them, but was expressed in and through the masses themselves. What he failed to take account of was the determinism that inheres specifically and uniquely in the 'human material' as such. His theory could not accommodate a class of factors irreducible to the pure logic of the class struggle and capable of a sometimes decisive influence. He tended to reduce to the 'vertical' class struggle, by force if necessary, every factor in social movements which might appear unconnected with this struggle. If there seemed to be in the struggle of the 'oppressed nationalities' something more and something other than the pure and simple class struggle, Marx held that this 'something else' had no influence comparable to that of the class struggle itself. But we cannot help remarking that, from the historical point of view, the frequency of crowd manifestations (which are characteristic of both the acute and the chronic phase of revolutionary periods) is generally a presage of war, as though the two phenomena were normally adjacent in time. So it must be said that since revolution and war engender and prolong and complicate one another, they present characteristics which Marx's work does little to prepare us to understand. It is, indeed, always vain to consider facts solely in the light of their origins; for it leaves the facts still there to be considered in themselves.[1]

If it be admitted that there were national currents in the 19th century which cannot be fully accounted for by reducing them to social currents, which are themselves reducible purely and simply to phases of the class struggle, then it follows that the Marxist explanations of social excitability are not adequate; we must look to other schools. The point at issue is not whether national movements are secondary in relation to the class struggle, but whether they possess a describable phenomenological aspect and an analysable psychological significance of their own. For example, it is difficult to avoid seeing that the revolutions of 'forty-eight were *also* an outbreak of particularisms.

Crowd behaviour and the upsurge of the masses present psychological

[1] When the 'rudimentary forms of religious life' have been revealed something which is not rudimentary remains—namely, the very precise fact that 'religion' (the elementary evolutionary approach to it is now considerably out of date) is strictly an original phenomenon in relation to its rudimentary forms and, so to speak, in virtue of its difference from them.

characteristics which do not come under the study of the 'substructure' or of class struggles, as such; they constitute a sort of 'mixed datum' which the socialist intellectuals of the 19th century tended to ignore. But this censorship was lifted by the work of Georges Sorel at the beginning of the 20th century. When the partitions of society are removed, its constituent monads become more susceptible to the influences of an environment which has itself become much more fluid. The individual is subjected to contagions and 'psychological epidemics'. Thus, a man who at a given moment is hardly conscious of his national particularity will show by his behaviour at a later date that he has become sensitively aware of it. He has caught a contagion, been swept into a current, and has reacted rather like an iron filing in a magnetic field. There is an element of contagion in mass excitement. Before long, all the chief preoccupations of this individual will be expressed for him through this current; and in extreme cases—which, as we know, are not rare—the collective current will become the unifying principle upon which his whole personality is integrated. He will have been profoundly changed and affectively reorganised. He will have been the subject or field, so to speak, of a series of displacements, projections, and transferences, and will have altered his 'fixations'. But the current which activates and transforms him only exists because there are other individuals like him, *whose affective energy is, as it were, the actual substance of the current*. Secular religions manipulate affective energy in rather the same way that capitalism manipulates bank-notes and credit; but the 20th-century secular religions have merely carried on the work of the particularist and social movements of the 19th. To certain Christian writers[1] the word 'demon' comes naturally when they are writing about crowds. It is the property of demons to be able to change their shape; and, to pursue the metaphor, the collective or crowd demons appear quite different from the demons that inhabit individuals. But they are really the same ones in a new shape; for there are no other demons than the ones we carry in our own breasts. But the crowd, and the secular religion, and the Party, are liberators of demons; in this sense—that, whereas the affective forces are held in check and subdued under the rule of the individual personality and kept down to individual proportions by other forces and equilibrating powers, they find release and the chance to multiply and proliferate without restraint in those vast *phenomena of resonance*, the secular religion and the Party. The result is manifested in space and time by the crowds at meetings and processions or, as they are called today, demonstrations. They are in fact demonstrations of affective forces. Personality, within the limits of the individual, is organised. One aspect of this organisation is the *mental*; and in

[1] cf. especially M. Ph. de Félice: *Foules en délire, extases collectives* (Paris, 1948).

crowd states the mental is more or less inhibited. To the mental belongs that very control which seems to be abolished in the crowd, but which is characteristic of the organisation of the personality within the limits of the individual. *The critical faculty is pre-eminently an individual function*. The action of those control mechanisms which physiologists locate in the cortex appears to be suspended when men are in a crowd state, so that the affective and nervous system seems to be abandoned and to abandon the entire individual to affective and nervous contagion. Impulses are awakened and 'activated' while the forces that work to restrain them in the individual are weakened. The repercussions of these impulses are increased as by an effect of resonance; and this effect of the crowd state resembles the effects of other intoxications.[1] The crowd state is not altogether a waking state. It annihilates the differences between individuals, to the profit of what is common to them all. Each individual becomes more receptive; and certain ones reveal an exceptional aptitude for *transmitting* contagion. This special capacity for passing on the germ of infection is revealed to them, then and there, as a vocation.[2]

* * * *

What we call *totalitarianism* is like a cross-roads, or centre of a star or a wheel. The roads that lead to it may start from widely divergent points. Hitler's Germany reached it through fighting communism, and it is by no means certain that if German communism had triumphed it would not have taken the same road. Russia and Germany reached much the same position during the 'thirties, although they had so little in common and had different histories and started from quite different points. *Totalitarianism is the pattern obtained when these dissimilar traits converge*; and this pattern not only helps us to understand both the Russia and the Germany of the 'thirties, each by reference to the other, but it also enables us to recognise the corresponding lines in other historical configurations.

'*Assimilation* is a transformation from the different to the like, from the other to the same',[3] and *convergence* bears the same relation to assimilation as the moving to the motionless. 'A group of transformations is said to be *convergent* when its effect is to produce a growing resemblance among the elements in transformation.'[4] We shall use the

[1] Alluding, in another place, to the powerful effect of human 'vibrations', and perhaps of human influences whose exact nature is unknown, we once wrote concerning the crowd that the other, in large doses, is a drug'.

[2] In any crowd there are special adepts of the crowd state, natural crowd subjects. The number of such 'transmitting stations' present in a crowd gives it its particular character and its active properties.

[3] Lalande, *Vocabulaire technique et critique de la philosophie*. [4] ibid.

term *movement of convergence* to describe the movement by which events or systems or different realities, such as the psychological development of the aspirations of an individual and the corresponding development of those of an historically existing group, *seem to move together to meet one another*. This is what happens when an individual 'projects' into a real, objectively existing group the ideal group which satisfies his psychic need.[1] In such a case one of the facts is subjective and the other objective, but in the case of totalitarianism there are two comprehensive and homogeneous social facts. Between 1930 and 1940 there occurred a very striking example of the *phenomenon of convergence*. The Russian revolution had put an end to the last of the old absolutisms; Hitler's movement was loudly proclaiming that it would save 'the soul of Germany' from 'Jews, western capitalists, and Asiatic bolshevism' (to recall the language of Nazism). Russia had no part in the European and Western cultural sphere; it owed neither civilisation nor Christianity to Rome, but derived its culture from the Byzantine tradition. Up to the 15th century Russia, in Western eyes, was simply the plain across which 'ethnic whirlwinds' came sweeping—Attila, Genghis Khan, and Tamburlaine being the most formidable examples. After the 15th century there were some contacts with the West, but it can still be said that in the first half of the 17th century Russia was not a part of Europe. This is proved by the fact that she took no part in the Thirty Years War; she was not yet in a position to claim her share in the spoils of Germany. The quarrel was settled without her and the treaties of Westphalia were a purely western affair. When Peter the Great arose in the European firmament it was at first in order to learn from Europe, and one cannot say that he brought Russia into the sphere of European culture. Russia was a world of its own, and participated only superficially, through its oligarchy, in the Western world. (The destruction of this oligarchy by the revolution alienated Russia still further from the West; the French language, for example, practically disappeared with those who spoke it.) But from the time of Peter the Great Russia was sufficiently European to intervene in Europe and to send her armies as far as Zürich at the end of the 18th century and as far as Paris when Napoleon fell, but not sufficiently so to become herself a part of Europe. Nicholas II reacted away from Europe, which he identified with liberalism, and after his death the same mistrust prevailed, though it varied in degree; and printed matter from the West continued to be carefully filtered. On the revolutionary side, the liberals and Marxists were studying in Europe at the turn of the century, but a large part of the opposition preferred to stay at home for the inspiration which would eventually give rise to a new régime. It may

[1] See Chapter 10 above.

have seemed that the success of the Marxists in the October Revolution was a victory for the Western revolutionary wing. But what was the effect of their rise to power upon relations with Europe? A renewal of suspicion. Europe was now anathema as capitalist and not as 'progressive', but she was still anathema and would remain so; there was no real change of attitude, although the justifications for the attitude were totally different. With the rise of Stalin and his totalitarian régime, there was an even more rigid censorship of everything coming from the West; more rigid than under the Tsars, because it had the means to be. The difference of régime between Europe and Russia remained the same and, after the interlude of the revolution, there was an absolutist régime in Russia just as there had been a hundred years before. It is true that, owing to communism, there is more communication than under the Tsars between Russia and the rest of the world, but it is only, so to speak, one-way communication.

Germany belongs to the European sphere. Before the 19th century she belonged to Europe as much as France or Spain or Italy did[1]; and during that century German thought, in its creative period before Bismarck's unification of the country, fertilised the whole of Europe. (The Bismarckian outlook was as antipathetic to Nietzsche as it would have been to Hegel, Hölderlin, and the great romantic historians.) Germany had possessed feudal and princely traditions and mercantile towns, and had always been in touch with Italy and the rest of Christendom. But in Russia the monarchy did not arise out of the nobility, like a feudal monarchy; on the contrary, it was the monarchy that created the nobles. Nobility was derived from function, and the seignorial powers of the provincial governors were exercised in the Tsar's name. The Tsar could give or take away thousands of acres of land and tens of thousands of 'souls'.

In the West it was the feudal nobility who created liberty, by defending their own against their suzerains and by securing guarantees for it. The English *magna carta* was the outcome of the Barons' War; and the tradition of liberty in France was born of the fruitful tension between the lawyers of the Third Estate on the one hand, whose brains were at the king's service for restraining the feudal power and putting into practice the traditions derived from Roman law, and on the other hand the great vassals whose aim it was to prevent the king's power from becoming anything more than a suzerainty. The Hundred Years War cut through the tangle of feudal relationships which had made the suzerain of England more powerful on the continent than his French

[1] This is only strictly true of the old romanised provinces and of Austria. It is less true of east Germany, which was a later addition, of the 12th and 13th centuries, and was more a 'colonial', seignorial, and territorial domain.

overlord. But the whole of the later middle age was a period of wars for liberty. Everywhere status or privilege was being defended, attempts being made to extract guarantees from the most powerful, and alliances being formed against the most dangerous. The French communes allied themselves with the king because the feudal power was more dangerous and the king's support favoured the growth of commerce and industry; but reversals of alliance and the offer of support to the highest bidder were everywhere common practice. The net result was, however, that the varied and changeable feudal scene, within which the new urban powers arose, performed the function, up to the 17th century, of a school of liberty. It also exhibited a great deal of 'social spontaneity'. The various human groups looked out for themselves, and it was only the peasantry who lagged behind and remained passive subjects of history longer than the others.[1] The Third Estate circulated both articles of commerce and ideas throughout Europe; it produced clerks, lawyers, bankers, merchants, captains of industry, and corsairs. The fact is that the periods represented in France as periods of despotism, thanks to an historical convention evolved during the Third Republic, were periods of very great social vitality; and the so-called despot had in reality to reckon with vigorous opposition, which frequently compelled him to give way. Moreover, the monarchy was accepted, and there were even times when it was unanimously accepted, so far as one can judge, by a general social consensus of opinion. At such times, not only did no better alternative than monarchy seem conceivable, but no alternative was conceivable at all. So at that time republicanism was regarded as no more than one of the possible régimes for a *city-state*—though the most desirable in the opinion of J.-J. Rousseau, himself a *citizen* of Geneva and, thanks to this quality, privileged over strangers like the citizens of the ancient cities. The historical concept of liberty in Europe was born of the struggles of those social categories that were historically the most active in claiming franchises, rights, privileges, and a special status for themselves. Thus, the bourgeois of the French towns, relying on help from the king, fought against territorial feudalism, the great vassals struggled to keep on equal terms with the king, the merchants strove to make money, and the lawyers strove for a social position and for the reality of power (it was under the shelter of the monarchy that they learned how to conquer the nobles). The Church struggled to preserve and extend the Christian faith and to acquire and keep the *real* foundations of power; it fought in every field—in the universities and through its Orders: militant or mendicant, contemplative or learned, charitable or missionary. Liberty in Europe has its origin in an extraordinary social vitality—a vitality appertaining to society itself—which

[1] But peasant risings also occurred; the *jacquerie* of 1358, for example.

is expressed in the initiative and pertinacity of a number of societies within society. Liberties were only won by conquest and could only be maintained by their constant exercise, and this was also true of the liberty to express one's thoughts. In the fight for this liberty the leaders of the assault were on more than one occasion burned alive; but in the 18th century the main army occupied the position without being exposed to any great danger from the so-called despotism of the *ancien régime*. The first of the 'intellectuals' who suffered under the revolution and the Empire were in reality the victims of the very forces which they themselves had helped to unleash.

* * *

At about the same time during the 'thirties Germany and Russia began to exhibit comparable social traits, including coercive methods which were identical for their victims and also, in a certain sense, for those who applied them; and this phenomenon of convergence is the more remarkable because of the different historical background from which the two totalitarianisms emerged. But there is, all the same, one common feature in their two histories, which becomes apparent if we compare the Germany of 1848 with the Russia of 1917: *in both cases the bourgeoisie was weak*.

The French monarchy had great difficulty in asserting itself against an active feudalism, and its success was due to its support by the vigorous bourgeoisie of the rapidly developing commercial towns. The higher clergy, although their origin was in the feudal nobility, were not historically identified with it; they were sometimes with the king against the nobles and sometimes with the Pope against either king or nobles, and more often still their support was divided between the other parties. The economy of the towns gradually became that of the monarchy; the towns were the focal points, and their trade soon penetrated the entire country, so that they ended by controlling the feudal economy. Thus the great feudal domains ceased to be self-sufficient, and the feudal lords found themselves dependent upon the urban economy for the satisfaction of needs which the urban economy itself had created. Some of the great bourgeois towns became *centres*, and the centralisation of the monarchy was based upon them. After the Hundred Years War none of the great vassals could be indifferent to what was happening at the court. Europe was beginning to conceive a model of the State which seemed to have been borrowed by Italy from the ancient world; and it was to Italy that the French looked for this model.

But at the time when a centralised monarchy was arising in France out of the urban economy, the German towns that had grown up along the Rhine and in the north, as a result of the fall of Novgorod and Kiev and the revival in the 12th century of the great Mediterranean trade route, were without protection against the territorial, seignorial, and feudal system that engulfed them. For there was no monarchy, and indeed its absence is the outstanding characteristic of Germany. Instead, the great princes of the Church ruled their own separate, and particularist, States, and elected the suzerain in concert with the other great vassals. The Golden Bull of 1356 regulated the election of emperors during four centuries. A central power of this kind was far from being an urban or in any sense a bourgeois power, but on the contrary it drove the towns to seek protection from the princes, whether ecclesiastical or lay. The commercial cities of Germany did not become the centre of a country unified under an urban economy, but remained as enclaves within a feudal and seignorial system.

These considerations do something to reduce the distance between the points of departure of Germany and Russia in their convergence towards totalitarianism. Right up to the 19th century in Germany the urban economy remained an enclave within the seignorial system, and the towns were protected by princes, in the full oppressive sense of the word 'protection'. But when the glories of Novgorod and Kiev had become a memory and no new breeze of trade came to revive them, Russia lay open to successive waves of Turanian invasion; and when the invasions had passed she lived, being essentially a flat and open country with no made roads and chiefly dependent upon river transport, by extension, and not by intension, like those peoples which worked intensively to civilise themselves because they were contained within barriers which they could not cross. Russian civilisation is extensive, not intensive[1]; its empire was extended by a natural progress along the great rivers towards the ocean boundaries. Apart from the steppe, the chief feature of Russia was 'a dense forest within which, even in the 17th century, the towns and villages between (for example) Smolensk and Moscow [were like] larger or smaller clearings'. With Peter the Great the Baltic was reached, and with Catherine II the Black Sea. The monarchy rested upon the boyars, who were warriors and *appanaged* high officials (that is to say, they ruled over immense areas of land and great numbers of 'souls'); and the functionaries who rose to high positions in the Tsar's service were created boyars by endowment. This happened too quickly for any real class opposition to develop between them and the boyars. Russia, therefore, was a territorial and seignorial despotism which gradually became, without losing these characteristics, a despotism of officials.

[1] cf. Stählin, *La Russie des origines à la naissance de Pierre le Grand* (Paris, 1946). On this point, Stählin cites Ratzel and Hettner.

The history of Germany, on the other hand, produced a sort of intermediate form between Russian and Western society. Historians generally speak of two Germanies: the old romanised provinces of the west, and the colonial lands, retaken from the Slavs after the beginning of the 12th century, in the east. But this colonisation planted the seed of what was to become, in the 19th century, a unified Germany, for it was the common work of Germans from all other parts of the country—local feudal lords, from dukes and margraves downwards, emigrant peasants from the west, and the militant Orders. Retrospectively, their combined work can be seen as the foundation of German unity. In 1226 the Polish nobles appealed to the Teutonic Knights for help against the Borussians and in the event they received no better treatment than the Borussians themselves at the hands of their rescuers. The structure of this Germany was seignorial and territorial; the small squires of Elbe and Spree and the descendants of the Teutonic Knights coalesced to form a single class of military lords, and eventually reduced to serfdom the free peasants whose labour had reclaimed the soil of eastern Germany. This was the social milieu[1] which gave birth to the Prussian State; and it was upon the Prussian State that German unity was based, and not upon the urban economy of the west and the Hanseatic towns, whose bourgeoisie was fundamentally similar to that of the Flemish, French, and Italian towns. The German bourgeoisie could look for support neither to the clergy nor to the monarchy under which territories and peoples were grouped; it was confined to a subordinate status within a primarily seignorial system. The junkers of the Spree and the descendants of the Teutonic Knights were finally amalgamated in the Prussian State, which was itself founded upon the Electorate of Brandenburg and upon the addition, in the early 18th century, of East Prussia to the other possessions of the Elector, who assumed the crown at Königsberg. The basis of the State was the alliance between the new monarchy and the great domains; the king was surrounded by fighting squires, and below them the official and bourgeois classes and the peasantry were strictly and hierarchically ordered in a system efficiently adapted for war. From the first, Prussian industry, like that of Russia, was a protected industry, in which Prussian initiative was officially encouraged. The bourgeoisie was not a power conscious of its own identity, nor was it tempted to oppose the nobility. Having absorbed Silesia under Frederick II, Prussia was established on the left bank of the Rhine by the Allies of 1815, and thenceforth it was Prussia and the Prussian system that ruled what was to

[1] Luther's reforms reinforced the power of the sovereigns at the expense of all the other rising social forces. Lutheranism made subordination to the prince the first duty of his subjects, and encouraged the princes to round off their estates by encroaching upon Church property.

become, after 1850, the most highly industrialised area of Europe. When, in the 20th century, the old seignorial and territorial Prussia began to lose itself in an over-industrialised Germany, the weight of the western German capitalist bourgeoisie made itself felt; but the Prussian system remained untouched by the conflict of interest between the western free-trade capitalists and the eastern junkers. The Prussian military caste remained at the head of the State; and the bourgeoisie which had been in strict tutelage in the Middle Ages developed into a capitalism which felt quite at home within an authoritarian Empire. It was more interested in organisation than in free competition. (Indeed, German history to some extent missed the anarchic phase of capitalism; organisation was already becoming an important problem at the time when German capitalism developed.)

Since the great agricultural industry of eastern Germany was tending to become industrialised at the same time, there was comparative harmony within the Prussian system between the two great components of the new German Empire. There was no irremediable conflict between the giant industrial combines, which accelerated Germany's economic unification, and the Prussian type of hierarchical governmental structure. The bureaucratic administration by which the King of Prussia established his position as Emperor of Germany was copied from the Prussian model, and provided the backbone of the new State. The eastern lands to whose colonisation the whole of Germany had contributed now repaid their debt, and Prussia created Germany just as Germany, between the 12th and the 18th centuries, had created Prussia. The liberal bourgeoisie of the universities was polarised to the Prussian-model bureaucracy. There is nothing in Germany to correspond to the type of university members in the French educational system who criticise 'authority' and make jokes about the 'society' of which they are supposed to be pillars, and the army in which they must serve, and the very régime itself of which they are the typical products. On the contrary, the eastern junkers, the southern democrats, and the western Catholics were all subdued to the same pattern by the working of the 'gigantic' industry of the Wilhelm period, because it was identified with the power of Germany from which they all benefited. By 1907 one-half of the entire German population was employed in industry and commerce. The super-industrialisation of Germany did not much affect the political character of the German bourgeoisie, which remained in tutelage in spite of its powerful initiatives in the fields of invention, technique, and organisation. Only, instead of being protected by the dynastic princes, it was now protected by the Kaiser's State, a complex apparatus whose composite structure held together Kaiser and people, bourgeois interests and working-class claims, and the old political

States. It kept its power thanks to the opposition of parties and the local particularisms over against which it stood as the symbol of unity. After the fall of the Kaiser's State, at the time of the Dawes plan, German capitalism—having become 'Americanised' and still more highly organised—was protected by international high finance until the coming of Hitler's Reich. Hitler put it back under the control of an even stronger State power, but left intact the profit motive and the jurisdiction of the capitalists and high authorities of finance and industry.

German unity, as we have seen, was achieved by the Prussianisation of Germany, just as the kingdom of Prussia had been created by the efforts of all the rest of Germany. But Germany in 1914 and Russia in the nineteen-thirties had this in common, that for both of them the most vivid historical form upon which they could model themselves was a seignorial and territorial despotism. In neither country had there been a revolution of the Third Estate; in both of them the initiative had come in effect from above, and in both of them it was a seignorial and territorial despotism that supplied the prototype for the power that presided over the integration of a State system and a giant industry. The essential difference lies in the western history of West Germany, to which nothing in Russia corresponds.

We see, then, that the converging routes of Russia and Germany towards totalitarianism do not start, by any means, from totally dissimiliar points. But the fact that the two starting-points bear certain resemblances to each other does not mean that it is only societies whose history contains a strong element of seignorial and territorial despotism that are threatened with totalitarianism. It is certain that the weakness of the bourgeoisie, though different in degree and kind, was a determining factor in both cases. The two great triumphs of totalitarianism have both been in societies in which the Third Estate had shown little sign of historical vitality; these societies were also relatively amorphous, the lack of clearly defined shape being due, in the case of Russia, to a chronological disparity[1] with Europe, and in the case of the Weimar Republic to disintegration. The proletarianisation of the German middle classes, which began, in the time of the Kaisers, owing to the intensified over-industrialisation of Germany and also to the organised,

[1] I mean by this that in a sense Russian history and European history, although they interact to contribute to universal history, are not of 'the same age', and may even be regarded as different species of the sociological fauna. Many of the characteristic features of European history have no counterpart in Russia: the feudal, communal, and monarchical wars, the struggle of the less-favoured orders against the royal authority and of the orders among themselves, the distinction between temporal and spiritual, the Renaissance, the Reformation, Humanism, Classicism, a Capitalism fostered by private initiative. In so far as these exist or have existed in Russia, they came to her from outside, as they did also to America. But America is really linked to them, for Americans are directly descended from the Reformation and from the maritime and commercial and exploring genius of Europe.

aggressive, and almost seignorial character of German capitalism, was accelerated after the defeat of 1918—by inflation, unemployment, the growing number of *Luftmenschen*, and the general social instability which produced 'marginal men' who repudiated the traditional social and moral codes. The Dawes plan revived a German capitalism more organised and concentrated than ever; and proletarianisation was still proceeding unchecked when Germany was hit by the world capitalist crisis around 1930. This crisis restored to favour the autarkic and nationalist theories of capitalism which had periodically made themselves felt in German economic thought from the time of Frederick List and more particularly from the later days of the Kaisers. All this tended to increase the *mass* element in society at the expense of the classes; and the more so because it took place in a land where individual initiative had always been subordinate to social discipline and obedience to leaders (as much so in the social-democratic party as in the administration and the army). In such an environment the disorder resulting from the disintegration of classes creates masses which are especially suited to form the human material of an absolutist type of régime. The authoritarian and hierarchical relationships inherited from the preceding epoch remained as a prototype in the historical psyche of the German people; and it was demonstrated by events, in Germany and Russia alike, that a certain type of relationship, inherited by the present from the past, will persist even though the past be regarded as dead, or even if its abolition is the avowed social object.[1]

Proletarianisation, the process by which people become 'unclassed', produces the *mass*. So the 'organised proletariat' did not gain new adherents as a result of the disintegration of social classes in the Germany of the 'thirties, but, on the contrary, the capitalist crisis unclassed a part of the proletariat itself along with a part of the middle classes. Unemployed proletarians sometimes became 'disorganised', but unemployed petty bourgeois seldom became proletarianised; their consciousness, instead of reflecting their social condition, resisted it. When proletarians become unclassed through unemployment, they no longer conform to the laws upon which Marx's prophecy of revolution was based. They are no longer proletarians in the modern but rather in the classical sense of the word. They draw unemployment pay, go to the cinema and to 'monster demonstrations', read the papers, and adapt themselves to a state of undernourishment. They are available, as a mass formation, for the subversive enterprises which turn society into a battlefield. A gulf appears between those who have work and those who have not. The assured conditions of life of the party or trade-

[1] This fact can also be observed in the relationship of Jacobinism and its successor, Bonapartism, to the monarchical centralisation of the *ancien régime*.

union bureaucrat draw a brutally sharp line between him and the unemployed man. Meanwhile, those who no longer have a place in any class at all become increasingly indifferent to the fate of the proletariat; and society appears to be crumbling into fragments. But the social being itself resists this fragmentation, and there are blind and clumsy attempts by the massed crowds to find substitutes for the broken or obsolete forms of social organisation. Men who are reduced to a state of animal privation flock towards anything that promises a certain human warmth; and this will be something that has already served in the past as a focus for mass concentration. It exerts a direct and violent attraction; and an attraction of this kind has a compelling force of a different order from that possessed by a system of ideas. This explains why pre-existing systems of ideas have so little weight against the trends that lead to totalitarianism. It is as though society itself, at the moment when a majority of its members are struggling for bare existence on any conditions, were trying to safeguard its own existence by a structural simplification.

In each of the two totalitarian societies of the 'thirties the Third Estate was weak; its function of social vanguard had been performed in Russia, from the 19th century onwards, by the intelligentsia—in other words, by men nourished on *imported* ideas. The Russian Revolution was a revolution of the intelligentsia, and was possible because the mass of the peasants wanted peace and land and because the proletariat was relatively very small and easily permeable by the revolutionaries; it owed its success to the fact that Europe was occupied elsewhere in destroying itself. The Germany of 1933 had *acquired*, what was a datum in the Russia of 1917, a state of social amorphousness: the war, the inflation, the crisis, and unemployment had unclassed sufficient numbers to create a *mass* which could polarise the rest of society as soon as it had become self-coherent. We have noted the weakness of the German Third Estate in comparison with the French. The case is typified by Prussia, in which the 'estate' of the officials remained subordinate to the military nobility, whereas in France, at the very climax of her military history, the higher ranks of the army were invaded by the expanding Third Estate. This explains why Marx's address of 1850 (dual power, permanent revolution, systematic outbidding of the liberals and the left) was able to provide Lenin with an invaluable tactical programme; neither in the Germany of 1850 nor in the Russia of 1914 was there any force corresponding to the 'vanguard of the Third Estate' in France in 1789. The French Revolution was a bourgeois revolution because the bourgeoisie, as it was called, with insufficient precision, was alone in profiting from it; but in fact it was a *revolution of the Third Estate* and led by the advance guard of the Third Estate (for example, the lawyer

Robespierre, the surgeon Marat, the writer Saint-Just). And what was the significance of their demand for a dictatorship of merit and virtue? They were trying to accelerate the necessary social function of circulation of the élites, which was hampered by the resistance of the privileged. Thus there is something profoundly reasonable in the French Revolution; and this is precisely what later revolutions have not imitated. We can also learn from the French Revolution that when an oligarchy is defeated or finally driven from the field of history, the leaders of the victorious forces are not demiurges capable of impressing their image upon succeeding history. Power is seized by those who are ready to seize it. When a ruling oligarchy falls, the vacant functions will be assumed by the group most fitted to perform them, and this even though the functions have been profoundly transformed. What happens is a *readjustment*. In the universal or general character of the principles proclaimed by the French revolutionaries, I find something much more reasonable than in the assertion of the class character of a revolution. Successful revolutionaries are not entitled to say more than this: we have dispossessed a ruling oligarchy of its powers, and these powers will now be exercised by new men and new groups, whose quality will be tested by the use they make of them. It is courting disillusion to proclaim in advance the dictatorship of a class; and in order not to recognise this fact today one needs to be either a dreamer or a fanatic (though, as we know well, the one does not exclude the other). All that can reasonably be promised is that the circulation of the élites will be made as effective as possible. (I do not suggest, and do not think, that one must never go beyond the reasonable; but to denigrate it on principle is to deliver oneself bound hand and foot to the unconscious. Without the unconscious nothing can be done, but to surrender to it at the very moment when one is supposed to be finally establishing order is to sacrifice intention without a struggle to the reality that devours it.)

The lack of a bourgeoisie, and therefore of any adequate previous circulation of wealth and ideas, was responsible for some of the major features of the Russian development of a new despotic, 'Islamic', and tyrannical *Imperium*. But another feature was possessed, in differing degrees, both by the 19th-century Germany which gave birth to Marxism and by the 20th-century Russia which used Marxism to create a new 'Islam'; and that was a lack, in comparison with the rest of Europe, of social spontaneity and fertility. In Germany, social spontaneity had been stifled by the principalities and by the stultifying principle of the Electorate, which made it impossible for the Emperor to reform the Empire. The Habsburg monarchy was reduced to managing its dynastic affairs in the same way as the other monarchies derived from feudalism, though it managed them better: it was confined to maintaining in Germany a situation favourable, or at least not compromising, to the successful management of those affairs. It had no influence upon the solution of the German problem, other than a retarding action, and the problem was settled by the power of Prussia and France in indifference or opposition to the wishes of Austria. Germany was the creation of the French Revolution and the two Napoleons and Prussia, but also of the poets and thinkers beyond the Rhine. By the beginning of the 20th century the capitalist development of Germany was the first in all Europe, but it was the Prussian military power that carried the German bourgeoisie to success. The fact that it accepted first the Weimar Republic and then Hitler proves that this bourgeoisie, no doubt because it had always been a 'protected class', was incapable of historic initiative. Its mission was purely economic, and today it seems to be merging into a class of high administrators. The historic initiative of the Third Estate was a specifically French phenomenon. (It is true that England also shows a high degree of social continuity; but they have erred who tried to imitate her, for she is inimitable.)

Russia achieved in the 20th century the revolution without a bourgeoisie that Germany had missed in 1848–50, and therefore it is no historical paradox that the Marxist strategy should have succeeded in the 20th century in Russia but not in Germany. The problem was to make use of a weak bourgeoisie for overthrowing a feudal absolutism, and then to get rid of the bourgeoisie. The fact that this Marxist strategy, conceived for the Germany of 1848, was rich in lessons for the Russia of 1917 implies a certain resemblance between the two régimes. If Germany in 1848 had been racked by a foreign war, the highest hopes would have been justified. Had not Marx, a little earlier, been dreaming aloud of a German revolution ushered in by a Gallic cock-crow?

But in 1848 the proletariat was still rudimentary, and the bourgeoisie still undeveloped and too submissive to its social superiors; the Marxist strategy was not even attempted. When it was applied in Russia in 1917 it only succeeded thanks to the war, and it led to a reinforced despotism, a militant secular religion, and a tyranny, which implies a continuous state of internal war. *Both Russian and German totalitarianism were the creation of societies that had never had a Third Estate with vigorous leadership or a militant bourgeoisie.* In both the Romanov and the Hohenzollern empires the dominant class consisted of landed proprietors to whom the monarchical bureaucracy was subordinate. (Prussia was to some extent a seignorial State.) The tactics worked out by Marx for the Germany of 1850 were less appropriate in 1914 for Germany than for Russia; and the less so because the German Marxists were formed intellectually by Marx's *Capital* and considered that his work before

1850 was not truly Marxist. The lesson to be drawn from this is that the tactics of 1850 are *effective against a weak opponent*. They could not be seriously attempted in 1850 because the enemy was far from being sufficiently weak; they succeeded in Russia in 1917 because he was. Nor can it be said that they are out of date today, because in France and in Italy the communists have an enfeebled enemy to deal with.

* * * *

The outstanding characteristic of 20th-century absolutism, as manifested in Russia and Germany, is its combination of a *tyranny* with an 'Islam'; this means that the political, which had become effectively secularised between the time of Machiavelli and Lenin, is *reconsecrated*. The new absolutism recombines the political, the economic, and the spiritual powers, which the preceding age had tended to keep separate.

With the triumph of the Counter-Reformation Catholicism survived the great schism, but Christendom was broken. It was not only that the secession of the Protestants removed from the Pope's jurisdiction the whole of England, a great part of Germany, and a small part of France, but there were other signs that the times were changing: Jansenism, Gallicanism, and a subterranean offensive of epicurean and libertine ideas.[1]

At the end of the 17th century no one either at court or in town still believed in the divine right of kings, who were expected to justify themselves by virtue. 'Without money, honour is but vanity', says one of Molière's characters, and another of them, Don Louis, reproaches his son, Don Juan, for misdemeanours (seduction, desertion, debt), which were little more than a noble's prerogatives at the beginning of the century.[2] The secularising process was enormously accelerated by the

[1] Let Gassendi, the Chevalier de Méré, de Saint-Evremond, and even the great Condé himself bear witness. And the same state of affairs is attested both by the vogue of ostentatious piety and by the vogue of licentious manners (of which the king himself set the example until the régime of La Maintenon). When the Court of Louis XIV became strict, it was rather in the manner of a beauty who compensates by austerity in old age for the licence of her gay youth.

The violence of the attacks on 'libertinism' proves that it must have been a serious problem. Famous authors attacked hypocritical piety, insisting that their motive was love of true piety. But all the pious, whether true or false, drew the line at Molière's *Tartuffe*. It was only in the teeth of fierce resistance that Molière was able to get permission to produce the play, and then only after having rewritten it several times. It is worth remarking that the cabal of the pious was led by the Prince de Conti, a reformed libertine. It is equally worth remarking that Molière's *Don Juan* is spared by heaven during his libertinage but blasted as soon as he appears in the cloak of piety. La Bruyère raises suspicions about the court's appearance of pious conformism by daring to define a pious man as a man who would conform to atheism if the king were an atheist. And what are we to say of Fontenelle and the 'modernists' entrenched in the Academy, who foreshadow the 18th-century spirit?

[2] Molière makes no bones about translating Tirso de Molina's data into bourgeois terms.

French Revolution and the victorious Napoleonic tyranny, and it continued through the 19th century in spite of the counter-offensive and reactions of the first fifty years, in spite of the Holy Alliance and the 'system' of Metternich. Louis Philippe was regarded by all as the typical bourgeois usurper who made poets regret the great military usurper. At the end of the century there was a new emperor in Germany and a king of all Italy; the former retained something of the old prestige because the German Third Estate had never rebelled against the values of the nobility, and in Italy the King of Piedmont was accepted by the patriots because they were concerned, above all, to get a united Italy. But the old monarchies never recovered what they had lost; the religious sanction was a thing of the past. Only the Habsburg and Ottoman empires remained as survivals. Belgium and Holland had constitutional and parliamentary monarchies on the English model, and if the kings of the new nations detached from the Ottoman empire were authoritarian, this was only because the countries they reigned over were unripe for the English system. Russia, the latest arrival in the 'Concert of Europe', escaped the general tendency because she was kept apart from Europe by her geography, her history, her Byzantine religion, and her Asiatic peoples. But the fact that she escaped it made her an anachronism in 19th-century Europe. Not even conservatives looked upon the 'gendarme of reaction' as an example; to them, too, Russia appeared barbarous.

With the dawn of the 20th century the process of secularisation of power seemed to be complete. Those socialists who were enthusiastic about the Russian Revolution saw in it the *year one* of a new era in which the divine sanction of power would be no more than an historical memory. But the contrary happened, and a new cycle of opposite tendency seems to be beginning. We have already seen the rise of new absolutisms. The liberal State in the 19th century was concerned that order and prosperity should be enjoyed by commerce and industry, and by its citizens in their private lives, by everything, in a word, that was not the State; ideally, the State was to efface itself and leave society to the free play of the 'struggle for existence' and 'natural selection' among businesses and men. In the absolutism of the old régime the divine right of kings was founded upon the Catholic religion (the king, at his consecration, was entrusted by God with the charge of his peoples),[1] but Russian absolutism in the 20th century seems to be born of a religion which is, as it were, unconscious of itself. Being 'scientific', Marxism is identified in the minds of Marxists with 'science', the supreme intellectual authority of the 19th century, and it is as science that it claims the right

[1] The French sovereign owed his sanctity to the consecration at Reims, where he was anointed by a high servant of Christ.

to rule and to impose itself (hence the 'Islamic' character of the communist Campaign). Marxism cannot openly claim sacredness, because it is based upon the denial of the sacred. In principle, it is the contrary of the sacred, it is the *true* (but we may wonder whether truth really needs to be imposed by an 'Islam'). In reality, the Marxist *Weltanschauung* passes by a *sacred contagion* to the 'caliphs' who impose it upon the world: and that is how Stalin becomes the 'Commander of the Faithful'. The power he wields was derived in theory from a doctrine, but became the power of a few individuals, with a tendency to be concentrated in a single man; it thus converges towards the same point as the power of Hitler, which he claimed to hold from the unconscious and the irrational. Hitler declared himself the personification of Germanism and the white race, and pointed to his successes as a proof of his direct 'inspiration'. He is like the pure product of a 'consecratory process'. With an education based upon the anti-semitic pamphlets that circulated in Austria at the beginning of the century, he commanded the obedience of the most expert technicians and the most methodical scientists of perhaps the most advanced country in Europe in science and technology. Those who had dealings with him did not feel themselves in the presence of a controlled or balanced personality; he was essentially 'receptive', a perfect specimen of the 'crowd subject', and in effect he appeared, and no doubt was only first revealed to himself, at the 'hour of the crowd', the hour of distress, collapse, and confusion. His mission, he said, was to produce order from chaos. But, in fact, he was the link between chaos and chaos, he was the man through whom one war engendered another, the man who perfected chaos by making it appear as order, efficiency, and organisation. The *Wehrmacht*, the nobility, and the industrial magnates, those who still represented an order of some kind, or the memory of one, were repelled by him; and they saw clearly. For although they could agree when he spoke to them of order and authority, what could it mean if *such a man* was to play the leading part?

In the end, the times being what they were, he was accepted, though not without a bad conscience, by the representatives of the former German élites; but every now and then they drew back, waiting for his first failure. . . . The series of his triumphs continued uninterrupted. They went along with him, and took advantage, hoping the chance would come later to put things on a 'normal' basis. But at last fortune reversed the hour-glass and infallibility began to work the other way; what became inevitable was not victory but the disaster which would restore the man of chaos back to chaos. It is like a revival, in the industrial age, of the magical origins of monarchy—a brutal rebuff to rational 'enlightenment'. In the realm of the unconscious, Hitler is at home. But in the end, for all his cynicism, he is destroyed by the very powers that gave him his strength, he falls a victim to the furies whom it was his achievement to unleash. Various 'intellectuals' explained and rationalised his position in works which, doubtless, the master did not examine. He sought no doctrinal justification for his power. Hitler's reign of the unconscious was a sort of volcanic sovereignty, an eruption of the instinctive German force, in whose name and as the expression of which he claimed the central power. By contrast, the power of Lenin, and later of Stalin, is rooted in the point where Marxist doctrine and Russian reality meet.

* * * *

The superficial application of scientific and 'American' methods could stimulate the Russian masses, but Germany, in the heart of Europe, where science and the techniques for exploiting it had come to birth, was no longer capable of such a youthful and barbaric enthusiasm. So the movement in Germany which corresponded to Russian communism and 'converged' with it (we describe the convergence as 'totalitarianism') could not employ the cult of machinery or the mystique of progress to 'activate' the masses. The Germans, like the French and the English, were familiar with scientific techniques, and could not be expected to deify them. So with Hitler Germany turned towards its own subconscious[1] and released its own 'demons'. In spite of appearances, the Germans are not simple enough to swallow a cheap ideology; and we can see today that the 'movement' was essentially a nihilism. Its own leaders, and all who had dealings with them, have underlined this fact even more clearly than its opponents. Along with a complete indifference to ideology there went a sort of instinctive faith in pure irrationality—and not on the part of Hitler alone, for there were ideologues in the universities who marched in step with the self-taught leader. Such ideology as there was did not rise above the level of thematics and hysterical justifications. The latter were inconsistent with one another,[2] and little effort was made to rationalise them. The way in which they were systematised was itself irrational; it was an example of the discontinuity which seemed to preside over the essentially instinctive German form of totalitarianism—'they have no theory', as the German

[1] This subconscious does not stop at the frontiers of Germany; the whole of Europe, and of mankind, is concerned—and more deeply than by the immediate effects upon its destiny of this particular, and now obsolete, manifestation.

[2] cf., in addition to Hitler's *Mein Kampf*, Von Salomon, *Les Réprouvés* and *La Ville*; Hermann Rauschning, *Germany's Revolution of Destruction* and *Hitler Speaks* (Engl. trans.; London, 1939); Gisevius, *To the Bitter End* (Engl. trans.; London, 1948). Dozens of other references could be given, especially the records of the Nuremburg trials. cf. also G. M. Gilbert, *Nuremburg Diary* (London, 1948), and B. H. Liddell Hart, *The Other Side of the Hill* (London, 1948).

communists said. The Hitlerites appropriated every theme in Germany that could serve them, every one that could be made to 'converge' in the slightest degree with their intentions of the moment.[1] Hence the predominance of unstable myths and fluid dogmas, perverted by the interpretations they were made to serve; and all of them in chaotic evolution until the final collapse.

The two great totalitarian chiefs of the 1930s were very different from one another. The Russian appears, in virtue of his personal history itself and the manner of his rise to power, as the personification of an order, whereas the German personified a chaos and a *débâcle*. Hitler's *hubris* and extravagance were so theatrically displayed as to obscure the real convergence of characteristics by which we can identify both in him and in Stalin the type of the modern tyrant of the first half of the 20th century.

The tyrants of the Greek and Italian cities were often men of unique qualities[2]; but the 20th-century tyrant owes his position less to the qualities by which he differs from others than to those by which he expresses, so to speak, the collective character. (That he does, in fact, possess aptitude and talent must be admitted, if only on the principle of sufficient reason; he could not do what he has done unless he were capable of doing it.) It is as though 20th-century absolutism were unconsciously influenced by the same aspirations of the lowly as 19th-century democracy; the representative figure is not related intellectually to those he represents, but in an unconscious way. He represents the mass in the sense of *resembling* it, so that it recognises itself in him and can enjoy the illusion of obeying itself in its obedience to him; in this way it feels it is its own master. This new kind of tyrant, an emanation from the depth of the mass, resembles it in its most massive aspect. He conveys the impression of a force that is almost or quite undifferentiated, a sort of quantitative power. (One has only to compare Stalin or Hitler with Napoleon Bonaparte, the last of the tyrants and *condottieri* of a quite different age, to understand immediately what is meant.) The 20th-century 'leaders' are at the head of both an 'Islam' and a tyranny; they claim, or are claimed, to be the incarnation of a race (and a people), like Hitler, or of a class (and an empire), like Stalin. The figure of Stalin is a comprehensive symbol: professional revolutionary, son of the

[1] Zoological materialism, Pan-Germanism, geopolitics, war between States in place of war between classes, 'aryanism' versus 'semitism', Prussian socialism versus Western capitalism and Asiatic bolshevism, 'proletarian' nations versus 'capitalist' nations, 'blood and soil' versus 'mind and money', 'Nordic idealism, liberty, and democracy' versus French softness and corruption, racial purity versus impurity, a people with roots versus frontierless finance, and finally, at the last moment, the defence of Europe (of which they themselves were the oppressors and partial destroyers) against 'Jews, Anglo-Saxons, and bolshevism'.

[2] Though there were also inconspicuous tyrants, such as Cosimo de Medici.

people, father of the people (and of the peoples), leader of the world proletariat and of the professional revolutionaries all over the world, who make the questionable claim to be the agents of the proletariat and are, unquestionably, the agents of Stalin. The modern tyrant regards himself as the equivalent, on the affective (not the political or intellectual) plane, of the chosen leader of a democracy. Chosen he certainly is, but in his case the word must be given its religious meaning. The autocracy of the tyrant is like a democracy that has sunk to the unconscious and instinctive level. Unlike the great personalities of the Italian Renaissance, so admired by Jacob Burckhardt and Nietzsche, the modern tyrants merge with their function instead of standing out from it and making, as it were, a contrast with it. They are leaders not because they are men of finer essence but, on the contrary, because they represent the popular essence itself, concentrated in an individual. They personify the concentration of power. Twentieth-century absolutism, which seems at times to give a man more power than any one man has ever before held, is nevertheless not a *personal* power. The tyrant is the incarnation of the party, and is identified with that enterprise which is also a Church. His face is, literally, the face of the party. The party's enemies are his enemies, and vice versa; his life's work is to ensure that the identification holds and, if possible, becomes closer. To be a tyrant in antiquity meant to be raised above the factions, but the modern tyrant identifies himself with one of them; and this faction becomes the State, *while still retaining the main characteristics of a faction*—and having become the State, it engulfs and imprisons the rest of society. The ancient tyrants were often 'free thinkers', indifferent to the factional disputes[1]; and there is really no reason why a modern tyrant should not be the same. Nevertheless, he 'participates' in his faction, and is touched by what touches it. So he can never allow himself to *appear* detached. The Greek and Italian tyrants seem to have wanted to be sovereign personalities, and if their power shone with the brilliance of personality it had also its fragility: but the modern tyrant is much more like an actor playing a star part than an original character. His very face and person are stylised and socialised; his life-story, become legendary during his life-time, is so written as to fulfil an unconscious demand of the masses. He 'represents' a certain *style of man*, and his language is the language of the mass. The very substance of his speeches is moulded and assimilated to the techniques by which they are diffused and by which they acquire or enhance their obsessive power: truisms, recital of facts,

[1] It was certainly one of Napoleon's assets that during the Revolution he was not deeply involved in the passions of the French, but was, so to speak, organically alien to their passionate factions. His rise was steady and untroubled because he took account of passions and prejudices only as a great strategist takes account of the conditions for a battle—as objective data relating to the problem of action.

repetition, assertions so gross that their very enormity dispenses them from the test of proof, appeals to elementary sentiments and motives and attitudes (fear, attack, rights, defence, pæans of victory, threats, displays of innocence, displays of toughness).

* * * *

In the 18th century men began to exalt 'natural reason'; everything was to be reasoned about and explained. In the following century it was hoped that the light of reason would illuminate everyone, and the reasonings and explanations would be available to all. What school does for children, the press was to do for adults, so that everyone would enjoy the benefits of Reason and Enlightenment. The sacred was expected to vanish without leaving a trace after it had been explained away by all the books and pamphlets and newspapers which, with the later addition of the broadcast and the film, were the typical means of expression of the period. But these very same means of expression were used in the 20th century for reintroducing the sacred into politics. In the democratic and capitalist 19th century there was a vast and incessant outpouring of words, but in the 20th, with ever-increasing technical resources for their diffusion, the words seemed to proliferate automatically and multiply by the million; and the very instruments of enlightenment upon which it was hoped to establish the 'reign of reason' turned in the 20th century into propaganda vehicles for secular religion, up-to-date fetishism, and leader worship.

The techniques evolved by modern industry enable what would have been no more than a tyranny in earlier ages to become a totalitarian absolutism.

Even the most tyrannical of the ancient tyrants could not be totalitarian in more than intention, because he lacked the means for getting control of his subjects' actions and thoughts. But the modern tyrant has unprecedented possibilities for obtaining such control, thanks partly to the modern techniques at his disposal and partly to the destruction of many of the traditional bonds between human beings and of the sentiments underlying them. He is thus able to obtain a sort of total control. The children's minds are moulded at school, and the adults are exposed to the unremitting propaganda of meetings, newspapers, wireless, cinema, and poster publicity: the whole technique of capitalist advertising is called upon. Totalitarianism maintains itself by its power of initiating, amplifying, and intensifying 'psychological epidemics': obsession, phobia, impulsive action or non-action, fear, and hate. It conditions men's reflexes for delation or aggression, and stimulates the psychological mechanisms conducive to the desired action and behaviour.[1] The minds of individuals become stereotyped by the simple process of repetition, and collective neuroses and psychoses are enabled to propagate and intensify themselves as it were automatically. Exposed to the pressure of unremitting suggestion by the obsessive technique of press and wireless, 'totalitarian man', as an *individual*, begins to experience and to accommodate himself to affective states which properly belong to the *mass*, and the distinction between the individual in possession of his critical faculty and the individual rendered acutely suggestible by the 'crowd psychological state' tends to disappear. There is continuity between the two states of mind, and the individual becomes, as it were, *contaminated* by the mass.

In the industrial countries, with their thickly populated urban areas, each individual is intensively and continuously exposed to the pressure of the environment, and in such areas the human element in the environment is a very powerful and concentrated influence. Consequently, the mind of the individual, or, more specifically, its *organisation*, which is what makes him an individual person, is pitted against a suggestion and a pressure which are too strong for it; the intensity and volume of the pressure and the force of the suggestion are on a different scale from the individual's equipment for resisting and criticising them. Collective impulses and inhibitions are a part of his life, and soon become irresistible or indispensable. *The technique of bombardment by words, systematically and obsessively employed, can disorganise and then radically reorganise the minds of men subjected to it.* In a totalitarian régime the techniques by which the individual reintegrates himself become a monopoly of the central power, and the personal element, which every highly developed human being evolves by his work upon himself, is reduced in importance. These techniques are used in such a way as to strengthen the already powerful forces of social interaction and interattraction, and to widen the scope and control the direction of these forces. Reflexes of justification are gradually substituted for reflexes of criticism, until the individual's power to resist or arrest the prevailing trends has become atrophied. In totalitarian man the power of going against the stream is abolished.

The author of *The Elementary Forms of the Religious Life* [2] depicted 'primitive' man in subjection to extreme social constraints, and he contrasted this condition with that of 'civilised' man, in the society of which he himself was the sociologist. According to him, the latter possessed an 'organic' and the former only a 'mechanical' solidarity.

[1] M. Serge Tchakotine (*Le Viol des foules par la propagande politique*, Gallimard, 1940) describes this as 'psychological slavery', and calls the totalitarian man with his 'guided mentality' a 'psychic automaton'.

[2] Durkheim (Engl. trans.; London, 1915).

So the transition from liberalism to totalitarianism would be a 'regression' towards the primitive social form.[1] We must observe that if the 'primitive', as conceived by the French school of sociology, 'bathes' in the 'collective thought' of his clan or tribe, it is at least his real thought and not imposed upon him from outside. It is the very form of lived experience, because the individual and the social, for him, are each implicit in the other; whereas the propaganda of totalitarianism imposes upon its subjects abstractions which gradually become felt and lived experiences but which begin by being forced upon them by external constraint. In this, totalitarianism is continuing and exaggerating the work of capitalism. The 'lies of the press' were invented by capitalism, but it was reserved for totalitarianism to give them forced currency, backed by the power of the State.

The abstract formulas inculcated by obsessive propaganda become transformed into suggestions, and the constraint imposed by words is reinforced by action. Urban man in a totalitarian civilisation is exposed to the maximum force of social interaction and inter-attraction in a *prescribed direction*.

Thus the individual, 'contaminated' by the mass and moulded to the image of the leader, is 'formed' during his most malleable period, and it is easy to see how vastly the totalitarian formation differs from that provided by the culture (or *Bildung*) of earlier systems. The 'average man' of totalitarianism will be a quite different person from the 'average man' of liberal and capitalist democracy. The totalitarian system works by inducement as well as by constraint; a pedagogic technique of repetition inculcates the pattern of the desirable, the correct procedure and behaviour for achieving success,[2] and the kind of enjoyment to be derived from it. It is a method of training the human animal, not fully planned in advance but gradually brought to perfection. By the sustained application of these methods a '*totalitarian man*' can be produced who differs in a number of ways from the other types of *homo sapiens* extant in the world at the same time. Looking at him from outside the totalitarian camp, there is a tendency to regard the totalitarian man as a victim of 'oppression'; but this is to underestimate the plasticity of human nature. Very often he is not oppressed, because good care has been taken to ensure that he shall feel different needs and desires from those who so regard him. This is the case, at least, so long as he is effectively exposed to the pressure and suggestion of the totalitarian system. But it is true that the slaves of the concentration

[1] But this kind of evolutionary conception gives rise to vain speculations more often than it helps to solve historical problems.

[2] The best way to learn about a society is to study what are the *real* conditions for succeeding in it.

camps, who are the classic example of totalitarian victims, tend to escape the formative influence (by being too far below it) to the extent that their treatment desocialises them and 'takes them out of history'.

The phenomena of totalitarianism are at once the cause and the effect of a decline of individual responsibility, which is in striking contrast with the moral maxims and norms of the liberal period. The régime of the concentration camps sought and found the point at which the individual can no longer maintain his personal and organised hierarchy of values and responsibilities. Once this point has been reached, the concentration camps tend to transform the person into something that is no longer a person, and in so doing they merely extend and intensify, by hot-house methods, the process of decline of personality and responsibility which may be observed in other modern societies, not merely the totalitarian ones but those which, like our own, have been particularly exposed to totalitarian influences.[1] In a society where individuals are as manifestly the product of circumstances as the bubbles of marsh gas, it is difficult to feel personal hatred, and feelings tend to become simplified. If people are noxious, it is because they are doing what they must do in order to live; they are seen as functions rather than faces. The man who believes himself to have retained some sense of personal responsibility will feel—if he has never been tortured or lived in a concentration camp—that he has merely been lucky and has no grounds for taking any credit; and as a result of this he becomes incapacitated for judging others. Not having suffered them himself, how can he judge the pressures to which others have been subjected? And even if he has himself suffered, how can he be sure that his suffering was the same as theirs? He cannot feel much confidence in such an insecure criterion. Perhaps he has been lucky even in his trials, for how can he feel certain that he would have resisted certain temptations if he had been older, or younger? On the whole, he suspects that any indignation he may feel at the behaviour of others may be merely facile.

Totalitarianism has inherited the organisational techniques of capitalism, but the high degree of organisation made available to it by capitalist development is used for different ends. The progress and triumphs of capitalism are turned to controlling, with maximum efficiency, the movements of men and the circulation of goods, and also to repressive and police techniques, and terror, and the 'conditioning of minds'. It is only because modern tyranny is able to be totalitarian, thanks to the technical means at its disposal, that it is able to overrun enormous countries and even to penetrate beyond their frontiers while at the same time retaining some of the features of the ancient city

[1] For more than ten years these influences have been strongly at work upon us, both from Russia and from Germany.

tyranny. Today, a world tyranny is feasible. The totalitarian police possesses the surest and most efficient means, not only for destruction but also for the rapid transmission of information and orders. Moreover, in Russian totalitarianism, which has had the time to become and now is the most 'advanced' specimen of the type, the State holds all its subjects at its mercy. Being the only employer, it can deprive them of work; controlling the supply of all the necessaries of life, it can banish an individual from society and compel his surrender by withholding his ration card. It can order the movements of individuals and groups; indeed, there can be no group migrations except those ordered by the State, and they are on a considerable scale. It also controls travel; no one may come or go without its permission. And since it allows no one to avoid the common task or even to relax from it, no one is allowed to leave except for approved reasons.

We have already described, in political terms, the phenomenon of concentration of power in Russia.[1] Economic, religious, and political power, which were kept distinct in the liberal era, are all combined at the summit of the pyramid, where it is for a few men to know and act and judge and decide about everything. Ultimately, power of every kind resides in the leader. In Hitler's Germany the leader had no use for any kind of ideological justification. Not that he forbade it—on the contrary—but the sacred was embodied in him as a fact. In communism, however, the 'Islamic' character is more marked. There is a 'Koran'[2]; the wheat has been separated from the chaff, the canon from the apocryphal material. Marx and Lenin have their place in the canon along with Stalin, but not Trotsky or Bukharin, whose infamy resembles that of Simon Magus.

During the 19th century power was, in theory, more and more bound by the letter of a constitution, but in the 20th century it is breaking free. At the summit, where all powers converge, they are redistributed on purely functional principles. Economic power (the power of control over economic life) and political power, and the power to prescribe what everyone must believe, no longer represent separate spheres; whether such-and-such a power is exercised by such-and-such a man or men, or by others, depends upon functional requirements, and a man may pass from one function to another which, by our standards, is totally unconnected with it. Equally, there are combinations of functions which we would regard as quite different from one another.

A few men are in control of a State which aims to predetermine, by

[1] Part I, Chapter 5.

[2] In a country of so high a culture as Germany, it was not possible for *Mein Kampf* to fill the role of a Koran. Educated Germans could only, at the best, accept the book with strong mental reservations; but they accepted its effect upon the man in the street, keeping out of the way themselves or waiting until they could turn events to their advantage.

planning, the entire life of a society. (There were some Nazis who hoped that it would be possible, by systematic eugenics and selection, to predetermine biologically the individual members of society.) Thus power exerts a direct effect upon economics, and we are at the opposite pole to the classical liberal economic theory with its 'objective economic laws' which must be respected. The capitalist criterion of economic yield is subordinated to considerations of the development of power—a 'regression' which throws light upon the nature of economics itself.

The Nazis did not interfere with capitalist profits, but they imposed a four-year plan upon German industry, which meant that private initiative was tolerated only in so far as it conformed with the plan and could be fitted into it smoothly and without loss. Although the capitalists and their high officials and experts retained the direction in their own hands, their position tended, by a phenomenon of convergence, more and more to resemble[1] that of the higher ranks in the Russian State system. By the same phenomenon of convergence, there is a tendency to resemblance between the supreme planners of the two totalitarian states, although Germany retained private property while Russia suppressed it. In fact, the Hitlerian State did already control the functioning and use of the principal means of production, exchange, and communication, and with the war its control reached the maximum of rigour. By its exchange-control and double currency it had full power over Germany's foreign trade; and its policy of barter and bilateral agreements ensured it the monopoly of all large-scale transactions and gave it the full disposal of the national economy. The convergence between the German and the Russian system is obvious; both of them rejected the laws of the world market, and in neither of them was there a hard-and-fast line between the political and the economic sphere. Hitler used intimidation to impose such commercial treaties as were necessary to his pursuit of political power. Once the war began, his 'occupation money', which was given forced currency, was backed only by the power of Germany as manifested in her victories, and not by a gold reserve; between his economy and his power there was complete continuity and, as it were, convertibility—a state of affairs totally alien to classical liberal economics. There had already been a softening of economic rigidity through the development of credit and the interaction between the flow of wealth and changes of opinion; and the possibilities of action were thereby greatly increased. Thenceforward it may be said that the spheres of religion and politics and economics were permeable by one another to such an extent that none of them could be accurately described in the terms that were applicable to them in the 19th century. The new masters found the life of the collectivity as wax in their hands:

[1] This is the basic theme of Burnham's *Managerial Revolution*.

economic laws still existed, and were governed by facts, but the masters could control the facts. What they had to reckon with was not so much human resistance as the risk that a changing world might upset their calculations. Where gold is supplanted by force, the economic motive of profit is supplanted by the will-to-power and intimidation. If the need to live does not spur the workers to sufficient production, it becomes possible to substitute for it the fear of dying; and if labour costs are too high, they can be reduced by making men work in 'labour camps'.

* * * *

Islam has provided the type of the society in which the political and the sacred are indissolubly merged. The law of the Koran was religious, political, and civil all in one; and an infidel could be no more than a *tributary*. In history and in law he appeared as an object, but not as a participating subject; and the Ottoman empire was interested in the children of infidels only because they could be recruited as janissaries. During the great period of Islamic conquests the State, in so far as it existed in our sense of the word, *participated* in the sacred doctrine of the prophet and was its embodiment and life. The companions of the prophet, partakers in the revolutionary legitimacy, did not constitute a Church; nor do they in the secular religions inherent in 20th-century absolutisms, but the power of the prophetic élite (which is what the party's 'summit' is at the moment when the new State is created) is all the more absolute for being, as it were, a condensation of the power of the whole of society. And the leader represents the extreme point of condensation.

Having received Christianity from Byzantium, it would seem that Russia has also copied the Byzantine example of interpenetration between Church and State, which allowed the Cæsar to intervene in dogmatic and conciliar questions from inside the Church, as it were, instead of acting from without like the monarchs of the West. When, in 753, Constantine V secured the condemnation of the ikons at the Council of Hieria, the opposing party was punished for rebellion both against the Empire and against God himself; and there was little distinction between the two rebellions. The Great Comrade in the Kremlin today is rightly regarded as the leader not only of the Russian communist party but also of the 'world proletariat' (which means, of all the other communist parties). Since the war he has remained Generalissimo, but he is still also the head of the administration, in virtue of his function as secretary of the Party. His 'natural attributes' as described in official pronouncements and encomiums include 'genius', 'well-beloved', etc. By this concentration of power he resembles, even more than the Tsar, the Cæsar of Byzantium. From the 10th century it was the aim of the grand dukes of Kiev to imitate the Byzantine Basileus; and the Byzantine origin of the Russian model of sovereignty is indicated by the very word Tsar (Cæsar). A people of pagan Slavs formed a barrier between the State of Kiev and the West; and Novgorod's commercial relations with the outside world during its great days did not last long enough to counterbalance its secular contact with Byzantium. The historian[1] who defined the Byzantine empire as an 'artificial creation' which governed twenty different nationalities, uniting them under the motto 'one master and one Faith', was perhaps aware that the definition could be applied without much alteration to Soviet Russia, which recalls both Byzantium, in which orthodoxy[2] and nationality were identified, and also those nations, of which ancient Jewry is the type, which are at the same time a people and a Church. The Islamic communities, for which religious and warlike activities were one and the same, are also an example of this type. As 'Islams', both the Russian communist campaign and the Pan-German 'Aryan' campaign would in principle subdue the whole world, which they hope to dominate, to this 'mystical participation' of an orthodoxy with an historic people—and more particularly with the high élite of this people, in which (according to Hitler's system) the Race, and (according to the Russian system) the Marxist doctrine, or in other words 'Science', is held to be incarnate. The community of those who know 'the way of salvation' thus reappears in a modern, secular-

[1] Charles Diehl.

[2] The 'general line' comes in a direct line from Byzantium. There is convergence between Russian history and the necessities of the great modern tyranny of the industrial age. In 1547 Ivan the Terrible crowned himself Tsar, or Emperor, of the Roman East; and not long before, the monk Theophilus of Pskov had written to the Grand Duke Basil: 'Two Romes have already fallen; and now Moscow is the third Rome. There will not be a fourth.' The same accent, in a more modern key, can be heard in Dostoevsky (cf. the speech on Pushkin). The general line is the *consensus*, as defined by the supreme authorities, of all actions and all thoughts. The proclaimed necessity for such a consensus explains a number of specifically Russian totalitarian features. 'Class statistics' and the re-writing of history (which was also a characteristic feature of ancient China) are manifestations of orthodoxy. The State's truth must be believed; and since there is no fundamental distinction between the spiritual and the temporal, thought that is in contradiction with act cannot be tolerated. It must be exorcised.

Thus, in the great spectacular judicial displays, the specifically Russian propensity for public confession is exploited—a propensity which is not derived from Byzantinism but grew up later among sects like the Old Believers and the Dukhobors. The 'educational' aspect of the so-called trials of those who are rejected from the general line and the total consensus reveals a convergence between Byzantinism and the simplified scientism imported from the West. In Russia the latter becomes still simpler and more 'scientific'. The accused, who are represented as having always lied, must be considered truthful for the first time when they confess. To believe their confessions is obligatory, on pain of diverging from the general line. The convergence between so-called scientific utilitarianism and the Byzantinism of the general line consists in this: that the accused man is always made use of. If he is not executed, he is made to work for the five-year plan; and if he is executed, his death is exploited as propaganda.

ised version (in which the future does duty for the 'Beyond'). Such a community is the collective repository of this immense and all-important knowledge, and is symbolically represented in the person of the leader. Infidels will be overcome with the aid of 'science' and 'technics'; and hence the unquestionably magical resonance of such words as 'dialectic'.

To be communist and to be Russian are two states between which there is participation, so that any offence suffered by communism will also affect Russia, and vice versa; and each is moved to vengeance for any moral injury to the other. Any such wrong offends the communal psyche, which is composed of the psyches of all the faithful; it touches them all, and each of them reacts individually to the offence. There is here something other and more than an interaction between the individual and the social. The conception of an individual psyche and a social psyche in contrast to one another is too static, for each of them only represents one limited view of a *circulation of energy*. It is better to regard them, for the sake of comparison, as communicating vessels rather than as closed systems. Each of them is created by the other, and fed by it; but each assimilates and transforms what the other gives it, and is itself the product of this assimilation and transformation.

It is easy to understand the value of orthodoxy in a secular religion, for orthodoxy is simply the intellectual representation of a *consensus*, which is the very foundation of strength and victory. Unanimity is desired, and the idea that there could be unanimity in error is intolerable—which is not to say that it is impossible, but it is the kind of thought that is repressed, censored, and exorcised. A man who harbours such ideas is a danger to the community. At the trials of Zinoviev and Kamenev, and later of Bukharin, the fundamental issue was: Is it possible to be right in opposition to the Party? And suppose a man really is in the right against the Party, is not this the essence of criminality? If, being in the right, he is mentally opposed to the Party's actions, he has at least that much in common with the enemy; and this is the first link in the chain which connects the secret opposition with the enemy's world. Moreover, what could be more demoralising than the example of a man who is in the right against the Party and outside the Party? If the Party deprives such a man of his thought and of his life as well, surely it is only taking what belongs to it, for all his power and authority came to him through the *circulation of energy*, and by the use he makes of them he is diverting away from the Party energies to which it has a right. Alain used to tell his students at the Lycée Henri-IV that it is right to withhold assent from the tyrant. But secular religions, and the tyrannies which support them, draw their life from this assent, and they regard as a menace anyone who refuses it. They are created out of their subjects' psychological energy, and if its refusal became general they would be destroyed. Secular religion and tyranny demand to be *acknowledged.* By definition, they cannot allow 'interior freedom'; or if they do tolerate such a menace it is only under duress, and only so long as they have no option.

If the head of the State is also the Commander of the Faithful, then the political and the sacred cannot be kept apart. The result is that in totalitarian societies the judgment which strikes the dissenter does not seem to be contingent or dependent upon human and personal wills; it seems *inevitable*. It is the 'irreversible movement of history', something higher than and incommensurable with any individual factor. The dissenter is trodden down beneath the march of history. It is truly a case of 'belief in impersonal and omnipresent forces', and everything seems to be so calculated as to make the man at the base of the pyramid feel himself as impotent against the will of the Party as against the stars in their courses. (But since this is only true in so far as he believes it, every possible method is employed to enforce the belief.) The man who succeeds in swimming with the historical current can take advantage of its power and indulge, behind the impersonal mask which lends him temporarily the face of necessity itself, the needs of his 'all-too-human' nature. But it sometimes happens that even the mighty stumble in their turn and 'fall out of history'. . . . In the countries where they are the most strictly obeyed, secular religions do not emerge from the depths; they are imposed from above. The faith, the myths, and the dogmas are handed down from the summit.

* * * *

In so far as 20th-century absolutism is a tyranny, its political dynamic is essentially the same as that of the ancient tyrannies. But totalitarianism brings a new and original feature to tyranny by identifying the political with the sacred. It appears as a secular religion of militant 'Islamic' type: the distinction between politics, religion, and economics is abolished. Power is concentrated and is also, at first, undifferentiated. . . . But totalitarianism, in fact, is simply the realisation of the ideal to which the ancient tyrannies aspired. (They came near to achieving it in the small cities, whose citizens, attached to the place of their birth by religious ties, could be kept permanently under the eye of the tyrant or his mercenaries, unless they went into exile.) But modern industrial techniques not only make it possible to treat an enormous country in the same way that the most stringent tyrant of the 8th century B.C. could treat some little city or island of the Ægean, but also make it possible to go much further. By 'tests' and techniques of investigation, a whole population can be card-indexed with full details; all the main facts of the individual's past history, and his relations with other people, and even his aptitudes and tendencies, can be ascertained and listed. The testing of reflexes is already current practice, and the technique for measuring what the 19th century called 'intellectual capacity' is ready for use. The totalitarian State can train and condition the reflexes of the human animal almost from birth; and an important part of his education is purely and simply an application of these training methods. From birth to death, thanks to the technique of bombardment by words, the individual is kept under the influence of his trainers, like a small child or a performing animal. He must accept what the State inculcates without ever being allowed to think freely about it.[1]

In serious cases—for example, when the government is dealing with a refractory individual—suggestibility can be increased by the administration of chemical doses which have the effect of entirely destroying the subject's resistance to suggestion. In other words, when psychology fails the inquisitors of secular religion and State are free to resort to physiology—to say nothing of torture, which has never ceased to be employed, more or less secretly, by every police force in the world.[2]

Now, for the first time, instead of being used in conformity with the accepted standards of society, which are implicitly approved by everyone, all these techniques can be applied at the will of a small omnipotent and 'omniscient' group of men, a group in which *power* and the *sacred* are concentrated and made manifest to the eyes of all.

There is a second point of difference between 20th-century absolutism and the ancient tyrannies; namely that the modern tyranny is in subjection to its own methods. We have already seen that in modern absolutisms the leader is not distinguished, as many former tyrants were, by the *difference* between himself and his subjects, but is, on the contrary, like the embodied essence of what they all have in common. The 20th-century tyrant is a 'popular star' and his personal character is obscured; and this is equally true whether he sets himself up as a magician in control of 'hidden forces' and in direct contact, so to speak, with the subconscious, or whether he is simply the personification of the Party, his personal features being used as the trade-mark of 'God and Co.' This seems to mean that the former relation between man as a *person* and his human means of action has broken down; it is as though the means had become so powerful that the temptation to use them is irresistible, and thus the capacity to choose between them, selecting one method and rejecting another, is abolished. Totalitarianism is a sort of dictatorship of means. From its first beginnings, as we have seen,

[1] On the day when we are unable to think freely about material presented to us, Western culture will be a thing of the past. There are other possible cultures. . . .

[2] cf. A. Mellor, *La Torture*.

tyranny never accepted the principle of self-constraint or recognised the existence of 'invisible barriers'. It was because the ancient tyrants over-rode the sacred conventions of their day that their name was execrated. The tyrant's subjects, no less than the dispossessed oligarchy, were still attached to the ancient gods, and were shocked in their souls by his impiety. The illegitimacy of the tyranny became connected in their minds with its cruelty, and the two have remained connected in history.

In contrast to the ancient tyrants, the 20th-century tyrant rehabilitates the sacred, but in an unrecognisable form which is hateful both to those who are attached to the older forms and to those who would like to have it in a less oppressive form. Since, however, the religion to which the modern tyrant adheres is a secular one, it has no scruples about the use of temporal means. It is itself temporal. The Inquisition, whose last fires were burning at the time of the Counter-Reformation, was not perhaps a phenomenon inherent in what one might call the essence of Christianity, but it happened all the same; and in a secular religion it could happen without coming into conflict with any doctrinal or other internal obstacle. Marx never denied that violent means would be used, and squeamishness was to be discouraged. Technical and industrial progress has placed unprecedented means at the disposal of those who work for the triumph of a secular religion; and they are ill-equipped for rejecting such means. It seems as if the mere existence of these means[1] creates an irresistible urge to employ them[2] and subjects men to a new determinism—which cannot exactly be described as inhuman, since the force it exerts is derived from man himself, and it is he who supplies its source of energy.[3] It is their own power that men call inhuman when

[1] Which, it is fair to note, are also in existence in the United States, and are currently employed by gangsters and by the police who are in daily contact with them. But in American society this is a peripheral zone, and in the interior a different climate seems to prevail. The existence of religious traditions and of a profound belief in individual opportunity, and also the very structure of this federal Republic, are a guarantee that these gangster methods are not the act of an omnipotent State, or of an omniscient 'political class', at war with its own citizens. There is no secular religion. The State belongs to the citizens and not to any secular religion; it is an organism in which all have an interest because it guarantees to all men their opportunity. Admittedly this is only the theory, or the 'political formula', as Mosca would say, but it has the value of a regulating standard by which aberrations are recognised as aberrations. The theory represents the good, and, in relation to it, evil—though it does exist—appears as evil and not as the remedy for evil. When attempts are made to excuse or justify evil, the standard they refer to is the good. We may add that, in another way, the very existence of these contradictions is *also* a guarantee that America is not totalitarian.

[2] I refrain from discussing here the 'trials' which are characteristic features of Russian totalitarianism and the communist secular religion. They call for separate and detailed study.

[3] In this and the preceding chapter we have been concerned with the circulation and transformation of energy, adopting a point of view from which the distinction between psychology and sociology appears superficial. This point of view goes beyond the perspectives which show the individual as separate from society, or psychology from sociology.

they find themselves crushed by it as individuals. Psychological forces are not confined within the limits of the individual. The individual's organisation of these forces is his psychological individuality; but individuality can be compared only to the visible part of an iceberg. The farther we go below the surface, the weaker is the unifying and, as it were, centralising power of the individual principle. As we have seen, an ideology is a ruse by which the top of the iceberg deceives the lower part—and the converse is also true.

In fact, when objectively examined, the means employed reveal that the ends are of the same nature as themselves and quite unlike the proclaimed end—which is always, in one form or another, the 'realisation of the Good'. The end, which is of the same nature as the means (at the lower level the distinction between the two does not exist), is censored at the higher, or official, levels, both of the 'Islamic' community and of the individual's consciousness (between which there is no hard-and-fast line, for it is the same energy that is being circulated and transformed).

Twentieth-century absolutism, therefore, differs from the ancient forms of tyranny as realisation differs from intention, so greatly do the means at its disposal increase its power of territorial expansion and its psychological intensity. In a word, it is thanks to its *organisation* that modern tyranny makes the ancient tyrannies and despotisms appear, by comparison, imperfectly tyrannical and despotic. It is organisation that puts a world of difference between pre-capitalist and post-capitalist tyranny. The latter is called totalitarian because the capitalist era has revealed that it is possible to organise and rationalise *everything*. It is clear in retrospect that the weakness of organisation in the old tyrannies and despotisms was an effective safeguard of liberty; in other words, the way was kept open for new possibilities. But totalitarianism can organise on a world scale with the same thoroughness as capitalism can organise a factory. When the Arab and Islamic conquests reached their maximum extent, stretching from the Indus to the Garonne, it was quite impossible to achieve centralisation; but capitalism has made centralisation possible over an even vaster area.

This is the cause of another difference between ancient despotism and modern tyranny: the effective opposition now occurs at a different point in the system. In the Achemenid and Ottoman empires the governors of remote provinces could proclaim themselves independent and reject the despot's authority. But in contemporary absolutism, owing to the concentration of power, the strongest possibilities of opposition exist in the neighbourhood of the summit and not at the periphery, as in the old despotisms, nor at the base among the lower social strata (which is where the dissident communists would wish them to be). In comparison with liberal society, the possibility of opposition has shifted from below upwards. The maximum possibility is at that part of the summit occupied by the high personnel of the police,[1] who have the whole system as it were under their hand. So the concentration of power which is inherent in such a system may one day prove fatal to it.

In the totalitarian world, what Hegel and the early Marx called civil society, in which 'each individual is the sum of his needs', no longer exists. But though civil society as such can no longer be distinguished, man is still none the less 'the sum of his needs', and it is by his needs that the totalitarian State holds him, just as he is held, according to Marx, by the 'eunuch of industry'[2] in the capitalist régime.

'Every human weakness,' said Marx, 'binds man to the priest because it is the point where the priest can get access to his heart'; and in the same way the secular religion and the totalitarian State get their hold upon men through all those needs which reveal the weakness and precariousness of the human condition. It is the same principle that Marx noted in capitalist society: every need implies dependence. In the totalitarian régime the State alone is independent, and its independence is a system built upon the dependence of individuals. There can be no social success outside the system, so everything that the man of today links with social success is also bound up with the system, and more particularly the satisfaction of the fundamental needs: hunger, love, conquest, protection, the possession (or the illusion of possession) of things and people, and the desire to be free from petty necessities. The State is the sole employer and the universal punisher. Like a father, who may be affectionate or sadistic, it can feed or starve the individual; it may promote him to the higher spheres of social responsibility, or it may degrade him to the hell of the concentration camps, where the most gifted man can be automatically reduced by depriving him of calories. The power of money in capitalist society arises from the fact that it is universally desired as being, in principle, the means of satisfying every passion[3] and every need; thus money comes to be sought for in place of the goods that it procures, and the means appears to replace, and does in fact to some extent replace, the end (or, if it be preferred, there is a sort of dialectical transition from end to means). But in capitalism this universal means, or common measure, which tends to usurp the reality of

[1] cf. Chapter 5. [2] Marx, *Nationalökonomie und Philosophie*.

[3] We assume this here for the sake of simplicity. It is not uncommon in contemporary society for women to love a man who personifies in their eyes the power of money or social influence. Since this power is physically identified with the man, it is pointless to ask if they would love him without the power. (There has been a displacement and intellectualisation of the attribute of virility, which is power; and even if the man in question is not particularly 'virile', he is still the personification of power.) We may say that the man is loved *because of* his power or his money, but it would be false to conclude from this that he is not loved. The love is *conditioned* by the power, but it is a mistake to confuse love with the conditions of love.

the ends it pursues, is *in circulation*; it is mobile. It is only in the imagination of the believer who is at war with it that capitalism is a being endowed with will and purpose; though it can indeed be argued that such a view is not entirely false. To regard capitalism in this way may help to throw light on certain aspects of it. But up to now there has never been, and there still is not, any group of men who act as a general directing staff for capitalism as a whole. If such a general staff were ever discovered, and if its activities were of exactly the same kind as those of the communist Islam's general staff, then we should have to find another name for capitalism. It would have lost one of its essential characteristics. For the dictatorship of money never was, and is not, the result of a conscious, predetermined plan; it simply happened as a by-product of men's activities and efforts. Money certainly does represent energy or, as Marx said, 'alienated human essence'; but it is not a being endowed with self-consciousness. On the other hand, the activities of the Campaign against capitalism are predetermined and planned; where the Campaign holds full sway, the power to which it subjects its adherents is not blind, like the power of money; it is the power of a system which is embodied in living men. This system, as manifested in the realm of action, *is* the communist Campaign. But the transition from the régime of omnipotent money to a system embodied in living beings brings no alleviation but rather an aggravation of the tyranny to which men are subjected. Who could pretend that totalitarianism, taken as a whole, is less oppressive than capitalism?[1] On the contrary, the inherent tendency of capitalism to increase the dependence of the great majority is itself increased and accelerated by totalitarianism. It is brought into full consciousness. Totalitarianism inherits all capitalism's methods and many of its characteristics, but not its *liberal* characteristic, the most human of all even in its inhumanity. So totalitarianism can be said to co-ordinate into a single system all the aspects of human dependence which are characteristic of the industrial age; unified by totalitarianism, human dependence appears as a single total phenomenon. The tyranny is inherent within the society, and is seen not only in its attitude towards other societies nor only in the citizens' attitude towards the authorities, towards one another, and towards themselves, for it exists both as an 'objective' structure on the social and historical plane, *and also in the individual, in the form of ideas, beliefs, behaviour, outlook on the world, and style of life*. The individual psyche and the collective psyche are one, and not two. As Nietzsche observed, society reveals

[1] It may be objected that totalitarianism is only a phase or 'transitional dictatorship', which is essentially the Marxist position. But if we agree to this objection we agree to totalitarianism. Once again we are forced to perceive that there is no real communication between those within the system and those who remain outside it; and this lack of communication enables us to diagnose the presence of religion.

what the individual hides (and the individual reveals what society hides)[1]; and from the observations of psychiatrists and psycho-analysts concerning individuals we can perhaps learn a great deal more about society than the psychiatrists and psycho-analysts themselves would suspect.

* * * *

What does western Europe owe to the fact that it possessed a strong Third Estate? Metaphorically speaking, the answer is: a social soil of great fertility, a soil which nourished and invigorated the idea of liberty. It was thanks to the communal struggle of the commercial bourgeoisie of the Western cities against feudalism that the monarchs were able to reduce and confine the feudal nobles to the status of courtiers. In this sense, Western history is the history of the struggle for liberty or opportunity. Each element of society struggled against any of the others that obstructed its opportunities; the kings against the feudal nobles and the nobles against the kings; the nobles against one another and the kings against one another; the commons against the nobles; and finally, in France, the Third Estate (led by its historically conscious and technically informed vanguard) against the *ancien régime*—a hierarchy of estates which was withholding official recognition from a state of affairs which already existed in fact. The Third Estate summed up in itself and was in a sense the historical representative of the centuries of struggle in Europe for liberty, or opportunity; and when its vitality exploded like a train of powder across Europe from 1793 to 1815 it was like a final upshoot of the essential fertility of the historical and social soil. The *ancien régime* was a plurality of social groups which had grown from below upwards and which combined together so as to form a country. Between the groups the monarchy acted as arbitrator, and in France it powerfully assisted the growth of the Third Estate. The various privileged orders, the corporations and guilds, the provincial assemblies, the religious sects (such as Jansenism), the intellectual groups, the rivalry in the provinces between the king's agents and the local magnates—all this bears witness to a vigorous society and a fertile social soil. When the Third Estate made its revolution, the universality of its claim, which has since been so much criticised, was really the sign of a certain wisdom. It claimed equal rights—in other words, equality of opportunity for talent; and although this turned out in fact to mean the bourgeoisie, as Marxists were later to call it, the claim remains much more valid than the claim put forward by the Russian revolutionaries, who seized power in the name of the proletariat. For it is impossible that the proletariat should ever exercise power, as a correct analysis of

[1] This might be called a sociological example of the principle of communicating vessels.

the two words power and proletariat is by itself sufficient to show. The resulting absolutism merely gives factual proof of the theoretical error.

Whereas the bourgeois revolution was the culmination of a period of social fertility, the totalitarian revolutions of the 20th century appear today rather as the reaction of societies threatened with dissolution: there is an immediate concentration of power at the summit, while below it all is in confusion and disarray. And the disorder is only ended by the initiative of the supreme authority, which imposes rigid cadres of a military type upon the whole of society from top to bottom.

History seems to show that there are periods of social fertility when a society produces forms which appear to grow, like trees, from below upwards; this was how there grew up, after the great invasions, the turbulent feudalism of western Europe; its towns, its great religious orders, its cathedrals, its urban civilisation along the great routes of communication and trade, and its arts and crafts and culture. Then there follows a period of stability: the dynastic State with its orders or estates, in which there is a comparative equilibrium between the still antagonistic forces; and in spite of the frequent and varied crises this was the situation during the apogee of the great Western monarchies. At such times, and viewed from a distance, the different warring elements appear like the members and organs of a single organism. After this come periods of crisis when, in spite of great social developments, the social soil seems to become impoverished; and the 19th and 20th centuries, with their mechanical progress, perhaps represent a period of this kind. New social groups still appear, such as the trade unions, but the social soil seems less rich. Groups of thinkers of the activist type urge the affective energies of individuals all in one direction, and the collectivity is increasingly subject to influences that seem to be external and to be the product of exhaustion rather than of strength—or perhaps of a tired strength, passive rather than active. Social structures are simplified, classes become indefinite and merge into the masses, separate powers coalesce, and society is reconstituted on simpler lines: army, administration, and public welfare. The weaker societies do not accomplish the whole process by themselves; it is imposed upon them. Societies that have become amorphous tend more and more to be forced into rigid moulds, and they begin to resemble one another to the point of merging into a single society. (In other words, the process involves a horizontal as well as a vertical simplification.) And in the non-totalitarian societies 'converging' phenomena begin to appear.

In our view, the totalitarian State is simply *the lowest and most disastrous way of adapting to this latter-day, autumnal social situation*; it is not a fatality imposed by history, and, indeed, any such notion is strictly meaningless. It is merely the most facile solution, and it has been able to prevail, though only for a short time, in an unstable society with a weak and 'sheltered' Third Estate, namely Germany, and also for a longer period in Russia, which is socially as well as geographically a vast open plain. It is only through 'cultural loans' that the Russian absolutism acquired its means of action; as in the days of the first Ivans, the State is still struggling to bring society to birth—and from this point of view the Russian revolution is not so much a breach of continuity as a very sharp acceleration both of historical rhythm and of the circulation of élites. The extension of such a system by force up to the shores of the Atlantic would involve an unmitigated lowering of civilisation. But this is no reason why it should not happen. What *is* a reason, however, is that Europe, though sore beset from within, is protected from the imminent Russian expansion by the power of America.

The sterility of the social soil is the cause of the complete disappearance in totalitarian régimes of all 'intermediate bodies'. They are replaced by forms which may superficially resemble them but which are organically different because they are inspired from above. Even the family offers no resistance to the State authority, which completely breaks it up by enrolling children in youth organisations and parents in adult organisations, and making it a civic duty for both to place the service of the State before family solidarity. In other societies, to denounce one's parents may be a hideous crime or an act of Roman virtue, but in this one it is an automatic social obligation, a mere act of conformity, and a profitable one from the point of view of enlightened self-interest; in short, a normal thing to do. And the fact that the family group may at any time be abruptly separated by transfers of labour or deportations gives the final touch to the special sociological character of the 'totalitarian' family.

* * * *

The resort to collective myth and the appeal to historic memories were not invented by the 20th-century movements. All through the 19th century there runs a thread of nostalgia for past glories and hopes of *risorgimento*. The peoples were to be awoken and transformed into nations; and poets, thinkers, men of letters, and agitators, inspired by the myths which they themselves created and formulated, endeavoured to impart them to the masses—because, as Marx said, it is by penetrating the masses that an idea becomes a force. Thus, in what is called fascism, we find that the most activist or (since our subject compels us to put a strain upon words) the most 'activising' of these mythical and legendary images are syncretised.[1] The succession of inconsistent

[1] The same phenomenon occurs in Stalinism, but more slowly and later, because it has had to pass through a Marxist and internationalist phase during which the myths are repressed.

attitudes, the conflicting images or representations, and the contradictory heroisms acquire an emotional homogeneity from the common possession of a certain 'activising power'. Myth for myth, there is nothing in Italian fascism, for example, that was not also in the *risorgimento*. But the fascists did not propose to leave these myths to artists, professors, and journalists; they wanted to connect them to the dynamism of the masses, in that region where there is continuity between imagination and act. If the masses are deeply penetrated, a psychic level is reached at which there is no inhibiting or arresting influence between feeling and doing, and the 'activating myth' can produce its maximum effect. This explains the swift and sure progress of Hitler and Mussolini in their rise to power. But, in its place, the economic explanation is equally true, because it explains why the masses are in a condition to respond to the reactivation of these myths. The historical riches of western Europe are so great that the reactivation of a country's historical myths is the only means by which any great movement can succeed. The Stalinists are well aware of this, and in France they appeal not only to the Commune (although it was patriotic) and to the Revolution (although it was opposed, on the whole, to the very idea of class), but also to Joan of Arc and even to Louis XIV. If Napoleon had not invaded Moscow at the head of an 'international army', perhaps they would appeal to him also; but Charlemagne, Emperor of the West, is of no use to them at all. Their aim is to appropriate the country's heritage. And this is what every great movement must do; it has no choice but to appeal to the people's historic memories, to those historical representations which still possess affective value and whose reactivation can be expected to reactivate the masses. That is why every great movement in France is bound in fact to appeal to the French Revolution as a period of greatness.[1] And the French Revolution is close to us, it is still active in our hearts; and all the more so because it satisfies the intellect today much better than a class revolution which would condemn the majority of Frenchmen to a sort of historical purgatory. It may be that the French Revolution—which is simply an assertion of the necessity for the circulation of the élites—has still to complete its work. The appeal to tradition must be to a still living tradition; and only a tradition as live as the French Revolution can shake French hedonism, that hedonism of the post-liberal era which coquettes with misfortune, learning to play amid the ruins and to grow rich on the black market.

In the European countries with a rich past and a complex history, the great movements of the 20th century can only sustain their vitality by a

[1] Pointing out, for example, that in the country of Saint-Just a revolutionary cannot be a systematic liar, or belong to a 'foreign faction', or be the perpetual accomplice of an alien tyrant. When such representations are revivified, they become *active*.

return to the sources; and this is what gives the European, and particularly the French, Stalinists their distinctive colour. It compels them to reconcile yet another contradiction, and this can easily be done by adroitness of argument and verbal manipulation; for it is a purely intellectual contradiction, and has no weight against the simple need of strengthening modern incentives by combining them with historical ones. It is a typical operation of affective mass 'logic', and one of the most successful.

In all the great historical countries of Europe there is a tradition of legendary and 'sacred' history which every movement of social recomposition must take into account. In these countries children are familiarised in their most impressionable years with a whole repertory of historical attitudes and legendary representations, whose memory is an exaltation and a spur throughout their lives. The great movements of the 20th century—including Stalinism, except for its Leninist phase during Lenin's own life-time—were made possible by the work of 19th-century writers, poets, thinkers, and romantics, *mediated* through the popularisers who followed them. The resulting images created a language understood by the masses, a language based upon representations familiar to them from their early schooldays. It is noteworthy that the men who have handled this language the most skilfully—Hitler, Mussolini, Stalin—were men who in their youth never got much beyond the elementary school stage. Being on a level with the mass, their language was immediately comprehensible to it; and they, and those around them, had the gift for vulgarising the more ambitious theoretical representations which they later acquired. In this way they constructed a whole popular philosophy and history, rewritten for mass consumption and perfectly adapted for its object, and making use of crude and simplified, but 'activated', images.

The 20th century presents a series of 'transitional dictatorships'—in Russia, Lenin and the Politburo, and then Stalin; in Italy Mussolini; and in Germany, Hitler. They are, in fact, three varieties, or more precisely three variants, of the same sociological species. They are three tyrannies in the strict meaning we have assigned to the term: a faction and its leader requiring a repressive apparatus to maintain themselves in power.

From the purely political point of view the situation at first recalls the Convention, that is to say, the first dictatorial phase of the French Revolution, which ended with the more stable dictatorship of Napoleon Bonaparte. It contracts several phases of the French Revolution into one, as though there were a sort of 'acceleration of history' to be taken into account. In 'backward' Russia the functional political equivalent of our revolution was a revolution of the intelligentsia (or, if it be preferred, of the most completely and effectively 'activised' elements of the vanguard of the intelligentsia). In the movements farther west, in countries of older civilisation, richer history, and more fertile social and historical soil, namely in Italian fascism and German national socialism, this 'clean-sweeping' phase of the Russian revolution was not repeated. In those countries a clean sweep is seen as a vast and uncompensated destruction of wealth; and even Hitlerism, whose destructive character is unquestioned, had consciously to lay its chief emphasis upon historical and 'sacred' and legendary motifs. Stalinism itself, if it triumphed in one of these countries, would have to make a show of doing the same; for it is one of the conditions of success. The break with the preceding liberal democracy, even if it is a superficial democracy like the Italian and, still more, the German, affects the content much more than it affects the forms of the constitution; so it is easy to make a show of continuing to respect the forms. The transition is from a more or less parliamentary liberal democracy to what Proudhon called 'compact democracy'. In a polemic[1] against Louis Blanc and the 'communists' of that time, Proudhon defined this term in the following formulas which are borrowed (so he says) from the ancient form of absolutism: undivided power; all-absorbing centralisation; individual, collective, and regional thought held to be schismatic and therefore systematically destroyed; inquisitorial police. In effect, the State based upon the party system is replaced by the one-party State. The old forms are rendered obsolete by *attack from within*, for the psychological tendencies which triumph in the new régime are already at work within the old. Multiplicity and competition give place to unity and monopoly, and this is hailed as a triumph for the 'will of the masses'. The proof, or rather the emotional demonstration, is given in monster parades and processions and meetings. The conscious will of the leader and his staff is represented as the unconscious will of the masses.

Hitler claimed to supply a better and profounder interpretation than universal suffrage of the people's will, and he also claimed to *be* the people's answer; he was united with the Party in a state of 'participation', and the Party was united with the people, so he himself, through the Party, was in a state of 'participation' with the people. In this way democracy becomes a physical state; and this was the original idea behind the confused and tenuous Hitlerian theory of 'Race'. The Führer is the embodied consciousness of the Race, and therefore also its conscience. He is the incarnation of the community's Fate, and in his personal existence, which from being obscure has become spectacular, he 'plays' (in both senses of the word) the destiny of the people in the arena of history. By expanding a people into a race, the tyranny can

[1] *Capacité politique des classes ouvrières.*

acquire the additional prestige of an 'Islam'; it can make recruits outside its frontiers and exert a disruptive influence in neighbouring communities by disaffecting a part of their population in the name of 'racial purity'. Thus the 'spirit of the race' is set free, and the community can worship itself in it; finding the transcendent within the immanent, and at the same time disciplining itself and increasing its production. Such a revolution represents, on the one hand, an acceleration of the circulation of élites and, on the other, a modification of the type that rises in the process. The new élites have been described as 'mass élites'; they are less civilised and cruder than the élites whom they forcibly displace, and at least equally astute—but with a different astuteness, elementary and childish, which at first gives them the advantage when pitted in diplomacy against the élites of communities of the older type. The latter, indeed, are quite disarmed until they have learned to adapt themselves. The new élites are men who began at the bottom of the ladder and have had to fight hard for their position, instead of stepping into it naturally like the diplomats of democratic countries, who have usually prepared for their careers by university study and examinations. Whatever qualities they lack, they have a certain energy and toughness. The term 'fascism' is still applied in the West to two phenomena, one German and the other Italian, which differ in many ways; but it refers to what the two have in common. To begin with, they occurred in old historic Western countries which had once had a very rich social soil and still retained many traces of this fertility, which could not be obliterated overnight. Both the mythology and the propaganda of fascism bear witness to the persistence, in societies that had relapsed into a comparatively amorphous state, of historical forms whose remaining vitality it is hard to estimate with accuracy. (In Germany the series of shocks that had broken society down were defeat in war, unemployment of the demobilised soldiers due to the country's diminished economic activity, inflation, and general crisis.) It is as though fascism were the gross reaction of nations in danger of disappearing from history; a reaction of the elementary will to survival. The most active social elements were the first to react politically, and it was their irruption into political life that gave the fascist movements their special character. They knew nothing of political customs, rules, or doctrine; as political products of a social disequilibrium, their aspiration was order, but their programme was to follow their bent. The historical unconscious and the social law of gravity obtained free play, untrammelled by any of the traditional and conventional forms; but the appearance of these forms remained although their content was increasingly disregarded. Germany and Italy, however, are very far from being new countries, and their social soil itself appears to have a resistant power.

Thus, although the people had been reduced to an amorphous mass-population, which flowed into the rigid mould of the victorious single party and the institutions it established, there nevertheless persisted, behind the totalitarian façade, a host of individual and group rivalries which were fed by older rivalries between different localities or traditional authorities. The old forms were still alive and had merely compromised with the new régime. This is what the Wehrmacht did in Germany, and also the capitalist and landowning classes. Hitlerism was less totalitarian than Stalinism; a trace of Germany's earlier history survived in the feuds and rivalries of individuals and interests.

In those western European countries where Stalinism is strong enough to be a danger but not strong enough to carry the day, it is opposed by the growth of authoritarian movements which resemble it in their preoccupation with efficiency and in their contempt for the old liberal ways—which, in their opinion, are ways leading straight to defeat when the enemy is totalitarian. That section of the older élites which is historically the most exhausted will tend to favour whatever movement is the least disturbing to its habits, but the remainder prepares to fight. In countries where there is no danger or threat of communism there have been no fascist movements, nor even any with the smallest resemblance to fascism. In England, which has not been attacked nor had to defend itself, both attitudes are deprecated; but English liberalism has been sheltered from the continental storms, with the result that the English have failed to develop any 'pathological clairvoyance' in these matters. When they advocate the kind of liberal solutions which they themselves have been able to apply, they seem to be missing the point. The fact is, of course, that their survival as Englishmen is not—or is not yet—in danger.

The typical and virulent form of fascism has been seen in countries afflicted with an inferiority complex in the matter of imperialism; countries which obtained only a small share, in proportion to their technical development and population, when the world was divided up among the European powers in the late 19th and early 20th centuries. The German Jews would no doubt have had less to suffer if Germany had possessed as many colonies as France.

Further, it can be said that fascism and national socialism came on the scene both to expose and to remedy the emotional inadequacy of 'democratic socialism'. Fascism, in the wider sense, is a reaction against all the consequences of industrialism, socialism included. Its *content* was already present in 19th-century nationalism, which asserted the uniqueness of a particular group of men as distinct from others, and not the solidarity of all men reduced to a uniform way of life. There are two movements by which it is possible to trace the entire history of

Europe in the first half of the 20th century, and the tyrannies of the period are without exception the product of these movements. One is the *nationalist* movement (or movements, for multiplicity is an irreducible constituent characteristic of this type of particularism); and the other is the *social* movement, which is essentially the impulse to transform political democracy into economic democracy. One is a movement for national, and the other is a movement for social, emancipation. The nationalist movement expresses the will (in both the metaphysical and the biological sense of the word) of 'particular unities', such as nations, peoples, and races, to obtain recognition, in the Hegelian sense, of their own particularity; and the will is the more intense because they feel that this particularity has been slighted by foreign domination. The desire for liberty is felt, above all, as a desire for collective self-determination. It is one of the major traits of the history of the present century that this demand for recognition of particularity or particularism, as such, has occurred not so much in Europe as in the rest of the world. In Europe, indeed, a tendency towards unification is beginning to appear, but in those parts of the world that have been awoken by contact with the aggressive colonising activities of Europe local particularisms have been reborn, or even created, through the study of European history by colonial peoples and the imitation of European models by their intelligentsia.

In the 19th century the two great movements, social and nationalist, though intellectually incompatible, were emotionally allied; each of them stirred the peoples to an awakening, and the results of this awakening, when the peoples had been truly turned into masses, were the phenomena which form the subject of this book. In both movements we find the same relation of the 'mass élites' to the mass and of the mass to the leaders, and the same popular agitations; both movements lead to the formation of a party and a secular religion, and to the birth of an 'Islam'. Moreover, it is only so far as the two movements cease to be incompatible and begin to unite that totalitarianism can come into being. The specific absolutism of the 20th century became possible from the moment when these two movements combined into one, the moment when the national leader and the social leader were the same man. This movement occurred while the Bolsheviks were still fighting against the Whites and against the masked intervention of the Entente, though the fact was not appreciated until much later. But honour where honour is due—Lenin takes precedence of Mussolini.

CHAPTER 13

The Totalitarian Dynamic

IN totalitarian régimes the concentration of social power is accompanied by a restriction of individual opportunity. The activity of individuals is canalised by the State, with the purpose of concentrating all available energy into a sort of one-way drive. Impoverishment of the individual psyche seems to be a condition of the concentration of social power. The force that generates historic and world-changing initiatives is the energy of living men, and this it is that Power seeks to monopolise. It was quite otherwise in Renaissance Italy, for example, which was anarchic and fragmentary and continually at war with itself in every sphere: faction struggles in the cities, and war between the cities themselves, and war against the 'barbarians' in which one *signoria* or another would be allied with the enemy. It was a sporadic and fickle war, which never became a war of all Italians against all 'barbarians'. Far from being a 'one-way' flow, energy was expended at the source; it neutralised, squandered, and destroyed itself. It was the hey-day of individuality. But in the totalitarian system there is a wholesale requisitioning of energy which makes it impossible for it to be displayed in the incomparable manner of the Italian Renaissance. It is from this requisitioned energy that totalitarian foreign policy derives what contemporary observers have called its *dynamic*. This totalitarian dynamic does not arise from any superiority of energy among the population of a totalitarian State, as individuals, over the inhabitants of a non-totalitarian country of comparable size and population. On the contrary, it is the result of a psychological *economy*, a more stringent control and concentration of the energy available. The leaders, in whom all power is concentrated, have a far greater capital of energy at their disposal than the officials and delegates of a people governed on the principle of representative democracy. That is why they are able so easily to create basic industries and plant for the conversion of primary power, and to use them for the production of goods which they are free to withhold from the majority of their subjects for the sake of building up the State power.[1] We have seen that in totalitarian Russia and Germany the

[1] It will suffice to recall here the Soviet and Japanese policy of dumping (Japan may be regarded from this point of view as a totalitarian State), and the symbolic choice in Germany

State is essentially an 'apparatus of power'. But the power has to come from somewhere, and there is in fact only one source of power. The totalitarian dynamic depends upon the existence and installation of an apparatus of power which draws energy from the place where it is found, in individuals, and stores it up; and the potential of energy thus accumulated is placed, thanks to the concentration of power, at the discretion and disposal of a very small number of men.

The 'collective' energy put into operation by the totalitarian dynamic does not resemble the energies from which it is derived (if we consider them as they appear on the level or on the scale, so to speak, of the individual). We see here the effect[1] which is described by Marxists as the 'transformation of quantity into quality'; we see also once again that it is a sort of 'principle of communicating vessels' which causes the social whole to appear as something which is other than the sum of its parts. There is nothing in the whole that is not also in the parts, and yet everything in the whole is different from everything in the parts. Social reality has its own specific character, and it is tempting to explain it by some process comparable to the transformation of energy. But this is still too simple, for there is less difference between work, heat, and light than there is between the energy expended by the individual and the energy exploited on the collective level. The totalitarian dynamic involves a particular method of exploiting energy. In other societies the mere absence of an apparatus of power, and of the concentration of power that it implies, enables individual energies to be expended on the individual level, for the benefit of limited groups or in conflict with one another; the separate energies remain scattered, and are not converted into the single collective energy which makes the totalitarian dynamic.

More than once in the 20th century war has compelled the canalisation and transformation and concentration of energy by societies of the relaxed type in which energy enjoyed free play and could expend itself where it chose; and this energy brought the victory to societies which, at the beginning of the war, had been less concentrated and were less equipped with 'one-way' dynamism than their opponents. This was how the democracies succeeded in winning the two world wars of the first half of the 20th century. We see here a sort of reversal of cause and effect: war has the effect of making a non-totalitarian society largely totalitarian, but a totalitarian dynamic was the cause of the war. Being by definition *turned outwards*, the totalitarian dynamic is essentially

between 'guns or butter'—between immediate enjoyment and future power. Soviet Russia faced exactly the same alternative and made the same choice when it gave heavy industry precedence over light industry, and production for power precedence over consumption goods. The famous alternative propounded by Goering makes the relation between 'dynamic' and 'restrictions' clear to everyone.

[1] Using the word as it is used in such expressions as 'Joule effect' or 'Compton effect'.

aggressive; and the result is that it stimulates energy in the outside world to resist it. When the non-totalitarian protagonists try to organise themselves for defence, their efforts at first make a pitiable showing compared with the totalitarians'; and some of them may be unable to pass the test, but those which do succeed in passing it find in the end—at the very moment when totalitarianism has no reserves of energy to call on and can no longer convert individual into collective energy—that they are in no way inferior to the totalitarians in dynamic aggressiveness. If the non-totalitarian societies possess a sufficient 'material basis' and a certain minimum of moral assets (community of life and traditions, and a sufficiently widespread will to preserve this community and the values inherent in the traditions), they have a greater power than the totalitarians for converting individual energies into collective energy; and therefore—provided the conversion 'works'—they possess a stronger potential of aggressiveness. This explains why they 'recover themselves' during a war. But the recovery cannot occur unless it has time to do so, and therefore the non-totalitarian society must be protected from the immediate aggression of its initially more powerful enemy. This condition was fulfilled in the last war, for England[1] and the United States.

The mere existence and presence of a great totalitarian dynamic, born of a previous war, is itself a factor making for war. It subjects those whom it threatens to a real historic *test*: it either breaks them down or else it compels them to recover themselves, and it compels this recovery precisely to the extent that it fails to break them down. This is the mechanism that produced national socialism as a retort to bolshevism, or 'anti-bolshevik bolshevism'. The way to overcome bolshevism is indicated by bolshevism itself; it reveals its chief enemies to themselves and seems to leave them no alternative but to imitate its own methods. Employing, for its own part, whatever methods are most effective without regard to their consequences (except from the point of view of efficiency), it corrupts the historical atmosphere. In establishing the supremacy of *means* it also promotes the whole attitude of mind associated with those means, raising it from the subconscious to the level of consciousness. It founds secular religions and makes messianic promises; and only the promise of paradise is sufficient to excuse acts of war in peace-time, and the horrors of concentration camps and judicial torture, and the revival of slavery. Thus there comes to be a direct relation between eschatology and villainy.

* * * *

[1] It was no doubt the last occasion in history in which the English Channel will constitute an obstacle.

If the tone of politics and diplomacy altered during the 19th century it was because forces which had been kept under in the preceding century began to be able to express themselves. In the ordered society of the *ancien régime* the men who controlled or set the tone in politics were selected from among the most cultured members of society; they were men for whom good manners implied emotional control. Court discipline imposed self-control, promoted integration, and favoured the possessors of these qualities. But when the society of orders broke down it became possible for a certain number of men who had not undergone this discipline to intervene in the direction of affairs; *appetites* and *feelings* began to be more openly displayed in politics, and notably such feelings as indignation and moral reprobation. Impulse began to play a larger part, for the plebeian is more emotive and more 'natural', and either lacks certain habits of restraint, inhibition, and control, or else possesses them in a less degree. He is capable of 'regrettable' reactions, and also of regretting them later, or of forgetting them. So the tone of diplomacy became bourgeois, and then petty bourgeois (the protagonists influenced one another). But the 20th century was to take a further step.

* * * *

The totalitarian dynamic is all of one piece. Totalitarian foreign policy shocks and disconcerts liberal diplomats by a brusqueness which does violence to their habits of thought and behaviour and upsets their rhythm. Many factors combined to give the statesmen and diplomats of the bourgeois democracies an inevitable preference for indirect methods and an unhurried rhythm of work: the diplomatic traditions inherited from dynastic Europe, the natural caution of the democracies, which makes their governments anxious above all not to appear to the electorate as war-mongers, and the fact that the free circulation of printed matter of every tendency makes it impossible to keep the electorate so much in the dark as the subjects of a totalitarian State. But sudden changes of policy and directness of method present little difficulty for a régime which controls public opinion as openly as it controls everything else; the representatives of such a régime are not hampered in their business or made cautious by resistance or impediments in their own country, whereas Western politicians are obliged to manœuvre and have to prepare carefully before dealing with internal opposition. This is not by any means to say, however, that the democrats have a monopoly of ruse and the totalitarians a monopoly of brutal frankness. Indeed, there is even more trickery on the totalitarian side, but the tricks are different; and they have more of them up their sleeve. Thus, if a totalitarian Cæsar is truly resolved upon peace, his very absolutism is supposed to give us grounds for hope; and 'democrats' go on hoping, in a confused way, that the 'leader' will rally his people to peace even more easily than he would rally them to war.

The totalitarians can manœuvre more swiftly and have therefore the advantage of surprise. They are easily able to confuse an opponent who is obliged to prepare every move long in advance; and when the opponent is faced with an ultimatum he can only temporise, and is all the more inclined to do so if it is already too late for temporising. If he postpones his reply, the irreparable occurs and the moment for action has passed; he can only console himself with the promise to do better next time. This was the technique of Hitler's policy of annexations in time of peace, which made war inevitable. The German militarists would certainly not have undertaken a war while an intact Czechoslovakia could threaten Berlin; and Hitler's diplomacy removed this pretext for opposition. Achievements of this kind finally drove the opposition underground, for if all the world gave way to Hitler how could the German militarists hold out? When the Politburo decided to bring Czechoslovakia to heel in February 1948, it knew it was not risking war, and also had reasons to fear that the operation might become impossible if it were not carried through at once. Having secured a base for aggression, the time is ripe for launching a 'peace offensive'.

* * * *

This sort of policy is inherent, is *given*, in the structure of totalitarian régimes. There is a race between the willed convergence of all the social forces into a state of cohesion and their latent tendency to diverge, a tendency which can only be kept latent by appeals to the 'external danger' or the fear of 'encirclement' by the enemies of the 'great constructive work'. In the depths of totalitarian society there is always a centrifugal tendency, a desire for stability and repose, for release from the tyranny and for the decentralisation of its apparatus; and these latent desires can only be prevented from manifesting themselves by being continually forestalled. The government must always be a step ahead, to keep them in check. And this competition in speed, this incessant strain of holding together a collection of forces which would tend to scatter if not firmly held, is at the same time a race for world hegemony, because it is external opposition that can make the internal opposition critically dangerous, and vice versa. It is hardly possible nowadays to be defeated by external power alone (except where there is a very great disproportion of strength); there must be pressure both within and without. The race for hegemony appears to the historian as an endurance test; and the presence of totalitarianism is one of the signs that the 20th century is an age of wars, for tyranny never appears in history unaccompanied by revolutionary agitation and war. It often represents the transition from the one to the other. The existence of totalitarian régimes would seem to betoken a chronic state of war, in which the outbreak of wars in the strict sense of the word serves merely to mark the more critical stages.

* * * *

From all this it follows that totalitarian policy [1] must keep the initiative at any cost. The adversary must be overwhelmed by events; he must manifestly lose the initiative, and with it the confidence that comes from the sense of being able to influence the course of affairs. To this end he must be infected with the sense of impotence of the spectator who can do nothing but look on at the very events which touch him most closely; and totalitarian diplomacy, supplemented, characteristically, by propaganda, is directed to demoralising the adversary by the demonstration that 'events are moving too swiftly for him'. Hence the technique of blowing first hot and then cold, by which opponents are systematically confused and kept in suspense. In this connection, certain characteristics of the 'sensational' press of the 'capitalist' countries are extremely useful to the totalitarian foreign policy. Totalitarian diplomacy and propaganda frequently test the psychological resistance of the opponents they propose to disintegrate by suddenly switching from war talk to peace talk, in the hope of obtaining from 'cowardly relief' what they were unable to achieve by menaces. Another of their objects is to enable their friends to continue to maintain, without too great implausibility, that 'an agreement is possible' with the totalitarians and that their latest promises can be believed, that they really are going to check their course and call a halt. (Even during their most outrageous exploits the 'gleam of hope' must be kept alive.) Now, in order to be what it is, the sensational press must find something every day to make a sensation, and what can be more sensational than to reveal the imminence of total war in a period of comparative peace, or to discover that agreement is on the point of being reached in the midst of an acute phase of 'psychological' war? Totalitarian diplomacy would lose one of its trump cards if the democratic powers were to forbid their newspapers to be quite so sensational at certain times. The freedom of the press in their opponents' countries is in some ways extremely useful to the totalitarians. It is precisely this

[1] We have not attempted here the systematic study of totalitarian foreign policy. It is a study that remains to be undertaken; but it is sufficient for our purpose to recall certain features which are, in any case, certain to be present in everyone's memory.

freedom that gives such value to the lack of freedom in their own countries, enabling them, by the technique of blowing hot and cold, to elicit the extent of the desire for 'peace at any price' among their opponents—who, for their part, have no such means of information. If, in spite of everything, their opponents continue to hope against hope, it is a good sign. It then becomes possible to exploit the human tendency to confuse desire—in this case the desire for peace at any price—with reality. The technique consists in keeping the desire supplied with illusions to attach itself to.

The Russian 'peace offensive' of May 1948 will be remembered. Six months before the American presidential election there began a campaign of playing upon the American people's desire for peace, a desire which can be expressed in the United States not only in speech and writing but also by the vote; that is to say, in the choice of leaders. (As is well known, the American Constitution confers very wide powers upon the President.) Communist propaganda designated Mr. Wallace as the 'man of peace'. The converging effort of communist propaganda and Russian diplomacy seemed to be directed to imbuing the greatest possible number of American electors with the illusion that American-Russian negotiations would lead to a real peace, a peace of understanding, if only they would put Mr. Wallace in charge of them on the American side. Thus the American citizens' will to peace was to be made to work in favour of the candidate whom, rightly or wrongly,[1] the totalitarians expected to be most useful to themselves.[2] Their only concern was that the man elected should be the one who would make it easiest for them to prepare their next onslaught. Thus the opposition in a pluralist democracy between party and party, interest and interest, illusion and illusion, is turned to the advantage of totalitarianism, which exerts the whole weight of its pressure against the enemy's line of least resistance.

The democratic leaders are 'reasonable men', in the commercial sense of the word. They talk business; their aim is to reach an agreement from which all will benefit in return for concessions all round. But absolutism is not reasonable, or it acknowledges a different kind of reason. There is no bargaining with militant fanatics, for there is an unbridgeable gulf between the commercial and the warrior mentality. The democratic leaders genuinely believe in the possibility of agreement; it is inherent in their conception of the world that 'men can come to an understanding'.

[1] It is no business of mine to have an opinion about this.

[2] In the event, the totalitarian propaganda seems to have achieved the opposite of its intention. Mr. Wallace came to be regarded, in the minds of many electors, as 'Stalin's candidate'.

But the fact is that the political world today is not unlike the world of physics, in which everything is pressure, resistance, action and reaction of forces. If the communist 'hand' becomes weak, then the totalitarian player will be obliged to lower his bid. But it seems certain that he will never do so unless and until he has no alternative. He will not surrender the hope of destroying his adversary until he has lost all chance of fulfilling it. So it was with Hitler, and so it is with the Russian leaders of the communist 'Islam'.

If once they lose the initiative, the 20th-century tyrants feel themselves menaced by the 'internal danger'; and the play of interlocking forces in their system is so narrowly adjusted that the menace is a real one. Russia cannot afford to throw away the communist card, not merely because no real power would ever sacrifice so valuable a trump but also because by losing it she would risk losing all. She would in effect lose the whole justification for her tyranny; and a 20th-century tyranny is endangered by the mere fact of losing its justification. Without war, the machine will begin to run down; and there is even the danger that the tyranny may one day throw itself into war in order to keep the machine running. Only if it fears war more than anything else can this possibility be excluded.

One can see, therefore, why the leaders of 'dynamic' régimes are so profoundly averse to committing themselves *genuinely* (though not to signing treaties, in fact quite the contrary). It is probable that, although the Stalinist régime does not correspond to the communist ideal, it would put itself in mortal danger by making agreements which emptied this ideal of all its significance.

* * * *

'An oath made to the infidel is not binding'; so the allies of the Campaign, whether they be political parties, groups, individuals, or States, are by definition fair game for exploitation. 'The Party of the proletariat', said Lenin, 'must get hold of the liberal at the moment when he is prepared to take an inch, and force him to take an ell. If he resists, we shall advance without him, and over him.' That is how the obsolete social species are dealt with. The Campaign has its mission, and may not tie its hands or do anything that could be seriously damaging to the mission. It is only the others, those who have no 'historic mission', who are, or can be, bound by an alliance. Indirectly, the exploited allies do contribute to the accomplishment of History. But History can do nothing for them; it sweeps them away with majestic disdain. Having served their turn, they are cast into outer darkness; for when the 'historical process' has no further use for them they become noxious. An alliance is only a 'moment' in the historical process, and is soon left behind as the process develops; and the formation of 'unnatural' alliances only goes to show that History pursues a devious course.

But is it, in fact, possible to make an alliance with someone who recognises no obligations except towards himself? It can be argued, truly, that the Campaign recognises obligations towards the Proletariat. But what is the Proletariat but a higher being, a mythical being, whose will it is the function of the Campaign to interpret and formulate and make prevail? The Campaign has the right to deceive the Proletariat itself, in the name of the Proletariat, and to betray and exploit real proletarians both economically and politically for the sake of the Idea of the Proletariat—an Idea of whose truth the Campaign is the sole repository. (This is part of the constituent faith of the Campaign.) So what the newspapers call Machiavellism and political realism are simply the natural consequences of the faith. But it is impossible not to notice how admirably the secular religion is adapted to the will to power of an élite, so that the two are completely identified in action and can only be separated by an intellectual analysis.

The Campaign knows no rules, and hence its specifically 'plebeian' emotional style, which is noticeable already in Marx.[1] As regards the enemy, it is ruthless and cynical about the treatment which is coming to him and which, however cruel, he will richly deserve. But when it comes to themselves, communists release a really unquenchable flow of indignant self-pity. If the enemy speaks realistically and cynically, they protest like pious old ladies or howl with self-commiseration. But the next moment they are cynics again, because the next moment they are talking about the enemy. In this mood, liquidations are referred to as casually as the week's laundry, or else there are horrific threats of damnation and death. The specifically communist *pathos* is derived from that mixture of sentimental indignation and 'realistic' cynicism which, it cannot be denied, appears already in the prose of Marx and Engels and Lenin. Is communism playing a doleful tune, or treating us to hagiography and holy pictures? If so, it is speaking of Russia or the Comrades. Change the subject and, hey presto, it is foaming at the mouth and roaring like a man-eater.

This special type of 'Machiavellism' succeeds in combining with traditional Machiavellism all the new amenities of an industrial age. The permanent procedure is adapted to the new situations of an age of mass phenomena, which is also an age of justifications and ideologies; an age in which implacable Power accepts the convention that it should 'explain' everything to all men, addressing itself to their reflexes and

[1] Or even in our own *sans-culottes*, in its blend of mawkishness and ferocity; but they did not include the pedantry as well.

not to their judgment. Thus the totalitarians make a point of accusing their enemies of the kind of behaviour which they know they themselves will be accused of[1]; and there is nothing the communist fears so much as the socialist or former communist who has had enough experience of communist methods to be able to use them himself.

So communists are always ready to charge their opponents with doing precisely what they themselves do, or intend to do as soon as they can. Stalin,[2] for example, accused Zinoviev and Kamenev of doing the very thing that he himself was going to do when he liquidated them: '. . . an amputation policy is full of dangers . . . today one is amputated, another tomorrow, a third the day after. What will be left of the Party in the end? Zinoviev . . . demands Bukharin's blood. We will not let you have it.' Everyone knows what happened later to both of them. The Stalinist is equally ready to appropriate his enemy's ideas, in order to sabotage them or else to put them into practice before his enemy can; he is thus able to destroy his enemy with the very weapon for whose use he is indebted to him. This is what happened to the ideas of Trotsky and the opposition concerning industrialisation and planning. When the authors have been liquidated, the executioners take the credit for their ideas.

Members of the Campaign have another favourite trick which consists in pushing everyone who is not with them farther to the right; this is done by attacking enemies on the 'right' and on the 'left' indiscriminately, by pretending to see no difference between them and therefore identifying them with one another. (An example of this is the theory of social-fascism, which did sterling service in Germany by identifying social-democracy with fascism.) But the Campaign's general staff is well aware of the process by which the leaders of the Campaign, both inside and outside Russia, become a new élite possessed of greater power, where it can be exercised, than that of the 19th-century bourgeois élites; and it is extremely anxious that this process should not be statistically verified. To obscure it, all the Campaign's resources are employed to impose an ideology according to which the Campaign, as the permanent representative of the hypostatised proletariat, is as far to the 'left' as it is possible to be; and from this it is deduced that anyone else who claims to be 'left-wing' is in reality, whether consciously or not, a 'right-winger'. Here it will be seen that the terms 'right' and 'left'

[1] On 28 February 1948, after the communist coup in Czechoslovakia, a staff writer in *L'Humanité* announced: 'The nations have had enough of this kind of thing . . . we are all of us tired of being oppressed by the will of the foreigner.' Next day the *Populaire* commented: 'The whole art of . . . (the writer in *L'Humanité*) consists in asking himself what his opponents are likely to say about any situation he proposes to defend, and then coolly appropriating their arguments and comments for his own use.'

[2] cf. Souvarine, *Stalin*, p. 406.

are illegitimately regarded as absolutes although they are in fact extremely relative, to say the least.[1] But from this abuse of terms a regular mythology of cardinal points is evolved, with a fabulous fauna of 'deviations'[2] described as 'leftist' or 'rightist' according to circumstances—and sometimes as both. This geometrical imagery is liable to turn into a very sinister farce. In the trial of Zinoviev and Kamenev there was talk of 'parallel centres'; and the purpose behind all this fantasmagoria, this peremptory handling of the cardinal points, is to guard the 'left' flank of the Campaign, to make it immune to attack from the 'left' by identifying all its opponents with the 'right' and the 'past', and with 'reaction' and 'capitalism'. Anyone who accepts this mythical geometry is reduced to admitting that if he is not a communist he must be a 'rightist'. The technique of journalistic falsehood, whether by distortion or suppression of the truth, has not penetrated everywhere in the capitalist world (its application in the scientific sector, for example, has proved difficult), but in communism it is generalised. For the purposes of the Campaign new truths are fabricated from day to day by specialists whose function it is to impose them wherever possible, by suggestion or by terror. Blind, deaf, and dumb whenever it is convenient, communism regards information as a means of power; a view which is certainly true but hardly seems to take sufficient account of the special nature of this means. The Campaign would appear to be taking a sort of revenge upon truth and, even if there were no other signs, we could deduce its real nature from its strategy of deceit. Or is it a transfiguration of the truth? If so, we may feel that a transfiguration of this kind is the fruit of a wretched and degraded age, and that the right word for it is deformation. Is it possible for a believer to lie when championing his faith? Perhaps he will tell falsehoods, but that is not the same thing. One has only to read the history written in Russia today.[3] There are no longer any facts except when the Campaign has an immediate use for them; there are only ideas, images, and words. But anyone who shows that he does not take these ideas and images and words for facts is incurring the risk of punishment. The conformity between the technique of journalistic falsehood and the totalitarian style is profound.

* * * *

[1] How can one be to the right or to the left of anything except in relation to something else? How can there be an absolute right or left? Sentimental politics can be compared to a qualitative physics.

[2] Tail-endism, adventurism, leftism, right opportunism, etc., etc.

[3] cf. the role attributed to the 'Trotskyist-Bukharinists' in the October Revolution and the first years of the régime in the *History of the U.S.S.R.* used by Soviet secondary schools (ed. by A. M. Pankratova, text approved by the Historical Institute of the Academy of Sciences of the U.S.S.R., Moscow, 1943–46); in the same work a number of inventions which have always been credited to western Europe or America are claimed for Russia.

Both the ancient monarchies and the nation-States of the 19th century used to make annexations; a sovereign would rob his neighbour of a province, add it to his own patrimony, and hand it on to his own heirs. Until the first world war, annexations were the normal conclusion of a war. But in mid-20th century we are in an age of *penetrations*, which are effected by economic power, political manipulation, and intellectual bullying. Before the official outbreak of war there is a preliminary penetration; the attacking power mobilises within the enemy's own territory, and the purpose of this opening manœuvre is to dislocate the enemy's organisation and thus facilitate its destruction in the succeeding phase. If there is any resistance, this latter operation is primarily military, but when it has been completed there begins a second penetration, of a different type. The earlier one was not very profound; its aim was to disturb and upset and undermine. But the second is an operation in depth, which plants its roots in the conquered territory; its purpose is to make the conquest an irreversible and irreparably accomplished fact. This phase is accompanied by a thorough reorganisation of the population and the ownership of property, and of the methods of production and exchange. The 20th-century conqueror must attach to himself a part of the penetrated population, by linking their interest inextricably with his own. The change of system is symbolised by the execution of one or two important men who represent the régime marked for destruction, and everything is got rid of which too much recalls the days when the tyrant was not, or was not sufficiently, feared. The tyrant alters the very structure of the society he is working upon; and, since it is necessary to attach a part of the population inescapably to himself, his second penetration is *subversive* in its results. The penetrated territory is despoiled and exploited in such a way as to bring advantages to a section of its inhabitants. Thus the conqueror gets whole social strata under his patronage. Groups as well as individuals, for whom he has opened the way to powers and pleasures, are irrevocably compromised and attached organically to the régime, whose overthrow would mean that they would lose everything.

Stalin's penetration has a practical advantage over Hitler's in that it does not openly offend the peoples to be colonised. Having no doctrine of zoological predestination, communism does not claim dominion for a master race over slave races. The federal form of the Union of Soviet Socialist Republics makes it constitutionally applicable to the entire world. It can absorb everything—though whether it can digest what it absorbs only history will show. The constitution of the communist party also is such as to enable it to spread over the whole world and to recruit local leaders of every race. Up to now, however, this universal machine has served the interests of soviet particularism; the régime imposed by Russia upon those European countries that are not in a position to resist is not intended to develop them along their own lines; it organises them as buffer States and strategic bases. The fundamental policy seems to be an economic and, even more, a strategic opportunism: not only the economic exploitation of the 'protected' countries but also the winning over of a part of their population so that the Russian influence may take root, and so that power may always be in the hands of men who can refuse Russia nothing. Within these limits national feelings and particularisms may be respected, flattered, and even encouraged. A new social differentiation cannot emerge until the succeeding phase. It takes time; and although we can now recognise it in Russia, the 'frontier States' have not yet reached the point. The leaders of the communist parties are still in fact a mixture of revolutionary chief, totalitarian agent, and democratic champion. Local requirements decide which of these three types shall predominate.

At its higher levels the communist party appears to be a sort of open élite (though the Russian élite is tending to become, at the summit, a closed caste); an élite which can extend itself horizontally, while closing vertically, in the same manner as the Union of Republics whose nerve system it is. Russian expansion can count upon an organisation everywhere whose original motive force is the revolt of proletarians against their conditions; and there are specialists of agitation to ensure that all discontents are canalised and centralised within the organisation.

Totalitarian penetration has certain resemblances to the colonial penetrations of the preceding age. We are familiar by now with the main outlines of Russia's policy in the neighbouring countries which the war delivered into her hands: a government of communists and selected or approved non-communists, which obeys the Politburo, and uses the judicial and police systems, without changing their outward appearance but merely assigning them new tasks, for the liquidation of the Campaign's avowed or suspected enemies. The first weapon is the trial (or execution without trial) for collaboration, which achieves the liquidation of one part of the potential opposition with the assistance of the other. Then for those who resisted the Germans[1] there are trials for espionage or high treason. At elections, the desired results are assured by means of pressure of every kind, but an opposition is still, for the time being, allowed. There is selection and organisation of 'model' opponents, as at Lublin in 1944 when a new social-democratic party was fabricated in which the leading socialists were quickly brought to heel; and there are 'patriotic fronts', in which the non-communists are hedged around by communists armed with powerful arguments, such as the proximity of Russia, the ever-menacing danger of treason trials,

[1] e.g. Petkov, in Bulgaria.

and the fact that the State apparatus is in their hands at a time when everything—production and distribution, material and intellectual life—is controlled by the State. The fact that it is no longer autonomous only makes the State apparatus the more oppressive. By a succession of purges the system is worn down to the point where all possibility of organised resistance has vanished. The latest, and classic, example of the working of 'dyarchy' is the *coup d'état* by the police in Prague in February 1948. Police, 'action committees', and national front are simultaneously mobilised; and while the patriotic and national fronts eliminate or absorb all the country's other organisations, the communists eliminate or absorb all the other political parties within the fronts. The former élites are 'politically expropriated'.[1] At the moment of attack the defence is paralysed from within. Such was the plan which, in combination with outside pressure from Russia, worked successfully at Prague in February 1948. But most of the key positions of the State had already been occupied after the liberation, thanks to a wave of assault in which communists and non-communists took part more or less indiscriminately as allies; and this had the result of creating a confusion of loyalties on the personal plane. Now, in this kind of relationship between totalitarians and others who belong to less rigid systems, a conflict of loyalties works in favour of those with the most consistent outlook, those for whom there is always something that takes precedence of their personal situation. From such a state of affairs, therefore, the communists have much to hope. As Hitler complacently reveals in *Mein Kampf*, totalitarian diplomacy adopts a principle of the Cartesian method; it subdivides its problems as much as possible. To announce one's intentions may stir up an effective opposition to them; so Hitler divided his annexation of Czechoslovakia into three separate operations. And, to keep to the same example, Stalin also began by recognising the status of Czechoslovakia as a Western democracy. But the communists, whose hands were free, were able to absorb or annihilate the socialists, who were exposed to Russian as well as communist pressure. It was still possible, however, to resort to free elections of the Western type, but the *coup d'état* eliminated this danger and, along with it, the people who personified the 'Western' democratic character of the State. Beneš resigned and Masaryk perished. All the satellite States were brought to heel by a similar process: police measures, purges, treason trials. This is not a phenomenon of convergence but of synchronisation and *Gleichschaltung*. The enfeebled enemy is broken down by a combination of pressures: from without and from within, from the State apparatus which has been 'colonised' by the enemy and swollen by the confluence of economic with political power, and also from the masses organised

[1] As M. N. Clarion puts it (*Le Glacis soviétique*, Paris, 1948).

by the Party and 'activated' by propaganda. A preliminary weakening of resistances has been effected by the purges and 'patriotic' confiscations inflicted upon former Hitlerian collaborationists; and the resistance organisations have been colonised as the State apparatus is destined to be. Such is the model for what Western journalists describe as 'prefabricated revolution'.

The fundamental condition for 20th-century revolution is the preliminary weakening of the enemy. But the disproportion of strength between the country undergoing the revolution and the empire which imposes it is so great as to obliterate all trace of the factor which was regarded, until socialism became bolshevised, as the very hall-mark of revolution, namely the initiative from below. Twentieth-century revolution is simply a particular form of foreign intervention. The communist leaders in Bulgaria, Roumania, Hungary, and Poland were for practical purposes members of the soviet bureaucracy; most of them had had Comintern careers and had lived in Russia. While organising these countries strategically, the Russians also draw profits from them; from those that were on Russia's side in the war the Red Army collected booty and, in addition, by the seizure of German property the Russian Super-State automatically became the leading capitalist in these countries after their 'liberation' from capitalism. So the standard of living of the masses in the countries overrun by the Campaign is still kept at a low level, but it is calculated that the emotional satisfaction accruing from the political expropriation of the former élites will to some extent make up for any deficiency in material rations.[1] This totalitarian confidence trick is common both to Russia and to the régimes known as fascist. Such, then, are the up-to-date methods by which a country is ruthlessly fleeced with an unconvincing show of decorum. When necessary, as at Prague, the membership statistics of political parties, former resistance movements, and trade unions are added together to give an impression of mass unanimity; but these functionally heterogeneous units are largely composed of the same individuals, so the same numbers are added together more than once to produce the totals.

There can be no standing still for the Campaign, which has given a new meaning to the old aspiration that Moscow shall be the third Rome. It can only advance or give ground, for immobility or marking time are not in its nature.

This nature is the specific nature of 20th-century powers. Both functionally and organically, Hitler's campaign followed the lines of the communist Campaign, which resembles it in being an *expansion*. It seems that nothing short of the total domination of the planet can appease

[1] What happened in Yugoslavia shows that there is a point beyond which this calculation cannot be relied on.

these amorphous Powers which grow by spreading, like a stain of oil, destroying or assimilating whatever lies in their path. To an imperialism of this kind there are no natural bounds, for it is trying to establish the reign of something which replaces every absolute and seeks to fill the role itself.

* * * *

The evolution of the theory and practice of the revolutionary 'nucleus' can be traced down to our own time from the origins of the Campaign and the 'creative' epoch which is reflected in *What is to be Done?* Revolutionary nuclei were first needed for mobilising and manipulating the masses; but even at that time Lenin was writing: 'We must have "our own men" everywhere . . . among all social strata and in all positions from which we can learn the inner springs of our State mechanism', and indeed the role of the spy who acts a part in order to encompass the ruin of those whom he seems to be serving is an immemorial one. It was not invented by Bakunin and his associates, who attempted nucleation within every group they could reach. But with the change of tactics in 1934 the scope for nucleation was increased and extended, and towards the end of the second world war its field of operations became vast. The 'responsible' communists induce the electors to vote for a 'controlled economy' and to support measures giving the State control over the greatest possible number of social activities[1]; they then introduce their own men into the bureaucracy called into existence by such measures; they also seduce or corrupt, so far as they can, any officials who are susceptible to blackmail for past mistakes or to bribes for ambition; and in all these ways they manage to *simplify the data* of the problem of capturing power. To open assault, or even legal conquest of power by electoral majority, they add a gradual and surreptitious penetration, a silent capture of the posts of control, and ultimately (though this remains to be achieved) a quiet but forcible ascendancy over the entire life of a collectivity. All that is necessary is to plant a sufficient number of sympathisers and satellites in the right places, and when once this has been done the Campaign's electoral offensives can be synchronised with the action of those bureaucratic mechanisms of the State which have been 'taken in hand'. Further, control has to be obtained over the distribution and allocation of consumer goods and over the favours granted to individuals by a new type of State whose economic substructure is entirely immune from the competitive risk of 'natural selection' in business. Pressure can thus be brought to bear both upon the industrial-

[1] This is not to imply any criticism of such measures in themselves. We are merely noting the use to which the Stalinists put certain reforms, which would work out quite differently if the Stalinists were not what they are.

ists and upon their employees, thanks to the control obtained over the supply of raw materials to the former and over the various methods of rationing and distribution to the latter; and the Party's affiliated bodies or the communist-controlled public utility corporations receive State subventions which help them to recruit personnel and strengthen their power of control and action. Operated on a grand scale in east Europe (among the countries on the Soviet frontier), along with purges to liquidate as many non-communists as possible, this system[1] quickly turned a number of States into 'clients' whose independence had become purely nominal and which were destined, barring accidents, to become in due course frankly incorporated. The same system was also applied in France and Italy, though with less success because there was no direct military pressure from Russia and because it was necessary, at first, to take account of aspirations other than those towards totalitarianism. Nevertheless, the task was vigorously pursued, thanks to the strength of the communist party at the time[2]; but the fact that France is not on the borders of Russia made a certain amount of compromise and co-operation with others inevitable for the communists. The essential was to establish a régime which enabled them both to continue to invade the State apparatus and also to insure themselves against possible counter-attacks. The Stalinists seem, in effect, to have made a tacit compromise[3] with other political groups which thought a similar régime would be to their interest but were not so well placed for drawing advantage from it. In a society where the State power is growing, the occupation of key-positions which control distribution and allocations makes it easier to gain political adherents and to win elections. The old-style insurrectionary seizure of power is replaced by the presentation, at the right moment, of an accomplished fact, emphasised by carefully orchestrated 'mass agitation' which conforms to a prearranged scenario; and followed by a general consolidation of power. This was the plan which succeeded in Czechoslovakia in February–March 1948. It presupposes that the opposition is already paralysed and unable to react; and in this the French situation differs from the Czech. The communists no longer possess the means for paralysing their opponents in advance. Their opponents have powerful allies outside.

But where the process follows its normal course, it ends in the overthrow of the representative and parliamentary democracy which protects a minority and prevents the majority from liquidating it when circumstances allow. The 'superstructure' becomes an anachronism in a

[1] More direct forms of pressure were also used.

[2] A strength which it owed to the valour and sacrifices of its militants in the struggle against German totalitarianism.

[3] A treaty of partition. This sort of compromise simply registers the relative strength of the participants.

society where the State is completely dominant, and parliament is reduced to a mere assembly for registering accomplished fact—until it disappears altogether. This makes possible a complete change in communist tactics; for those who control a State, which controls the country's economy, have both capital and industry in their power, and may, according to circumstances, either leave an important sector of private industry untouched or else suppress it only by degrees. From the liberal view, the victory of politics over economics appears to be the end of liberalism. It is, in any case, the installation of a new political élite, formed partly at the expense of the old; but the destruction of the old élite as a dominant oligarchy does not necessarily affect all its individual members. As a class, the old oligarchy no longer exists, but those elements of it which are suitable are 'taken into partnership' by the new powers.

Entire social categories and classes can be liquidated, or consolidated, or turned into privileged groups, by those who have achieved economic power through control of the mechanisms of the State; and in this way a new social differentiation can be substituted for the old.

Further, it is necessary to instal as many Party officials as possible in positions in the State service, and in this way they are rewarded by the State for services rendered primarily to the Party.[1] This applies not only to ministers and members of parliament, for that goes without saying, but also to the directors of 'organisms' of every kind. They are communists at the State's expense, conquerors receiving tribute before they have conquered. The economic, administrative, and legal apparatus are all made use of as far as possible for winning over individuals and destroying or 'colonising' minor groups and associations. Thus the power of the totalitarians arises from the fact that they can mobilise a part of the State itself, at the same time and as well as their 'action committees' throughout the country, for the subjugation of that part of the State which still resists, or might resist, their double pressure converging from above and from below.

If the Campaign relied only upon its accomplices, it could be dealt with, in spite of its vast network extending over the whole world, by nothing more than police operations. But the strength of communism, and its originality, come from the disinterested militants and sympathisers. The whole edifice would collapse like a sawn tree-trunk if their sympathy and faith became untenable; but they will not become untenable while the remote inner citadel remains intact—that magic citadel within which evil is transformed to good, fact into myth, history into legend, and the steppes of Russia into paradise.

[1] In their own minds this distinction does not exist. Whoever works for the Party is working for the State; and if he begins by destroying the State, it is only in order to reconstruct it the better. Or so they say.

From the intellectual point of view, the errors of Marxism are often partial truths; and if they are pressed further their partiality is corrected and the truth appears. If we mention such a true dynamic as psychological energy, for example, we shall be accused of idealism; but in fact we are only taking realities into account. As a war machine, Russia might be conquered; but to defeat communism by arms alone would not be to defeat it in men's minds. It is a religion, and where we find it wanting it is for us to supply something better. If, as is to be feared, it comes to fighting, the force of arms will not be without avail; but neither will it be sufficient. We all know that arms cannot settle every problem, and in the hierarchy of energy the psychic takes precedence of the atomic. Whoever forgets this will pay a heavy price.

Though it be statistically true that individuals are attracted to power and organisation and force by the promise of deliverance from the anxieties of a world where every uncertainty is a threat, and though it be true that we can explain in this way the political behaviour of the majority of men, it would nevertheless be an error of method to ignore the motives of the pure. *For the motives of the pure are the justifications of the rest*, and it is not uncommon for the latter to live up to their justifications at decisive moments, behaving disinterestedly from interested motives. The man who is not pure can sometimes surpass himself in order to deceive; and it is a man's act, and not his intention, that makes him a hero.

To understand a movement it is indispensable to understand the psychology of its sincere believers, for in a sense the whole thing depends on them. Politics, in Péguy's sense, could not exist without a mystique; the former being simply the exploitation of the latter and therefore dependent upon it. Without believers the Campaign would be practically defeated, for their fervour is one of the motive forces of its machine; and it is an error of positivism to underestimate this source of energy. That there is conditioning by the economic substructure is of course true, but it *is* only conditioning. The Campaign, in fact, cannot be understood solely through its believers nor solely through its officials. If there had been no martyrs, the 'collaborator' could not pretend to be touched by grace; and if no one had been killed it would not be possible to exploit the dead. History is made by men in whom motives of this kind are incarnated, and who do not shrink from the consequences of their acts. We have already made it clear that we believe these motives can be revealed by an 'historical psycho-analysis'; but no matter what psychological motivations may be revealed in it after the event, the moral myth itself is effective on the historical plane. It is only after the event that the motivations become clear, and they are only intelligible to a small number, who cannot convey to the majority any understanding of their methods; whereas the effects of the compulsive power of spilt blood and of the infectious enthusiasm of faith are immediate and durable. What inspires the sympathiser's sympathy for the movement is its past—a past which colours the present. So whoever fights against communism is also fighting against a myth; and troops which are trained for war against an army are not thereby equipped to deal with a myth or a secret society.

The significance of the efforts by the communists' headquarters to stimulate and inflame agitation is sufficiently clear. As far as the regular cadres are concerned, organisation takes first place; but it would be ineffective unless a certain religious temperature were maintained. There must be some fanaticism, and a faith in the ultimate objectives of the movement; and also, among the rank and file of 'history's infantry', the belief that the methods of the Campaign are in fact consistent with its objectives. Only so is it possible to maintain the sympathisers in a state in which they can go on sympathising. The claims of labour must be tirelessly pressed (this is easy enough), hope must be fed and lies disseminated—lies and obsessions.

A social form like this, multi-dimensional and totalitarian as it is, reveals in its own nature and characteristics the nature and characteristics of the struggle in progress; it is symptomatic of our troubled age. *The question at issue is posed simultaneously on every level.* The mere existence of the Campaign reveals a chronic condition of war, in which the wars of armies—which in the 20th century take the form of general, world-wide military crises—only represent the acuter phases.

For the Campaign there is no such thing as a bilateral compact, there is only the tactical retreat; concession implies no renunciation of the thing conceded, and what is held to commit the other party to a contract does not commit the communist. Where ends are different, means are different: in the Western democracies tolerance is still alive, and in a general way the existence of the *other* and the different is admitted, but for the Campaign everything that appears to obstruct or delay its progress towards absolute political, economic, and religious supremacy is a thing to be destroyed as quickly as possible, and by whatever means are most efficacious for the purpose. The choice of weapons is governed exclusively by their effectiveness. Both the Campaign and the totalitarian régime, which is its centre of gravity, are precarious; the Stalinists feel themselves to be in danger so long as anything remains unabsorbed, and they cannot admit that anything which they threaten is not to the same extent a threat to themselves. There is mortal danger for the Campaign (or so the communists imagine) in any limitation, other than a tactical and temporary one, of its objectives, or of the tasks which it offers to the energy of its supporters or the hopes with which it inflames their minds, or indeed in the mere existence *elsewhere* (for the existence of an 'elsewhere' is not permissible) of *alternative* solutions to its own. There is an organic connection between its world-wide expansive thrust and an almost intolerable internal constraint. They are simply two aspects of the same thing, and any setback to the external dynamic will also weaken the internal constraint. The supreme principle and *ultima ratio* is to keep on advancing at all costs. In the eyes of its leaders, the Campaign represents upon a world scale the dilemma: 'Eat or be eaten'; and this explains its omnivorous character. Its anxiety-state causes it to project into its enemies characteristics which are really its own. Hitherto the religion of these enemies has not prescribed the extermination of the Campaign in the way that communism implies the destruction of private capitalism and of the individual ownership of the means of production and exchange; and if any such doctrine came to be held it could only be as a reaction to shock. So the mere existence of the new totalitarian régimes, in which the religious, political, military, and economic powers are combined as one power, takes us into a new world in which it is impossible to avoid imitating them to the extent necessary for combating them. Simply by compelling the opponent to fight, they compel him to resemble themselves; and there is no graver problem today than the problem of keeping this resemblance down to a minimum.

Any totalitarian enterprise involves individual terror and collective frenzy, both internally and externally; the frenzy being the cause of the terror. And within the totalitarian State the anxiety of the individual is exaggerated to the point where he can only find refuge in the collective —a way of 'socialising humanity' which Marx does not appear to have foreseen. For the totalitarian dynamic success and existence are the same thing. Not to advance means to retreat; and it is necessary to believe that the outside world harbours all the forces of evil, for otherwise the totalitarian dynamic cannot be justified in its home country. By its total rejection of the idea of neutrality it keeps the world in a state of war: whoever is not with it is against it, and 'to be outside communism is to be anti-communist'. By making it obligatory to choose, totalitarianism tends to present the entire historical life of its time in the form of a choice. For the believer no true peace is conceivable until *after* the Campaign has triumphed in every sphere; and since the kind of war which ended with an annexation of territory has been replaced by a new kind, whose purpose is not only the acquisition of wealth and raw materials but also the total possession of human beings, the aims of propaganda have been extended. It goes farther than the promotion of obsessions and tries to make men *possessed*. The object of the Campaign is not territory and tribute, but the absolute possession of men all over the world. There is nothing that can halt the Campaign until its limit has been reached, and its only limit is the determined resistance of an opponent of the same type.

* * * *

The unity and self-consistency of a campaign of this kind, which operates simultaneously on many different levels and in several dimensions, are revealed in its strategy; there is a converging dynamic, a concentration of all its methods and tactics towards a single centre, which is *total* success. This success means the victory both of a totalitarian State and of a secular religion, a success which would include all the possible forms of victory: the submission of the whole world to an élite which recruits and perpetuates itself by co-option, and the submission of this élite to a supreme general staff. Such a victory is prepared for by converging attacks and combined operations. But combined operations in the ordinary military sense are conducted only on the military level. Strategy hitherto has always been plane. Today, however, the traditional methods of war have been amplified in depth by such additions as the following: the art of directing the flow of resentments and of re-orienting emotions and reactions, the art of inducing psychological 'identifications', the cultivation of good and bad consciences, inferiority feelings, compensation mechanisms, obsessions, and phobias, the propagation of general hysterical, destructive, and self-destructive impulses, and of individual and collective complexes. In other words, contemporary war and strategy include the dimension of psychology. Specifically military operations may be no more than the final and decisive phase of a campaign which has relied exclusively upon psychological techniques for the greater part of its progress. The effect of raids by air-borne troops upon vital centres can be enormously increased by the presence among the enemy of 'sympathisers' who have prepared the ground and helped to paralyse the defence beforehand from within. For such purposes the religion supplies secret agents who work unpaid and are, or can be if properly handled, more reliable than paid ones; and their subterranean action, combined with organisation and the psychological weapon and the air arm, may predetermine the employment of other arms and the occasions for their use and even the necessity or otherwise of using them at all.

War changes its character with the changes in character of the war-making powers; and the wars of today are no longer waged for the interests of closed units like the feudal suzerainties and the dynastic and national States of the West. Our description of the Campaign will have made sufficiently clear that it is not national; no unity comparable to the dynastic States and their successors, the national States, of the three preceding centuries, is composed by the countries under Russian domination—the Eurasian bloc over which the Soviet State holds direct sway, and the fringe of vassal countries which are being strategically and economically annexed pending their complete absorption. The older States were based upon a population rooted in the soil of the country, the community of manners and way of life produced by a long period of living together, and a common conception of the Sacred[1] and, consequently, of the more or less sacred character of the State. But the last-named foundation was worn away during the 19th century.

Nevertheless, the class war did not replace the war of State and nation in the 20th century. To think so is to over-simplify what is really happening. It is only according to the Marxist reading of the facts that the Campaign is a class campaign; and, since Marxism does not provide the key to decipher the whole text, it misinterprets the part it can read. In the real history of the Campaign only one type of action and one kind of agent conforms to the Marxist theoretical position; and neither of them suffices for the needs of communist expansion. The real value of the working class to the Campaign is as raw material.[2] The Campaign is the working-up of this raw material, but not of it alone. It is not only among the working class that resentments and aggressive impulses and hatred and greed have been stimulated and harnessed to the Campaign's purposes; the strategy, being *total*, must take into account the *whole* of the field that is to be attacked and surrounded. Stalinism cannot be reduced to a campaign for the benefit of the working class. That is not what it is, either in Russia or outside Russia; and the ideology which would make it so is disproved by the facts. Nor is it true that the bolshevik general staff was composed of prophets or chiefs of a priestly order. If socialism has become a religion, and if the Russian revolution has played a determining role in the development of the religious spirit, it is because the bolsheviks, and later the Stalinists, have found it useful to employ a weapon which, though extraordinarily effective, is only one of the weapons in their armoury.

Because the Campaign has not relinquished any of the weapons which contributed to its power, it must necessarily operate in several dimensions; and it can be predicted that any resistance it meets with and fails to suppress will also be compelled by the force of circumstances to organise itself in more than one dimension, thus transforming itself so as to become more effective and united in the sphere of action. (The ideal being to acquire the advantages of unification while avoiding the

[1] Or the memory of such a conception, whose historical effect endures for some time.

[2] The colonial and semi-colonial 'masses' are also raw material, and often a more malleable one. And even more so the intelligentsia which is prepared to 'lead' the masses.

uniformity which involves a lowering of the potential of affective energy; this potential is a function of the initial diversity.)

The Campaign is not confined within frontiers, nor is modern war so strictly confined within temporal limits as the wars of the past, which were bounded before and after by periods of peace. At the end of the first world war a number of small local wars were still in progress: the Greco-Turkish war, the Russian Civil War, the German *Freikorps* in the Baltic States, the struggle for Trieste, the German, Hungarian, and Italian 'revolutions', the abortive risings in Bulgaria and Finland. And the same is true of the second world war. The heads of States did not meet round a table to revise the map of the world. There was no treating with the vanquished, and there is no confidence in the series of agreements between the victors, which quickly became out of date. War was not replaced by peace, it merely cooled down; but nothing came to an end except the great continent-wide military operations. After the cessation of hostilities, the Campaign continued to employ, even more vigorously than before, all its old familiar tactics: religious propaganda, psychological aggression, exploitation of every difficulty in every country not under the Campaign's control. The danger of war is the danger of a gradual, though intermittent, rise in the temperature of the 'cold war'. At a certain point a general war of the same type as the last could break out—a general war which might be lost or won almost before it had started. But it is also possible that other, and localised, forms of war may occur instead.

The strength of patriotic motives has been somewhat undermined everywhere in contemporary civilisation, and there are many men who are no longer unreflectingly moved to fight for 'a plot of earth'. In 1914 the reigning élites were accused by revolutionaries of exploiting patriotism for the sake of other interests; and today one may with equal justice suspect the communist staff of exploiting the workers' 'class motives'[1] for the sake of a campaign which is so remote from those motives that it can only be connected with them by a filtering and distortion of the truth which amounts to plain fiction.

We are now living in a state which is neither war nor peace. The cold war can be heated up, but so long as the Campaign is in existence it can never be abolished in favour of a final peace, in the true sense of concord or *homonoia*. A state of equilibrium, however, is possible of attainment, for the Campaign can only advance as far as the point where it encounters real resistance; and this resistance may be such as to make the risk of war too terrifying.

But it may at certain times be to the Campaign's interest to reduce the temperature of the cold war; though this can only mean a truce dur-

[1] Or the colonial peoples' aspirations to independence.

ing which another more active phase of the war is being prepared. At any given moment there are always a few points where the chronic state of war is acutely manifested, but these manifestations may be localised or brief. In a state of latent war, whose sporadic and local manifestations are partly internal and partly external, the most conspicuous warlike acts are usually not military; more often they are social or, more exactly, of mixed origin (acts of sabotage and damage, waves of strikes which are *controlled*, not as regards the claims advanced but as regards their moment of outbreak). Psychological techniques, for manipulating and predisposing the masses, gain in importance. The whole art consists in creating a predisposition, whether for acceptance or for resistance. The masses have to be persuaded and a new art of persuasion, with its appropriate rhetoric, is developed. This rhetoric is transmitted by the familiar obsessive techniques (wireless, newspaper, rumours, slogans, the orienting of resentments and aggressive impulses in the direction most damaging to the enemy), and its purpose is to promote and cultivate in the masses a predisposition and a specialised tendency to behave in whatever way is strategically desirable at a given moment. But since the political situation is not static it is sometimes necessary to cultivate a new predisposition, which may conflict with the old until it has been firmly implanted in its stead. And all this is strictly a mass operation; the results aimed at are statistical and can only be obtained by playing upon large numbers.

* * * *

The Campaign finds itself obliged to undertake a sort of 'counter-education' which encourages mental discontinuity, discourages memory, and dissipates attention. Above all, its appeal is emotional; it creates vivid impressions and entices the masses, under the influence of these impressions, to commit *irrevocable acts*. The sincere and naïve educational ideals of the early days of communism are increasingly supplanted by a technique of predisposing and sensitizing the masses to react to those stimuli which will provoke the actions required of them. Communists who have outgrown the awkward age of educational naïveté are now able to acknowledge the existence of motives opposed to their own, and do their best to turn them to advantage. It is a question of convincing those who can be convinced and making use of everybody. The methods are at bottom the same as those employed by the old politicians of the mature and, indeed, the ancient democracies, for Cicero knew all about them; but they have undergone a double transformation—from local to world politics and from the individual to the mass level. The purpose is to persuade large groups of men holding certain sentiments in common to adopt the behaviour required of them, while distracting their attention from the fact that they will thus be serving a power which is *alien* to their interests or feelings. It is not too difficult, for men are always ready enough to repress troublesome thoughts. There may be not only inconsistency but actual contradiction between the motives for which men are fighting and the motives of those who are making use of them; but it is enough for the latter that the two should converge towards the same result. It may sometimes happen that a motive is too strong to be checked after it has served its turn, but this is a risk that has to be taken; and it must be admitted that these operations have, up to now at any rate, been very successful.

The combatant who is materially the better armed may fail for the want of this *psychagogic* art by which alone combined operations can be extended to the immaterial dimension. It can be brought to bear upon all men alike, and it works upon them in the mass on the emotional level. Psychological impulses have always played an indirect part in military action; but this new art can 'manipulate' them directly. It can thus undermine the power of armies from within and disorientate the traditional view of treachery. It supports any tendency that leads the individual to destroy his own traditions. The revolt of son against father and the revolt of any man against any authority which represses him by setting reality against his wishes are made to assist the triumph of a new 'Father', a new Authority, and a new Reality, which are more repressive still. It is the most tyrannical tyranny of the century which mobilises men's resistance to tyranny in all the rest of the world. Such, in mid-20th century, is the *mystification* in which the idea of revolution has become involved.

In a country that has been 'prepared' it is possible for an airborne company, or even a section, to destroy a dam or a vital production centre in half an hour and then vanish without a trace. A treatise on war may be entirely correct as far as it goes, but if it omits one of the contemporary dimensions, then all its partial truths are in danger of being falsified. Of what value is the speed and accuracy of a radio-directed projectile unless the scientist who invents it, the technician and engineer who make it, and the soldiers who use it *can be relied on*? Suppose the enemy is inside the soldier himself?

The world in which the written and spoken word can still circulate freely may fall a victim to this structural characteristic if it lacks the necessary determination to convert it into a guarantee of victory. For in a free country ideas can circulate, and consequently attitudes can be disseminated, by a kind of osmosis. (By ideas we mean, in this context, psychological states expressed in certain kinds of behaviour, irrespective of how they are formulated intellectually.) Latent rebellion may thus become contagious, and military action may be counteracted by a hate-offensive. (It is not impossible, when one comes to think of it, that this kind of offensive also should be 'radio-directed'.) Frontiers are ill-defended if the frontier-guards are unreliable, and it is of little avail to watch over a territory if some of those in charge of it are *predisposed* to assist the enemy instead of fighting him.

The motive and purpose of the revolution was the seizure of power by the 'plebs', according to Blanqui, or the 'proletariat', according to Marx. But for both these thinkers the revolution itself was morally unconditioned; in their eyes all other historical phenomena should be progressively conditioned by it. They had, indeed, no meaning apart from the revolution, and were good or bad only in relation to its purposes. But by now the motives and aims of the revolution are undeniably corrupted; they are taken for granted as parts of a *total strategy* within which they are only one element among others, one means to be combined with others in the pursuit of the over-all objective. Mobilisation within the enemy's territory has been a feature of war throughout the ages, but modern techniques for the diffusion of verbal propaganda increase the scale and extent of the operation so much as to alter its very nature. There is full scope for the characteristic 20th-century art of collective suggestion. In 1918 the war of propaganda was won by the allies, especially England, and President Wilson; but with the Russian revolution a religious factor was introduced which radically transformed the basis of the art, and the communist Campaign, which from the outset considered itself at war with the rest of the world (regarding a nominally peaceful period as no more than a tactical respite), was able to combine the age-old tactic of mobilisation behind the enemy's lines with the new kind of psychological warfare made possible by the advances in journalistic and radio technique. This psychological war is something more than the propaganda war between the belligerents of 1914–18. Today the workers behind the enemy's lines are psychologically stimulated by a faith of the Islamic type. Socialists, 'men of the myth', and 'believers in the Revolution' are the victims of a mystification. The absolute which was to condition all the rest is now no more than a technique for sowing discord among the enemy; it is only one weapon in the military arsenal among others, such as panslavism, pacifism, and the Orthodox Church guided by reliable bishops. But it still remains the best weapon.

CHAPTER 14

Projections of the Sacred

WE have always been told that politics and religion were disparate, that the functions of the political and the sacred were as distinct in society as are the functions of respiration and assimilation in the human organism. In the liberal age they were regarded as two separate categories of modern Western thought in the same way that the faculties of ideation and sensibility are two distinct psychological categories. For each of these categories there were appropriate sciences and disciplines: religious history and general history, the comparative study, or science, of religion and the comparative study, or science, of politics. Not only did these studies deal with different subjects, but they implied a different turn of mind and a different intellectual approach; and no doubt the dichotomy was scientifically necessary, for it represented the dissociative, analytical approach without which there can be no science in any domain. 'Religious facts' introduce us to a domain where man is defined by his radical insufficiency and by his awareness of it. The aim of religion, on the collective level, and of mysticism, on the individual level, is to transcend those individual limitations which condemn man to be no more than an individual; and for this reason some modern writers have felt justified in including together in one class the generally recognised religious phenomena and certain others which they call 'inferior forms of mysticism',[1] such as the effect of drugs and the ecstasies arising from the 'crowd state' and collective hysteria and reciprocal suggestion. In all three cases there is transcendence, or attempted transcendence, of individual limitations.

It is an entirely different domain from the political; for politics, in principle, is the continual search for a middle term, an attempt to mediate between the desirable and the possible, between conflicting human aspirations and historical realities. Between the two, certain possibilities emerge which the man of politics transforms into concrete plans; and once he has begun to put a plan into execution, he is in the domain of the real where the morality of the intention, as Nietzsche said, is only a pre-morality. He declines to take refuge in being right in defiance of the facts. In politics there are no excuses or alibis or exten-

[1] cf. Philippe de Félice, op. cit., and *Poisons sacrés, extases divines* (Paris, 1938).

uating circumstances; and it is in contrast with the solidity and fullness of the political world that the world of the 'beautiful soul' appears insubstantial. Men who are caught up in politics are not grateful for anyone's good intentions, and take no account of them. Indeed, good intentions which produce no effect will not be remembered, but only the actions of those who are active.

We do not intend to reject the distinction between the political and the sacred, any more than we propose to regard it as ultimately valid. History shows us régimes and periods in which the two are distinct, or at least are tending to become so, and others in which they tend to merge together. Not that in either case the political and the sacred are distinct functions with their own more or less distinctive organs; but *the political function is sometimes more and sometimes less identified with the sacred.* It must be noted, however, that the deconsecration of power has never been complete even in the most reputedly irreligious periods and régimes. According to the accepted 'political formula' of the age, political power has never been regarded as sacred in the plutocratic parliamentary liberal democracies of the 19th and 20th centuries, but this does not mean that the human tendency to consecrate politics has been abolished; it is only repressed. The farther we go from utilitarianism and scientific balance of power calculations, in other words, the more we allow politics to be coloured by human emotions, the more strongly the influence of the sacred will flourish. For example, there is an element of the sacred in the 19th-century conception of the *nation*—in its great men, its symbols, its glorious deeds; and in other régimes and periods the sacredness of power is equally clearly expressed, in beliefs which may differ among themselves but whose common historical lineage can be traced.

It is easy to recognise the descent, from ancient Egypt to 20th-century Russia, of the concept of the sacredness of power. On his passage through Egypt, Alexander the Great did not disdain to be invested by the priests of Ammon with the Pharaohs' religious authority, and it was later transmitted to the hellenistic monarchy of the Ptolemies. Then, when the mediterranean world was unified, the hellenised Egyptian monarch became the perfect model of the beneficent and tutelary sovereign (*ἐνεϱγέτης, σωτήϱ*) of a universal tutelary State; and the Roman Cæsar quickly became divine in those parts of the empire where the people's affectivity endowed power with sacredness. While he was still only *imperator*, *tribunus plebis*, and *princeps senatus* at Rome, he was already a god in Egypt and the East. The conception of a divine emperor was sometimes eclipsed and sometimes varied, but it persisted as a more or less constant theme from Julius Cæsar, who claimed descent from Venus, to Constantine, who was both a high priest of the State religion and also held his power from Christ. Caligula, the 'living god', married his own sister, like the Pharaohs; Hadrian, the hellenist, took the title of Olympian from the sun-god Jupiter, but also imposed upon the whole empire the Egyptian cult of Serapis—a god whom he himself, although almost a complete sceptic, eminently represented; Aurelian, who deduced the divine character of the monarchy from the solar cult, even claimed to legislate upon Christian dogma. Diocletian had been unable to create religious unity in the empire against Christianity, but Constantine succeeded by founding it upon Christianity; and historians have remarked that it was at this moment that Christian minds became possessed of the idea of the divine right of kings, which is itself far older than Christianity.

In this form the notion of the sacredness of monarchy remained a constant of Western political thought, as is seen in Charlemagne and in the Germanic Holy Roman Empire, and it was preserved intact at Byzantium, whence the grand dukes of Moscow arrogated it to themselves. Later, when the chief dynastic States of the West became great monarchies, the theory of the divine right of kings appeared again in various forms.

During the Italian Renaissance there emerged, most clearly in Machiavelli's works, what was to remain the Western conception of politics until the rise of the 20th-century secular religions. Politics were freed from all religious and magical context, and became a technique based upon knowledge, that is upon logic and experience, to the exclusion of any kind of supernatural revelation. It was the art of attaining certain previously defined objectives by the most appropriate means, and its first law was the adaptation of the means to the end in view. Machiavelli's principles were adopted by the European chancelleries. The art of politics resembles that of medicine in being based upon knowledge, but not upon complete knowledge; and the art consists in knowing when and where to apply it. (Thus political theory is at the same time both futile and weighty.) Art presupposes an artist, who must know how to combine inspiration with knowledge, and how and when to intervene. There is much in common between a medical and a political diagnosis; the politician, like the doctor, must possess knowledge, and the ability to choose and the power to act. In dynastic Europe, from the end of the religious wars until the French Revolution, high politics came to resemble a game of chess played by men who were all members of the same élite and, in general, of the same class—nobles and princes of the Church. There were moments when the game could only be carried on by changing boards, which meant substituting military for diplomatic play. But the military game was played by professional armies, while the rest of the population could continue to pursue its own business. Armies were composed of mercenaries, men who enjoyed fighting, and ne'er-do-wells, reinforced by a few poor wretches pressed for service and a few simpletons recruited in taverns. The civil populations suffered nothing from them, unless they had the misfortune to inhabit the scene of operations; not that they escaped the consequences of a war, but these were much less severe than nowadays. After the French Revolution, however, the picture changes.

* * * *

The 17th-century libertines and free-thinkers were succeeded in the 18th, throughout Europe, by the 'philosophers', who thought that Christianity and the Church could not survive the belief in the literal truth of Genesis, which the 'progress of enlightenment' would destroy by a rigorous historical and philological criticism. The protagonists of the enlightenment resumed, after a lapse of several decades, the ambitious programme of the Oratorian Simon[1]; they made a great to-do of proving the physical impossibility of miracles, and pointed out the strong resemblance between the miracles in different religions and the similarity of the excellent arguments (the very ones used by unbelievers) with which each religion combated the miraculous and supernatural claims of all the others. In the 19th century, while the historical and philological criticism was developed, there grew up also a psychological criticism, converging with the historical; it was less precise and less scrupulous, and therefore all the more easily disseminated. The principles of this new method, which claimed to find an historical and natural origin for the belief in supernatural and super-historical events, were established by Feuerbach. After its abstract phase in the 18th century, the critical spirit became more concrete in the 19th: the combined historical, philological, and psychological methods revealed the immense part played by 'luck' in the development of religions and the tendency of every Church and every faith to persist in its being, just like all the secular institutions. It was pointed out that dogma, doctrine, and belief appear to be used, in fact, to perpetuate *mundane* institutions, practices, and societies; the presence of the 'all too human' was detected everywhere, in orthodoxies as well as heresies. The critical spirit made use of definitions, scientific verifications, and established facts, as so many weapons; it attacked the realm of dogma by dissociating and dissolving its components, detaching them from one another and exposing them to the light of common day. And while traditional religion was undermined among the educated classes by these methods, the same result was produced among the most uprooted section of the people by

[1] *Histoire Critique du Vieux Testament* (Rotterdam, 1685).

the process of proletarianisation in the towns in which they were massed.

Did this mean that the hopes of the 18th-century philosophers, and of their rationalist-optimist successors of the 19th and even the 20th century, were about to be fulfilled? 'Religion will pass away by a process as inexorable as growth.' Freud's words, which are a last lingering echo of the *Aufklärung*, express in a tone already 'dated' a state of mind which his own work, with that of many of his predecessors and contemporaries, was going to render obsolete; they derive from the illusion that religion disappears into oblivion, or evaporates, when confronted with science. According to this illusion, the two cannot co-exist in a world that has become 'enlightened'. It is true that the classes which live by trading in either commodities or words were increasingly permeated by the philosophy of the enlightenment and by utilitarianism; and it is true that the uprooted persons who composed the 19th-century masses were lost to traditional religion when the old society of orders, which was organically linked with it, fell to pieces. But all this was not sufficient, as the 19th century believed it would be, to put an end to the history of religion. The human situations to which religion, myth, revelation, and epiphany correspond have not ceased to arise as frequently as ever.

Those who overestimate the force of rational argument and persuasion are making the very mistake of which psycho-analysis accuses philosophy. No one has demonstrated more clearly than Freud that enlightened therapy is not in itself sufficient (the reductive critical, or even psycho-analytical, method is purely destructive and offers nothing in place of what it takes away); although indispensable, it is either inadequate or disastrous unless it is connected with a quite different order of reality—and this is what Freud himself calls 'transference'. If the treatment succeeds, it is not through the mere fact of making the patient conscious, or more conscious, of his trouble.

In western Europe how have the consequences been manifested of this two-fold disaffection from traditional religion—among the 'enlightened' classes infected by 'philosophy' and among the uprooted peasants who have become the proletarian mass? It would appear that the fervour and energy released by the obsolescence of religious beliefs are attached to new objects. A new sacred seems gradually to be formed in compensation for the loss of the old beliefs. The new links by which men slowly become aware of being bound together, the links which express their actual condition, acquire an entirely new affective value, though not by any means an unprecedented one. It seems that, instead of disappearing, the sacred is projected elsewhere. Three great myths then demonstrate their supreme influence over the Western sensibility. They are not the only ones, but they dominate and attract and absorb all the others which are less powerful. These are the myths of the Nation (or Race) and of the Individual and of the Species. The last-named had already appeared towards the end of the 18th century in the form of the 'human race'; didactic, flattering, optimistic, and harsh by turns, it eventually assumed the ironic but on the whole benign countenance of 'philosophy' and the warlike one of the revolution. But in the 19th century it took on yet another aspect, though still promising future bliss, as socialism or *messianism of the human race*. Marx's mythical proletariat was the vehicle of this messianism of the species; it was in order to reach the Promised Land of the Species that the dangers and ambushes of the narrow revolutionary defile must be faced. Between the Species, mostly in exile at present, and the promised land it is the proletariat that intercedes and mediates. Those who do not belong to the proletariat must adhere to it and serve it. There is no other salvation.

In the first half of the 19th century, in a soil harrowed by the imperial wars, the myth of the individual, the one and only and inimitable, flowered nostalgically in the poets and their readers. It was for the individual's salvation that Christianity had discovered and peopled the beyond; and romanticism is the lament of the individual who has lost this hope. The renewed vitality of historical study is a consequence of the waning belief in the immortality of the soul. One is tempted to say that everything that was withdrawn from the other world came to enrich and dramatise the historical world, where it appears in the full light of day—a tragic testimony to the prowess of modern man.

In the literature of romanticism the aspiration to transcend individual limitations could find no satisfaction but only the most modest and disappointing and ephemeral, and finally the most irritating, of substitutes. It was effective only for the few and only for a short time; it was much less than a dream because it lacked the dream's power to banish reality. Romanticism is simply religious nostalgia in a mental universe which excludes religion or which, at any rate, is younger than religion and can live neither with it nor without it. The impossibility and the contradiction are expressed in a tone of purest, most authentic anguish. That romanticism is a dead-end is proved by the fact that it expresses itself exclusively in the form of art, and especially (and perhaps only) in literature—for romantic painting is painting before it is romanticism.[1] The yearning to transcend the limits of the individual leads to a comic catastrophe or to an insane one; and, indeed, the two do not necessarily exclude one another. In such a rarefied atmosphere the sacred could not re-establish itself. It can only attach itself to what really does bind men together with this-worldly bonds, earthly bonds which are like a revenge taken by the earth itself. What most appeals to men who long, con-

[1] cf. André Malraux, *The Psychology of Art* (Eng. trans., 1949).

sciously or unconsciously, to forget human insufficiency and to transcend their personal limitations, is the promise of social solidarity and collective euphoria. The first traces of the myth which later became national unity appear during the European, and more particularly the German, wars of independence against Napoleon. It is as though an attempt were being made to compensate for the failure of immortality by turning to the durable and long-lived, to the permanent character, stamped in flesh and soil, of this or that variety of the human species. In this way an appeal was made simultaneously to two powerful and often antagonistic and mutually destructive motives: the sociability which makes men come together and the anti-social tendency which opposes one man to another and urges him to assert his personal particularity and impose it in a fight to the death. From the middle of the 19th century, nationalism spread like an epidemic. Man asserted himself and worshipped himself, neither as individual nor as species, but as a variety of the species. When the French Revolution hurled the word Nation against the monarchs who were attacking it from every side, this intoxicating word was not one of those which express a hope, or option on the future, and are still void of concrete meaning; it was an historical reality. The French nation was already an established fact, though for the Germans and Italians and other peoples of central and eastern Europe the nation was still a myth of the future. And this is why the French nationalism of the 19th and 20th centuries has always been somewhat artificial and was never so vibrant and disturbing and frenzied as German, Italian, or Balkan nationalism.

From the second half of the 19th century national demands began to make themselves heard not only in literature but also in history, as witness the fact that the manual of history has become one of the modern successors of the catechism. The 19th century was an age of missions. While Marx was creating the mission of the proletariat, every nation in process of formation was claiming to have its own mission, and finding at least one, if not more; and the older nations, too, were reasserting their missions.

There is nothing new in this will, held in common by an entire category of men, to form a whole or unity; or, rather, this single will animating all the members of a group is new only as regards the character of the group, which is based on historical and racial community. Indeed, the sentiment which animated tribal religion and the ancient city cults can easily be recognised in it. Socrates gives it expression in the *Apologia* when he prefers to drink the hemlock rather than become a city-less man. But in its new appearance this religion of particularity is profoundly changed, both in content and scope.

The agitated period when the society of orders was collapsing produced mobs and violence and tended to emphasise the animal characteristics which differentiate one variety of the human species from another, and especially from the variety by which it is oppressed. Being emotionally easy to identify, these animal characteristics form a tie which everyone can feel; and thus the most common quality of all—that of resembling other people—becomes a sign of elective grace.

Here once again we find a pattern which can be traced many times among the ever-changing lines of history. Men cannot foresee all the consequences of their acts. It is true that the course of events is determined by the conscious aims which guide men's actions—as the Homeric gods pointed out to their favourites the enemy to be attacked; but the results do not correspond to the intentions. In the real world intentions do not watch like gods or guardian angels over the actions they inspire. What happens is the resultant of various forces operating in obedience to physical law. There is no complicity or secret alliance between idea and force; and force is in no way morally committed to idea. Forces are not moral but physical, in the strict sense of the word φύσις, or nature; and ideas are metaphysical. The belief that intentions are causes is a relic of anthropomorphic and magical thought; good intentions have no efficacity in themselves and provide no guarantee of good results. Everyone must have noticed in his own life that the acts of his ill-wishers have sometimes been beneficial to him and vice versa; some of our friends do us no good and some of our enemies are valuable. The conscious aim of the 18th-century protagonists of Reason and Enlightenment was the reconciliation of all men in a luminous world swept clean of all the contradictions from which they suffered. Once the despots (kings) and knaves (priests) had been cleared away, all religion and all the 'evil forces of superstition' would melt like clouds; and when the peoples had been freed from superstition the relations between men would be regulated by Reason. But we find a very different world when we look from the conscious aims of the *philosophes* to the historical results of their philosophy (which was itself determined by factors of which they were quite unaware). As men of ideas, the *philosophes* misjudged the power of the idea; they failed to see that when an idea appears to become a real historical force it does so thanks to an energy received from below and not from above; this energy is not, or is not solely, derived from conscious good intentions but also from all the licence and rationalisation and indulgence that the intentions may cover. All they knew of the idea was the idea itself; they knew nothing of what surrounded it. If the history of the 19th century is examined it will be seen that the sacred was not destroyed but displaced. The national myths and cults which make the 19th century the age of nationalities resemble the tribal myths and cults and also those myths and cults of the Polis which existed in the cities of the ancient world before it was unified by Rome and before the appearance of Christianity, the universal religion of the individual. This religion inherited the universality of the empire and transferred it, during the political schisms which followed the period of unification, from the temporal sphere to the spiritual. 'Particularist' psychological tendencies were obscured while the unification held, but they can be detected, even while semi-latent, in many a rebellion and religious heresy; and historians have had no difficulty in recognising 'national demands' behind the heresies in the countries of the Byzantine Christian empire subdued by Islam. At the end of the middle ages particularist sentiments revived again in the newly flourishing cities, but were thwarted by the feudal system, with its uncertain territorial boundaries, and by the œcumenical claims of Catholicism. The French Revolution, however, was thought to announce the approaching triumph of the human race; but what actually happened? What was the effect of the three-fold process of the de-Christianisation of the élites, or a part of them, by 'philosophy', the Napoleonic wars and the resistances they provoked in Europe, and finally the industrial revolution which de-Christianised the masses as the *Aufklärung* had de-Christianised the surface of society? What happened was that sacredness began to adhere to the immanent instead of the transcendent; it was projected upon man instead of God. The sacred was formed anew around what may be called two poles of association: myths of the Species and myths of the group. With nationalism the ancient tribal and city myths and cults were revived and also surpassed. They were no longer the same myths and cults, but new ones attached to similar psychological constellations. And at the same time there was foreshadowed in the work of the early socialist thinkers a messianism of the human Species—whose virulence was neutralised at first in the 19th century by the admixture of political liberalism, then in its hey-day, but was to erupt in the 20th century as the communist 'Islam'. The 'philosophy' of the 18th century did not lead to the realisation or triumph of the benign and exalted conceptions which inspired it. On the contrary, its criticism seems to have prepared the way for myths of a very different kind. The whole tenor of 18th-century 'philosophic' thought was against the partitioning of humanity, whether horizontally into belligerent kingdoms or vertically into a hierarchy of orders which 'reason' could not justify. Superficially, it inclined towards a sort of serene cosmopolitanism, a dictatorship of the lucid and communicable which would banish everything tortuous or obscure. It was confident that intellectual clarity could overcome all opposition; and the biggest obstacle was the Church, which took some rude buffets from the French Revolution. But it turned out that the following age, the 19th century, was a profoundly contradictory one. In the economic sphere it conformed to the 18th-century aspirations; by multiplying, extending, developing, and diversifying the processes of exchange it did in fact bring men closer together and disseminate clear and easily communicable ideas. But at the same time there was a reappearance of psychological constellations formerly associated with paganism and with the familial, tribal, and city gods, the objects of local cults of blood and soil. It seemed as though the past were not really past, as though the old cults were only repressed and not abolished, and could reappear in new disguises. Instead of being endowed with infinite potentialities, the historical psyche seemed to dispose of only a limited number of patterns.[1]

When Christianity won the final round against the mystery religions in the Roman Empire, it saved the individual from dereliction; it attracted individuals because it was concerned with individual salvation. But in the 19th century the 'group mysticisms' (the mystique of the limited group and the mystique of the Species) returned to the offensive; and unlike the group mysticisms of the ancient world the modern ones are mystiques of immanence, and are therefore a crude and imperfect form of mysticism. Thus in our day both the Species and the collectivity are conceived in a much more rudimentary way than in the ancient mediterranean civilisation.

Christianity is a religion of sin because sin only exists on the level of the individual. Collectivities will not admit the idea of sin, because they have no *super-ego*; or, if they have one, it counts for very much less. In the 19th century the American people were genuinely religious; but it did not prevent them from exterminating the Indians, although this was judged a crime by all the finer consciences among them and they could never have reconciled themselves to a comparable crime on the individual level. Collectivities never commit crimes, they leave them to the individual; and any attempt by propaganda to bring a collectivity to a sense of guilt is doomed to failure. *Collectivities see their sins as their mission.*

The attraction exerted upon men by the group was all the more powerful in the 19th century because it was possible to form groups unrestricted by the social divisions of the old society, such as the orders and guilds which partially satisfied the group instinct, and uncontrolled by the individualist principle of religion (which, though still œcumenical, was no longer powerful). The characteristic 19th-century group is

[1] The subject should be pursued much farther and an attempt made to define and determine 'effects', in the sense in which the word is used in physics and psychology alike; its study has given rise to the theory of 'archetypes', which lies beyond the limits of our present subject.

the nation. It was Christianity, with the Greek tradition interpreted through humanism, that bestowed upon the individual in the Western world the ability to value himself irrespective of group judgments, though these were still powerful and in fact the last word is always with them. And in the 19th century the group judgment vigorously reasserted itself. Even the most individualistic assertions of a Stirner or a Nietzsche rise from the depths of a sort of ocean of despair; and in the 20th century the domination of group judgments was even more forcibly and effectively imposed. As a general rule, even the 'superior' individual[1] of our own day will judge himself by what one might call 'group standards'. This is truer today than in the 19th century, and it was truer then than in the 16th. In the 19th century there arose from the depths of society *an egoism which was not directed towards the ego*; the individual came increasingly under the jurisdiction of group judgments, not merely in reference to other men but also in reference to himself. And with the technical progress in the methods for diffusing speech entire groups speaking the same language are beginning to hold the same beliefs, opinions, and prejudices. The individual is no longer shielded from this invasion by intermediate groups; and the 'aristocrats' who ignore the existence of any opinion outside their own aristocracy are now a negligible minority.

Thus there was developed in the 19th century an unprecedented trend towards solidarity of opinion, which is a factor favourable to war.

Group particularism was an early development and occupied an inferior position in the psyche; but in the 19th century it seems to have been freed from the influence of the antagonistic elements that kept it down. The individualistic universalism of Christianity lost influence, and this meant that the hellenic element also was weakened—that same hellenic element which, in the early centuries of Christianity, had raised a Jewish heresy to the level of the Universal. When the individual was chosen to be the vehicle of the universal, it was a triumph over every particularism.

Mankind was profoundly and universally stirred by the French Revolution and the break-up of the society of orders. In humanity's stormy periods there are always currents which rise up from the depths of the past, and in the 20th century one of these millenary currents brought to the surface the ancient solar symbol of the swastika. Nineteenth-century particularism had been only national, but the 20th century went farther and invoked not merely the soil but blood as well. Particularisms of blood and soil poured over Europe like a tidal-wave from antiquity, and overflowed upon the rest of the world. Contact with Europe's armed and (in the *material* sense of the word) civilising

[1]There are exceptions, but they prove the rule.

invaders reawakened and stimulated the particularisms of the colonial countries. The Europeans taught the yellow and black intelligentsias not only their techniques, their science, and their history, but their nationalism as well; and this at a time when they were creating the very situations which, in the nature of things, bring nationalism to birth.

* * * *

Emancipators are ignorant of the nature of the real forces they liberate, and therefore they are subdued by them. (These forces are, in the strict sense of the word, *lower*; they were overlaid, and now they rise to the surface.) So ideology is resorted to, to save the situation; it shields men's minds from the painful thought that what they are doing is not what they would, and that what they would they are not doing.[1] Professional emancipators, from Voltaire to Freud and from Hugo to his modern epigones, decline to know—or to act upon the knowledge—that for the vast majority of mankind the desire for light is a minor motive which only serves as a cloak for other and deeper impulses. Why does humanist culture point to the Greeks, and especially the Athenians, as leaders of humanity? Because they created an athletic and individualistic civilisation in which the desire for light was certainly more powerful than it has ever been elsewhere.

Simultaneously with the mystiques of the limited group there was a revival, from the middle of the 19th century, of a sort of mystique of the Species—a mystique of the entire human group, but considered as a species. And in this groping mysticism of the species the cosmopolitan hopes of the 18th century were combined with infinitely more profound and ancient impulses. These impulses, which may be thousands of years old, are a legacy from prehistoric times when man, the prey of other animal species and of the elements, may have felt an instinctive urge to come to the help of any creature of the same kind as himself.

* * * *

When it was discovered in the 18th century that gods and 'supernatural powers' owed their existence to men's belief in them, this was thought to mean the end of divinity and the supernatural. It was only a matter of time and the gods still hidden in popular superstition would be exorcised by exposure to the light, or so it was supposed; and the general progress of humanity as a whole towards the highest levels revealed by the light of reason would sweep away all the gods and super-

[1] It is possible today to know much more about this; but there is a strong resistance to such knowledge.

natural powers. It was believed that the gods and their powers had been created by man; but it did not yet occur to anyone that the creation of gods and powers was a human function, and a vital one, and that its repression would have disturbing effects both in the life of the individual and of the collectivity. It was reserved for the 19th and 20th centuries to begin the exploration of dynamic psychology. The 18th century would not have been reluctant to acknowledge the omnipotence of Eros; but it was some time before his ubiquity was recognised. The more intrepid champions of the 18th-century critical spirit were suspicious of the 'pietistic' theory of the functional need for an object to respect, admire, and adore; they scented in it a lingering trace of the Church's influence. So the function was anathematised as a whole and banished from consciousness. And then it was that reason began to develop its own fanaticisms. It is an understatement to say that the French Revolution gave a poor example of the tolerance that had been so much extolled before it began; revolutionary intolerance soon made people regret the intolerance which had been attributed to 'despotism'. The process, commenced by 18th-century intellectual criticism, of banishing the irrational from consciousness to the subconscious was continued in the 19th century by the industrial revolution. The increasing rationalisation of social life in the 19th and 20th centuries did for the masses what 18th-century rationalism had done for a part of the élite. But to drive it completely into the subconscious is not merely to fail to destroy the irrational, it is to offer it an impregnable stronghold from which it can counter-attack while enjoying immunity from direct intellectual criticism. A society which ceases to purge itself of the irrational by means of ceremonial enthusiasms puts itself increasingly at the mercy of the irrational; failing to understand their real import, it rationalises irrational manifestations which become all the more dangerous for being believed to be the opposite of what they really are. So once again, as in the past, historical complexes are able to mobilise psychological energy and get control of individuals, instead of being controlled by them; and the energy thus concentrated produces, wherever the resistance to it is weak, an effective equivalent of the gods and supernatural powers which are supposed to have been consigned to oblivion for ever. The national and social collective passions of the 19th century hardened in the 20th into secular religions; but it happened so gradually that no one was aware at any given moment of a transition from the profane to the sacred. The communist believer of today is under the impression that he weighs the pros and cons of a question like any other man; but one of the scales will always be the heavier, even with nothing in it.

* * * *

The first intimations of this mystique of the Species date from the 18th century. The Stoic phrase *caritas generis humani* was used to express the new aspirations, and it was for the *human race* that the French Revolution proposed to legislate. In the same century the word 'philanthropy' came into its own. Emancipation was the order of the day, and since all men were to be emancipated it really meant the emancipation of the Species. Thinkers later described as socialists, namely Saint-Simon and Charles Fourier, were thinking of Humanity, Man, and Society, all of which are myths of unity. For some of the romantics the People began to mean the entire human race. The question arises whether all this is leading to a decisive modification of the conscious human psyche. Could there be a revolutionary psychological change which would endow the Species itself with consciousness? A disintegration and reintegration on such a scale would not be without precedent, for the Roman world was the scene of an equally revolutionary and total shift of emphasis when the city cults were replaced by the universal religion of the individual. Nineteenth-century man had the choice of two great religious ways: a return to the cult of the limited group, which was foreshadowed in the claims of national particularisms, or an advance towards a religion of the Species, which corresponds, perhaps, to even older archetypes. Viewed with detachment and in the light of scientific progress, the position of man in Christianity appears utterly contradictory. Aspiration for eternal life is aspiration for life. We are, however, endowed with a very long—if not eternal—duration; but we possess it as a species and not as individuals. And the individual desires for himself this eternity, or rather this very long duration, which belongs to the species. His deep aspiration would be satisfied if individual consciousness were replaced by species-consciousness. But consciousness pertains to the individual and duration pertains to the species; and it seems that consciousness is essentially linked with finitude. By progressively shifting the accent away from the individual, by discovering in history something other than the individual, and by emphasising this discovery, Western thought seems to be obscurely groping towards an end which appears absurd, although there are really no grounds for pronouncing it impossible: namely, to deprive the individual of consciousness, that is to say, of his purposes and his aspirations of fulfilling them, and to transfer it to the species. This would solve the tragic and fundamental dilemma by which man is racked and crucified: his aspiration as an individual to the endless life which he feels himself to possess as a species. Christianity came to protest against the idea of a life of misery ending in blank nothingness; it gave human life a meaning, and introduced the impossible, perhaps, to overthrow the absurd. The problem is to release what must die from its longing to survive. A consciousness of the species is almost inconceivable, but to declare it impossible would be a lapse from intellectual integrity. If such a psychic revolution occurred its aim would be the same as Christianity's: to conquer death. Is it impossible for the species to rediscover consciousness? It may be that the individual only appeared when the species had reached a certain stage of evolution and had already a long history behind it. From the scientific point of view the individual is a function of physical and chemical relations which can be mathematically expressed; he is an equilibrium bounded on each side by disequilibrium. And within these boundaries which he cannot transgress without ceasing to exist he is perpetually changing. If he is revived and resurrected, what will it be that lives again?

Would it be possible, by an asceticism probably more rigorous than any hitherto known to humanity, to prise away from the individual his consciousness and his human perspective and transfer them to the Species? And what result would this kind of asceticism and discipline produce? It would not be a dialectic of ideas, like Plato's, which promotes the soul of the beautiful body into a beautiful soul, and thus leads it to its goal which is the Good. The new religion we are discussing is not a dialectic of ideas; it is a dialectic for reducing the flesh itself, the living flesh of man. The elements of a religion of the species seem already to exist in suspension in the societies of today, just as the elements of Christianity existed in the mediterranean world while it was being unified by Cæsar. And the problem has not changed, it is the conquest of death. Christianity solved it by making death no longer a death. It turned death into the true life. The life of this world, it said, was shot through with death, whereas the life of the beyond, for those who achieved salvation, was *Life*. Ever since the 19th century it would appear as though western Europe, faced with the same problem, the decline and ruin of the sacred (only in this case it was the death of God and not of *a* god), were dimly groping towards a new answer. Now that humanity is ceasing to believe in the great hope of the individual after death (since the 19th century what has become of the belief of the best Christians in hell?), the problem is to prevent the consciousness of death, the consciousness that 'it is I who die',[1] from arresting humanity's progress. And the answer which is beginning to be obscurely formulated is one that has been made before and elsewhere, but in other forms. It is that the barriers of the individual must be destroyed, for it is *only* the individual who dies. Thus, if consciousness could cease to be confined to the limits of the individual, if the individual could *attach* himself to the supra-individual, then death would not matter. It would be the death only of what is mortal. It would be simple mortality. For what is

[1] As André Malraux puts it (*La Voie Royale*).

tragic in our destiny, both particular and universal, is that we are exposed to what seems to us to be an original injustice. We can accept that what is mortal should die, but its death seems to involve also the death of what ought not to die; for we are no longer able to believe that what we most value is immune from death. But other religions have taught that the valuable must be kept separate from the perishable; and in this the 'living Buddhas' have succeeded, so Buddhism asserts. The asceticism inspired by this faith endeavours to negate the most certain properties of the living being. The 'voluntary centres' aspire to a dominion (which modern science has not yet conceded them) over the sympathetic system; the adept claims to check the flow of his blood, to postpone and choose the hour of death, to defy the law of gravity. But these can only be accessory phenomena, exploiting the field of the magician (or the technician). Romanticism was the last echo of outcast individualism; and the 'existentialist' philosophies in their turn are the last echoes of romanticism. (True to their origin, they are literary to the core.) All of them are caught in the impasse of death.[1] For if the individual has no future—until his death—except to be an individual, then freedom is nothing but the freedom to revolve in a closed circle, galloping round and round like a circus horse until death brings the turn to an end. But Christianity broke the circle by teaching men to die joyfully because this life was nothing but a preparation.

Disillusioned with the individual, Western thought since the 19th century has been tentatively seeking some other solution than the Christian. It is tending towards an integrally new religious 'alienation' by which the death-doomed individual is stripped of his *value*. To speak of a reintegration of man's nature is to abandon history for eschatology. Man is not static or stable; it is not in his nature to let himself be. Irredeemably bestial, and yet an indomitable creator of gods, his withdrawal into himself must be either a resort to eschatology, which means mysticism, or a lapse into animality; or else, unfortunately, the two together and both of them unconscious. Like Christianity and like Buddhism, the still inchoate aspiration towards a religion of the Species undoubtedly demands an almost superhuman asceticism; and if men were to attempt it they would have to follow a different road from that of Christianity and the Christian civilisation. Such a new departure might seem to us to be a violation of the very nature of man, and so it would be; but the same is true of Christianity itself, and no doubt it is in the nature of man to do violence to himself. There would be no such thing as history unless man had been incessantly questioning and violating his own nature. There are inventions in religion as in other things; and whether we call it a transference, a displacement, a

[1] Except 'Christian existentialism', which addresses itself only to Christians.

reversal, or a conversion of energy, a new mode of life is always a new mode of life.

The aspiration towards a religion and a civilisation of the Species was betrayed, however, almost from the start. In the romantic messianism of the early socialist thinkers a new 'pathos' was dimly discernible. When Feuerbach speaks of 'Man' it is the Species that he has in mind. And when socialism, towards the end of the 19th century, asserted its 'scientific' pretensions and the efficacy of its teaching, it took on the significance of a doctrine of sociological predestination. By a process of dialectical mystification (to use the 'mystifying' language itself), the Proletariat, with its satellite intellectuals, was made the supreme Intercessor for the Species, and the seeds were sown of the doctrine which would make the party the supreme Intercessor for the Proletariat. We see here an example, much cruder and harsher than any to be found in the working of modern democracy, of what may be called the 'fallacy of *representation*'. The relationship established is quite unlike the constitutional one between elector and elected; it much more resembles what M. Lucien Lévy-Bruhl called 'mystic participation'—the very thing which Marx, in his Promethean desire to deflate and reduce the sacred, called a mystification. Facile, elementary, and over-simplified, this representative principle contradicts the profound impulse which it claims to express. It can only be described as a crude piece of jugglery. If there is any value in Marx's polemic, based on Hegel and Feuerbach, against religious alienation and mystification, its chief value is as a criticism of Marx himself.

Marxist communism contains a myth of the Species. It aspires to create the unity of the Species against all the lesser groups to which the individual has hitherto been subordinated. Today the heritage of Christ is disputed, and there will be wars of succession, an age of struggle for the unification of the Species, an essentially *revolutionary* age. And after it the Species will renew its war upon 'Nature', but with immensely increased power because it will no longer be in conflict with itself.

But this myth neglects the fact that man is not an *imperium in imperio*; he too is 'nature'. If Nature is to be subdued by man, will she not also be triumphing in man—which is to say, triumphing over man? Would a new and more sociable animal species emerge, resembling the insects in its stricter subordination of the individual to the species? Nietzsche desired the elevation of the type man through a new absolutism which would subdue the human raw material to the good pleasure and inspiration of future legislators whose plans would embrace millennia. But he did not entirely desert the path of the personal religions and the civilisation of the individual. He was not interested in the individual but in individuals, and therefore he sacrificed quantity to quality. He was not concerned with the Species.

The myth of the Species in communist propaganda and ideology shows us an aspiration perverted and degraded into a justification. To abstract the individuals who compose it is to endow the Species with transcendence; but, in fact, the Species is only accessible through the individuals. Hypostatised as an abstraction, it becomes a transcendent and all-devouring entity; and to immolate existing individuals for the sake of future individuals—or of the Species (the ambiguity is of the essence of mythical thinking)—is to feed this transcendent entity with human sacrifices. But if the whole chain is present in each of its links, if the individual and the species are each immanent in the other, then this immolation of individuals may be the destruction of the Species as well. . . .

From 'utopian socialism' to Stalin, the history of this aspiration is a history of decadence. Marxist communism is the aggressive caricature of a religion of the Species. Day by day it pronounces, in the blended accents of executioner and pedant, the *damnation* of thousands of men whom it declares to have no further significance or value, except negatively, because the 'historical process' has made them obsolete: the men in concentration camps and the prosperous men who will join them tomorrow, and all those who have to be reduced or liquidated in one way or another, such as the other social classes, the generations who are 'too old to understand' and, finally, all those communists who are guilty of deviations,

Here the contrast is striking between communism and Christianity. For the Christian a man is a neighbour, a soul to be saved; but for communism, in its meanness of spirit, and in contradiction to Nietzsche's dictum, man is too often a thing to be *reduced*. Christianity speaks to every man personally—'*de te res agitur*'—and does not treat us as mere fodder for 'History'. With an incomparable decisiveness it took to itself the universal and individual desire for victory over death; and by this it did not mean that we must sacrifice ourselves for the sake of some great anonymous victory by and on behalf of men unknown to us. Those who call themselves the champions of a religion and civilisation of the Species have so far only shown us its sanguinary caricature; and if in the future there is debate between those who uphold personal religion and those who champion the Species, the example of the latter's present-day champions will be of no assistance.

* * * *

The idea of a 'perfect' state of affairs and of 'perfect beings' corresponds to an archetype which has inspired many types of religion from the immobile *askesis* of Indian sages to the messianic and millenary faiths of zealots. The 'perfect state' is sometimes projected into the past (the golden age) and sometimes into the future (the last judgment, the classless society) and sometimes into both—as in the case of the cyclical theories of the Eternal Recurrence. The idea of recurrence reconciles the past and the future and goes beyond them both.

To aspire to an absolute culmination and to imagine the attainment of the extreme limit is probably inherent in the psychological structure of most, if not of all, of the races of the human Species. In this aspiration Freud thought to recognise the influence of Thanatos,[1] whom he conceived as presiding, jointly with Eros, over the transformations of desire; the two deities being in perpetual conflict. (This is a powerful example of the 'dualistic' archetype, projected in the guise of a 'metapsychological' interpretation which certainly contains some truth.) The repetitiveness of the Eternal Recurrence expresses, even more profoundly than the idea of a return to the non-differentiated, the imperious desire for equilibrium and stability and absolute repose. It represents the nostalgia for a condition, quite outside any kind of life, undisturbed by the first beginnings of the tendency to differentiation.

It is impossible to ignore entirely these considerations when we examine the psychological structure of paradises. In the classless society, for example, humanity is to be brought to perfect homogeneity and unity through the suppression of social differentiation; and when this culmination has been reached there will be no longer, it seems, any line of demarcation between what is today imaginary and what is not. 'Man (i.e. the Species) will develop in every way'; and surely it would be a crime against the Species to refuse to employ any means whatsoever in order to reach such a goal?

We can now form some idea of the remoteness in time and the psychological depth of the origin of Marx's 'realisation of philosophy' (for this was his interpretation of the Hegelian goal of 'History'). All the troubles arising from human *differences* will be abolished when humanity has become homogeneous. The classless society is the most recent of the active and aggressive conceptions of the perfect state. But is it an end, a final condition of glory? Or is it a beginning as well as an end, the commencement of a new cycle? Engels held that 'primitive communism' was the first state of Humanity; and perhaps the new homogeneity will be succeeded by a new differentiation. . . . Or will there be an unprecedented break with everything we know as human or can foresee—a new dispensation about which we can say nothing at all and can only maintain a religious silence? It must surely be impossible to see the classless society face to face, for how could the weak

[1] More 'scientifically' he calls it the death instinct. Cf. *Beyond the Pleasure Principle*.

human eyes of the believer penetrate that zone of glory? And how much the less our own. . . . We shall not attempt to decide whether the 'instinct of the absolute' is the same as the 'instinct of death'. We shall confine our exploration to more limited fields.

We have so sharply isolated the eschatological element in the communist religion that the faithful will refuse to recognise it; and those who make a profession of 'objectivity' will perhaps accuse us of lacking that quality. It is true that ideology has performed its special task by adapting[1] the eschatological representations to the state of mind of a society in which the use of scientific techniques has established the supremacy of science, a society in which reverence for the scientific spirit is obligatory. But the religious tenor of the ideological representations is manifest in the effects they produce.

In every society, what is called civilisation is based upon the repression, diversion, and canalisation—in a word, the utilisation—of the impulses of the participating members, and not only the disinherited but also the élites, who, in general, enjoy more satisfactions but have also more self-restraint. Thus, in addition to the horizontal strife between societies and the more or less latent vertical strife within them, called by Marx the 'class-struggle', there is also a more general strife within each individual. Man strives as much against himself as against others; a struggle of the instincts, which is no less significant than the struggles between States and classes. History is a product of these three warring factors, as the examination of any major historical phenomenon will reveal. In every society, then, there is not only a latent resentment of class against class, but also of individuals against the apparatus of constraint which is a condition of civilisation; and hence there is always a good chance of success, though especially in certain periods, for any propaganda which combines a promise to the disinherited of a share in the good things of which they feel deprived with a promise to the individual of a release from social constraints. Propaganda of this kind points forward to the promised age and land in which those differentiations will cease to exist, by which today the 'few' are separated from the 'many' and those who command from those who obey. The malcontent and the disinherited can share alike in this vision of a time when the individual will have no grievance against a society which no longer oppresses him, and the disinherited no resentment against a culture of which he is no longer deprived. The aspiration for a society in which goods are owned in common unites with the aspiration for a régime not founded upon the restraint of impulses; and in order to find plausibility in this blessed prospect one has only to forget how the benefits of culture are really earned—a thing which it is pleasanter to forget than to

[1] An example of the phenomenon of convergence.

remember. The whole world will be transformed with increasing speed as the boundaries of this society of less work and more play are extended. Society will be no longer in any way divided against itself, because the reasons for conflict with others will disappear at the same time as the reasons for self-conflict. All the powers of humanity being devoted to the common task, none of them will be distracted from it by fratricidal strife; there will be no more victims of the class war and no more victims of society. To sum up, the Freudian *super-ego* and the Freudian *id* will no longer be distinct—and the barriers between desire and reality will collapse.

What is the meaning of the 'image' of the U.S.S.R. that was formed in the communist psyche during the 1920s? It is this: an historical fact converged with an eschatological representation and *focused* it. The U.S.S.R. was represented as *the beginning of the great event*. Even though the U.S.S.R. has nothing in common with the great event and all that it implies, it is nevertheless a necessary preliminary to all those things. If it departs from them, it is only in order to approach them better. If it seems to favour a thing, it is only so as to extirpate it the more thoroughly; if it seems to destroy a thing, it is only so as to restore it in more glorious form. In this connection an extraordinarily distorted and simplified form of the Hegelian dialectic is used with great effect; it is a *deus ex machina* which turns every denial of the ideal into a superior affirmation of it. Though frustrations and prohibitions and privations are redoubled, would it not be a crime to object when they are the precursory signs of humanity's golden age? The purpose is nothing less than to rescue the Species as a whole from anxiety and distress; and only *hard facts* can provide the foundations for the dogma of a materialist religion of the human species.

But the present day has brought to light the damaging contradiction within the materialist religions: they have never succeeded in protecting themselves from collision with hostile fact. And this failure is inherent in their nature. In Feuerbach the postulate of the 'mission' of the Species was all the more inviolable for being implicit, which is why Marx and Engels valued this thinker so highly; they knew how much they owed him. Marx's philosophy in his younger days before the Communist Manifesto is deeply tinged, in spite of himself, with religious aspiration. Born of religion, his philosophy passes through 'political economy' to return to its source. And in communism it was the technical political element, on the one hand, and the religious, on the other, that were to grow continually stronger at the expense of the philosophical element.

But the communist 'Islam' no longer represents the religion of the Species, except to betray it; all the resources of suggestion are now required to disguise the fact that it is nothing but a hastily patched-up doctrine of predestination. Christianity triumphed in the ancient world because of its emotional appeal, because affectivity found in it the most complete satisfaction. But communism is far from providing a similar satisfaction today; its very structure forbids it even to make the attempt. If it exists, it is nothing but itself. If it is not itself, it ceases to exist.

* * * *

A universal religion undoubtedly performs, in its time and place, a function equivalent to that of a psycho-analytic catharsis on the grand scale. Psycho-analysis, in fact, is merely one method among others of providing a substitute when religion is not fulfilling this social function —and it is an extremely costly substitute, for it has to be applied individually in each separate case; but, like religion, it does offer a cure by the release of energy. In the religions of the past, the divinity in one form or another was set over against man, as object in face of subject; and the cult of the divinity operated a discharge of energies whose repression within the individual psyche would have been dangerous for the individual. By facilitating their transference the cult fixed these energies and made them amenable to control. When religion is strong and not undermined by scepticism, it exorcises the unconscious much more thoroughly than psycho-analysis, which, as we have said, is at best only a social palliative. The only aim of psycho-analysis is to adapt man to life by dissolving the elements in him which resist adaptation (to analyse means to resolve, and the therapy may be compared to the resolution of a mathematical problem); even when the transference succeeds,[1] it does not fully appease that hunger for an object to adore and respect which the present system of human relationships usually represses and perverts. (Secular religion does satisfy this hunger and is therefore, to that extent, more successful than psycho-analysis.) According to Jung, religious cults bear implicit and, as it were, unconscious witness to the fact of a circulation of energy (he calls it an 'energising cycle'); and it is by studying the human functions they perform, and not the myths they evoke, that we shall understand their human significance. The results of the reductive criticism inspired by the 'philosophy of enlightenment' were disappointing to its enthusiasts because they did not appreciate this distinction. If we destroy a thing we must put something in its place; and if we fail to replace what we destroy, we shall find that we have not in fact destroyed but only *displaced* it. When a religion declines or loses ground to another the same principle applies, irrespective of the value we may attach to the new or the old religion:

[1] A successful transference is not a cure, but a preliminary condition of cure. It gives the individual a second chance.

there are similar psychological displacements, fusions, deviations, identifications, and transferences. And, moreover, as the psychoanalysts justly remark, 'psychological energy is wayward'. It cannot be diverted like a water-course; there are directions in which it will not flow; and the time-factor also enters in to increase the difficulty. This is a point upon which two types of men are equally deluded: those who believe that a myth can be promoted and imposed on the grand scale simply because it is wished, and those who believe that a god can be maintained beyond his time *in order to keep away a worse one*. There can hardly be a clearer proof that a god is dead than this reason for keeping him alive. The days of the gods participate in historical time, and in its irreversibility.

But it is none the less true that religion can never be defeated by the weapons of enlightened philosophy; and if this does not convince critics of the vanity of criticism, it is because they stop too soon. The anti-religious criticism of religions left their *function* out of account. Man is all the more at the mercy of the unconscious when he is unaware of the need to be on his guard; and as a result he becomes more self-estranged than ever and an increasingly desperate note of hypocrisy is detectable in his ideologies. From the point of view of the historian, it is true, Christianity has already been several religions.[1] The profound mutual incomprehension between Byzantines and Crusaders in the first crusade was partly a question of religion; and what was there in common psychologically between the reawakening Christianity of the 10th to 12th centuries and the religion of the catacombs? *Can we speak of the same religion when the psyche is so different?*

In the 19th and 20th centuries 'Man' did not grow as fast as his own powers. The more he dominates surrounding nature, the more he is dominated by nature within him. But it is true that these propositions lose their beautiful simplicity when his contemporary social differentiations are carefully, i.e. historically, examined. There is no doubt, however, that Western man in the 20th century is *on the whole* not so superior (to say the least) in comparison with 17th-century man as 20th-century machines are superior to those of the 17th century. Inequalities within society are perhaps less great, but who would dare to assert that a comparison between the 'higher' levels would give the 20th century the advantage?

It is significant that 20th-century tyrants are much less *individualised* than 17th-century kings. The latter were much more spontaneous and much more responsible for their actions. Modern tyrants possess many more machines, but cannot stop them so easily. Intelligent retreat was not possible for Hitler as it was for Frederick II; and Napoleon was not

[1] Thinkers as different as Oswald Spengler and Professor Guignebert agree about this.

lost in the turmoil he created, but remained an individual. The totalitarian tyrant, on the other hand, seems to be literally nothing compared to the forces he can unleash. There has certainly been a decline of individual responsibility; individual men today, whoever they may be, are not thought capable of resisting the sort of pressures that can be brought to bear on them. And if man can no longer be counted upon, the consequences must be far-reaching indeed.

* * * *

In the 18th century the Church and the Monarchy were 'exposed' by *philosophes* and encyclopedists. Reason became the Absolute to which everything else stands as relative, and upon it a universalism of the human race was to be established. But in the 19th century Reason itself came under criticism. It was seen to be a solvent which could destroy faith but could not, in any vital sense, replace it. Applying itself to history, criticism then began to challenge reason's eternal status; it discovered reason to be historical and, at the same time, superficial. The historical and the various were no longer considered as inferior to reason but as part of it. All that the 18th century had taken apart was put together again. Schopenhauer 'unmasked' the primordial will to live behind the façade of reason, and began to make contacts with Eastern thought. From him, Nietzsche took over the will to live and examined it from every side; and we find it again, unrecognisable, in the work of Freud at the end of the century under the name of *libido*. This metaphysical idea[1] offered an approach to the study of the emotions and of affective dynamics, thanks to which psychology will at last begin to deserve its name.

In exposing the pretensions of 'eternal reason' Marx was already anticipating the psycho-analytic mode of thought; behind every ideal and rationalisation and convention and fiction he proposed to reveal a social complex, an aggressive and defensive system. But he concerned himself only with historical and collective phenomena, whereas the psycho-analysts reveal the impulses behind individual and biological characteristics. Thus a real analysis is made of the ideas, the values, and the standards which men are required to acknowledge. An attempt is made to resolve them, and *solve* them, so that they no longer appear to belong to a higher order of things or to represent any greater degree of necessity than the 'subjectivity' which they claim to regulate. Like plants and animals, they are simply products of environment.

These successive 'debunkings' might be said to lead to pure nihilism, were it not that the poison contains its own antidote. For nihilism, too,

[1] It is one of those initial assumptions which require further examination.

can be debunked. At the heart of nihilism, as of despair, there lies an unjustifiable certainty; for if nothing is true, then the proposition that nothing is true is as uncertain as any other proposition. It is like an unstable chemical substance which destroys itself as it creates itself.

Criticism began by attacking falsehood for the sake of truth and evil for the sake of good, because the false was masquerading as the true and the evil as the good. But in the end every truth had been revealed as falsehood and every good as evil. So if nothing remains that can be trusted, then all we can do is to debunk this 'nothing'. By exposing the situations hidden behind ideas and the impulses disguised by values, it was discovered that criticism was nothing but a debunking machine. It was backed by no standards and could be used by anyone for any purpose. But what was de-bunked was not destroyed, but only displaced; and myth reappeared in new forms to nerve the arms of the iconoclasts themselves. . . . In all this zeal for profanation there is something infinitely unrewarding. We destroy only what we ourselves have made. Man gave and man takes away. To unmask a thing does not mean to lift a veil that exists outside ourselves, it means to withdraw our confidence so that an idea loses the attractive power with which we ourselves had endowed it. In this way we do not liberate ourselves from myth but only from *a* myth; and we shall experience again in the future the effects of our myth-making and deifying propensity.

To be a god-maker is not to be a god. When man is man, he creates gods; when he sets himself up as God, he becomes a beast. Like a comet, man is in trajectory, and to stop at the highest point is to fall to the depths. When perfect virtue and absolute justice are the order of the day, angelic theory is accompanied by bestial practice: virtue and the guillotine, ideological heaven and concentration-camp hell—the complementary contraries of Heraclitus.

Mental health depends upon free access to the sources of energy, upon unimpeded communication between the conscious and what is called the subconscious; in the same way, social health demands that the myth-making and deifying instinct should not be blindly repressed. It is a force within us, and to negate it is to deprive us of a dimension. But there is no chance of our escaping the implacable and sterilising furnace of the truth, and therefore it behoves the most lucid among us to try to discern, at any given moment of history, the motive of its disintegrating action.

* * * *

That intellectualist criticism should lead to totalitarianism seems a paradox to the abstract intelligence, but not to psychology. The general repression of the deificatory or god-making impulse is not the same thing as its abolition. We do not know what the effect of abolishing it would be; but we do know that its repression during a period familiar to us (for it dates from the 18th century to our own day) has been accompanied by an outbreak of the crudest sort of myths, against which the very men who were boasting of their freedom from old superstitions have seemed to be defenceless.

The modern techniques for rapid transmission and circulation of words have encouraged a general tendency to economise intellectual effort; and even professional intellectuals, though they have more knowledge than ever, seem to have less judgment. It appears that the repression of the god-making instinct in the 18th, 19th, and 20th centuries has resulted in a *displacement* of the sacred. There has been a revival of familiar archetypes tricked out in the fashions of today: the classless society, the millennial Reich, doctrines of biological and sociological predestination, the mission of the proletariat or the aryan race or some other race. A superficial and inadequate use of the critical function, and the great game of debunking, seem to have cleared the ground to make room . . . for what? For a renaissance of archetypes from the remote depths of the past.

What has happened is that men have 'exposed' and 'unmasked' everything to the point of stripping human existence itself of all meaning or significance. Our existence has no longer any guarantees or any obligations. The objectivity in whose name everything was condemned as subjective in the 19th century now fails us in its turn. Instead of providing a real and solid foundation, it leaves man believing himself arbitrarily condemned to inhabit a certain environment as an arbitrary specimen of a certain human type. 'Why these things and not others?' Objectivity has gone the same way as eternal reason. Human behaviour appears as the resultant of a number of strains and pressures from different directions. We still hear a lot of talk about liberty; but the only liberty we really should ask for is to go against the line of least resistance. We are always free to go with it.

* * * *

Now we reach the stage of political nihilism; German national socialism exhibits perfectly the convergence between 'active' nihilism among the élite and 'passive' nihilism in the masses. It will be remembered that a wave of conversions and 'self-committals'[1] preceded it. The 'committed' individual is very often a symptom of the growth of nihilism among intellectuals. To commit oneself is to become attached to something that is already strong and on the march to victory—

[1] Conversions to national socialism and communism, and even some to Catholicism.

something that is immune from the implicit criticism of nullity by which the newly-committed condemn themselves. The communist party and the proletariat represent for them that power from which their nihilism gave them the sense of being excluded; and they have often not enough critical sense left to be able to criticise a pro or a con, a party line or objective, which in fact is quite as open to criticism, to say the least, as all the things they are so proud of having debunked. Proceeding in a circular course from destruction to destruction, the critical faculty has at last destroyed itself. Totalitarian solutions combine the seductions of simplicity, extremism, and even absurdity; and it becomes possible, by means of auto-suggestion, to reach the pitch of fanaticism: 'Since nothing is better than anything else, why should I refrain from this?' If nothing is defensible, then everything is legitimate; and if all things are equal, one may choose to do anything. All ideas are equally valueless, so choice can be governed by power instead of thought. Nihilism reduces all values to the same level; in other words, it introduces equality into the essentially unequal, and is therefore in this sense absurd. But it was nihilism in this sense that played into the hands of Hitler and, later, of communism.[1] The general destruction of confidence having spared nothing, all that remains is an intolerable void—which must be escaped from at all costs. To escape into communism is to join a great campaign which solidly exists and progresses, and which represents 'something one can do'. To 'commit oneself' and to 'collaborate'[2] might be described as the same action in differing circumstances. But there is a psychological and moral difference: one is committed before victory, and one collaborates after it. In committing oneself there is an illusion of choice, but in collaboration there is an illusion of having no choice. It is essentially a difference of timing. To commit oneself is to forestall events; but the zeal of collaborators is all the more intense for being belated.

Every sort of confidence having been undermined, and every form of life, whether social, historical, or individual, appearing arbitrary, the way is clear for the belief that social life and human relationships can be based upon a consent obtained automatically by coercion.

In the *Will to Power*, Nietzsche prophetically describes the evolution of nihilism. In the first stage values are detached from reality, for the world-as-it-is is unworthy to exist and the world-as-it-should-be does not exist. The existing world is condemned in the name of an anti-

[1] This is the active nihilism of the intellectuals (there is also a complementary *passive* nihilism of the masses). *Nota bene:* This nihilism is not openly avowed, and in order to practise it the point of departure must be a profession of faith whose apparent content is anything but nihilistic. Not that it deceives anybody.

[2] These words should not be taken in any condemnatory or discreditable sense. We are concerned with contemporary social facts and historical categories.

world or other-world. The next stage is to condemn the other-world also. The nihilists now forget that they have lost the right to depreciate existence in the name of values which they have also depreciated; they soon fall victims to the crudest myths and most compelling realities, and are immediately obliged to exhibit all the external signs, if nothing more, of a 'simple faith'. These signs would have astonished their fathers, whose critical faculty they hold in such contempt.

Secular religions take full advantage of the arts of slander and depreciation practised by the nihilist intellectuals who change sides to join them, and the destructive action of their criticism thus comes under the control of the totalitarian enterprise. It requires skill to make use of it, for the method consists in poisoning society with poisons secreted by itself while shielding the poisoner from their effects. Totalitarianism must assist the enemy's own self-destruction by maintaining the virulence of depreciatory criticism, while protecting itself against it.

Now the 'values' of this criticism are valid, *a fortiori*, against secular religion and totalitarianism; and it might well happen that totalitarianism should fail to control this formidable criticism, which was born in the West and against which the West is therefore to some extent immunised. That the totalitarians fear such a failure is revealed in their fear of the free circulation of ideas.

The nihilist state of mind, in which, as Nietzsche says, man can no longer relate himself to positive values, can only be changed from within; the faith and the myths to which it predisposes a man are cruder and more vulnerable than those he has abandoned, *but it cannot be overcome by retreating from them*. The 'values' of depreciatory criticism can only be effectively combated by those who have seen deeply into them, for they alone understand them and become immune to their poison. Thus, those who overcome nihilism will be precisely those who appear as nihilists to the superficial observer. Nihilism needs to be carried to the extreme, and it will then be found that it is at least as vulnerable to criticism as all the things it has criticised.

The mental process that produces nihilism has its point of departure in myth, and in the end it returns to it. Today as in former times, *mutatis mutandis*, it is myths that group men together and inspire them and incite them to action.

But history is something more than a process of ripping open dolls and turning them over to shake out the sawdust; it is also the midwife of values. There is nothing that can force us to doubt the 'fruitfulness of action'; and it is the fact that we are still conscious today in the West of man's propensity for self-change that inspires our resistance to any ideal of a closed society of the insect type and any campaign which, though advocating in principle the socialisation of man, would in practice sacrifice man to socialisation.

History and the historical mind cannot be accused of making anyone a nihilist who was not already on the way to become one; for there is nothing that history more clearly emphasises than man's inventiveness. Man is, above all, *the animal which finds a way out*.

History continually shows us man refusing to be imprisoned within the terms of an 'insoluble' problem, and performing a creative act which renders the problem obsolete. Creativity cuts the Gordian knot and abolishes the problem. In real history there are fewer 'problems' than is thought, and more examples of situations saved by creative acts. A 'problem' is a situation reflected upon and brought into full consciousness; and therefore it often happens that its insoluble character is co-extensive with the problem itself. A problem may pose itself in such a way that we can only solve it by drawing upon the resources of our own consciousness.

CHAPTER 15

What is a Revolution?

THE diverse histories of nations and of the intercourse between city and city and nation and nation become intelligible when once the general 'sphere of culture' which embraces them has been understood. So history is always the *total* history of a certain 'world', and comprises both the horizontal history of a culture (inter-State wars) and its vertical history (class struggles). These two histories interpenetrate, and, indeed, it is only by analysis that they can be separated from a third, which is the history of culture itself.[1] The frontiers of art, religion, philosophy, science, and technics are not those of a State except—and the exception is vital—when the frontiers of a single State coincide with those of a culture. In such a case the 'sphere of culture' can be said to be politically homogeneous; instead of multiplicity, there is unity. There are several examples of this: the mediterranean world from Augustus to the 5th century A.D.; the Chinese empire of Shih-Huang-Ti which lasted altogether from 221 B.C. until the great invasions[2]; India in the time of the Guptas and in the 5th century A.D.; and the Moslem empire of the Great Moguls from the 16th to the 18th century. The history of each of these worlds is a history of alternate multiplicity and unity; and the same is true of other spheres of culture (for we have mentioned only the largest and most varied, the most clearly defined and, in the old French sense of the word, most *civilised*; in a word, the most perfect of them). There are at least two periods of history when the State of the Pharaohs was at the very summit among States: the early centuries of the 3rd millennium B.C., and at the apogee of the New Theban kingdom. But the history of Egypt's successive periods of greatness is not self-enclosed like that of the universal empire of China or Rome. The Egyptian delta is both a part of the mediterranean world and also a promontory of Asia; and there was an exchange of influences and a

[1] The marvels of culture come to birth in a definite place, but they often develop in other places. They give birth in their turn and intermingle and disseminate themselves in new and unrecognisable forms throughout the world they are transforming. The dynamic history of Greek culture is the history of its birth and incessant transformations.

[2] Between the 4th and 6th centuries A.D. China was again united under the Sui dynasty and remained so during the 7th and part of the 8th century. And there were to be two other more or less complete unifications of the Sinic 'world'.

mutual interdependence—a sort of historical osmosis. The different spheres finally merged and became part of the hellenistic and Roman world. And the Parthian kingdom became, as it were, an in-between world opening upon four different cultures.

* * * *

Empires like these, whether or not they deserve the name of universal States, come into existence during periods of unity which are preceded and followed by periods of dispersion and multiplicity. The passage from multiplicity to unity[1] and then back to multiplicity can be observed in every 'historical world'.

History is not merely the history of wars between States, or of the class struggle, or of a self-contained culture. Barbarian invasion is an historical factor as important as war between States or classes; it is the *intervention* of peoples hitherto excluded from the civilised world. No historical world has escaped this type of intervention, but it occurs in different ways. It may be an irresistible 'ethnic whirlwind', a whole people on the march, with their carts and children and cattle; but the invaders are not necessarily nomadic barbarians. The Spaniards who put an end to the Aztec and Inca civilisations were the contemporaries of Titian, Lucas van Leyden and Guillaume Budé. It is a world in expansion flowing over another world, and each of them appears 'barbarous' to the other. Ever since the 16th century Europe has been systematically intervening in the rest of the world, and the tempo of intervention was accelerated in the 19th century when the United States began to participate. This universal and systematic intervention of the white man, with his overwhelming technical superiority, has unified the whole world in the external and material sense. As Frobenius says, the globe has been encircled; and, as Toynbee says, the colonial peoples now stand in the same relation to Western society as the barbarians did to Rome. He applies the same description to both—*external proletariat*.

The *internal proletariat*,[2] according to Toynbee, includes all the disinherited and malcontent elements of a given world, in addition to the

[1] Or if not to unity, at least to a less complicated multiplicity. The emergence of a particular State, later becoming universal, may be taken as the dividing line between an 'historic people' or *Kulturvolk* and a *Naturvolk*, as they are called by the Germans, who first made the distinction.

[2] Toynbee holds that the Christian religion is primarily the creation of the internal proletariat. But in fact it was largely the work of the external ('Syriac') proletariat which was interiorised when the Roman world was unified; whereas epic poetry comes from the barbarian external proletariat. But it would be interesting to know whether this last statement, which is very convincing as regards the Indo-Europeans, is equally true for other peoples.

proletariat in the Marxian sense; and communist practice seems to bear out this theory, for its propaganda is aimed at all the disinherited and malcontent as well as the Marxian proletariat, and is as much concerned with the external proletariat (the colonial peoples) as with the internal. Its purpose is to organise converging thrusts of rebellion which the bolshevik general staff can synchronise with its own activities on the horizontal plane of inter-State war.

Europeans have spread their arts of peace and war among the peripheral peoples and created intelligentsias; they have recruited these 'barbarians' to fight in their own wars, and in addition to teaching them the use of machines and weapons, they have taught them nationalism and socialism. They have drawn the peripheral peoples into the orbit of their own political quarrels.

* * * *

The word *Revolution* has many meanings. When it is used in a certain sense it is not rigidly confined to that sense, but still partakes of an affective and motive force derived from all the other meanings. Certain kinds of word are privileged in this way. In speaking or writing the sense is determined by the context, by what precedes and follows the word; but, whatever the context, the word seems to overflow the precise and definite meaning assigned to it. There are overtones of all the other meanings; *participating* in one another, they make their power and presence felt. The word has a power which always goes beyond any meaning which can be assigned to it *hic et nunc*, and this power so profoundly modifies the word's function in any given discourse that it modifies the nature of the discourse itself. Whoever makes intentional use of such a word will always go beyond his original thought; he will be seduced by the properties of the word. Writers are well acquainted with these peculiarities of language, and sometimes they use a word with the intention of 'playing upon' its alternative meanings. The literary craftsman will often select the phrase *most charged with meaning*. Words are material endowed with certain properties before the writer begins to use them; and it is his knowledge of these properties which makes the man of letters a particular kind of artist. As a painter uses line and colour, the writer uses the semantic material of words, phrases, and syntax. His art consists precisely in understanding his particular medium and the facilities it offers for the expression of his 'genius'[1]; and if he invents new words he takes into account the emotional effect of their sound when spoken. The language of science, on the other hand, tends to be a language of fixed symbols, like algebra; it deprives words

[1] Using the word in the Latin and not the romantic sense.

of any associations irrelevant to the exact purpose for which they are required.[1] But man's everyday speech is too deeply involved with his life to be anything like an algebraic language.

Now let us examine the meanings attached, in the 19th and 20th centuries, to the word 'revolution'. It is a great change—both in the world and in people. It is the overthrow of a régime, the break-up of a certain 'state of affairs' and a certain 'order'.

Reading Marx chronologically, it is possible to trace the rise of the psychological constellation which was to fix the sense of the word 'revolution' as it is still used today by communist believers. The idea of a transition from a certain historical condition to its *opposite* dates from before the 19th century. The French Revolution pointed the antithesis between the powerful and the wretched, the rich and the poor, and emphasised the doctrine that the first should be last and the last first. And the word 'proletariat' was revived from Roman history. Marx was concerned to define the precise identity of the 'last' who were to become the 'first', and it is noteworthy that the idea of the proletariat precedes in his writings any actual knowledge of the proletariat as an historical reality.[2] The Hegelian dialectic allows him to *fix* the archetype, for if contrary is succeeded by contrary the appearance of the proletariat becomes a metaphysical inevitability. To clothe it in flesh, Marx worked out a complete sociology. He found in the French socialists, whom he knew through Ludwig von Stein's book, the actual *material* of the dialectic whose form he had learned from Hegel. The society which 'negates the human essence', in the person of and by the mere existence of the proletarian, turns the proletariat itself into the negation of the society which produced it. The proletarian, then, is the negation of society, and a proletariat without class-consciousness is a sort of passive negation; but it cannot long remain so, because, according to Marx, there is no such thing as a realm of ideas distinct from the realm of facts, and even pure idealist fantasy is rich in factual significance. By entering into the masses, an idea becomes a force; and the proletariat's awareness of its own situation becomes an 'objective' aspect of the historical process. But the revolutionary must work to arouse the proletariat's consciousness and be prepared to recognise if necessary that it is not yet awake. He must be confident, however; for his own efforts are also a part of History. It is part of History's plan that men must take pains, for although History will inevitably unfold in a certain

[1] As the logical positivists have perceived, it is the weakness of what is called philosophy nowadays that its words are not algebraic symbols, although this is what the very nature of speculation requires them to be. Philosophers attempt to meet the difficulty by inventing neologisms, but they are unsupported by any solid reference such as is available for a scientific neologism.

[2] cf. all the pre-1848 texts.

manner, *this will not happen without pain*; and the trouble involved is part of the historical process. By becoming the active negation of society the proletariat transforms evolution into revolution; and finally Marx deduces that capitalism bears within itself its own negation, that its own evolution produces the element that negates it. And it is a part of the process that this element should be endowed with historical activity. Marx took the idea of evolution from Hegel and Darwin, but it was to Hegel alone that he owed his intellectual justification of revolution. He obtained it by the transition from quantity to quality[1]: the theory that a sufficient accumulation of quantitative variations culminates in a qualitative change. Thus the proletariat is at its highest point of activity at the moment of transition from one social state to its opposite. Evolution becomes revolution; the evolution of capitalism culminates in the revolutionary transition to socialism. Such is the elaborately intellectual formulation of the process by which the last become first and the first last. Observe how the Hegelian dialectic is used to *clothe* a messianic archetype and an eschatological theme. Deprived of human essence, the proletariat overturns everything and takes the human essence entirely to itself. Having reconciled Hegel and Feuerbach, Marx goes beyond them both, and it is 'Man' who now takes his destiny into his own hands; but it is only because he has previously been excluded from humanity that he is able to do so.[2] By a dialectic similar to that of sin and redemption, the man who has had least part in humanity becomes the completely human man; but the first state is a condition of the second, just as redemption would be meaningless unless there had first been sin. The eschatological theme is revealed in this catastrophic reversal and transformation. It is an apocalypse, an *end of the world*. The revolution is the *great ordeal*—a sort of spontaneous last judgment, without a judge or a judgment seat; it will confirm and elect the good—the proletariat and its servants—by the same test which destroys the power of the wicked. Catastrophically conceived, the revolution is the day of wrath and the day of dread, the transition from the old order to the new, and not merely a change of political régime. Through the revolution we pass from this world to the 'world to come'; passing through the ordeal, we leave behind us the accustomed order of things (which is evolution, the slow accumulation of infinitely small quantitative changes). With his adventist outlook Marx expected the revolution: it would break out during a particularly severe capitalist crisis—the severest yet, and the *last*. Observation reveals that crises are a con-

[1] *Science of Logic*, Vol. I, Bk. I, Section III, Chapter II, B. (Engl. trans., 1929), 'Nodal line of measure relations'.

[2] cf. Hegel, *The Phenomenology of Mind* (Engl. trans.; London, 1910), Vol. I, p. 175; 'Lordship and Bondage'.

stituent factor of capitalism, and thus the observed economic phenomenon converges with the adventist state of mind; each seeks the other out, the one objective and the other subjective, and at every crisis they touch. At the revolution, or final crisis, they should combine. This is the ordeal that precedes the installation of the Human Species, elect at last in its entirety, in the promised land of the classless society. The new order turns the old order upside down and is its negation. The last become the first, and through the grace of the Proletariat, the elect of the Human Species, the entire Species is saved at last.

The first examples of the archetypal figure expressed in this passional constellation are to be found in Babylonian, Persian, and Jewish eschatology; but the intellectual elements have changed out of all recognition. It is the emotional pattern of the intellectual elements—in other words, the constellation itself—that is familiar. Communism, as a secular religion, is still imbued with the religious ideas which our civilisation inherited, through Rome, from the 'Syriac' world. But those elements which reveal the purely eschatological form of the archetype are censored or disguised in the believer's psyche; they take on an appearance of homogeneity[1] with the historical environment of the 19th- and 20th-century civilisation. The secular religion disguises the fact that it is a religion[2]; and, indeed, it is inherent in its nature to pretend to be something else. But it gives itself away by using 'logical arguments' and 'arguments drawn from reality' which only *appear* to be, and are not in fact, of the same nature as the arguments that are usually so described. When put to the test, their true psychological origin is revealed; they prove to be beyond the reach of the logic and reality to which they *apparently* refer. The infectious character of such ideas is not the effect of their intellectual tendency as such, but of what lies behind it.

It can be seen from Marx's earliest writings onwards how eschatology is bound up with the technical political theme, and an analysis of communist religious behaviour will clearly reveal the links between the two. The eschatology is hidden behind the political technique; revolution is a matter for action, and eschatology has only to provide the simple, axiomatic certainties which action will make prevail. If this cannot be achieved, the next best thing is to provoke the required actions by mobilising the appropriate incentives for them. In the speeches and writings of believers there is no apparent distinction between the eschatological representations and the historical observations among which they occur. Nevertheless, the revolution means the establishment of the supremacy of ends. In the meantime, however, although there are

[1] Again a phenomenon of convergence.

[2] Certain Islamic sects exhibit a similar behaviour, as when a heresy disguises itself as orthodoxy.

revolutionary trends and revolutionary periods, the flowing tide is followed by the ebb. But the crises which are characteristic of capitalism become more and more severe, and the influence of the 20th-century world wars works in the same direction; it is through them that the crises foreseen by Marx produce their effects. The Russian revolution gave a factual demonstration of the superiority of a general war over a capitalist crisis as midwife for revolution; and this in no way contradicts the Marxian theory, for Marxists regard war as the last resort of a capitalism trying desperately to find the way out of an impasse and escape its doom. It amounts to the same thing, whether the revolution is produced by a capitalist crisis or by the war to which capitalism has resorted to forestall the crisis. And the believer is quite undisturbed by the fact that there were wars before capitalism ever existed. It is enough for him to reply that in those days there were other forms of exploitation of man by man. And if you object that the end of what is now called capitalism would not necessarily mean the end of war, the believer takes refuge in a world where you cannot follow him. He has an understanding with History, from which you are excluded. He leaves you floundering in your world of error, separated from him by the gates of the historical hell.

* * * *

It is possible, however, to treat revolution as a concept like any other. The word can be used to describe an alteration in the balance of power between men or groups of men, a change of scale or general shift of values. For revolutions are, in fact, transitions. The historical 'world' changes; it becomes a different world, and yet it is still the same. The transition in the Greek world, from the 8th to the 6th and even the 5th centuries B.C., from the ascendancy of the *γένη* to the city tyrannies and democracies, can be called a revolution. The word can be applied to the general transformation and crisis by which a society passes from multiplicity to unity—a phenomenon which also implies its opposite, the passage from unity to multiplicity. In fact, they precede and follow one another; the one being a supreme effort towards integration and homogeneity and the other a final disintegration and dispersion. In the Roman world the first phase appears as the transition from the Republic to the rule of the Cæsars, the multiplicity and diversity of mediterranean life being unified under the Empire; and the second is the decomposition of the World State of the Cæsars, whence a new diversity was slowly to emerge. People are more inclined to use the word revolution for the former type of critical phases—for the integrating process which precedes a long period of unity—than for the final disintegration which is the prelude to the birth of a new culture. In either case it is a 'time of troubles', as Arnold Toynbee says. But we shall conform to the unconscious custom and reserve the word *revolutionary* for the troubles of the transitional periods from diversity to unity (or to a lesser degree of multiplicity); for the transition from Republic to Cæsarism[1] we shall use the term 'Roman revolution'. Between the latter period and our own time there are many analogies, as anyone can verify.

In a diversified and multiple 'historical world' (composed horizontally of different peoples and vertically of different social classes), an increase in the solidarity between its constituent elements shows that this world is undergoing a process of integration; but this solidarity is reflected in the interdependence of crises. The troubles are spread and diffused and tend to become universal.

When the original *gentes* of a small Latin city defended themselves against the assaults of newcomers and only yielded if the secession of a part was threatening the existence of the whole and playing into the hands of the external enemy, this was the first historical sketch of what was later to be called the Roman conquest. The rural middle classes, first of Rome and then of the whole of Italy, were mobilised. The *nobilitas*, the senatorial oligarchy of the *patres*, began by taking the lion's share of the conquest. As soon as possible, it held the East to ransom; it rounded off its estates in Italy, at the expense of that same class of small freeholders which it had led to victory; it extended its *possessio* over the *ager publicus*, again at the expense of the freeholders and the Italian allies. Pasture replaced arable cultivation at the same time as the patrimonial estates became *latifundia* and slave labour replaced free. The small freeholders became proletarianised and joined the urban plebs at Rome, while their place was taken by 'barbarians' whom defeat had reduced to slavery. And at the same time there arose the new class of businessmen who farmed out the taxation of conquered countries, mulcted them for their own profit, and became a 'money power'.

Excluded from high political life by the oligarchy, their money gave them the power to intervene in politics, if only to defend their wealth and their opportunities for increasing it. At the same time the military were becoming aware of their power and the businessmen took advantage, for the maintenance of their own position, of the antagonisms between the generals and the oligarchy, from which generals were usually, though not always, recruited. When Marius began to recruit 'proletarians', the army, composed now mainly of proletarians and

[1] More precisely, from the Second Punic War (it was in 215 B.C., after the battle of Cannæ, that the associations of tax-collectors appeared) to the return of Octavius to Rome after the battle of Actium and the conquest of Egypt (A.D. 30). But the rise of a civilisation, or even the opening of a period, is not a transition from not-being to being. A civilisation, or a period, has no definite starting-point. At a given moment it is *there*; and all that can be done is to fix its birth between two limiting dates.

mercenaries, became the personal army of the *Imperator*. 'There is no assembly and no magistracy with the power to separate Marius from his soldiers.' The age of armies was also an age of 'gangs'. Rome was held for Marius by Saturninus and Glaucia; and while Marius, at Gafsa, was perpetrating for the first time the destruction of an entire town and selling its whole population into slavery, the bands of Saturninus and Glaucia terrorised the city and used the *lex majestatis* to destroy what remained of the old republican way of life. By intimidation and corruption, blackmail and violence, they perfected the technique of electoral manipulation, and by their command of the streets they made it impossible to oppose their own candidate. Sulla triumphed over the followers of Marius by similar methods, and added to them the weapon of proscription, which caused many estates to change hands. In the next period the bands of Clodius and Milo rationalised the system of Saturninus and Glaucia, and Cæsar and Pompey succeeded to Marius and Sulla. Conquest followed conquest among the Eastern kingdoms and in the barbarian West, while at home there were slave revolts on a huge scale, starting from the *latifundia* or the gladiatorial schools. The rural middle class declined in numbers; Italy was losing her population. Twice the very existence of Rome was threatened by slave insurrections. In Sicily the surviving small freeholders made common cause with the rebellious slaves. Piracy at sea kept pace with banditry on land, and large-scale expeditions were necessary to deal with both. The enfranchised slaves, who paid rent to the masters who 'settled' them, were alien to the Roman way of life; they changed the character of the plebs itself and were a symptom of the new mass age. This new plebs sold its votes and was insatiable for bread and circuses, whilst, *at the same time*, there was every kind of rebellion and agitation among the disinherited. Society was fluid and the régime transitory. Groups and individuals asserted their will to live in conflicts of every kind.

It was a struggle for the *imperium mundi*, a struggle throughout the mediterranean world as well as at Rome, and the stake was world-exploitation—but in whose interest? The competitors were the senatorial oligarchy, the men of money, and the generals; for the Gracchi had not succeeeded in modifying the nature of political power when they turned for support to the original rural plebs.

Every revolt was quelled in turn, whether it was the revolt of Italian allies claiming equal rights, or of foreign potentates or peoples, or of rebellious slaves. To begin with, the spoils were shared between the highly placed members of the oligarchy, the moneyed men who profited from the victories, and the war chieftains whose power grew out of the State's danger. The sources of power were exploited by all who found them within reach and had the necessary ability; it was to this that they devoted their considerable talents. The power of words, as the career of Cicero proves, was irrevocably committed to the service of power and its interests, and Rome was occupied by well-organised gangs representing the interests of the different generals who were competing for the conquest of the world. Soon the only real powers were money and the professional army attached to its leader; and these powers, the only real protagonists, *vitiated from within* every institution and every movement of reform. Constitutional and legislative measures were merely successful or unsuccessful manœuvres in the struggle, and there was no longer any real distinction between internal and external politics. The rival *Imperatores* requisitioned against one another the assistance of subject or 'protected' foreign cities and rulers. But while the struggle was being waged by every means and everywhere, a concentration of power was taking place. Cæsar, as high priest and claiming descent from Venus, finally envisaged a sacred monarchy like that of the Ptolemies. The 'Roman revolution' took the form of a complete upheaval of power and property relations at the same time that Rome was putting the world to sack; and the plebs' share of the booty was only bread and circuses.

This period of interdependent crises and general diffusion of troubles finally reached a sort of saturation-point, at which there began a new period of unity and general peace. The world reached that state of order for which everyone had been longing in the last days of the Republic. The new society was not perfect, but it was comparatively stable and peaceful. Disorders and the causes of disorder were localised, and the race for wealth came under the control of central authority. Order was imposed up to the frontiers of the 'world'; and these frontiers were cleared from time to time and dykes erected to keep back the unpredictable human tide that continued to beat against the Empire's confines. During the *pax Romana*, war was no more than the guarding of the 'limit': colonial military settlements, patrols, expeditions against the Parthians.[1] The revolution was over, but the golden age had not arrived. The world was still this mundane world.

During revolution all the great forms and categories of social activity are progressively deprived of their autonomy; foreign war and civil war, foreign policy and domestic policy, economics and politics and religion —they all cease to be independent of one another. More and more everything 'hangs together', and this involves, both for individuals and groups, an ever-increasing stress and strain. The greater interdependence between men and between groups is experienced by each individual man and group as an increased vulnerability, and finally the whole world is a vast sensitive area of friction and counter-friction. Interaction between microcosm and macrocosm, individual and society, substruc-

[1] To keep control of the silk route; but this object was never achieved.

ture and superstructure, becomes dizzyingly swift, and men are swept along with it uncomprehending. World solidarity manifests itself as individual suffering. There is no longer a 'synthesis of values and aims' enabling each human group and each individual to 'find a place for everything'; and ethics breaks apart into incompatible duties; 'values in isolation make war upon one another', contending for the individual—and within him. The historian can break the general crisis down into a series of particular crises at definite times and places; but the crises determine and modify one another, and their interdependence is both spatial and temporal. The ancient psyche is stirring to change, and as yet nothing has come to fill the void left by the things it has cast away. Needs are ill-formulated and must satisfy themselves where and how they can. The *beliefs* on which society was founded no longer command organic assent, but are attacked or defended on grounds of interest; the great social impulses in the psyche which these beliefs represent are openly destroyed by criticism—and are abandoned even by those who are insensitive to criticism. This is what is happening, in 20th-century Europe, to the impulses of the liberal age. The State, in other words the regulating function, is becoming the great purveyor of goods and services, and it is to the higher positions in this apparatus of power that the ambitious are increasingly attracted. Political groups are turning into associations for perfecting empirically the best methods for winning these positions.

In such periods, when the old basis of society is becoming undependable and fluid and is giving place to a state of transition, the criticism of everything upon which the old, and no longer satisfactory, state of affairs was based becomes unrestrained. The old conception of the sacred, the old institutions and social ideals, are all rejected. As a natural complement to the spread of scepticism, there is an outbreak of immature mysticism—'the alliance of scepticism and nostalgia'. Side by side with nihilism (the state of psychological 'availability', which means that one is available for *anything*), there emerges in various forms a nostalgia for social *consensus*. In its longing for unity, the psyche will feed upon the grossest counterfeits of it: the golden age or the day of glory. This is the meaning of the myths, which are already in decline, of revolution and the classless society. The controls exercised by the psyche in the preceding age having lost their power of integration, the war between isolated values is fought not only between men but within the psyche itself, which is no longer unified by adherence to a cosmic, and social, order. The new 'conceptions of the world', which attempt to fill the place of that order, are merely conceptual, and therefore fragile.

Crisis consists of a series of crises and revolution of a series of revolutions and wars. As a result of the interdependence of crises and wars the 'inferior'[1] elements and the peripheral elements (Toynbee's 'internal' and 'external' proletariats) both enter into a state of turmoil. But, in truth, they can hardly now be described as 'inferior' or 'external'; they have been drawn into the circuit and become a part of history—which previously passed them over or passed them by. Not that the 'advent' of either of them is likely; but in the selection of new élites their existence will have to be taken into account. While the Roman world was being forged into unity, the external proletariat was either kept at a distance in the wild regions at the edge of the civilised world or else transformed into an internal proletariat by enslavement, which could be, and often was, followed by emancipation. Natural obstacles[2] made it impossible for neighbouring civilisations (in practice, India and China) to interfere. The barbarians were in fact a buffer between the three empires, which were therefore only able to act upon one another indirectly; by resisting or yielding to the barbarian pressure each of them helped or hindered the invasion of the others, and at any given moment the weakest barrier was the most easily forced.

In relation to the peripheral peoples, or external proletariat, the dividing-up and economic exploitation of the Western world by Europe, which began in the 16th century and reached an unprecedented acceleration in the 19th, played the same part in our 'revolution' as the Roman conquest played in the transition from multiplicity to unity of the mediterranean world.

Historians are able to treat the history of Chinese civilisation separately from that of mediterranean civilisation because it was impossible for one 'historical world' to impinge directly upon the life of another. But today, when industrial and financial techniques of European origin encompass the globe, such intervention has become possible. Europe itself facilitates the intervention of the colonial peoples in European life by teaching their intelligentsias how to use the means of power and all the other most easily communicable skills and customs of its own civilisation. It also recruits soldiers from among the colonial peoples. In so far as there can still be separate worlds,[3] intervention by one world in the life of another is simply a question of power. But in fact it can no longer be said that there are distinct and separate civilisations in the sense that the empire of the Cæsars was distinct and separate from the China of the Han dynasty; these two could trade together—and they might have combined to make war on the Parthians, though the project

[1] This is not a value judgment; it indicates only the *position* which these elements occupy.

[2] That is to say, natural obstacles in the proper sense of the word—seas and deserts that could not be crossed with the means of transport then available, and also large and sparsely inhabited regions.

[3] Different worlds can still be psychologically distinct, although in contact with one another; but there cannot be material isolation.

was abandoned—but they did not directly impinge on one another. The different units today are unified by a common technique and are 'in contact', as war reporters say, on all fronts. In Russia the Marxism imported from Europe has not only transformed the Tsarist empire but also serves as a pretext for the new empire's interference in the affairs of the rest of the world. The new Russian empire is a determining factor in the communist campaign, which would be a totally different thing without it. In the revolution now in progress, seen from Europe and from the European point of view, both the internal and the external proletariat are simultaneously in agitation, and there is permanent interference by a psychologically alien empire and civilisation. The psyche is evolved by history, and although the histories of Russia and Europe have always *touched*, they have remained distinct from one another. Like Japan, Russia has selected and filtered the cultural traits she borrowed, being careful to adapt them to her own psyche; they acquire a different significance and are no longer the same except in appearance.[1] The unrest and agitation of the internal and external proletariat are synchronised and organised and, what is more, this is done by and for the sake of a great empire which is also a 'Super-State' within whose rigid frame a whole 'society of peoples' is both constrained and oppressed, but also given expression. This exploitation of unrest is a systematic form of disguised warfare. Whereas the Roman revolution was a transition from multiplicity to unity inside a sort of sealed vessel, within the limits of a *single* world, our revolution is both a revolution and an invasion as well. Whenever the Russians go too far there is danger of an American counter-attack. The interdependence of crises means not only that war and revolution reciprocally determine one another, but that the whole world is thrown into turmoil and mobilised. Increasingly, war becomes identified with world war; it vitally involves all the great powers. And just as every internal war tends to become generalised, so general wars come to resemble civil wars. The historical field has widened, and Europe has correspondingly shrunk. From the 18th century to the present day the European's range of anxieties has spiralled outwards, and now we are no longer concerned with 'a world' but with the world. A revolution—the long crisis by which a multiplicity becomes a unity—can no longer take place within a 'sealed vessel', in one part of the world, not even in a whole continent. The interdependence of troubles is a universal interdependence.

Revolution is an historical process which leads not to the gates of

[1] For example, the externals of justice clearly perform a different function (witness the great Russian trials); and socialism, which was regarded in 19th-century Europe as the extension of democracy from the political to the economic sphere, is in Russia innocent of any effective control from below.

paradise but to a world similar to the one we know except that many of the things in it, including the psyche itself, have changed.

By what groups will goods and services be distributed and shared, and how will these groups be composed? For whom, or for whose profit, will things be distributed? What human relations will really be changed? And what will be the cultural significance of the change? What sort of new order will it be in which men will *accept* their status, and how will it guarantee the circulation of élites? These are the real questions, which reveal what is really at stake in the battle.

* * * *

The phase of multiplicity and diversity contrasts with the phase of unity and homogeneity. But there is another contrast: namely, that between consensus and convergence on the one hand and dissension and divergence on the other. It is important not to confuse the second contrasting pair with the first. Thus in the mediterranean world of the 2nd and 1st centuries B.C. there was a maximum of divergence and at the same time an accelerated tendency towards unity and away from multiplicity.[1]

[1] The early Middle Ages, when Christendom was at its zenith, were an age of multiplicity. It was then, as Spengler says, that a new psyche began to 'awaken'. An age of multiplicity is an age of awakening; and dispersion is the first stage in the development of societies. According to Spengler, 'civilisation' is the end of a 'culture'.

Needless to say, we do not accept Spengler's analogy between culture (in the broad sense; the culture which ends by becoming a civilisation) and the biological individual. This analogy gives world history an impossible rigidity. It reduces all such phenomena as cultural 'loans' and cultural influences to the status of *pseudomorphoses*, and makes it impossible to conceive culture as a procreative phenomenon or to recognise that cultures can be fertile and can interbreed. For the fact is that a culture often draws its constituent elements from another culture; and it is in the choices it makes among the vital elements it receives from another culture that we can first trace the character of a new culture that is coming to birth. The idea, which was prevalent from the 16th century onwards, that European civilisation derives from Greece and Rome cannot be unreservedly accepted, but is certainly not without some foundation.

The high medieval Christianity of Cluny and Citeaux and Clairvaux, of Romanesque architecture and the legends of the Round Table, the Christianity of the awakening Western psyche, was not the Syriac Christianity of the catacombs; but it could not have existed unless the other had existed first. The early Christianity *generated* the later. It is true that the statues of the Florentine *Arte della Lana* make the female saints look like the Tuscan peasant women who are still to be seen at Florence with their donkeys on market-day, but this does not mean that Christianity is only a word, with incommensurably different meanings at different times. There is little resemblance between the Hildebrandine papacy and the Church of the catacombs, but Hildebrand's authority was made possible by that early Syriac phenomenon, of which the medieval psyche could no longer even form a conception. A culture is a sort of mosaic of seeds, and when it comes to an end the mosaic is shattered and the seeds disperse. Many are already sterile, but some will develop in a new environment and will *belong* to it. As living principles, they will be part of a new culture, but the new culture will be linked to the former one by innumerable fibres. These links extend in space as well as in time. The expression Roman Gaul has a real meaning (in spite of the

Broadly speaking, any age may be called revolutionary in which the increasing diffusion of troubles is approaching saturation-point. Dissension and divergence are reaching their maximum extension. The first stage of the integration of an 'historical world' is an exacerbation of antagonisms, both on the horizontal plane between States, individuals, and groups, and on the vertical plane of class conflicts. Society is no longer *accepted* by the majority; and an increasing number of men begin to lose their sense of 'belonging' either to the social order or to the world order. Society becomes, to an ever greater extent and at last completely, an arbitrary arrangement or, better, a succession of arrangements, which no longer deserve the name of 'society'. Legitimacy lapses, and among the successive 'states of society' or arbitrary social configurations, which are no sooner formed than they dissolve again, the individual is like Ulysses in the storm. He learns not to sail against the wind; and favourable winds mean 'success'. The role of circumstances in making or marring a man's career seems to increase while the role of responsibility diminishes; and in such times the great man is one who, in addition to his other gifts, possesses the gift of discerning the 'favourable moment'. Cæsar awaited this moment before breaking with Pompey and Crassus; he knew when it was necessary to make concessions, and when his wife was scandalously compromised he knew how to turn the disgrace to his own greater glory. To their other virtues the greatest men of such times seem to add an infallible knowledge and gift of social navigation; and in such men this science and art do not take the place of character but, on the contrary, enable character to tell. Cicero's great talents did not save him from being continually at the mercy of events, nor could they save him from destruction when a temporary alliance was formed between the great men he had successively betrayed. When the individual no longer feels himself integrated within an order, he seeks provisional substitutes for it: the shelter of a faction or any safe situation which will help him to cope with all the difficult ones. When the ocean of society is in turmoil it becomes more and more difficult to feel oneself organically at home in it and more and more necessary to watch the swell and undertow, the

unresolved controversy as to the relative weight of Roman and Gallic factors). The great legists at the dawn of French history were marvellously at home with Roman law, and this was not so anywhere else. Even the notion of *human rights*, as proclaimed by the French Revolution, was a Stoic seed that had lain for more than a thousand years concealed within the law. It suddenly sprouted again, but the flower was different; it bore no resemblance to the *caritas humani generis* which had budded in a harsh and twilight world and been worn by free men—who in the midst of abandonment still rejected the mysticism of women and slaves—with the characteristic tight-lipped serenity of Stoicism.

A criticism of Spengler would lead us far from our present subject. His virtue is in his vision and his style, and for this reason the severe and justified criticisms of his cavalier methods with history are beside the mark.

winds and adverse currents, and to predict the uncertain tides. But the situation appeals to the spirit of enterprise as well as caution. There are new opportunities, and with decision, courage, endurance, and luck much more may be achieved than in the preceding age. Swayed by fear or interest, the most exclusive groups and coteries relax their defences, and those who are bold enough can force their way in.

The date of birth of a revolution cannot be fixed like that of an individual, for the revolution is only perceptible when it is already in existence, and although it is logical to trace its 'causes' back to an indefinite past, it is necessary in practice to stop somewhere.

When an 'historical world' is going through an acute phase of dissension, there may be in one particular part of it a state of convergence which qualifies that part to undertake the general unification for its own profit. Today, when the process no longer takes place within a world but in the world as a whole, it is in Russia, the United States, and England that convergence is more manifest—though for very different and apparently opposite reasons—than in the other important areas (western Europe, for example) of the dawning world-civilisation. The United States and Russia,[1] moreover, possess greater material and human resources than the rest.

If we turn back to the Roman world, we find nowhere in it any comparable centres of consensus. Every part of the world seems to be simply a part of Rome; and the conflict all over the world was a Roman conflict—whether it took the form of rebellions by slaves or exploited allies, or of those wars between rival *Imperatores*, each supported by an army and a faction, which entirely voided of their original meaning any electoral proceedings which still took place at Rome. The struggle for power at Rome was *also* and simultaneously a struggle for world power. Continuity of internal and external policy degenerated into *confusion* between the two; and war was simply one among other political expedients, until finally it became the decisive one. It was with one another that Cæsar and Pompey, Octavius and Antony were at war. Everything else had already been dealt with. The victories recounted in a narrative with the title *De Bello Civili* were victories which determined the fate of a whole world.

At the most there can only be analogies between the revolutionary phases of two different 'worlds'; but these analogies are sufficient to endow the word revolution with a very different meaning from the

[1] Russia has a secular religion at her disposal. If she is inferior in atomic weapons, she makes up for it by the more advanced 'psychological' weapons which she owes to her privileged relation with a secular religion. If this secular religion were to decline or be withdrawn, Russia would not for a moment consider initiating, or even allowing herself to be drawn into, a world war. So the factor making for war is not Russia but 'communism' (in so far as it is possible to distinguish between the two).

eschatological and at the same time purely economic one paradoxically attributed to it by Marxists.

* * * *

When the 'Roman revolution' was complete, it ushered in a period of peace and order for every land, every people, and every society in the mediterranean world. But what do we mean by a universal State?[1] The expression may refer to an historical reality, but also to an ideal; and as an ideal it is the intellectual formulation of certain aspirations. There is convergence between the reality of the most perfect universal States, the only ones for which we use the name, and the aspirations of men at a certain point in the historical curve of their 'world'. Ideal and reality touch at certain points, though on either side of these points the usual counterpoint obtains. It is when it is close to reality that the ideal is most provocative of thoughts and plans and dreams.[2]

In the past a universal State arose out of the unification of an 'historical world'. In the Chinese or the Roman psyche the boundaries of the Chinese or the Roman Empire were identified with the boundaries of the earth itself, the *orbis terrarum*; they marked the limits of the inhabited world. Beyond the world and outside civilisation were the barbarians, living their strange and sinister life; and it was the responsibility of Emperor and army to keep them at bay. In the first two centuries A.D. scarcely anyone gave them a thought at Ephesus, Alexandria, or Hippo, or at Rome itself. For at that time they represented no sort of threat to the Empire.

[1] An expression systematically employed by Arnold Toynbee. Our own use of it will be more limited.

[2] The power of the ideal of unity is manifest today in the profusion of articles, speeches, and conferences on 'world government', the 'unity of mankind', 'world federation', 'world citizenship' (see postscript on page 334), and the 'unity' of continents which are still in fact in a state of multiplicity.

For the zealots of world unity, political power (the State) is merely a necessary organising function; they accept it perforce but without enthusiasm. It probably appears to them as a mere transitional phase, much like the phase through which, according to Engels (*The Origin of the Family, Private Property, and the State*), the State would pass in order to emerge as anarchy. They would prefer organisation without any State. Formerly it was the government of *a* world that was the issue; but today an ever swifter historical process with an ever-widening scope has made the problem of a single government for the whole world a topical one.

Another symptom: the great figures of our day have an international standing. In the 19th century it was not so. Dostoevsky was hardly known in western Europe during his life, and he began to be translated only when Nietzsche discovered the *Letters from the Underworld*. Between the 17th and the 20th centuries there has been a great change in this respect. The anglomania of the *philosophes* introduced Shakespeare's name to France; he was 'adapted' by Ducis in the first half of the 19th century, and translated by François Marie Victor Hugo in the second half. But today a writer can become world famous in his own life-time and when he has written only a few books. This happened to André Malraux after the publication of *Les conquérants*. All that was necessary was that the great theme of the age should be treated by a genius on a level with the age.

By defining a universal State as one whose frontiers coincide ideally with those of the world and actually with those of an 'historical world', we exclude certain States which Toynbee describes as universal: the Habsburg monarchy, the Napoleonic, the Ottoman, and the Russian Tsarist empires, and certain others.[1] The transitory empires of Napoleon and Charles V cannot be included among universal States,[2] but the Roman Empire of the Cæsars and the Han dynasty of China do satisfy our definition; they had no contacts with other spheres of culture or with one another, but only, in effect, with barbarians—who, if they were not exterminated or driven back, had to become vassals and be integrated in the Empire. Between these two worlds the Parthian kingdom ruled over the 'Syriac' sphere of culture. Being smaller and less clearly defined, it suffered attrition from the Roman power.

The specimens which compose the fauna of history are not so sharply individual as those which zoology can distinguish and classify. The 'perfect' individual is simply an 'ideal type' or pure form by reference to which the imperfect individuals who really exist can be classified. Thus it is legitimate to describe the Egypt of the first dynasties, and even the Egypt of the new empire, as an 'historical world'; but this world was formed around the valley of a river, and it opened upon the mediterranean world through the towns of the delta. So it cannot be said that the frontiers of the Egyptian State coincided with the frontiers of the inhabited world.

The Roman Empire is the one that most nearly resembles the model of the universal State, and this although it possessed some of the opposite characteristics.[3] And the fact that it is the only empire of which historians express surprise *that it did not last for ever* is an implicit admission that historians so regard it. Although their profession teaches them that every human institution is condemned to pass away, they seem to have more difficulty in admitting it where this particular institution is concerned; and perhaps this is because few human institutions have ever been so *complete*. For more than five hundred years the Roman Empire was the *modus vivendi* of men and nations.[4]

[1] Toynbee even includes the Tokugawa Shogunate of Japan, though it did barely more than create national unity. See the complete list in Somervell's abridgment of Toynbee's great work *A Study of History* (Oxford University Press, 1947).

[2] Nor, for the same reason, can the New Theban empire, although its internal policy and its style, when at its zenith, were those of a universal State.

[3] Characteristics upon which most historians are particularly inclined to dwell.

[4] It is a habit of historians to lament the deficiency of the laws of succession and the absence of an automatic *jus regnandi* to prevent the disorders and bloodshed which often accompanied the assumption of the highest office. But the explanation is that the highest office was a burden indeed—its holder was responsible for the continuation of the civilised world, and he became the guardian in chief, the guardian of guardians. It seems that the well-known tendency to depreciate what exists in favour of the non-existent obscured this

The Emperor was responsible for military command—in other words, for protecting civilisation from the barbarians—and also for maintaining order within the civilised world; for otherwise social life could not be carried on, nor fields and cattle be tended, nor men pursue their business. Very often it was the bravest leader of the bravest army who won the prize; and the difficulties he had to overcome on his way to power enabled him to demonstrate the very talents he would require when he had gained it. He was elected by his acts.

It is complained that political life came to an end under the Empire, but was the Empire the cause or the effect of this occurrence? Had not the political soil lost its fertility? The *scale* of history had changed, and the Greek cities had become mere provincial towns, owing such importance as some of them still possessed either to their trade or to their schools of philosophy. In the centuries of the *imperium mundi* municipal intrigues could count as nothing more than municipal intrigues; and since the highest power attached to the highest responsibility, the ambitious man who wished to dominate the pacified world was obliged to devote himself to war. The army was required for policing the frontiers of the world, and it fulfilled its task. There were abuses, of course; but Tacitus was really a scandal-monger.[1] And even Hegel[2] has been so unworthy of his own profundity as to write: '. . . Domitian [was] the grossest and most odious of tyrants, and yet Roman historians say that under him Rome enjoyed repose'—and he leaves it at that. But to confer repose is a great deal, and of how many tyrants can such a claim be made? It should be noted, moreover, that in the time of Domitian repose was one of the major needs. In other words, Domitian gave what was wanted. Accepted by everyone—apart from a few senators who still lamented the passing of oligarchy[3]—the universal State was the final bourn of the Revolution.

fact. For a man to become Emperor with the help of the Prætorian Guard was to take an unfair advantage of the valiant generals posted far away on the frontiers. But this handicap was more than once overcome. And the procedure by which Emperors adopted associates to be their successors was attended with good results. Men of the highest qualities—supermen, as Ferdinand Lot calls them (*La fin du monde antique et les débuts du moyen âge*, Paris, 1927)—wore themselves out on the frontier stations while Rome lived in luxury. These men really carried on their shoulders the burden of the civilised world, and most of the Emperors were equal to the task.

[1] 'Literature' and 'style' have much to answer for. And the bad work was carried on by moralists of the humanist and classical tradition and by 'opposition rhetoric'.

[2] *Lectures on the Philosophy of History*.

[3] The senatorial opposition was not a republican opposition. The republic was no longer possible, and chaos was to nobody's interest. By permanently overthrowing Cæsarism, the opposition would have achieved nothing except the displacement of the universal State's centre of gravity. The composition of the Senate had changed, and its opposition was class opposition; it had become an assembly of landowners and included many provincial members. The imperial power represented the Empire as a whole better than the State did.

It is remarkable that during four centuries of the univeral State there were no great slave insurrections. The important separatist risings at Palmyra, or in North Africa in Aurelian's reign, and the various revolts in Spain and Gaul, never put the Empire in danger for long, and it was their connection with the barbarian peril that made them comparatively serious. Both slave revolts and genuinely 'national' rebellion and resistance belong to the revolutionary period and not to that of the universal State.

Every race could live in peace and every religion flourish—except one, which took the initiative in intolerance. Caracalla extended Roman citizenship to all the Empire's inhabitants. Many slaves were emancipated and many measures taken to protect slaves against their masters, who had bought them and whose own interest it was to feed them at least well enough to keep them fit for work. Slavery became a much more tolerable condition than it had been during the preceding five hundred years. The gradual emergence of serfdom was accepted, compromised with, and finally promoted by, the State; but it was more tolerated than desired. The Emperors always mistrusted this dangerous accession of power to the great landowners which, in the West, was to grow to its full development upon the ruins of the Empire. Certainly the small freeholder had little defence against the great landowner; but the condition of the small freeholder was in any case not enviable.

This universal State had none of the characteristics of a uniform system to which men are forcibly constrained to adapt themselves. It took what it inherited, and organised it. It founded only a few new towns—far fewer than Alexander in his brief period of glory. It selected from among existing institutions those it found to be in working order and capable of adaptation to the new scale of the world. They were in existence and they were allowed to continue. The Empire's policy was not consistently liberal nor consistently centralising; it was opportunist. The economic liberalism of Rhodes, the State socialism of Pergamum, and what may be called the 'national workshops' of Ptolemaic Egypt, were all part of the Empire's heritage, and the Empire, as heir, conformed to the precedents and models handed down to it. The State, in fact, *had no prejudices*. In mining it tried both public and private enterprise as opportunity, profit, or necessity seemed to counsel; and it found the way to adapt certain hellenistic institutions for use all over the Empire (for example, the prefectships of towns, the *vigiles*, requisitions in kind). Certain measures taken by Cæsar and Augustus which became fundamental were examples of unconscious or non-doctrinaire socialism, as when Cæsar deprived the associations of tax-collectors of the right to assess tax rates, and thus reduced the influence of money in politics by suppressing cause and effect together.[1] The profit motive of the capitalist bourgeoisie remained as a necessary constituent of normal social life, but nothing more. It could no longer provoke war nor corrupt the central power, which was above corruption because nobody in the world was rich enough to buy it.

In general the Roman Empire managed to protect the interests of the disinherited without impairing that mainspring of commercial enterprise—inequality of wealth. Its measures of social justice were not pressed to the point of upsetting the economy and creating troubles greater than those they were designed to cure.

There is no necessary connection between social justice and a democratic form of government; a fact which is equally well demonstrated by certain examples from Egyptian and Chinese history. The inequality of wealth which is the mainspring of commercial republics is a stimulant, and the accumulation of capital by private initiative favours expansion and enterprise. So the democratic socialism of the 19th century linked together two aspirations which history shows to be antagonistic if not incompatible. Though in men's hearts there may be a necessary connection between justice and democracy, history does not confirm it. History shows that justice in the sense of equality has been imposed rather by universal absolutism than by universal suffrage.

The first image of democracy in the western European psyche was derived from the city, from the commercial republics of Greece and Italy as represented by their high achievements and their great men. In 4th-century Athens, which was equalitarian apart from occasional reactions, politics was the concern of a minority for whom democratic government was their life's occupation, because it left them little time for anything else. They were professional democrats for whom any change of régime would mean the loss of their livelihood. In the great modern democracies—especially in the United States and France, but also in Germany and Italy when and in so far as they were democratic—there have arisen by a 'normal' social differentiation and division of labour, groups of specialists to take in hand the business of universal suffrage; and by these qualified technicians the vote is influenced and inspired in such a way as to ensure the power of certain interests, which are not always or only money interests. For the latter interests, in the 19th century as in the Greek city-states, universal suffrage has always been a weapon for destroying the oligarchy of landowners.

In certain periods and for certain countries the democratic system is unquestionably the best; but it is none the less utopian to expect the

[1] He left the associations only the collection of customs (5 per cent.) at the frontiers and in certain parts of the Empire.

simultaneous achievement of absolute justice and popular sovereignty through universal suffrage.[1] The aspiration, however, is valuable as a standard, which is tested by real historical situations.

The universal State, then, is a State which can practise both liberalism and State control, either alternately or simultaneously; it is a free-enterprise State and a social-service State, as and when necessary; but it is neither the one nor the other except when necessary. Inevitably it makes mistakes, but its principle is sound. It did not emerge from the brains of professors and theorists but as a response to the needs of a world; the world had to continue and the universal State took responsibility for its continuance. The Emperor saw no need to suppress any part of the world, and no class or race was systematically exterminated. The oligarchy of landowners, for example, had been dominant in the past, and the property system throughout the life of the Empire still allowed it sufficient power to remain a potential political force. Yet if this oligarchy had returned to power at any time while the Empire was still strong, it would have meant a class domination which might have been fatal to the unity of the world. Again and again the Cæsars were compelled to use rigorous measures to restrain the oligarchy, but it was hydra-headed. Neither complete State control nor socialisation was economically practicable. Their effect upon the maritime cities through which the wealth of the Empire circulated would have been such as to hasten the Empire's collapse; the tendency of the great estates to rely upon their own self-sufficiency would have developed much sooner than it did; and the barbarians could not have been held at bay for so long. It is true that the Incas achieved State control in Peru, but theirs was only a land empire and a relatively poor country, and if this was socialism it was a socialism of penury.

The Roman Empire was not a 'class State', and it had no ideological problems, but only real ones. When Roman law drew upon Stoic ideas it was in order to deal with actual present situations and not to create new and unprecedented ones. In such a system it may be said that the avoidance of gratuitous error makes up for the lack of far-sighted vision. We may think that the Empire often found the wrong solutions, and the results prove it; but at least it never substituted false problems for the real ones. Contemporary minds are irritated by the Empire's

[1] *Differentiated* universal suffrage has never been tried, and the weakness of undifferentiated universal suffrage is that by presenting the elected representative with a blank cheque it obliges him, in principle, to have an opinion on every question; but in reality there will always be some electors who know more than their representative on any particular question and are better able to judge it. If the techniques of investigation were judiciously employed it would be possible today to improve our political régimes. It is true, no doubt, that a touch of irrationality is as necessary in government as a blank space in a picture or a blind spot in the eye. But when absurdity is taken for rationality the results can be decidedly harmful at certain times.

combination of empiricism and reasonableness; and, indeed, it was severely empirical and severely reasonable, whereas the social function of the modern intellectuals who feel such an antipathy for it is to rationalise and formulate passion. If a drop of blood is shed without being justified by an *idea*, they are beside themselves. Every massacre today must point a moral.

Like everything of human origin, the organs of the Empire were often overwhelmed by changes in the environment to which they could not be quickly enough adapted. They were far from perfect, but has anything ever been perfect? The problem of politics is the problem of finding the governmental system that is best adapted to a given world in a given situation. A good government can only remain so by continually modifying and correcting itself. In the long run, trial and error is the only method. But some of the troubles which faced the Roman Empire were impossible to cure with the means at its disposal. The swarms of barbarians which finally overwhelmed the universal State put a violently excessive strain upon its powers of assimilation; and the widespread political disaffection which accompanied the growth of Christianity was hardly the kind of phenomenon that a government can be expected to cope with. The universal Empire corresponded adequately to a given world situation, but the end of that situation meant the end of the Empire.

It is not the end of history when all frontiers are abolished and the world's 'final state' is reached. The universal State has its history. The first proof of this is that it comes to an end. But even if it had no end it would still have a history.

* * *

The masses represent insecurity personified. Being the live product of an insecure age, security is their great aspiration; and it was under the Severi that the dominant imperial policy of protection for the weak reached its maximum efficiency. The official class was made open to talent; any officer promoted from the ranks and any provincial could in theory reach the highest positions. This revolution which rewarded merit and created a hierarchy of talent was the work of absolutism; and several Emperors, including the greatest, such as Aurelian and Diocletian, were men who had begun life as provincial soldiers.

As Roman civilisation began to grow poorer, the State was compelled to exploit more carefully its human resources. The coming of the universal State implied an impoverishment of the social soil, which was to continue. There is no clearer sign of the weakening of real productive forces, in the full and profound sense of the word, than an epidemic of socialist measures. An age of economy begins, and intelligence and energy are increasingly devoted to *organising* society. The Severi protected the immense proletariat which had grown up during the 2nd century in the great metropolitan cities. Hundreds of senators and thousands of knights were exterminated by these African emperors, and their property seized. Municipal *curias* were rigorously subordinated to the central policy. Social security was organised; and the landed proprietors were made responsible for taxation (which was an additional source of power for them when the Empire began to collapse). Property tended more and more to become a social function. All the crafts were compulsorily grouped in syndicates subordinate to the State apparatus. The State banks financed the construction of enormous buildings on an American scale for the metropolitan cities. Public baths and spectacles became more lavish, and Rome was illuminated all night. The life of the plebs, the later plebs of the later period, was irresponsible and uncontrolled. The 'lazzarone' way of life became common; and while passive nihilism and 'practical materialism' were rife, mystery religions began to appeal to uneasy sensibilities in the upper class. There were men of superior quality who tried to overcome the world by ascetic disciplines; Stoicism inclines men of power towards State socialism and intellectual aristocrats towards detachment.

After its apogee, when it was more than two hundred and fifty years old, the universal State was inexorably drawn into decline. From then on it seemed to fall back below the level of history, for there remained only a handful of men who really lived at the centre of historic events. The remainder continued to make history, but on the animal rather than the historical level. In a unified and centralised world, history was only the history of the decisions of a few men and of the carrying out of those decisions. When the universal State was at its zenith politics did not exist. The State apparatus took men where it found them, and mechanically performed its function of protecting civilisation from the barbarians. But what is taking place in the depths of men's sensibility is a factor determining the next phase of history; and it would seem that the great majority of men at this time were neither affirming nor transmitting any great organic impulse. They seem to have gradually lost their sense of history, their memory. The formative influence upon their historical psyche had been the State which represented the 'final state of the world', and no earlier memories had any force. It was not to the Roman cults that Julian the Apostate appealed against Christianity, but to a hellenistic syncretism in which religion was emasculated by philosophy and philosophy was fuddled by religion.

Such was the culmination of the Roman universal State. Thenceforth it was progressively less able to *contain* the centrifugal forces, and its history is a history of decadence.

* * * *

In the 20th century historical power manifests itself on a *larger scale* than in the past. The collective beings of today which can exercise initiative, sovereignty, or independence in the full sense of the word, differ in form and even in structure from those of a hundred years ago; and the constituent elements of power have been becoming to an ever greater extent material and emotional ones, at the expense of the intellectual and qualitative and individual factors which counted in the 18th century.[1] It is upon material resources and sentiment that the two compact and concentrated 'great powers' of today rely; but they can hardly avoid regarding themselves as in some sense the inheritors of other elements which—although they fear them no longer or much less than they did—they have not ceased to admire.

Between the religious wars which racked Europe in the 16th century, and the world wars of the 20th, in which the issues at stake become clearer as the century advances, the European States which were first dynastic and later national have ceased to be the greatest powers in the field. Yet it was almost inconceivable in the 19th century that anything but a nation could support the apparatus of power which makes a State; and in the 18th century it was equally inconceivable that the State could be anything except a monarchy. Jean-Jacques Rousseau still believed, and said, that the republican system was appropriate only for cities; and when Robespierre was elected to the Constituent Assembly he had not yet become a republican. Power today cannot reach its full dimensions within the limits of the nation, and both the United States and Russia consist of a number of 'States' or 'Republics', each of which possesses its own organs, so that the State which represents American or Russian unity appears to be super-national. In the time of Philip II there was a distinction between the monarch's own kingdom and his colonial possessions, and there is a corresponding distinction in the 20th century, but with a difference. The possessions of the Spanish, French, Portuguese, and English crowns were far away; but the 20th-century Super-States, though they consisted originally of a sort of metropolis and some territory that could be colonised, differ from the old kingdoms in that the metropolis and the colonial territory are contiguous. The Russian empire adjoined the Principality of Moscow, and the territory

[1] cf. Paul Valéry, "La Crise de l'esprit" (1919): 'The tendency is to classify the habitable regions of the world in such a way that sheer physical mass and statistical data—figures of population, area, raw materials—will finally become the sole criteria of classification'; in *Variété* (Gallimard), 1924.

of the United States adjoined the English colonies of the Atlantic seaboard. So the geographical area covered by the new great powers is a *continuous* one, and the empire can expand by simple extension. There are no differences between the newly acquired and the 'metropolitan' territories comparable to those between the remote possessions of the King of Spain and his European domains. Instead of founding new nations across the sea, the modern great powers create new forms which begin to spread out into the surrounding space as simply and naturally as vegetation. In theory, the United States could accommodate more States and the Union of Soviet Socialist Republics unite together more 'socialist republics'. For their sovereignty does not inhere within a territory bounded by 'natural' or linguistic frontiers. The structure of these powers is not confined to any clear and intelligible pattern which limits its possible extension. The United States has been made what it is by emigrants of many tongues and races; and the Russian empire, which extends from Baltic to Pacific, and from the Arctic to Iran and India and China, has absorbed whole populations and cultural areas, including 'primitive' tribes as well as old historical countries like the ancient kingdom of Bokhara. Such empires are not confined by the sort of boundaries within which a common history makes an apparently indestructible alliance between a people and a territory. What they really are, or could be, is a 'society of peoples' linked together by a common State apparatus. Extending across a continuous area of continental dimensions and endowed with great material and human wealth, they presuppose a certain minimum of work for the exploitation of this wealth. As the latest arrivals on the historical scene, they have relied on their own efforts, in an area where there were no technically advanced historical peoples to compete with them, to organise the circulation and concentration of material and social wealth on a different scale from that of the old nations rooted in their own territories and hemmed in on all sides by other nations or by the sea. No matter what their régime, empires of this kind are specifically different from the European dynastic or national States. The British Commonwealth is a *family* of peoples, of whom all except the Indians are branches from the same stem. But the United States was formed by adding together a series of heterogeneous human elements: first Dutch and English, then African negroes imported as slaves, then Irish, German, Italian, and Polish, and finally Chinese and Japanese.[1]

The originally heterogeneous elements were brought together in the Tsarist empire in quite a different way. The empire had conquered northern Asia up to the Pacific without in any way modifying its population. The Tsar was emperor of all the Russias, in the plural; and today

[1] But the original Indian inhabitants of the country were eliminated.

the peoples of the Soviet Union are still only in the process of integration. In the United States integration has reached a higher stage, largely because there was less heterogeneity at the beginning; on more than one occasion there was conflict between the motives impelling the free citizens to unite together and their desire to retain complete liberty of action. In the British Commonwealth a minimum of community was only preserved at the price of a maximum of independence; the system was founded until recently upon the economic and maritime supremacy, and priority, of Great Britain, and this supremacy depended upon the system of bases all over the world which protected and secured the empire's communications. It was a system which presupposed, in its variety and dispersion, a diverse and pluralist and fragmented 'historical world' in which no great power could become so strong and widespread that its *mere presence* would upset the ingenious intellectually contrived equilibrium. In the 19th century the freedom of the seas and the maritime supremacy of Great Britain were practically synonymous terms. The Commonwealth depends upon the free will of the self-governing Dominions, each with its own administration, and belongs to a universe where equilibrium is maintained between a number of powers of moderate and calculable strength. The power of Britain's maritime and colonial rival, France, was balanced by the industrial and military (rather than naval) power of Germany; and until the 20th century it was always possible for Britain to restore equilibrium in Europe by leaning to one side or the other.

For more than two centuries the world was a prey to European expansion. At the most it could try to defend itself, for it was unable to counter-attack. In the 19th century the United States asked only to be allowed to develop in peace; it was fully occupied in exploring its own domains. It was not until the end of the century that it found itself continually running up against the older powers, and even then it was seeking only economic outlets. The image of 'overseas possessions', which has something in common with the annexation of provinces by which the European dynasties enlarged their patrimonies, does not exist in the American psyche, and is indeed positively repugnant to it. In fact, it is the very thing from which the United States has emancipated itself. All that the United States asks of the countries it penetrates is a political situation conducive to economic expansion; it is the 20th-century successor to Great Britain as the great power whose interests are served by economic liberty and the freedom of the seas.

By different routes the United States and Russia have arrived at similar positions of strength; we can see in them the first model or outline of the most recent and up-to-date form of power: a society of peoples whose political structure is a Super-State extending over an unbroken geographical area. This area contains vast material wealth which must be at least partially exploited as a preliminary to the expansion of power. A State of this kind is not a national State although a sentiment corresponding to national pride and particularism will flourish there, as everywhere else; its patriotism will be a sort of imperial patriotism. Russia includes many peoples and many races, and so does the United States, though in a different way; and in both of them there is a nucleus around which (using the word 'around' in a psychological and moral rather than a geographical sense) diversity has been brought to unity or, in other words, the empire has formed itself. In the 19th century the United States absorbed a part of the excess population of Europe—Irish, Germans, Italians, and Slavs; before that there had been the forced immigration of negro slaves, and later, at the end of the 19th century, the Chinese and Japanese immigration began.

Each of these two empires has established political unity over an area of continental dimensions in which it represents a concentrated system of power without precedent since the days of Rome. Coming after the Industrial Revolution, the methods at their disposal are also unprecedented. They possess greater power than their immediate neighbours, or indeed the rest of the world, and in relation to the rest they appear as vast and concentrated accumulations of power and the means of power. Each, in its own part of the world, tends to become a pole of attraction. They have been described as 'distributing centres', and it is true that they are accumulators and distributors of power and wealth. Each of them represents a certain type of organisation for converting a great quantity of raw material into production or consumption goods; and for each there is a certain system of distribution which corresponds to its particular structure.

The difference of historical scale and the disparity of potential between the new powers and the old is now such that the latter can neither do without the former nor offer any resistance to them. They can only escape from this situation by renouncing their own historical form and assuming a new one, which will enable them to operate in the same way as the modern great powers, which grew up in territories whose original population was sparse and helpless.

The structure of the new empires is sufficient to reveal the conditions for exercising full sovereignty in the second half of the 20th century. These conditions are fulfilled by both the great powers, each in its own way, and it is impossible to enjoy full sovereignty without conforming to them—though there are several ways of doing so. When power *on a new scale* appears in any historical world, certain formal modifications are necessarily imposed upon this world.[1] The old-style powers must

[1] In the long run, though with a varying time-lag in different cases.

either unite together and transform themselves to meet the new conditions of existence revealed by the appearance of the new powers; or else they must resign themselves to absorption and assimilation by these powers, which may be regarded both as creators of the new situation and as organisms adapted to it. To mobilise any considerable amount of material and human wealth in an autonomous circuit, and to control and co-ordinate the power and energy so obtained, this is a problem of organisation which presupposes an effective hierarchy of organisers, managers, and skilled workers, and also a certain amount of convergence of effort. The problem is solved by the United States and by Russia, each in a different way; and total sovereignty, which was formerly achieved by the city and by the dynastic, the national, and the universal State, is today dependent upon its successful solution. Powers which belong to a lower, and older, order of magnitude have lost their status since the new empires appeared, and their destiny now confronts them as a dilemma: Shall they adapt themselves (and there are several ways of doing so) to the new conditions to which the modern empires are successfully adapted—in Hegelian terms, shall they negate themselves by self-transformation and self-transcendence, resigning their existence in order to exist again—or shall they merge into one of the already existing systems?

The problem is not unprecedented, but typical. From the 4th century B.C. the Greek cities were confronted with a dilemma of destiny. They were unable to rise above the scale of city life. Every attempt at federation was thwarted by a double particularism: the powerful cities trying to assert hegemony over the others, and the weaker cities fighting to recover their lost independence.

The hellenic world was handicapped by the very perfection of an historic past which it was unable to surpass. The image of the *Polis* was deep in the citizens' historical psyche and coloured their political thought with aspirations for the hegemony or independence of their own city; and when they were confronted with power on a new scale and in a new form they could not adapt their historical vision quickly enough.[1] The Lamian war, after Alexander the Great's premature death, marked the beginning of a new dispersion; but Alexander's epic feats had already fused the western fringe of the Syriac world with the Greek. It was the Roman conquest that effected the transition to the next phase; through conquest and victory the Roman generals found the way to the new political form which they were to impose upon their own city and the rest of the world.

The nations of Europe should take warning from the Greek cities.

[1] In this connection it is striking that Clemenceau, after the victory of 1918, retired from political life and wrote a book on Demosthenes.

There is good reason to think that perfection of form is achieved in the political world, as in the animal, at the expense of adaptability. The shapeless has greater aptitude for taking new shapes, and those animal species which are most perfectly adapted to their environment are the least able to cope with changed conditions. Their perfection turns against them, for perfect adaptation to conditions that no longer exist appears as total aberration in the new environment. The study of palæontology suggests many examples of this in the history of the animal species.

To the European of today few historic spectacles seem so acutely tragic as the decline of the city-state in the Greek world. Demosthenes went on thinking exclusively in terms of the city at a time when the city's destiny manifestly depended on its ability to transcend city limitations. The dialectic of the situation is implied in the etymology of the word 'perfect'. To be perfected is to be completed or finally accomplished. Nothing attains to perfection until it is already finished.

But today there is a difference; it is a characteristic of our situation that we are conscious of it, and that our consciousness is itself a part of the situation and reveals a new aspect of it. A civilisation aware of its own mortality may perhaps not be mortal in the same way as others.

* * * *

If Napoleon had unified Europe it would have been more than Europe, for it would have included Russia. 'Europe,' he said, 'will be either republican or Cossack'; but a republican Europe would have included Russia and a Cossack Europe would have included the western nations. Napoleon made more than one remark which indicates that he saw himself as the expression of every positive and irrevocable achievement of the French Revolution. Intellectually he owed everything to the 18th century, and it was his grievance against the 'ideologues'—although he protected them—that they would not recognise him as Reason incarnate (which Hegel did). His empire corresponds to the conception of 'enlightened despotism'—'a despotism made necessary by the peoples' lack of enlightenment'. In his concordat with the Church he was simply recognising a real force; his 'enlightenment' did not run to fantasy. He was obliged to recognise and *make use of* power wherever he found it.

And Stalin's attitude towards the orthodox Church is the same. The fact that it held out against the attempts to extirpate it qualifies this Church to be accepted and treated with as a force. Like Napoleon, Satlin lives in a world of forces, where what cannot be destroyed must be made use of; and the method of utilising the Church was already laid down in the old policy by which the Tsars were the defenders of orthodox Christianity outside Russia. Once again, Stalin had only to follow in the Tsars' footsteps.

Tocqueville already foresaw in mid-19th century the change of historical scale that the 20th would bring, and he predicted who would reap the advantage—the United States and Russia, free enterprise and absolutism. This pair now present the world with a dilemma, which is complicated, but not in any way reduced, by Marxism and the success of Marxism in Russia. It is a dilemma which taxes all the resources of the intellect. Europe passed irrevocably beyond the limits of the European continent without first unifying itself. At the beginning of the 19th century it already held India and the Archipelago. The Chinese empire of the Manchus slumbered in anarchy, the United States was in its infancy, and the rest of America from Mexico to Tierra del Fuego was Spanish or Portuguese. The whole of Africa lay open to European enterprise. If Europe could have come to terms with itself, it might have aspired to the *imperium mundi*. The Germany of the Kaisers, united too late, came too late to share in the partitioning of the world and got only the crumbs. From the geographical centre of Europe it made two attempts, under Wilhelm II and Hitler, to unify Europe and overcome the maritime powers by submarine terror. It failed both times, and for the same military reasons (to say nothing of others): the coalition of their enemies, the impossibility of controlling the sea by submarines alone, and armed intervention by the new world. Twice in twenty-five years there have been Germans to entertain the preposterous idea of conquering simultaneously western Europe, Russia, and America. It is true that the leaders denied each time that this was their intention; but that was to be expected. Hitler hoped to succeed by *rapidity of movement*; with Russia neutralised by the 1939 pact and France knocked out by a lightning blow, England was to be appeased by moderation, no demands being made upon her.[1] It was calculated that she would be glad to get out of the war on such good terms, with the British Isles and the Commonwealth intact. It was even hoped that the European powers conquered on land could be made allies against the United States, which would not be inclined to intervene in Europe for the sole sake of Russia. In any case, American public opinion might not have tolerated it. This compact and monolithic Europe, in which the Mediterranean was only a big lake, would have had a firm grip on Africa and an eventual reckoning between the two continents could be postponed to a later date. It is legitimate to attribute some such plan to Hitler, although he never expounded it in so many words, because it is implied by his

[1] This is confirmed by Liddell Hart, *The Other Side of the Hill* (London, 1948).

actions so long as he could still control them and before he was overwhelmed by events. Everything depended on speed, and it was the weakness of the plan that its *tempo* could not be altered; Hitler required the collaboration of the rest of the world, and the cosmos itself, in keeping to his time-table. But a plan that makes no allowance for delays and accidents is madness. From the moment when England refused to stop fighting, in July 1940, the plan was out of step with events, and the discrepancy grew, at an irregular rate, until its final acceleration into catastrophe. By his actions Hitler experimentally and disastrously revealed the change that has occurred in the order of magnitude and in the very nature of power, and in the conditions for the exercise of total sovereignty.

Russia or America? It is by no means certain that our destiny is ruled by this dilemma. There are other possibilities. But America and Russia are in the forefront at this actual moment, and the present age, more than any previous one, is the slave of actuality. To what extent are these two empires qualified to compete in the race for the *imperium mundi*? The United States of America is at once a maritime and a territorial empire, but the Soviet empire is a typical territorial despotism which has not yet found an outlet to the open sea.[1] The seignorial Achemenid empire, that perfect example of a territorial despotism, failed to become a universal State through its inability to rule the sea; it was halted in its course, though not destroyed, by the Greek world, which consisted of nothing but a few coastal towns and islands. Salamis not only made Periclean Athens possible but also tested one of the conditions for the universal State. The second, and successful, attempt to found such a State was made by Rome; and it was because it was both a maritime and a territorial State that it was able to be both 'centralist' and liberal, combining a 'social service' policy with the policy of free enterprise.

[1] The defection of Marshal Tito has diminished the hope of access to the Adriatic; and it seems unlikely that Russia can completely absorb China, for the Chinese world has never yet been absorbed into an alien political form. The U.S.S.R. cannot provide the machines or experts needed for Chinese industrialisation, and China will seek them elsewhere. Once she is equipped, she will have no reason for implicit obedience to Moscow's directives. Mao Tse-tung's attempt to unify China repeats the same movements—from north to south, from west to east, and from the centre outwards—which have, on several occasions in history, preceded China's unification.

The first outlines of 'Red' or, if it be preferred, 'Democratic' China do not look like attempts to apply a system mechanically (cf. Harrison Forman, *Report from Red China*; New York, 1945); and it would be a mistake at present to regard Mao Tse-tung's victory as a mere extension of the Russian system up to the Pacific. The Chinese communists made use of the Russians, and no doubt the Russians will collect payment for services rendered; but 'Democratic' China is already in a position to insist that the price shall not be too high. At a certain degree of pressure Chinese xenophobia would, or will, come into play against the Russians.

The 20th-century totalitarian State stands in somewhat the same relation to the universal State as a secular religion to a universal religion; it expresses an aspiration, but at the same time perverts it. Totalitarianism is a caricature of the universal State. In its system, in its measures of repression, and in its 'physical liquidation of the opposition', it always takes the easiest way; it forces society into a rigid frame and cuts away whatever will not fit. It simplifies the problems of government by treating the governed as things—and neither rare nor precious ones at that; it uses them as part of its material resources. All this is in line with Russia's historical tradition, and the Tsars acted in the same way. But in extending beyond the regions historically linked with Tsarist domination the new Russian absolutism would run into serious difficulties—and particularly in western Europe. The reality of Russian domination would quickly be opposed by a section (not the most numerous, perhaps, but the most efficient) of the communists themselves, who would thus prove in practice—and personally learn—that they prefer a republican to a Cossack Europe. But it seems certain that no lesser emergency can put a stop to the tapping and diverting and canalising of psychological forces by which the communist secular religion is kept alive in our midst; a consideration which enables us to estimate with precision the limits of the power of this anti-religious hybrid form of religion.

* * * *

Europe's need of America is an obstacle to European unification; and so also is the systematic and indefatigable campaign of the communist 'Islam' to disintegrate Europe's historical form and structure. But there are other obstacles.

Today, as formerly, what Europe sees if she looks at herself is something like this: a diversity of peoples with diverse destinies, each with its own irreducibly distinctive cultural nuances, each of them expressing a tradition of immemorial historical grandeur associated with men and achievements so noble that the mere contemplation of them makes one proud to be a man. Every European in childhood identifies himself with particular heroes whose great deeds were for the most part performed against other European heroes of the same rank.

But that is not the whole story. Strange as it may seem, there exist not only negative but also positive obstacles to the unification of Europe. The European penetration into every part of the world proceeded very far while there was still no such thing as Europe. None of the deeds which express for us the greatness and value of Europe were performed by 'Europeans'. It was not 'Europeans' who explored and invented, conquered new lands and developed them, or disseminated religion and culture; it was Spaniards, Portuguese, Dutchmen, Englishmen, Frenchmen, and Germans—all of them perpetually in conflict with other Europeans and usually, though not always, chiefly concerned with this conflict. And it was not Europe, but Christians, who converted negroes and Chinese to Christianity. It is possible *after the event* to speak of 'Europe's mission', but it was not as Europe that she accomplished it, any more than Greece was ever Greece except in our history books. Europe began to go beyond herself, starting in the 15th century, before she had ever established her own identity. The Europe which made a unique mark in history and 'encircled the globe' appeared as Europe only to outsiders; in her own eyes she remained everywhere what she was at home—either English or French, Catholic or Protestant. To European eyes the birth of the United States was simply an incident in the Anglo-French conflict, and the rebel colonies were no more than a distant pawn in the game between the two most Christian kings. Today, if people are ready, for the sake of the ideal of a united Europe, to sacrifice any reality, however imperfect or precarious or liable to sudden collapse, one can only say 'those whom the Gods wish to destroy they first make mad'. It may be that a united Europe is a 'reactionary Utopia', a sort of lullaby to rock Europe to sleep. But what sort of sleep? A Europe that is no more than Europe is less than Europe, and if she dreams of such a thing she is dreaming of her own end. A Europe reduced to the geographical limits of Europe would be engulfed by a different system which holds the advantage of the historical initiative. But this is not to say that Europe must not be united; it is to say that the historical problem is a much vaster one than the mere organisation of the European peninsula. What has to be organised is a very much larger area, which contains peoples who differ from one another much more than the Europeans among themselves. In short, the organisation of Europe cannot stop at the frontiers of Europe. History confronts us with this dilemma: either Europe must create a society of peoples and an apparatus of power comparable to those of Russia and the United States, or else she will be absorbed sooner or later by one of the great empires at her gate. If a united Europe cannot afford to leave Africa out, why should we shrink from stating this problem in its own realistic terms? And if we continue to talk of Europe in the narrow sense, how can we expect that Africans will not begin to think of Africa in the same way? Europe must either become the nucleus of a society of peoples, a distributor of wealth, and an apparatus of power, or else the historical reality of her power (which lies to a great extent outside Europe) will collapse, and Europe, in the geographical sense, will be absorbed into some other system. To restrict the meaning of the word 'Europe' to the geographical area of that name is to make it mean 'the end of Europe'.

In either of the wars of the first half of the 20th century a victory for Germany would have meant the unification of Europe under German leadership. Europe would have taken form around the German nucleus as Russia was formed around Muscovy. Before 1914 European wars were possible; but the war of 1914—which might have led to the unification of Europe—was the first war on a *world* scale.

American intervention hastened the allied victory in that war and contributed to its decisive end; but it was only an intervention. In the second world war, however, which began like the previous one as a European show-down, America did more than intervene; far from being an auxiliary, she played the leading part. With the swifter historical tempo, the increased rapidity of communications, and the greater economic interdependence between different parts of the world, America is now directly concerned with what happens in Europe. She has reached a position of wealth and importance where it is impossible for her to hold aloof, and many of the best Americans are distressed at the weight of historical responsibility which, as they now suddenly realise, they are called upon to shoulder. They are more or less obliged, whether they will or no, to impose some of their ideas upon the world; but it can still be said that they are doing it with the utmost reluctance. Divided though she was, and modest (by contemporary standards) though the means at her disposal were, Europe succeeded in transforming the world; and now America finds herself committed in spite of herself to something like a race for the *imperium mundi*. It is certain that she would prefer a world settlement by mutual agreement. A warlike imperialistic struggle for hegemony is as alien to the traditions of youthful America as it is congenial to those of long-lived Europe. A hundred years after Napoleon the question of European unification was reopened by the war of 1914, and the war of 1939 seemed at first to be going to raise it again; but during the course of each of these wars it was lost among much wider issues. Neither the first nor the second world war solved the problem of uniting Europe, but each of them raised a more far-reaching problem: if not the unification of the world and a new *imperium mundi*, at least a vast *simplification of the map of the world*, and not merely of Europe. To put it briefly, the problem which arises today, and for which a possible solution could be found, is not the problem of uniting Europe but the question whether a third great society of peoples, connected with the American system but distinct from it, shall or shall not be founded.

The tragedies and problems of Europe in the 20th century are of more than European dimensions, and any attempt to deal with them as purely

European problems is doomed to failure. While European techniques[1] have been spreading round the world, a whole system of new and varied inter-relationships has been knitting it together: the remotest countries are now in sensitive contact with one another both economically and intellectually, and an event in any one place can produce the liveliest repercussions at the other end of the world. Something unprecedented is happening; in the economic and material sense the world is, as it were, 'coming of age'—and a sort of world unity is beginning to appear, though it is still a purely external and superficial unity.

When the first world war broke out our civilisation was already of such an age that it was really impossible for the war to be no more than a day of reckoning among Europeans. For the first time in three centuries Europe rent herself so dangerously as to raise the question of who should succeed to her heritage; and at the close of the two world wars it became obvious who were the real victors. It is true that on each occasion an alliance of Europeans celebrated its victory over other Europeans, but Europe lost both the wars. The change in the order of magnitude of power revealed new perspectives to the 'colonial peoples'.[2] They began to calculate the advantages to be reaped from communism in its aspect as a general conspiracy against western Europe; and in the same way the 'backward countries' began to wonder how much they could get from the United States, which was the first country in a position to exploit the whole world in the 20th century, as Europe had been the first to partition it in the nineteenth. America now has the greatest facilities for scientific research and the greatest number of research workers, scientists, and technicians from all over the world, and especially from Europe.

So we can see, and have seen, the two first world wars as the preliminary heats in a race for the *imperium mundi*. The final is still to come, and it cannot yet be foretold with certainty who will be the starters. Perhaps it will be possible, for a time, to hold a balance between the diversity which our psyche demands and a unification of the world on the material level alone.

A society of peoples comparable to Soviet Russia and the United States, and fully equal to them in material and human resources, a

[1] The word 'technique' is used here in the broadest sense. The coming into fashion in the 1920s of the 'globe-trotter' school of writing is significant. Blaise Cendrars and Paul Morand (*Rien que la terre*, *Du monde entier*, *Ouvert la nuit*, *Fermé la nuit*) are a symptom of the 'encirclement of the globe'. The uniformity of style of the entertainment palaces and 'open all night' establishments all over the world is a sign of the standardisation of humanity's material conditions. In addition to the chroniclers of private life, we now have our chroniclers of public life, and instead of the confessions of the 'child of the century', we have the century's own confessions.

[2] If Europe is to be worthy of her history, she must see herself as she is and not in wishful terms.

society of peoples including non-Europeans, so that the colonial empires would survive in a new form instead of being destroyed, such a society is less utopian than the ideal of a 'united Europe'. Pandit Nehru's achievement in bringing India voluntarily into the Commonwealth may perhaps be one of the greatest historic events of the 20th century.

* * * *

Every social aspiration today has its ideology and every collective passion has its slogan. A secular religion makes use of slogans in much the same way as a lama uses his prayer-wheel. People agitate for 'world organisation' and look forward to the age of organisation that will succeed the age of organisms. It is easy enough to reconcile diversity with unity—on paper.

Too many of the plans have this major drawback—that they presuppose that very goodwill which is their first requirement. But it can at least be said that there is an awakening consciousness of our common destiny and of the need to act before our destiny becomes our fate.

If every susceptibility has to be respected, no action is possible; but if no concessions can be made, then it is not worth while to act. The historical role of the State as the cohesive force of society is still needed in some form or other, and *self-interest* will only perform it under pressure of inexorable necessity—as witness the United States and Switzerland, neither of which had a painless birth. Will Europe be able to select only the positive qualities of the various nations—their culture and their strong links with overseas peoples—while rejecting their negative ones—their particularism and their interminable vendettas? To synthesise the contraries and achieve a *coincidentia oppositorum* is a problem for the European genius. And it is truly genius that it requires.

Day-dreams about world organisation have often a colour reminiscent of Proudhon; people prefer to talk about *organisation* rather than about a universal State, and the word is made to stand for an œcumenical peace which has no need to rely, as in the past, upon a universal State. Or rather, there is a desire for the universal State, which is the perfection of the existing State, and *at the same time* for the elimination of the State—a desire for social security and *also* for the suppression of bureaucracy. All this is natural enough; affectivity is essentially ambivalent, and even if reality imposes upon us a hierarchy of preferences, this does not alter the fact that our desires are what they are, whether acknowledged or unacknowledged. Social facts are 'natural' facts, without being things. Humanity is a fact of history, and therefore Time is of the essence of our situation. The time-factor subjects the human intelligence to a stern and continuous test; and each one of us has only a limited time in which to seek out the laws that govern the temporal. We can only picture the final phases of the revolution in which we are the actors by imagining them in terms of previous revolutions. The faint and wavering light that guides us is nothing more than an analogy between an earlier state of the world and a later state. The transition from multiplicity to a lesser degree of multiplicity, or to unity, can take place in an indefinite number of ways, and we have no fixed points for calculating its duration; therefore, although something very different is called for, even the crudest analogies can be of some assistance. Are we, then, living in the age of Marius, or even earlier, or in the age of Cæsar?[1] But when we speak of the acceleration of history we are really referring to what economists call a 'trend', and a 'reversal of the trend' is not inconceivable. No doubt we are approaching the end of an 'age of aggressive States', but in taking the long view there is always the risk of misjudging distances; a period of great wars is usual towards the end of an age of aggressive States, but even this cannot be taken as certain, and in any case it may be said that calculations which are only accurate to the nearest century cannot tell us much about the psyche of today. The word 'revolution' has no meaning except in an historical perspective, and the only analogy that helps us to place ourselves in such a perspective is one which embraces in a single curve a moment of the past and also the future it led to (in this sense, the analogy with the Roman world shows us the Cæsarian universal State as our own 'past future').

The contemporary mind is more at home when it can appeal exclusively to 'economic facts'. Extrapolation from a given series of figures is always possible, and the modern mind avails itself of the possibility. But the association of ideas upon which the operation rests is often unperceived: figures have acquired a status (which they were far from possessing in the early days of the Western psyche) as the hallmark of true knowledge. Mathematics, for example, and mathematical physics. An intellectual discipline that is not concerned with numerically expressible relations has difficulty today in securing recognition as a science. There is something reassuring about a numerical series—for its producer as well as for its consumers. But it is only in mathematics that a numerical series has absolute value[2]; anywhere else it is valid only within a practically closed system, and only to the extent that it is practically possible to exclude other factors.

But in politics, which is 'history in advance', it is not permissible to exclude the factor of the unknown. 'Guess the riddle or be devoured.' Politics, in fact, is destiny. (In revolutionary periods the doors of private life cannot be kept shut; the wind of any public storm blows them open.)

[1] Allowing for the change of scale between *a* world and *the* world.

[2] This proposition is stated without precision, for the sake of simplicity.

Yet the area of the predictable continues to grow. Planning is a specialisation of the faculty of foresight which can be dangerous; but on the other hand, if we refuse to make observations and predictions the situation becomes appalling, as it is free to do. If we repress what we cannot help suspecting we reinforce a barbarously hypocritical obscurantism; and to avoid doing this it is also desirable to re-examine periodically the meaning of the words we use.

There are people who think that a prediction which is not an interpretation of statistics is negligible. Such people sometimes write the word *civilisation* when it is really *economics* that they have in mind. But, in saying this, are we reacting too sharply against the still prevailing idea that there is really no common measure between the pre-machine age and our own world which is the result of an unprecedented acceleration of technical progress? I see at least two good reasons for refusing to be carried away by this idea. The first is that man has not succeeded in changing himself so much as he has changed his environment. By adding new determinisms to those which already existed he has not abolished the old ones; he has simply changed the situation within which they operate, so that they now assume new forms. In this new situation man's relation to society appears more clearly than ever as a special case of his general relation to 'nature'. The social element has become more definite and 'objective'; and hence the apparent primacy today of economics. But the characteristic properties of the human psyche—its successive modalities and its peculiar dialectic, its constants and variables—have not been eliminated; the action is taking place in another country, but the protagonists are the same. To make the social reducible 'in the last analysis' to the economic (as Marxists and inverted Marxists do) is to neglect the factors which were in existence before this objectification of the social; it is to ignore the factors which preceded and determined the new environment.[1]

The second reason follows from the first. If the sudden acceleration of technical progress and the arrival of the machine age are the result of a sort of mutation of the psyche, how can we be sure that another mutation, *in a different direction*, is not possible and perhaps imminent? Technical progress represents in relation to the psyche as a whole, a specialisation analogous to the hypertrophy of certain organs in extinct animal species. In any case, we have small reason—to say the least—for despising the past. The 20th century has neither the spontaneity of the twelfth nor the refinement of the eighteenth; it has seen a return of slavery (which was everywhere in decline in the 19th century) and of Assyrian methods of total war and displacements of population which neither Hellas in its fratricidal strife nor Rome in its harshest conquests

[1] Or were one of its determining causes.

ever systematically revived. War has always been a powerful instigator of technical progress (the converse is also true); and technical progress is a sign of intellectual specialisation rather than of a psychic mutation. The lessons of psychology and history therefore have their value; but does the interpretation of statistics provide a basis for valid prediction of future trends over a given period? The predictions of economists are indispensable and of absorbing interest. By all means let us consult them—but as experts and not as oracles. Colin Clark, for example, cannot be ignored, but it would be dangerous to regard him as infallible. That a prolonged study of statistical series should lead to a subjective feeling of certainty is quite understandable. The predictions of a great economist do reveal short-term probabilities. They apply to the most 'economically advanced' countries; but will they necessarily apply to other countries which are due to reach the same economic level in a given period of time? What about the non-economic 'differential factors' which nevertheless determine economic events? Are we entitled to neglect the 'non-economic determinants' of economics, and more particularly the reciprocal implications and *convertibility* between economics and power, which can initiate a cycle of economic energy-transformations?

It is always possible to eliminate certain factors by hypothesis, but there is no guarantee that these factors will allow themselves to be eliminated in reality. The contemporary mind is responsive to the idea of a purely economic determinism, but history does not support it. Every event and each individual at every moment is the product of a multiplicity of factors which are very far from having been sifted and rigorously distinguished from one another. In a time of troubles there is a maximum of interdependence between crises, and economics is compelled to eliminate all the non-economic aspects, for otherwise economic research would be impossible. But what sort of predictions could even the best-qualified economist have made about Russia at the beginning of this century? The more strictly and purely economic they had been, the more rigorously they excluded everything not deducible from well-established statistics, the further they would have been from the truth.

Marx failed to predict the increasing importance of the 'tertiary sector'[1] and the tendency in a highly evolved or, in his own terms, an 'advanced capitalist' economy, towards a progressive stabilisation of the secondary sector. In a highly differentiated economy of this kind the division of labour is carried so far that most men are in the position of children receiving their food daily from the distributive system. They

[1] In Colin Clark's terms the primary sector is concerned with strictly essential needs (agriculture, for example) and the secondary with industry. The third, or tertiary, sector is the sector that provides services (barbers, actors, ministers, porters, etc.).

can only get their daily bread through the functioning of highly complex and increasingly elaborate social mechanisms; and if these delicate mechanisms are upset by one of the classic disturbances of a revolutionary period (in the broad and at the same time special sense in which we use the word), the primary sector is liable suddenly to reassume its primordial importance. This is what happened in German-occupied Europe in the last war. Since the primary sector has only a limited capacity to absorb new personnel, the active population of the secondary and tertiary sectors cannot be transferred to it in sufficient numbers. Thus if a country's distributive mechanism is broken down by war and the country is not immediately reintegrated into another system, military conquest leads to the following dilemma: either the defeated must be immediately succoured and taken in hand by the victors, or else the greater part of the defeated population must be systematically 'displaced'. For the sake of completeness we must add that there is a third solution—extermination. The last war offered preliminary examples of all these methods.

In attempting to predict the tendencies that will govern the displacement of the active population, we must not systematically exclude the hypothesis of future wars, nor of a 'peace' which is merely the absence of general war but is nothing like a *pax œcumenica* (we are far from such a thing); to do so would be to exclude systematically certain elements which a purely intellectual calculation must take into account.

Predictions which rely upon economic determinism are calculations based upon an isolated factor, whose isolation is an arbitrary assumption. To neglect history and psychology would not only be a symptom of cultural disintegration but would also quite certainly falsify our view of the future.

Postscript to Chapter 15

TODAY, as in the past, there are men of goodwill who seek to achieve world unity and world organisation by a direct appeal to the 'masses'. The world is composed of men—so the argument seems to run—each of whom desires the maximum of comfort for himself and, first and foremost, the abolition of war. Why, it is asked, should not every man be at home in every country, and is not the existence of separate States and governments, which goes back through thousands of years of history, the most obvious and tangible impediment to this ideal? And what could be more desirable than a single organisation for the equal distribution of goods? Perhaps therefore, say the men of goodwill, the same measures should now be taken on a world scale as were taken in the 19th century by the nations: there should be a world constituent assembly to vote into existence a world constitution; and then there must be a world executive which will command world-wide obedience because—obviously—it will be acting in the interests of the whole world. But the argument is circular; they are postulating the minimum of agreement which it is their aim to achieve. They assume in advance that it is true that men can always be convinced by argument, and that the passions are quite amenable to reason. If you point out to the men of goodwill who talk in this way that history by no means confirms their assumptions, but points, like psychology, in quite a different direction, they are liable to become annoyed. They will start by questioning the credentials of history and psychology and then, leaving the objective for the subjective and the defensive for the offensive, they will reproach you for advocating, or at the very least for abetting, war. And this puts you on a dangerous spot, for it is easily within their power to inflame the minds of the simple against you, and it is to be feared that they are not the men to refrain from doing so. If you are convicted of treason against world unity and universal happiness and peace, and if the crowd agrees with the verdict—these things can happen very quickly nowadays—you are in some danger of being torn to pieces.

Simple and easily communicable thoughts are dangerous, and they have the additional property of conferring a good conscience upon those who hold them; and experience teaches us that the worst is to be feared when a good conscience of this kind is shared by a large and united body of men. In other words, crowd enthusiasms are generally not conducive to the creation of great works, or discoveries, or any new acquisitions of the kind that is conferred by knowledge and wisdom—both of which are patient and conscious of imperfection. These people are so impatient for our happiness that there is a danger of their being carried away. They are suspicious of governments, which might be a healthy mistrust, but it is disquieting that they are at least equally mistrustful of everyone who disagrees with them. And in their speeches they are accustomed (like most other people, it must be said) to credit their opponents with wickedness or folly and little else. Since they possess a monopoly of good intentions, how can yours be anything except bad? Their direct appeal to simple feelings leads, as so often before, to a notable advance in barbarity; and in a time so out of joint as ours it is unfortunately not possible to ignore them. It is necessary to pay attention to any man who can assemble an audience of a few thousands. We have all had a chance to observe how the proceedings open, but their sequel is not so easy to trace. Let us briefly examine it.

This enthusiasm for the 'world' is only able to be manifested in those parts of the world that are not totalitarian; and therefore it inevitably works against the intentions of its promoters, whatever they may be and even if they are transparently benign. It works for the disintegration of the world which is not—or is not yet—totalitarian. It converges, therefore (at least for a time, which happens to be the present), with the disintegrating activity of the totalitarian 'Islam'[1]; and from convergence to co-ordination it is only a step, and a step that is all the more easily taken if one is unaware—officially—of taking it.

And there is another point: suppose the propaganda succeeds in sweeping the masses off their feet and the pressure of 'world'-intoxicated mobs breaks through the partitions between nations. It is very possible that the ensuing disturbances will before long become of such a kind and so violent as to distort completely the intentions of their original (and well-meaning) instigators. Subversiveness on this scale may well provoke the intervention of the totalitarian State which has been fostering it, the purpose of the intervention being to forestall social disintegration at home while taking advantage of it abroad. And this would mean war.

It is possible to have reservations about the efficacy and appropriateness of undifferentiated universal suffrage for electing representative assemblies within Europe; and these reservations apply with even greater force as regards the world. Why should the counting of votes produce any better results when done on a world scale? World elections might merely raise absurdity to a higher power. Suppose it should be possible

[1] A modern Molière writing a contemporary *Tartuffe* would deprive himself of his surest effects if he failed to make his hero a 'progressive'.

to organise anti-State elections of this kind in the different States without provoking disturbances (which would be wars, for a civil war is a war), who can foretell what would happen? At the best it might be an abortive effort, on a much greater scale but of the same kind as the Frankfort assembly in Germany in 1848, or at the worst an incalculable subversive explosion which would be more than likely to end in war. How can the sorcerer's apprentices of 'world' magic provide any guarantee that the unleashing of the 'world' masses would not be an unleashing of war?

The thought of these 'world partisans' moves too fast for history; it relies too much upon goodwill and invests it with a purely imaginary supremacy. It seems to take for granted that the excellent motives consciously possessed by all of us are not opposed by any powerful forces of the kind that psycho-analysis tries to deal with by indirect approach and stratagem. In their zeal for mankind they seem to trust in the omnipotence of those 'enlightened' motives which every ideology so prominently displays. We may believe that much will be forgiven them, for they will easily be able to prove that they knew not what they did.

There are no better grounds, then, for accepting the over-simplifications of 'world' enthusiasts than those of the fanatics of nationalism and the zealots of race or class predestination.

Index

Achemenid Empire, 225, 324
Alain, 221
Alexander the Great, 265, 321

Bakunin, 252
Bismarck, 196
Blanc, Louis, 233
Blanqui and Blanquism, 37, 192, 263
Bourgeoisie, in France, 186, 197–8, 204; in Germany, 200–1; in Russia, 204–6; historical role of, 228–9
Buddhism, 279
Bukharin, N., 53, 57, 62, 98, 105
Burnham, J., 115

Cæsar, Julius, 26, 106, 265, 307
Cæsarism, 30, 34, 36, 300
Catholic Church, 54, 83
Catholics in popular front, 118
Charisma, 40
Charlemagne, 231, 266
Cheka, 62, 63, 76–7
Chicherin, G., 105
'Chosen class', 41, 42, 107
Christianity, 15, 18, 38, 273–4, 277, 279, 281, 285–6, 306n.
Cicero, 307
Circulation of élites, 14, 31, 74–5, 82–3, 205, 234
City state, 177–8, 313, 321–2
Class struggles, 11, 169, 259, 283, 293
Cold war, 260–1
Communist Campaign, 12–25, 50, 95, 99, 107, 113–19, 124, 227, 260–3, 305; world-wide aims of, 12, 28, 34, 61, 95, 126–7, 248–9, 257; Islamic character of, 19–22, 111, 131, 157–9, 182–4, 209, 220; military structure of, 27–8, 36, 106, 108; and democracy, 61, 253; techniques of, 244–7, 252–8
Communist International, 12, 16, 50, 51, 54–9, 89, 91, 93, 97–8, 100, 101, 105, 107, 108
Communist Manifesto, 11, 30
Communist parties, their hold on members, 38, 54, 96, 130, 145, 157; and Comintern, 56–9; development of, 89–92, 96, 98, 102, 107; careerism in, 92; and Russia, 248–9
Communist Party of the Soviet Union, 38, 47, 49, 50, 52–5, 87–9; structure of, 60–6, 75–6, 85, 97, 99; opposition in, 62, 67, 70–1; twelfth congress of, 64; fourteenth congress of, 70; relations with other communist parties, 89, 92–5, 99–100, 102, 108
Communist tactics, disruption from within, 15, 17–19, 21, 22, 101, 103, 104, 117; illegal apparatus, 36, 37, 57, 100; fractions, 37, 56, 117, 118, 252; dual power, 43, 47, 60; secret agents, 102, 106, 107, 113; popular front, 118–19
Comte, Auguste, 107, 124
Convention, the, 48–9, 179, 232
Counter-Reformation, the, 207
Crowd phenomena, 190–4
Czechoslovakia, 166, 241, 250, 253

Dawes plan, 202–3
Delusions, pathology of, 129, 133–44
Democracy, and communism, 61; origins of, 170–2, 313
Demosthenes, 322
Dimitrov, G., 97
Dogma in the 20th century, 153–5
Dostoevsky, 29, 52
Duclos, J., 94

Eastern Europe, and Russia, 166, 248–51, 253
'Economists', 30, 35
Europe, and Russia, 9, 15, 51, 52, 54, 55, 195–6, 305; unification of, 323, 325–7
Existentialism, 279

Fascism, 27, 68, 231; origins of, 234–6
Fatimids, 19
Feudalism, 196–8
Feuerbach, 163, 267, 280, 284
Fischer, Ruth, 102, 103
Forced labour, 13, 14, 38, 77–80, 81, 134
Fourier, 277
France, 94, 197–8; communist party of, 91, 231–2, 253
French Revolution, 147, 186, 191, 204–5, 231–2, 270, 274, 276, 296
Freud, 133, 136, 139–40, 152, 268
Frobenius, 294

Germany, 13, 104, 109, 200–2, 205; social-democratic party of, 29, 33, 44, 51, 109; trade unions in, 82; communist party of, 98, 103, 109, 118; bourgeoisie in, 198–200, 202–4, 206
G.P.U., 102
Gracchi, the, 26
Greece, ancient, 34; political power in, 168–74

Habsburg Empire, 205–6
Hegel and Hegelianism, 39, 51, 123, 125, 127, 132, 177, 297, 311
Hitler, 109, 110, 119, 160, 209–10, 211, 231, 233
Hoffmann, General, 47
Holy Roman Empire, 199, 219, 266

Ideology, 136–41, 275
India, 329
Industrial Revolution, 149, 164, 190
Inquisition, The, 224
Intellectuals, 112, 127, 131, 136
Islam, 15, 18, 19, 219

Jacobins, 37–49
Jaurès, 32, 50
Julian the Apostate, 316

Kamenev, 53, 62, 64, 70, 93
Kautsky, 35, 37, 51
Kerensky, 48, 60
Kierkegaard, 42n., 116, 123, 127
Kolarov, V., 97
Kun, Bela, 97
Kuusinen, O., 97

Leader, concept of, 145–6, 159–61, 211–13
Lenin, 9, 15, 24, 26, 40, 43, 44, 53, 57, 95, 98, 101, 105, 106, 108, 109, 112, 126, 143; programme of, 29–38, 46–8, 50, 204; and Kautsky, 51, 55; authority of, 63–4
Lévy-Bruhl, 147n., 148, 280
Liberalism, 20, 39, 164
Liebknecht, K., 46, 51
Luxemburg, R., 46, 51

Machiavelli and Machiavellism, 22, 117, 175, 245, 266
Mana, 124, 126
Manicheeism, 39
Marius, 26, 300–1
Martin de la Torre, 174
Marx and Marxism, 30, 34, 38, 43, 48, 50, 51, 58, 94, 108, 112, 114, 121, 130–2, 136, 149, 189, 226, 263, 280, 287, 296–8; and Russia, 9–10, 15–16, 26, 30; and permanent revolution, 33; eschatological character of, 35, 39–45, 112, 125, 126; and Jewish question, 41–2; popularised, 116; and proletariat, 107, 123, 156–7, 185; and Hegel, 127
Masses, phenomenon of, 147–8, 159, 187, 203–4, 315; spontaneity of, 30, 31, 104
Mazzini, 38
Mensheviks, 46, 47, 60
Messianism, 130, 134, 156–7; *see also* Marx
Michels, R., 33
Monarchy, Western, 179, 207–8, 266; Russian, 196
Money, in capitalist society, 226–7
Moscow trials, 68, 221
Mussolini, 64, 89, 166, 231, 232
Myths, nature and function of, 140, 146–52, 153, 230–2

Napoleon, 149, 161, 179, 211, 231, 322
National socialism, 27, 184–6, 210, 218; Islamic character of, 207, 220, 234, 289; world-wide aims of, 251
Nationalism, 62, 187–9, 269, 270–5
Nechaev, 33, 37, 100
Neuroses, social, 134–7, 143, 160, 161–3
Nietzsche, 127, 158, 161, 227, 274, 287, 290
Nihilism, 287–91

Okhrana, 38
Oligarchy, and revolution, 25–7, 205; Russian, 9; Roman, 26, 82, 300–1, 314
Orthodox Church, 322
Ottoman Empire, 165, 219, 225

Pareto, 31, 32, 33n.
'Permanent revolution', 43, 47
Persia, ancient, 167–8, 183
Peter the Great, 15, 52, 95, 195
Philosophes, the, 167, 267, 271, 287
Plato, 177
Plebs, impotence of, 26, 30, 34, 95, 106, 109
Plekhanov, 9, 31
Politburo, *see* Communist Party of the Soviet Union, structure of
Politics, secularisation of, 22, 23, 207–8, 266, *see also* Machiavelli; and the sacred, 144, 146, 167, 172, 207, 213, 222, 264–6; in ancient world, 167–70
Populism, 30, 44, 47
Projections, psychological, 129–31, 195
Proletariat, emergence of, 11, 14, 189; Marx and, 42, 43, 296; and communist campaign, 245; 'internal' and 'external', 294–5, 304–5

Proudhon, 40, 90, 233
Psycho-analysis, 139–40, 268, 285–7
Psychological warfare, 10, 21, 115, 117, 258, 261–3
Purges, Russian, 88, 99

Radek, 105
Rationalism, in the 18th century, 275–6, 285–9
Reformation, the, 128
Religion of the Species, 277–81, 284–5, 298
Renan, 141
Revolution, theory of, 9, 27, 33, 263, 296–9; strategy of, 9–10, 205, 251; and the individual, 302–3; of 1848, 43, 164, 192, 206; of 1905, 60
Robespierre, 317
Roman Empire, 15, 27, 34, 69, 299–302, 308–10; religions in, 21, 156, 277; oligarchy in, 26; as universal State, 310–13, 314–17
Romanticism, literary, 149, 269, 279
Rousseau, 179, 197, 317
Russia, and Europe, 9, 15, 51–5, 195–6, 305; social structure, 11, 12, 16, 17, 54–6, 65, 81; as super-state, 12, 55, 318–20; trade unions in, 14, 56, 60; industrialisation of, 15, 16–18, 26, 30, 55, 73; as an 'Islam', 19–20, 61, 183–4; Tsarist, 26, 30, 61, 67, 73, 164, 195, 198–9, 204, 318; intelligentsia in, 30, 35, 204, 232–3; terrorism in, 31; Soviets in, 47, 56, 60–2, 68–9; structure of power in, 62, 68, 75–6, 109, 217–18; bureaucracy in, 87–8, 94, 96–7; Byzantine heritage of, 195, 208, 219–20; communist party of, *see* Communist Party of the Soviet Union
Russian Revolution, 9, 12, 38, 46, 47, 50, 204, 206, 208, 230, 232–3, 299

Saint-Simon, 277
'Satellite men', 118
Schopenhauer, 127, 287
Science, prestige of, 140, 154, 208
Second International, 40, 50, 53
Second-and-a-half International, 52, 53
Secular religions, 16, 18, 130, 139, 144–6, 161–3, 221, 291, 329
Social-Democratic Party, Russian, 31, 35; *see also* Mensheviks
Socialism, Western, 11, 17, 49, 90, 96, 97, 109, 110, 115, 156, 269
Social-Revolutionary Party, 47
Socrates, 270
Sorel, 31, 32, 40, 50n., 53, 128, 145–7, 151, 193
Souvarine, 98
Soviet Union, Soviets, *see* Russia
Spain, 166
Spengler, 306n.
Spinoza, 161
Stalin, 64, 65, 86, 89, 98, 99, 110, 211–12; as leader, 19, 160; career of, 63, 65–6, 68, 69–70, 71–2; power of, 209, 219–20
Stendhal, 48
'Sympathisers', role of in communism, 104, 113, 114, 117, 119, 141, 252, 254–6
Syndicalism, 32; *see also* Sorel

Teutonic Knights, 200
Thorez, M., 94, 101
Tkachev, 29, 30, 33, 35
Tocqueville, A. de, 323
Totalitarianism, 13, 194, 198, 202, 227, 325; and war, 28, 239, 256–8; and liberalism, 39; techniques of, 96, 116, 213–17, 222–3; foreign policy of, 240–4
Toynbee, A., 145, 294
Trotsky, 9, 43, 46, 49, 50, 51, 53, 57, 62, 85, 105, 108; on Soviet bureaucracy, 55, 58, 89, 97, 98; in opposition, 64, 67–8, 70–2, 76
Tyranny, ancient, 170–7, 186; medieval, 175–6; modern, 177–81, 183, 186, 211–12, 222–5

Unemployment, 203–4
United States, 17; and Russia, 305; as super-state, 317–20; and Europe, 323, 325, 327
Universal State, the, 18, 20, 183, 293–4, 310, 314, 324–5, 329

Vico, 146–7, 150, 177
Voltaire, 179, 275

Wallace, Henry, 243
War, 1914–8, 28, 165, 260, 328; 1939–45, 165, 323
'World State', the, 334–6

Zinoviev, 53, 57, 62, 64, 93, 105, 108